THE
Splendid Art
OF
OPERA

THE
Splendid Art
OF
OPERA

A CONCISE HISTORY BY

Ethan Mordden

Methuen, New York

Library of Congress Cataloging in Publication Data

Mordden, Ethan
The splendid art of opera.

Bibliography: p.
Includes index.
1.   Opera—History and criticism.   I.   Title.
ML1700.M73   782.1'09   80-15647
ISBN 0-416-00731-7

First Edition

Published in the United States of America by
Methuen, Inc.
733 Third Avenue
New York, N.Y. 10017

To three teaching editors,
SHELDON MEYER, HUGH HOWARD, *and* DANIEL OKRENT

Acknowledgments

THE AUTHOR WISHES TO ACKNOWLEDGE THE ADVICE AND ENCOURAGEMENT of Marion Wheeler, who commissioned the book; of Sukey Howard, who inherited the project with the enthusiasm of a founding member; of designer David Rogers, who like all art persons advises me to "keep it short"; of Charles Suttoni, who read the text for errors and found more than a few; and of the formidable Mary Heathcote, who edited the manuscript with the certain precise literacy that contributes far more than most readers are probably aware. I salute Ms. Heathcote with admiration and gratitude.

Contents

List of Illustrations

Photographs courtesy of Opera News magazine and
Matthew Epstein, Columbia Artists Management, Inc.

Preface

THIS IS A CONCISE BUT COMPREHENSIVE HISTORY DESIGNED FOR THE nonexpert. I have tried to cover all the major events in the history of opera, and some colorful minor ones, taking in not only composition but changing production styles and the various cults of personality. I have also tried to reveal the conduits of form without dwelling too much on the clichés that everyone learns early in an operagoing career, so that the story will be informative but enjoyable rather than academic.

Because opera is a combination of at least two arts, theatre and song, it has a built-in conflict that most other arts don't have: which of the two is more strategic? I see opera's history as a ceaseless tug of war between the two. In some eras, either "good theatre" or "good music" takes precedence; in other eras, the two generate separate forms that confront and borrow from each other. That tug of war provides the book's perspective. Aesthetic revolution, sociopolitical influences, vogue, technical innovation, show-biz tactics, huzzahs and hisses, and George Frideric Handel's attempted defenestration of the imperious singer Francesca Cuzzoni provide the fun.

The spelling of Russian names and titles represents a phonography of the Russian sounds, not the halfhearted system normally seen in Roman letters. On the other hand, sometimes a dedicated system confuses more than it educates, and while all works are cited in their original title and (where appropriate) also in English translation (e.g., *Die Zauberflöte; The Magic Flute*), I have used the original and the translation interchangeably thereafter, to reflect common operaphile usage. Similarly, characters turn up both in their authentic opera names (Didone) and in English renderings (Dido). Why not be comfortable as well as exact? Parenthetical dates refer to the year of performance, not necessarily of composition; and please use the glossary at the back of the book when trapped in terminology.

—ETHAN MORDDEN

THE
Splendid Art
OF
OPERA

In the Beginning Was the Word

> *It seemed to me that the ancient Greeks and Romans (who, in the opinion of many, sang their tragedies throughout) must have used a kind of music more advanced than ordinary speech but less than the melody of singing, so as to take the shape of something midway between the two.*
> —JACOPO PERI,
> Preface to *Euridice*

THERE IS NO ONE PLACE TO START. BY GENERAL CONSENT, THE HISTORY of opera begins almost exactly in the year 1600 in Florence, yet specific instances of music theatre turn up as far back as the thirteenth century. There were religious pageants that sometimes took weeks to perform, with ecstatic choirs in "heaven" and crude buffoonery in "hell." There was the secular masque, no less spectacular, emphasizing dance and threaded on a plot line so feeble that it was more a theme than a story. Of the less expensive events there was the pastorale, originally a spoken theatre of nymphs, shepherds, and deities in the sensually sylvan glade but quickly popularized with songs and choruses. And there was the *intermedio*, or intermezzo, the dramatically superfluous "interval" slipped between the acts of a play to lighten the heart with vocal music, especially the irresistible madrigal, a song arranged for a small group of gracefully intertwined voices. The musical *intermedio* eventually became so popular that it ceased to slip into a play's intermissions and began to bombard them. "Once we had intermezzos to serve the plays," observed a playwright of the time. "Now we have plays to serve as

3

excuses for intermezzos."

The madrigals themselves, strung out in a vaguely narrative sequence, comprised yet another form of music theatre, the madrigal
comedy. This genre dealt with the doings of the archetypes of the
commedia dell'arte—Harlequin, Pantaloon, Isabella, and other lunatics
and lovers. (The madrigal comedies were not invariably staged, however, and even when they were the action was mimed by actors, not
the singers.) On the simplest level were the ballad comedies. These
were farces or informal pastorales built on extemporized jests and
sentiment and filled out with verses set to popular tunes. This genre
offers a classic citation, so old that its title predates modern French
spelling, Adam de la Hâle's *Li Gieus de Robin et de Marion* (The Play
of Robin and Marion), traced back to 1283 or 1284.

All these forms of theatre called for music to some degree, but
there is one reason why none of them qualifies as opera: music was
extra to their essence. Religious instruction, spectacle, ballet, comic
improvisation, or speech was the main event in all except the *intermedio*
and the madrigal comedy, and these were not music theatre but musical
vaudeville, sometimes staged. Opera, then, would be something new—
drama expressed entirely in music.

But the inventors of opera didn't think of their genre as new
so much as revived. Their original, they reckoned, was Greek tragedy.
The Greeks were supposed to have sung their dramas, not spoken
them, and although no Greek theatre scores had survived even in part,
presumably one could bring back their format through an informed
synthesis. The "classical studies" cult that emerged during the Renaissance received a powerful impetus when the West rediscovered Aris-
totle's *Poetics* in 1498, for this work focused Europe's ambitious but
free-form hellenophilia. Before, Greece and Rome as fountainheads
of art and science had comprised something of a style, even a vogue.
But with the *Poetics,* Greece and Rome offered a method, a series of
aesthetic concepts that boiled down to a first principle of strategic
simplicity: art imitates nature. And opera, when it began about 1600
as an intended reconstruction of Greek theatre, represented a revolt
against flamboyance, against everything in music and theatre that did
not pattern itself on the fundamental purity of a geometrical Grecian
universe of humankind in harmonious motion.

The practitioners of this reordered thinking were gentleman amateurs and a few professionals, joined by their common mission to
discuss, experiment, and perform. They were known collectively as
the Camerata, and included musicians and poets of distinction. But they
were theorists as well as—perhaps more than—artists. That can be

tricky: art gets nervous in code.

The Camerata began meeting sometime around 1580 in the palace of a Florentine nobleman named Giovanni de' Bardi, and slowly commenced formulating and publishing. One of them, Vincenzo Galilei (father of the astronomer), produced an attack on the complex excursions of sixteenth-century vocal music, the madrigal in particular. With several different vocal lines ceaselessly overlapping each other, with certain words emphasized over others, Galilei asked, how could one *understand* a given composition? One could listen to it, enjoy it—but could one hear it? It sighs, it chuckles, it glides, it growls, making musical but never textual sense. Was this natural? Was this imitative art? Certainly music for music's sake has its appeal. But let music serve as the engine of verbal communication—words and melody in solemn clarity. *Then* the emotions will stir!

Citing Plato as his authority, Galilei defined music as first the words, second the rhythm of those words as normally spoken, and only then the sound of musical notes assigned to the words. The ideal of the Camerata centered on one voice declaiming poetry in a musical approximation of the language, a spoken poetry distilled. We would call this monodic recitative; the Camerata referred to it simply as *le nuove musiche*, the new music. Galilei worked out some of the first examples, using as his texts excerpts from Dante's *Divine Comedy* and the Book of Lamentations (unfortunately, both of Galilei's works were lost). Other Camerata musicians developed samples of the new music; the next step, obviously, was to put forth the new music theatre, the *dramma in* (or *per*) *musica*.

Bardi was called to Rome and the Camerata moved to the house of Jacopo Corsi. It was there that the first opera was performed, before an invited audience sympathetic to Camerata ideals. The work was *Dafne*, text by Ottavio Rinuccini and music by Jacopo Peri with some bits by Corsi. The music has not survived, and there is some confusion about whether the premiere was in 1594 or 1597.* *Dafne* went over reasonably well, it seems, and in 1600 came *Euridice*, another Peri-Rinuccini collaboration, with some added music by Guilio Caccini, performed to help celebrate the marriage of Maria de' Medici to Henry IV of France. This work has survived, and gives a clear picture of opera in its earliest form. In terms of genre, the authors' sources were the pastorale and *intermedio*, the former for its setting and

---

* Musicologists thrill to such ambiguities, but it seems that 1597 is correct. The earlier figure derives from a misinterpretation of a statement that Peri made in his preface to the second *dramma in musica*, *Euridice*. On such sparks whole academies blaze.

characters, the latter for its inessential but pleasing musical miscellany. In terms of music, the voices carry the piece; the small orchestra is there almost exclusively to accompany the singers, who alternate passages of recitative with more "musical" passages, *arioso* (songlike) sections or choral songs. As the titles (*Dafne* and *Euridice*) show, the venue is an Arcadia self-consciously modeled on a Greek idyll.

Here music theatre dwelled like an enchanted idealist in the sacred wood, seeking world-order and doing no evil. All was rural and serene. In Rinuccini's *Euridice* libretto, Tragedy opens the work in an invocational prologue. Then the nymphs and shepherds take the stage to celebrate the marriage of Orpheus and Euridice. A messenger appears to tell of Euridice's death. Orpheus laments—but, encouraged by Venus, he descends to hell and pleads with Pluto for the return of his beloved. Pluto accedes, without putting the traditional condition on Euridice's return. Back in the green world, nymphs and shepherds retrieve their interrupted merrymaking in honor of the union of Orpheus and Euridice.

This was, unquestionably, music theatre, a *dramma in musica*. The novelty of the form intrigued its first audiences, and it argued forcefully for precision in verbal-musical composition. But there were drawbacks. First of all, these pastoral tales hardly constituted a revival of the austerely shattering Greek stage, with its friezelike disasters and psychologically commentative choruses. Both *Dafne* and *Euridice* employ messengers to keep physical wonder (Dafne's metamorphosis into a tree and Eurdice's death) offstage: this is neatly Greek. But the Greek worldview glimpses calamity in the struggle between mortals and destiny, whether that destiny be the work of human character or the devious pettiness of Olympians. In *Dafne* and *Euridice* there is no real turbulence. Euridice dead, Orpheus simply trudges into the underworld, asks for her back, and gets her. *Dafne*, at least, is a little more complex; its story of a virginal nymph so resistant to romance that she'd rather be a tree than share Apollo's bed hides a sermon on courtly love. In its prologue, Ovid comes forward to warn the spectator of the powers of love, and at the end the nymphs and shepherds, sobered by Dafne's transformation, pray to Cupid that they have learned their lesson—not to withhold their favors from those who would share them.

The worst drawback was the new music itself. When it allowed for an occasional chorus or a real verse of song, it pleased. But when it recited the text, so careful to keep the music from breaking free as *musical* expression, it was slow and intense and dull. Yet this recitation was the very basis on which opera was founded. A touch of song and a touch of spectacle (for the appearances of the gods on high) enlivened the performances, but they suffered from their constraining theories of verbal musicality, their fear of musical flying. For all their Greek inspiration, the men of the Camerata did not grasp the totality of Greek theatre. (They didn't even get the names right—the Roman Venus and Pluto for Aphrodite and Hades, for instance.)

Despite its flaws, the new music caught on; at any rate, creators in other Italian cities took up the form, holding to pastoral subjects. The *dramma in musica* lived on the delectation of the elite of the Italian courts, so there was no popular taste to answer to. But it was bulky and expensive, a very specialized field, and it traveled slowly; only the librettos, printed as a rule, were portable, and so the words were more durable than the music. Rinuccini's *Dafne*, the first opera libretto, was set several times in opera's early years, first by the Florentines Peri and Corsi, then by Marco da Gagliano in Mantua, in 1608.

In those days each Italian city headed a separate Italian state, and although we now speak of Italian opera as opposed to French or German, seventeenth-century Italian opera is better thought of as Florentine, Roman, or Venetian. There were distinctions in style. Performances were occasional and practitioners few, so continuity became highly centralized, dependent on what kind of work had already been done in each locale and who would write the next one. In Florence, naturally, the Camerata approach with its monotonous recitative dominated operatic thinking. In Rome, Emilio de' Cavalieri introduced the Camerata style in his *La Rappresentazione di Anima e di Corpo* (The Play of the Soul and the Body, 1600), a moralistic piece peopled by such characters as Time, Worldly Life, and Counsel. But the austere Florentine sound did not suit the clerics of the Vatican, used to the sumptuous in all things. Over a period of years, a Roman style grew out of the Florentine, whether in reverent works like Stefano Landi's *Sant' Alessio* (1632) or more savory secular projects like Domenico Mazzochi's *La Catena d'Adone* (The Chains of Adonis, 1626).

In Roman opera, despite a devotional overlay stressing Christian teaching, the emphasis lay on large choruses, lavish decor (for audiences of as many as three thousand, though performances remained private), and genuinely musical passages. The Florentine recitative was scanted, even hurried; those prelates wanted *music*. Not surprisingly, it was a Roman opera, the Adonis piece, that first catalogued its high points as "arias" in an index at the back of the score.

The word "aria" was not new. Even the proponents of the new music resorted to it in nonoperatic contexts—an album of vocal solos, say. But for purposes of narrative theatre, the aria was thought of

as counterproductive to dramatic flow. The aria is, essentially, a passage
which is musically constructed. Though the words may be of primary
importance, the shape of sound is defined by a musical—not a verbal—
verse. The Camerata feared the aria as interruptive, superfluous, and
unnatural. But it was needed. Without it, without some genuinely
musical organization, opera was mired in effete intensities. The Florentines sterilized opera even as they invented it. And their whole era
lasted exactly ten years.

It ended when Claudio Monteverdi and Alessandro Striggio wrote
Orfeo (1607). Monteverdi was the superior composer of his place and
time, and Striggio was very music-minded for a librettist—his father
had composed one of the first of the madrigal comedies, *Il Cicalemento
delle Donne al Bucato* (The Prattling of the Women Doing the
Laundry, 1567). Striggio's version of the Orpheus tale shoves Rinuccini's Florentine version into the wings of art history; here is a piece
fashioned for theatre. The libretto seeks calamity: this Orpheus is
warned not to look back on Euridice, and does, and loses her forever.
There is a sense of real human aspiration, not the amiable still life of
the Florentine *Euridice*. When Orpheus has hurdled the Styx and
forced his way into hell, a spirit chorus intones an unexpected presage
of the kind of thinking that the Enlightenment would publicize:

> *Nulla impresa per uom si tenta invano*
> *Nè contro a lui più sa natura armase . . .*
> (Man attempts no undertaking in vain;
> Neither does nature arm herself against him . . .)

Nature, in the Florentine pastorale, was what the world *was;* in *Orfeo*,
it is a condition that may be defied and conquered.

Striggio even wanted to use the authentic ending of the legend,
showing the hero ripped to pieces by Bacchantes. But this opera was
not yet prepared to deal with. Monteverdi overrode his collaborator,
setting a precedent for opera composition that would be observed
almost invariably thereafter: the composer has the muscle. In the opera
as finally composed, Apollo takes Orpheus to heaven. Significantly,
where *Dafne*'s prologue was sung by Ovid and *Euridice*'s by Tragedy
—two animas of verbal poetry—*Orfeo*'s prologue is sung by Music.
Revolution! But how could it have been otherwise? What is Orpheus
if not a wonder-singer, a musician to stimulate and soothe us? He must
sing, not the recitative of Florence, but true song, outpouring from
within the bounds of the statement, variation, and repetition with
which Western music makes its point, what might be called its listening
space. Thus, when seeking to enter hell, Orpheus must charm Charon

into rowing him across the Styx. How charm him? How else? Breaking away from the Camerata's dictum that the music serve the word directly and simply, Monteverdi gives his hero an aria impressively molded in ever more elaborate vocal embellishments. But note a paradox: Charon likes the song but likes his duty better—Orpheus shall not pass. It is not embellishment but simplicity after all that swings the deal, for, dropping all vocal gala, Orpheus cries out, "Give me back my beloved, gods of Tartarus!" The directness of this line neutralizes Charon as the decorated song could not, and Orpheus steals into hell to retrieve Euridice.

This is just a sample of the sophistication of Monteverdi's *Orfeo*. The work is full of innovations that were to become staples of operatic method: a relatively large orchestra and varied use of instrumentation, the building of scenes to climactic moments that depend on the use of music to characterize and enrich, the repetition of telling lines for irony or emphasis, the development of the orchestra as a collaborative commentator on the action. This is not to suggest that *Orfeo* is as tautly dramatic or as musically fulfilled as opera would be some centuries hence. But certain passages of it are so dramatic and musical that, given the historical context, the work is a wonder.

For example, it begins pleasantly, even limply, yet soon rises to a finely judged forcefulness. After Music's prologue, the first of five acts discloses a pastorale of solos and choruses, introducing Orpheus and Euridice but not making anything of them. Literally nothing happens. But in Act II, as the rustic pleasures continue, a soprano messenger, Silvia, enters to tell of Euridice's death, and here Monteverdi's very personal use of the Florentine recitative is remarkably eloquent, colored to express both a personal and public horror. It rises suspensefully to Silvia's revelation, riveting attention on Orpheus and his reaction. In the 1800s, the announcement would inspire a tumult in the orchestra; here, in silence, Orpheus merely sighs, *"Ohimè."* He is too stunned to move. Then Silvia tells how Euridice was bitten by a snake, onlookers comment sadly, and at last Orpheus begins his emotional solo, "You are dead, my life, and I breathe?" The act slowly draws to a close, and at the last moment Monteverdi repeats an orchestral passage familiar from its use as a lively *ritornello* (refrain) in the prologue. But now it sounds crestfallen and hopeless. Words can tell only so much; it is music that rounds out the scene.

The Monteverdi-Striggio *Orfeo* in effect founded a new school of opera, far richer than that of Florence or Rome. The piece was first performed in Mantua, but a few years later Monteverdi moved to Venice. There, as *maestro di capella* (director of music) at St. Mark's for thirty years, he and several other gifted composers and librettists created a mother lode of operatic formula that has yet to run dry— and whose examples, after three hundred years, are only now being revived in delighted amazement.

Venice's emergence as an opera capital in the mid-1600s depended not so much on a Venetian aesthetic as on a number of socioeconomic factors. Cultural ideology, civic morale, economics, and other such influences prompted responses in art as in life, though the art thought itself (as all art did then) entirely apolitical. In Rome the cynicism and worldliness of the fat Vatican City contributed to a Roman style in opera. In Paris later on in the century, imperial megalomania, *philosophe* intellectualism, and a more earthy worldliness would call for an entirely different kind of music theatre. In Venice, most worldly of all, a confluence of mercantile wealth, fertile musical traditions, and an international social life encouraged the flowering of a vital opera and nurtured it with constant support. Most significant, it was the Venetians who turned opera from a divine right of the ruling class into an everyday adventure of the general population on a one-man, one-ticket basis. In Venice, opera went public.

Venice was the logical site for the republicanization of the opera audience, for the town's bizarre congruence of capitalism and totalitarianism made it as open to the demotic style as it was closed to the democratic system. Venice was halfway to America: nobody could be president, but anybody could get rich. Often denounced by Rome for its secular tolerances—its gentleman's agreement to talk God, think Mammon, and mean Venice—the city in the lagoon boasted a Carnival season (from Christmas to Lent) that was considered the most notorious good time in Europe. In the 1600s Venice was already ancient and miasmic, a radiant slum. It was also the annual gathering place of thousands of Western opinion molders who would return home to London, Paris, and Vienna with enthralled reports of Venetian opera.

It had to enthrall. For once the public theatres were opened, opera ran on a paying basis, no longer a matter of invited audiences and doting patrons. In Florence it had been theory; in Rome it was moral spectacle. In Venice opera was, like everything else there, commerce. It had to please an audience that knew what it wanted: entertainment.

The model for Venetian opera remained the pastoral pseudo-Greek invention of the Florentines as musically redeveloped by Monteverdi. We know little of Monteverdi's first Venetian operas, *La Finta Pazza Licori* (Licori Feigns Madness, 1627), *Proserpina Rapita* (Proserpina Ravished, 1630), and *Adone* (Adonis, 1639), as the scores are lost. In 1639 Monteverdi even went to the in-those-days unusual trouble of reviving an old work, his *Arianna* (1608). But meanwhile the first public operation had been launched in 1637.

The theatre belonged to the noble Tron family, who rented it to two Romans, Benedetto Ferrari and Francesco Manelli. When this pair staged their opera, *Andromeda*, they threw the doors open to the public. Such was the appeal of the experiment that three other auditoriums followed suit in the next few years, and there were sixteen Venetian theatres (not all in use, however) by 1700.

As Romans, Ferrari and Manelli naturally brought some of the Roman aesthetic to Venice; their chief contribution to the local product was the use of comedy. This was a specialty then, not a convention, and seems to have been introduced into Roman opera by the librettist Guilio Rospigliosi (the future Pope Clement IX). The Florentines had naturally barred comedy from their music theatre, for one of their many grudges against the Italian musical stage of the late 1500s concerned the musical hedonism of the madrigal farces.

Yet comedy is a very potent naturalism, universal and earthy and disdainful of the ideals and ambiguities of tragic poetry that some audiences find hard to live up to. The Camerata developed opera precisely to essentialize the world in art. As we have seen, it was Monteverdi, in *Orfeo*, who eased the Camerata form into true theatre without losing the expressive dramatic potential of dramatic song—indeed, Monteverdi was the first to exploit that potential. And Monteverdi, we should note, knew the value of comedy as a contrast to (and, sometimes, an explication of) heroic action. His *La Finta Pazza Licori* is thought to have been the first comic opera, predating the Roman variety.

Venetian opera made farcical scenes and characters a regular feature, no doubt at least partly because the public clamored for them. True, the sensitive may have regretted the coarse edge that farce put onto pastoral romance. However, Venetian opera was popular, and popular can be very inclusive: martial love, courtly love, fleshly love, beauties and suitors, spinsters and satyrs. Centuries later Gustav Mahler would observe that the symphony must be "a whole world"; in a sense this also describes the scope of Venetian opera.

On the other hand, the style was relatively fixed, making for an unnaturally stable microcosm. Love provisioned the subject matter, with several couples working their way through an incredibly gnarled plot to an invariably happy ending, the reassuringly formalized *lieto fine*. The love plot feasted on absurd coincidences, disguises, and sudden changes of heart and ran blithely from place to place—a battlefield, say, then the courtyard of a harem, here a city, there the harem again, next a palace, lo a gallery of statues, on to the royal gardens, thence into prison, to someone's house, and to another garden for the finale.* Such peripatetics were standard, even welcome if the budget permitted spectacle. Here was born another term in the operatic catalogue, "machinery" (as in the *deus ex machina*), used, for example, to crank the gods in from heaven on a barouche of painted cloud.

Further complicating the action were the comic characters, subsidiary to the lovers and tending to the lower social orders, usually servants who, as members of a royal suite, had access to almost any scene. In Roman opera the comics were used protrusively, as a separate entity to relieve the moral gravity of the main action, but in Venetian opera they were integrated into the modal texture as part of the operatic "whole world." The most successful Venetian comic archetype was the Aged Duenna, sung by a man and played for a vulgar but often quite funny blend of virgin hag and man-chasing bacchante. When not taking stage for a ludicrous solo on the subject of sex or irritating the heroic characters, the duenna figure could be counted on to sing a lullaby to her mistress that would turn the whole persona upside down with music of haunting loveliness. (Another convention of operatic antiquity: the Slumber Scene.)

We moderns are not always sure when a Venetian librettist is playing it straight and when he's joking, which is one of the reasons why the current exhumation of the old operas is such an exciting business. Most of the other reasons are the music. Monteverdi taught the Venetians how to heighten the dramatic flow of the recitative with more abundantly musical passages and free use of vocal embellishment —why not *use* the voices?—and a growing interest in the songlike solo that would eventually take over as the aria.

Oddly, Monteverdi himself, so much more musical than the Florentines, seemed to grow closer to their style in his penultimate opera, *Il Ritorno d'Ulisse in Patria* (Ulysses Returns to His Homeland, 1641). For this adaptation of Homer, Monteverdi created what may be opera's first great heroine in the waiting wife Penelope; by comparison, all the Dafnes and Euridices are ciphers. But the music of this work in general returns us to the plangent stasis of the Camerata pastorale. Far livelier to modern taste are the operas of Monteverdi's Venetian contemporaries and successors, mainly Francesco Cavalli and Marc'antonio Cesti.

Cavalli's star has reascended lately. When Monteverdi died in 1643, Cavalli inherited the leadership of Venetian opera, writing some forty-

---

* This is the scene plot of Cavalli's *Erismena*.

The intensity of Venetian opera: Frederica von Stade and Richard Stilwell as Penelope and Ulysses reunited in Monteverdi's *Il Ritorno d'Ulisse in Patria*. Note the intimacy of the handclasp, gently edging Classical aplomb with Romantic involvement. The Baroque was a complex age. *(Guy Gravett)*

Cavalli's *Egisto* (1646) at Santa Fe, 1974. John Cox's production, in Allen Charles Klein's designs, set the diverse comings and goings on a disc inlaid with astrological signs, surrounding a tree with a miniature "universe" suspended above: a Renaissance world-order in miniature. The old conventions come off fresh today: (left to right) the duenna (Douglas Perry) advises an entranced lover (Brent Ellis); Love (Faith Esham), nymphs, and satyrs express the characteristic hot Baroque shazam; three nymphs cavort—nymph at left (Mariana Cristos) has got her frond out of sync; the love plots in full cry, with Love (far left) intervening. *Egisto*'s prologue is launched by Night (below), a fearsome warrior, faceless in his darkness; but he is succeeded, as the lights come up on CoxKleinworld, by Dawn (the incomparable Sheri Greenawald, right) a veritable tarot of loving beauty. *(Ken Howard, Santa Fe Opera; Greater Miami Opera Association)*

odd works of great charm if limited variety. Within that little whole world of gods, nobles, henchmen, and servants, Cavalli held a carnival. He has been called Monteverdi's pupil; this is disputed. But certainly he learned from the master as all Venetian musicians did: with his ears.

Opera's subject matter had moved from Ovidian pastorales into classical and Renaissance epic derived from Homer, Virgil, Ariosto, and Tasso. Occasionally librettists invented their own characters, but the stereotypes were observed. Sometimes the love plot became so complex that the opera might be half over before one had the relationships sorted out—and heroines' penchant for donning men's clothes and assumed names didn't make things easier. This detailed plotting showed the influence of the Spanish stage, at the time in full flower and famed for its multiplicity of times, places, and actions. The great Venetian librettist Giovanni Francesco Busenello specifically invoked "Spanish methods" in his preface to his libretto for Cavalli's *Didone* (1641), a very Venetian view of the tale of Dido and Aeneas. *Didone* is virtually a comedy, making so much of Didone's comically luckless suitor Iarba that at the end, when Enea has sailed away and Didone attempts suicide, Iarba not only stops her but talks her into accepting him after all. Of course a Venetian audience would generally anticipate a happy ending of some kind. Still, an odd air of amused cynicism lurks in the wings as the curtain falls on *Didone*.

There is no denying Cavalli's effortlesss lyricism. Even today, with audiences not acclimatized to the style, every decent Cavalli revival succeeds. And why not? When the subject is love, the art does not date. The comedy, too, is ecumenical. By happy chance a performance of Cavalli's *Erismena* (1655) at Berkeley, California, in 1968 turned up in an ancient English translation of unknown authorship. To see the love-tossed Aldimira consult the portraits of her two lovers and sing

> I languish
> In anguish
> Yet my torments,
> My torments,
> My torments content me;
> These flames that torment me
> Are no emblems of smart,
> But trophies of joy
> That I bear in my heart . . .

was to see not an antique but a novelty of warm humanity. (Note the repetition of "my torments," a typical resource of the word-proud seventeenth century.)

The Berkeley performance was excellent. But perhaps the high point of the Cavalli revival was reached at the Glyndebourne Festival's 1970 remounting of *Calisto* (1651), a pastorale comedy in which Giove (Jove) loves the nymph Calisto who loves Diana who loves Endimione. The lavish sensuality achieves a remarkable layered effect when Giove disguises himself as Diana to woo Calisto; the singer playing Diana must then double as Giove-as-Diana and sound like a man imitating a woman. A year later Glyndebourne improved its already dynamic production with singing actors of grand thrust and gritty soul. This *Calisto* burned, caressed, and frolicked: Ileana Cotrubas' bashful nymph, Teresa Kubiak's inflammable Giunone (Juno), a countertenor Endimione, the lecherous male crone right out of the old days, and, best of all, the startlingly ravishing Diana of Janet Baker.

Cavalli's contemporary Marc'antonio Cesti still awaits a full-scale revival, though authorities habitually cite his *Il Pomo d'Oro* (The Golden Apple, 1667), a spectacular adaptation of the judgment of Paris that was apparently composed so Leopold I of Austria could personally present the apple prize to his bride, the Infanta Margarita of Spain. In all, however, the masterpiece of the Venetian school belongs neither to Cavalli nor Cesti, but to Monteverdi; it is his last opera, *L'Incoronazione di Poppea* (The Coronation of Poppea, 1642).

Poppea is a double triumph, as dazzling for Busenello's libretto as for Monteverdi's music. In this work the two men threw wide the scope of their form, relying on the penetration of art rather than the simple lure of entertainment. It is notable that in *Poppea*, for the first time, the source of the plot was history rather than poetry; Busenello drew on Tacitus as opposed to the epic and myth that opera had previously purveyed (and all too slightly), so his characters are more human than ideal. His plot still ranges around love intrigues. But the intriguers are unpleasantly naturalistic—selfish, vindictive, pompous, grasping.

Poppea tells of the emperor Nero and his passion for Poppea. Though he is married, the two of them blithely dispose of all obstacles to his making her his queen. Nero's wife, Ottavia, is banished. His mentor Seneca, opposed to Poppea, is ordered to commit suicide. Meanwhile a subsidiary love plot involves Drusilla and Ottone—she loves him but he loves Poppea. Ottavia blackmails Ottone into murdering Poppea; the attempt fails, and Ottone too is banished. And Nero and his beloved celebrate the fulfillment of what the title promised: The Coronation of Poppea.

All the conventions are in place, but manipulated as integers in the dramatic equation. Thus the usual allegorical prologue is used *conceptually* to establish the omnipotence of Love, as compared to the reigns of Fortune and Virtue. "The world," sings Love, "changes at my signal." Busenello's libretto amounts to a set of variations on that theme. The immortals do not pop into the action capriciously, but serve the overall purpose; it is Love, for example, who foils Ottone's attempted assassination of Poppea. Even the use of disguise, when Ottone wears one of Drusilla's dresses for the attempt, is a logical maneuver rather than the superfluous decoration it so often is in the librettos set by Cavalli. The man-chasing-but-played-by-a-man duenna and the Slumber Scene, in these authors' hands, also rise above the age: Poppea's nurse Arnalta gets to sing the lullaby, and though she is unquestionably a comic grotesque, Monteverdi arranged the number, "Adagiati, Poppea" (Rest, Poppea), to music of eerie beauty, perfectly in keeping with the character yet one of the highlights of the score.

The librettos that preceded Busenello's are by no means uninspired. But not till *Poppea* did opera prove its ability to recreate and interpret life as Renaissance drama did. *Poppea* is various, earthy, ambivalent. There is the almost naturalistic opening of Act I, in which two soldiers discuss the Nero-Poppea affair and the state of Rome in general; the gravity and terror of Seneca's suicide; the ribald sparkle of Nero's duet with his friend Lucano, in praise of women and delight at Seneca's death; the duets of Nero and Poppea, each a musical comment on the state of their romance—first anxious, then hungry, then satisfied. The ease with which these two erotic reptiles address each other is disconcerting to a modern who prefers ancient art to be quaint and moldy:

> POPPEA: How sweet, Lord, how tender,
> This past night,
> Did you find the kisses of this mouth?
> NERO: So dear they hurt me.
> POPPEA: And the apples of these breasts?
> NERO: Your breasts deserve sweeter names.

So heavy is the sense of touch and taste in *Poppea* that directors of recent revivals can seldom resist garnishing the action with touches of nudity and overt sex. Actually, the music already carries that information; no wonder it sounds so fresh after more than three hundred years. In fact, despite the many difficulties involved in resurrecting early Baroque opera, *L'Incoronazione di Poppea* kept turning up at odd moments throughout the 1900s, long before the current vogue for Monteverdi got under way.

Let us not underestimate these difficulties. These operas are long. They can be cut, of course, but this is artistically objectionable and—because of the complicated plotting—not easy anyway. Too, there is that emoting recitative, which most ears find windy and monotonous. Moreover, as originally written these operas depend on a kind of voice we no longer have in stock, the male *castrato*. These were, as the word suggests, eunuchs, ruined as men in their youth so that the resulting brilliant voices would make them as artists in their maturity. Apparently the surgery—removal of the testes before puberty—augmented lung power and retained the burnished vocal tone of adolescence. The practice originated God knows how, but by the 1500s the *castrati* were celebrated as the wonders of court and Church choirs.

Technically the Church abhorred castration and prosecuted it severely. Once the deed was accomplished, however, there was nothing to do but accept the fact and welcome the phenomenon into the musical ranks. Early on the *castrati* found themselves a berth in opera, and by the time of Cavalli they were not only fixtures but the stars of the show. They took the lead male roles, relegating the wholly male tenor to supporting parts, and strutted through opera history until the late 1700s. By the early 1800s they were in eclipse; the last of the line, who sang in the Sistine Chapel, retired in 1913.

The question today is who is to sing the *castrati*'s parts when operas of their era are restaged. Modern companies substitute mezzo-sopranos, baritones, tenors, and the occasional countertenor, whose tone color is not as lustrous as a *castrato*'s but is at least comparably weird. Substitutions necessitate fooling around with the original keys and also affect the balance of voice types. If one looks on the Baroque revival as an exercise in fetching camp, the use of women in men's parts only adds to the sport. But if one considers a work like *Calisto* or *Poppea* genuine theatre, the confusion of sexuality is irritating.

The problem of orchestration is even more troublesome. Some of the instruments called for by Baroque composers are at present defunct; authenticity means raiding the museums just to outfit the players. Even worse, though a composer sometimes listed the instruments required for a given work, he never wrote out the orchestration. Manuscripts consist of vocal lines and a bass line for harmony: the various instrumental parts were improvised in rehearsals. These composers were not writing for posterity but for a specific occasion, with themselves officiating. Now that we have reached back and pulled them into the repertory, we have to introduce them to posterity osmotically, sensing more than knowing them. The entire orchestration has to be reconstituted by a musicologist—which puts something of a punk on one's authenticity.

A surprising number of musicians have labored at this thankless task. Monteverdi's *Il Ritorno d'Ulisse in Patria*, for instance, may be performed in at least seven different editions of varying fidelity to the author's true style. By far the most popular arranger in the field is Raymond Leppard, whose version of *Poppea* is the one that finally brought Venetian opera to international attention. Heavily cut, this *Poppea* has been denounced by purists, though reports of the revisionism in its scoring are exaggerated.

Moving from *Orfeo*, Monteverdi's first opera, to *Poppea*, his last, we have the beginnings of opera in miniature: from pastoral idyll to complex world of ambitions and disasters; from an experimental form in which music is supposedly secondary to the words to a forthright collaboration of music and text; from a sometime court diversion to public property. One thing is sure. As in almost all musical matters up to about 1700, the Italian road is the one taken, the Italian method the one taught and learned. First in Florence, then Rome, then Venice (and later Naples), the leadership in opera is always Italian. Now the news goes out to the rest of Europe, and other countries will have their opera, too. But will it be *theirs*, really, or just their version of the Italian model?

CHAPTER TWO

Italian Import Versus Local Product

*There is no Question but our
great Grand-children will be
very curious to know the Reason why their Forefathers used
to sit together like an audience
of foreigners in their own country, and to hear whole Plays
acted before them in a Tongue
which they did not understand.*
—JOSEPH ADDISON, *The Spectator*

THE 1600S SAW THE INVENTION AND DEVELOPMENT OF OPERA IN ITALY;
the 1700s saw the pan-European dissemination of Italian opera and its
struggle with attempts to rouse national operatic movements. In each
country the Italian-nationalist conflict grew out of the incompatibility
of alien and indigenous art forms. (Just as each land has its own relatively unexportable brand of, say, farce—Austria has Johann Nestroy,
Italy Eduardo de Filippo, England Ben Travers, America Kaufman and
Hart—so would each land want its own culturally assimilated kind of
opera. Wouldn't it?)

In each country the Italian-nationalist conflict ended differently.
In Germany and Austria, Italian opera simply absorbed all promising
German styles, until a national resurgence at the end of the eighteenth
century boiled up suddenly to absorb the Italian style, like Cronus
methodically eating his children until his son Zeus deposed him. In
England, types of Italian opera battled each other until the most flamboyant type disguised itself as the nonflamboyant, beef-and-puddingy
English oratorio, forcing English opera to go underground for a hundred and fifty years. In Russia, there was no native challenge to Italian

opera until the mid-1800s. And in France—where everything that hopes
to succeed had better be either French or a French pretender—a true
national style was concocted by an Italian, developed by a Frenchman,
attacked by pro-Italian Frenchmen, and at last saved and perfected—by
foreigners.

Paris was to become the European opera capital, wresting emi-
nence from Vienna and London and riding through the nineteenth
century on the characteristic French love of analysis and controversy.
The most thorough resistance to new music on record is French resistance (to Stravinsky's ballet *The Rite of Spring* at its premiere in
1913); the most devastating body of music criticism is French (it includes the bylines of Berlioz and Debussy). Elsewhere, when an opera
or symphony is performed, the public applauds or boos. In Paris they
parse.

The French got their first taste of opera in the 1640s and '50s, all
the work of Italians performed by Italian troupes. The public was
apathetic. With their background in the great drama of Jodelle, La
Péruse, Granier, Hardy, and de Rotrou (and the two Corneilles and
Scarron were very current just then), and their pronounced taste for
ballet, French audiences were both too intelligent and too lowbrow
to tolerate the Italian music theatre with its severe musicality. The
Italians liked to hear great singing; the French liked a simple tune and
thought nothing of humming along with the singers. Joseph Addison
compared the singers of French opera to "the Clerk of a Parish Church,
who serves only to raise the Psalm, and is afterwards drown'd in the
Musick of the Congregation."

What was music theatre to the French? Incidental decoration at
most, useful for ballet but irritating in drama. Music sensualized when
it should enhance, preened when it should humbly bow, and delighted
in such expedients as the *castrato* voice, so intolerable to dramatic credi-
bility. In Italy, and everywhere Italian opera became popular, music
was the engine of dramatic expression. To the French, casting cold
eyes on these imported operas, music got in the way. Even the glowing
Cavalli, several times heard in Paris at the behest of the Italian and
opera-loving Cardinal Mazarin, was not popular, though his *Ercole
Amante* (Hercules in Love, 1662), specially composed for Paris, won
some interest for the ballet sequences that were interpolated by a
Florentine émigré, Giambattista Lulli.

Or rather: Jean-Baptiste Lully. This former kitchen scullion,
opera's first great opportunist, Gallicized his outlook and created
French opera, *l'italien tout français*. Understanding that French culture
and royalist politics called for a certain kind of opera, Lully carefully

answered that call. He worked only with French librettists schooled in French theatre, editing them for French shape and direction. He drew extensively on ballet and spectacle. He celebrated Louis XIV as the hero of the time. He oversaw all aspects of production, applying plenty of his acquired French taste, and he intrigued ceaselessly to insure success, reputation, and an opera monopoly. And, mainly, he subordinated vocalism to declamation. If Italian opera was *dramma in musica*, Lully's operas were French drama *plus* music.

Actually Lully's were not the first French operas. After the continuous failure of the Italian operas, composer Robert Cambert and poet Pierre Perrin introduced an unpretentious French nymphs-and-shepherds opera in 1659, a work that for some reason bears a classification rather than a title, *La Pastorale d'Issy* (Issy being the place where it was performed). At Perrin's urging, Louis XIV let him and Cambert found an Académie d'Opéra with the public premiere, in Paris, of their *Pomone* (1671). Surprisingly Venetian in format, *Pomone* nevertheless went over well, so Cambert and Perrin followed it with *Les Peines et les Plaisirs de l'Amour* (The Pains and Pleasures of Love) a year later.

This was where Lully stepped in. He had been working in tandem with Molière, composing incidental scores for what was called the *comédie-ballet*, a play with some singing and dancing. Since these plays were becoming more and more musical, Lully realized that he was heading into opera anyway. He might as well be the royal composer. Callously, he took advantage of Perrin when he was down on his luck and wangled Louis' imprimatur for a new French opera company, the Académie Royale de Musique. Louis had not supported the Cambert-Perrin venture financially, nor would he underwrite Lully's troupe, but an imperial endorsement was in itself a kind of capital.

Scarcely had Lully and his collaborator, Philippe Quinault, launched their partnership than Perrin was dead of debt and despair and Cambert in voluntary exile in England. The field was clear. Lully held Louis' letters patent guaranteeing the Académie Royale the sole right to perform opera in France. For the next fifteen years, Lully and Quinault built up a stock of French opera that set tone and form with such popularity that for nearly a century it was artistic suicide to try to overturn their model.

Lully defined his new genre as *tragédie en musique*, or *tragédie lyrique*. The term is exactly comparable to the *dramma in musica* that the Camerata spoke of, but Lully's operas offered a vastly different theatre experience, even aside from the Gallic colorations cited above. For one thing, Lully's *tragédie* depended heavily on solid playwrighting, on clarity of action and fine theatre poetry. For another, Lully's intention of using music only to set off the text (reminiscent of the Camerata's plan) resulted in an elastic recitative capable of moving from a dryly musical declamation into chance arias and ensembles and back again with ease.

It seems that Lully had learned from Cavalli how to vary his recitative with song; the difference lies less in form than in approach. Lully's recitative is graver, more grandiose than Cavalli's and his fluidly vocal passages are more definitively musical. This flexible seesaw between the "verbal" motion of plot and "musical" expansion of character gives French opera its identity. Neither half of the plan overshadowed the other; each seemed to draw the other out, setting up a delicate tremor of texture. Thus while Italian opera was leaning more and more on a musical identity at the cost of good theatre, French opera as originated by Lully rooted itself in solid theatre thinking. Cavalli himself said, "Lully has the great quality of our classical century: he knows how to order."

Having set his aesthetics, Lully had little more to do; the rest was good taste and great dignity, a certain *gloire*, a lot of *amour*, and the framework of *le merveilleux*—turns, surprises, spectacle. A look at some of the titles of the virtually annual Lully-Quinault *tragédies en musique* reports on the pair's bias toward Greek subject matter: *Cadmus et Hermione* (1673), *Alceste* (1674), *Thésée* (1675), *Atys* (1675), *Proserpine* (1680), *Persée* (1682), *Phaëton* (1683). Later they branched out into medieval romance: *Amadis le Gaule* (1684), *Roland* (1685), *Armide et Renaud* (1686), the last offering one of Quinault's tightest librettos on a subject, cribbed from Tasso's *Gerusalemme Liberata*, that was to prove one of opera's most insistent plot premises: the devious sorceress and the ingenuous knight—will they get it on?

All these intrigues of gods and heroes served mainly as an excuse for obeisance to Baroque sociopolitical inertia—whatever was was right and each in his place. In the prologues to Venetian opera, allegorical figures representing Love or Beauty or Destiny fought for sovereignty over the mortal world, a primitive metaphysics. But in Lully's prologues sovereignty was royal and unquestioned. In the prologue to *Alceste* the Nymph of the Seine repeatedly asks, "Will the Hero whom I await never return?" And Glory, descending in a floating palace, tells her, "Your Hero is not far away." No, indeed. Louis XIV sat only yards distant in the audience, relishing the homage in his wig.

This *Alceste* was perhaps the most popular of Lully's operas. One of the few to include some comic byplay, it focused squarely on its glorious principals, their several kinds of love (conjugal, unrequited, and summertime), and the marvelous materialization of immortal beings with accompanying ballet. Quinault's source was Euripides, though the French lines lack the awesome power of the Greek stage and, as in Italy, catastrophe tended to resolve happily. *Alceste* does savor its comedy, though, introducing a couple right out of pastorale to vary the work's central proposition—true love is stronger than death—with a sweet little taste of false love. Alceste gives her life for her husband, but Céphise sings to her Straton of the delights of changing partners.

Unlike Venetian comedy, Quinault's has dignity. But its deftness surprises. After an interminable scene of mourning for the dead Alceste, we move into an unexpectedly festive-sounding underworld, whither Alcide has gone to fetch Alceste back. The Charon that Alcide meets is nothing like Monteverdi's. This one is singing merrily about the inevitability of death—"They come young or old . . . The Shepherd and the King"—and baiting the poor souls who can't pay his fare. Alcide forces his way into the boat and almost sinks it, ignoring Charon's complaints. Quinault's poetry here is too sharp to give only in translation:

> CHARON: *L'eau nous gagne, ma barque crève!*
> ALCIDE: *Allons, rame, dépêche, achève!*
> (We're foundering, my boat is gone!
> Come on, row, get there, on!)

With the king's choral and instrumental retainers on permanent call, Lully had grand forces to deploy, unlike the Venetian theatres, which had to break even or go broke. Also unlike the Italians, Lully kept his performers as anonymous as possible, centering attention on the work: on Lully. And, of course, as part of his plan for rationalizing opera, he wrote no parts for *castrati*—how could a half-man play a hero?

But how valuable to drama were the ballet sequences and elaborate visual effects that Lully approved? In 1677 Jean de la Fontaine set his fabulous pen to those monstrous novelties of the Académie, the "machines":

> *Souvent au plus beau char le contre-poids résiste;*
> *Un dieu pend à la corde et crie au machiniste;*
> *Un reste de forêt demeure dans la mer,*
> *Ou la moitié du ciel au milieu de l'enfer.*
> (The counterweights can't get the wagons to truck;
> A *deus* cries out that his *machina*'s stuck;
> A bit of the woods in the sea seems to dwell,
> Or a half of a heaven is squatting in hell.)

For all Lully and Quinault's devotion to the dramatic values learned from the spoken French stage, French opera obeyed rules of popularity as well as of good sense. This is an important point. Though tomes have been written about theories of opera composition, there is a line past which theory fades and creative instinct takes over, a line reached in an opera score somewhere on page two. For all one's recipe, there is a lot of hocus-pocus in the cookpot—something feels right and you go with it. So it turns out that the first Italian operas were not so perfectly "words first, rhythm next, music last" as they were planned to be. Nor were Lully's operas as imitative of the French spoken stage as they thought they were. They had the *atmosphere* of tragedy, yes (with, usually, a happy ending tacked on as reasonably as possible). An interest in a well-rhymed couplet, yes. A general insistence on logical plotting (i.e., none of the mistaken identity games that ran riot in Venice) also. And such was the theatrical (as opposed to musical) power of Lully's opera that it cruelly exposed singers who couldn't act. But in the end Lully was as fixed on the public's reaction as any showman. He gave them ballet and machinery, and that's where theory bows to circus. Lully was direct and reasonable but he was also—because he needed to be—monumentally gaudy.

Lully—this is entirely by the way—died a horribly original death. He habitually conducted with a heavy baton of the type used to deliver the three bonks that signal the rise of the curtain in a French theatre. Accidentally bonking his foot, he developed a nasty wound which became infected and finally felled him. Long after he had departed the scene, however, his works dominated the repertory and his spirit was invoked as the seen hand that had sculpted French opera. His successors' pieces were held up to his for comparison, unfavorably as a rule. Meanwhile, a change in taste rediscovered the pastorale and emphasized the already emphatic component of ballet; the operas of such as Pascal Colasse and André Campra yield a new item in French terminology, the *opéra-ballet*, lighter in tone than Lully's *tragédie* and often loosely plotted so as to allow dance and comedy a very free play. Still, how long could Lully's approach be respected as the one true serious French opera? Indefinitely, his supporters declared. And along came Rameau.

Jean-Philippe Rameau is one of the most underrated of composers. He may now be on the edge of revival, but in his day conservatives faithful to Lully tried to drive him from the stage. Despite them, Rameau gained the public's interest, then affection, and it must have been odd for the casual operagoer to read disgusted, outraged reviews of the latest Rameau opus and then learn at the box office that the alleged failure was totally sold out.

One was either *lulliste* or *ramiste*—for Lully or Rameau—and one compared them side by side, for Lully's operas still held the stage. Though accused of heinous novelty, Rameau believed himself to be tilling Lully's own field. He knew he was original but he respected tradition, and on the surface his operas retain most of Lully's conventions—the gala overture, the ballet sequences, the gods on their machines, the invocational prologue (though Rameau's are concise, directly related to the libretto, and eventually he dropped them altogether). One thing sets Rameau apart from Lully, and from all his contemporaries with the sole exception of Handel: the creative integrity of his music. In his use of orchestra and voices, in his pronounced musicodramatic gift, Rameau left Lully where he belonged, in the past. The *lullistes* condemned Rameau as too loud, too busy, too orchestral, too vocal. But Campra, a *ramiste*, took the same line with approval when he noted that Rameau's first opera, *Hippolyte et Aricie* (1733), had enough in it for ten operas by anyone else.

Rameau had waited fifty years before making his operatic debut. He was known for a treatise on harmony and works for harpsichord; where he got his flair is anybody's guess, but *Hippolyte* is a great work of theatre, as *ramiste* in its musical push as it is *lulliste* in format. An adaptation of Euripides' tale of Phaedra and her guilty love for her stepson, *Hippolyte* drew freely from Racine's *Phèdre* to feature a hero, Thésée, who really sounds like one—not because the librettist, Abbé Simon-Joseph Pellegrin, tells us so but because Rameau does.

No wonder the *lullistes* felt so threatened by Rameau. His music bent a qualified realism into the heroic, a grotesquerie into the comic, a hunger into the idyllic. For some, no amount of ballet—Rameau supplied plenty—could mitigate the sheer rhythmic drive of Rameau's motion or the emotional weight of his standing still. Lully was large but at least he was simple. Rameau was not simple. He created more than his audience could encompass, sometimes more than his performers could present, and his canon of some seventeen full-length *tragédies* and *opéra-ballets* shows great diversity of technique and genre.

Hippolyte et Aricie was not only Rameau's first opera but his most powerful. He never again attained such protagonistic boldness as in his portrayal of Thésée, nor such human villainy as in his Phèdre. But then he never tried to. For a complete turnaround, *Les Indes Galantes* (Love in the Indies, 1735) abandoned *tragédie* for *opéra-ballet*, rich with *divertissements* (incidental episodes of dance and song). *Opéra-ballet* was far more opera than ballet, and *Les Indes Galantes* offered a prologue and four one-act operas, all devolving on the power of love.

"Indies" here is a fat rubric denoting exoticland, as it takes in Turkey, Peru, Persia, and a peace-pipe ceremony in North America. Given opera's predilection for antique decor, it is noteworthy that the setting is modern, and amidst the spectacle of five different sets of native costume Rameau pursued his experiments in what music could add to text, as in his daring musical "tremors" during an earthquake scene. The usual critical hackles were raised at such reckless naturalism. "I am racked, flayed, dislocated!" one writer complained. Obviously Lully had shown good judgment in deleting from *Alceste*'s premiere one passage in the underworld scene in which the men's chorus imitated the barking of Cerberus.

Castor et Pollux (1737) returned Rameau to the Greek *tragédie*. It is less thrilling than *Hippolyte et Aricie*, more—perhaps harmonious. *Hippolyte* was made of confrontations and anger, scene upon scene; *Castor*'s characters are more in tune with each other. Their problems stem from outside forces rather than interpersonal hostilities, and because it brought out the soothing melodist in Rameau, many consider it his masterpiece. From the first, an air of hopefulness descends: another of Europe's countless meaningless Peaces had been signed a year before in Vienna, and Castor's prologue ignores the opera itself to urge a "make love not war" point of view upon its audience in an appeal to Venus to restrain the God of War.

Veering between *tragédie* and *opéra-ballet*, Rameau preserved Lully's theatrical effects while elaborating his own musical credo, which is why his quicksilver melodies suit modern taste better than Lully's turgid recitative does. The so-called ballet (actually another *opéra-ballet*) *Les Fêtes d'Hébé* (1739) achieves an amazing mosaic of genres in its prologue and three one-act salutes to poetry, music, and dance, respectively, despite a weak libretto. The prologue is a comedy, the poetry act a romance, the music act a *tragédie*, and the dance act a pastorale. Almost nothing happens in any of them, yet such is Rameau's dash that the evening holds together.

Easily the most entertaining of all Rameau's operas is *Platée* (1745), an *opéra-ballet* run amok on pranks and spoofs. Platée is the queen of a swamp; ugly beyond belief, she thinks herself irresistible to men. Jupiter, seeking to tease Juno out of her jealousy, arranges a mock courtship and wedding of Platée, which Juno will intrude on and which —when she gets a look at the "bride"—will give her a good laugh and reconcile her to her consort. Many analysts have likened Rameau's pastoral style to Watteau's, but Watteau's terrain never shook with such cruel badinage. Rameau deliberately overdoes everything; his indolent nymphs and sarcastic Olympians carry the pastorale over into lunacy. Zephyrs murmur and brooklets tinkle in other pastorales. In *Platée*, the heavens drip goo and frogs, donkeys, and angry birds raise a tumult.

Platée is a masterpiece, its one drawback being the nonstop ridicule of its heroine. She is fatuous, pushy, and impossibly self-absorbed; still, why pick on her? Perhaps to mitigate the sport, Rameau cast the lead role not for a woman but for a tenor *en travesti* (in drag). This is the most notable example of the Italian influence that had been creeping into French opera since Lully's death, for Platée is nothing less than the man-eating duenna of Venetian opera promoted to principal status.

This Italian influence is a major consideration in our discussion of the hundred years after *L'Incoronazione di Poppea*, the first unquestioned great event in opera. For while French opera was founded as a meticulously French institution, every other nation either worked out a compromise with the Italian model or gave in to it altogether. Now that we've seen what the impervious French were up to, let us consider coeval developments in Italian opera. To understand that main route is to know the whole map.

It will be clearest if we start with two generalizations. First, the earthy and the heroic in opera were separated into two mutually exclusive forms, *opera buffa* (comic opera) and *opera seria* (serious opera). Second, the careful creation of a musical texture capable of moving in and out of the declamatory, the songlike, and real song was overthrown by an exhaustive interest in song and disdain of everything else. The aria became supreme.

Two more generalizations. First, comic and serious opera were separated by the will of prominent literary men—not composers. Second, the collapse of the verbally beatified recitative and *arioso* and the rise of the aria was an accident that began to happen when Venice threw open the doors of a public opera house. Though librettists and composers both helped launch the "aria" opera, it was two noncreative groups who were most responsible. These were the public, who loved singing stars best when they were singing full-out; and the singers, who agreed with the public.

If the French liked a drama-oriented opera, the Italians preferred the music. The French would ask, "Is the libretto worth its stuff *as a play?* Can I hear the words? Will the singers promise not to obscure the music with vocal filigree? Will the machines and dancers fill out the theatrical concept so as to enrich the scene with wonder and beauty?" The Italians would ask, "Who's singing tonight?"

Opera in its pre-aria days brought out the best in singers. The recitative, slowly spinning out its musicophonic phrases, was ultimately tedious, but it did require singers of great expressive powers. The post-Monteverdi Italian public, however, cared less for textual intonation than for florid vocal thrills. They wanted trills, embellishments, high and low notes, variations, coloratura. They needed celebrity performers to fix on. Gradually the continuity of fame established certain singers as the focus of opera, and by the end of the eighteenth century they were so vital to the fortunes of a given performance that they wrested control from the composer and librettist.

From a rare aesthetic experiment spoken of in hushed tones by the few who were let in on it, opera had become a nightly diversion known to anyone who cared to make its acquaintance and take it for granted. Opera theatres functioned as public parties where art was only one of the attractions. Gossip, political intrigue, gambling, social climbing, and assorted beau monde pantywaisting formed a substantial fraction of an evening's business in the opera house. With so much going on, there was none of the silent concentration the public offers opera today. Many of the ticket holders were there only because the action was, and had little if any interest in hearing music. Even people who did have an interest didn't necessarily hear an opera from beginning to end. They came and went when convenient, slipping in and out of each others' boxes to pursue their diverse courses as pillars or termites of society. The composer and historian Charles Burney wrote in the 1770s of a performance in Milan, "The noise was abominable, except while two or three airs and a duet were singing, with which everyone was in raptures."

The raptures centered on the singing more than the airs—what the Italians call *bel canto*. Literally the word *canto* means both song and singing, but by the late 1600s the operagoing public trusted the teller, not the tale. Even those nations not sympathetic to the curious sound of the *castrato* voice began to accept, then delight in it—England, for instance, and Germany. As sheer phenomenon—for that's apparently what they were, novelty that never lost its ability to awe—the *castrati* simply elbowed everyone else out of the way, with the exception of the most gifted and tenacious sopranos.

Sopranos, baritones, basses, and the generally disdained tenor were after all human behind all the technique that teachers could drill into them, all the poetry that creators could invest them with, and all the roulades they could drum up by themselves. The *castrati* weren't quite human, it seems. Sounding glorious, they naturally usurped the visual glory as well, setting the custom for stage deportment based on egomania rather than character. During an aria, other singers in view respectfully (or contemptuously) retired upstage, and might join in the applause (or the heckling) at the close. Meanwhile the aria singer struck a pose, waited out the orchestral introduction, and let fly.

And that was opera, a show-biz treat inflated by singers' fees and sustained by the acclamations of the public. (The *castrato* Carlo Broschi, known as Farinelli, so moved one woman at a performance in London that she cried out, "One God, one Farinelli!") From devoted inceptions in the Italian cities and in Paris as music theatre, opera had turned into music circus in which the performers—whether aerialists, clowns, or even beasts—were the whole show. Opera was going decadent.

The generalizations stated a little earlier hold that the aria-izing of opera was partly accidental and partly willed. The accidental obtains in the tacit agreement between singers and public that *bel canto* be made the paramount condition of opera. The willed, oddly, attempted to rationalize opera and only succeeded in institutionalizing its irrationality.

How did that happen? The freewilling rationalists, being literary men, ordered opera through its libretto but not its music. They said, "The shape of opera lies in its words. Control the words and one controls opera." Wrong. The shape of opera lies in its music. Music sets tone, delineates action, explains character, rhapsodizes, hates, arranges, lures, loves and fights and dies. The music controls the words—we've seen it gently start to do so in Rameau. In music theatre, the words work through the music; music doesn't work through words. In those days as now, people flocked to opera without having the vaguest idea what the words meant and had a great time, even a fulfilling experience. Would they go if they couldn't hear the music?

The literary movement that attempted to clean opera up began in 1692 with the formation of the Arcadian Academy in Rome. This was an intellectuals' club with a pastoral theme (members took rustic pseudonyms) convened for conversation and thought; one topic was the haphazard nature of the opera libretto. The Arcadians saw in Italian opera—they had little access to the French model—a chaos of passions with pointlessly gnarled plots and a lack of moral structure. The singing star was still only on the rise then, so *bel canto* was not among their complaints. They worried about the material itself, opera as written and composed.

Not being composers, they couldn't do anything about the music. But as prominent or soon-to-be prominent literary men they could tighten the opera libretto. They outlawed the many subsidiary characters, comedy, supernatural effects, and verbal overstatement endemic to Venetian opera. From now on, *no diversions*—just a main plot and one subsidiary plot using perhaps six aristocratic principals and a few extras. They favored plots with a didactic serviceability, gilding them with a high quality of poetry. They abhorred violence, preferring "styles" of conflict rather than the real thing—many duels are threatened, few fought. And they broke all their scenes into causes and effects, the cause relegated to recitative and the effect formalized as the aria. (As the critic Willi Flemming later put it, "the recitative loads the gun, the aria fires it," meaning that the recitative moves the plot action and the aria develops character expression.) Unfortunately this recitative was not the resonant speech-song of Peri, Caccini, Monteverdi, and Cavalli, but a square-cut declamation of no musical value whatever, and sparsely accompanied (usually by harpsichord and/or cello). The aria, of course, was totally musical, a very Pegasus of song. Singers winged high, like deities— "One God, one Farinelli!"

The aria was rigidly structured. Called the *da capo* aria, it comprised three parts: a first section, a corollary or contrasting middle section, and the first section repeated *da capo* ("from the top"), this time with vocal decoration. Thus each singer's performance of a given aria was different, depending on his ability to prepare or even improvise the right shade of decoration, in pastel or earth tones according to character.

What about duets, trios, choruses and such, so necessary to relieve the monotony of the solo? There were very few, a duet sprinkled here and there, usually a "chorus" (actually an ensemble of all the principals) at the very end. Thus the "aria opera" played right into the hands of the singers, who would much rather have the stage to themselves than share a number with their colleagues. Worse yet, with the action largely worked out in arias, there was little chance for real drama, for any fast contraction of the plot. Everything was expansion, a long sequence of tiny concerts in which one character would express his mind and then exit, then another character would express his mind, and then exit. There was no flow, no drive, just a rhythm of lumps.

Because comedy was forbidden, this form of opera was called "serious": *opera seria*. It thought itself not just serious but heroic, using primarily historical characters, telling of their amorous and political intrigues in three acts, and winding it all up with a *lieto fine*, the still popular happy ending, preferably brought about by the gesture of a magnanimous tyrant. There were *Dido*s, *Xerxes*es, *Scipio*s, *Merope*s, *Cato*s, *Semiramis*es, *Montezuma*s, *Horace*s, *Alexander*s, *Caesar and Cleopatra*s, each with its step-by-step imbroglio of highborn figures and exit arias. More rules, more rigidity: each leading character gets five arias (but never two in a row); each aria should show a different emotional facet of the character (dignity, ecstasy, gallantry); there should be *aria cantabile* (the aria as expressive beauty) and *aria d'agilità* (the aria as daredevil stunt); the title character gets a delayed—therefore suspenseful—entrance. And so on.

Historians invariably describe the movement that created *opera seria* as a "reform." Was it one? Even when composers and librettists bent the rules, the form still amounted to mechanical punctilio, and complete performances of these highly episodic *opere serie* today strike us as hopelessly leaden, except for those few composed by men of insuperable genius, such as Handel. Apologists remind us that conventions of one era always seem silly to audiences of another era. Not true. All conventions are not equal—some are born silly and stay that way while others only take a little getting used to. We may never understand the friezelike stillness of the Greek stage, for instance, but we have no trouble with the Elizabethan habit of writing plays in verse. Indeed, great verse seems to focus great drama.

So let's not accede blindly to convention, but judge it—and *opera seria*'s conventions do not judge well. In throwing out the supernatural spectacle and placing importance on the literary quality of the librettos, the reformists did all right. However, in purging comedy they did not refine so much as impoverish, for comedy is one of theatre's most vital dynamics, a major leverage in prying realism out of the natural fantasy of the stage. They were idealists, no question. But they weren't musicians, and—much of their current press to the contrary—they weren't great dramatists.

On the other hand, they codified what was in some ways already coming about anyway. The infamous *da capo* aria was used, not invented, by the reformists. Even as they produced their first reform librettos in the early and middle 1690s, the aria opera was asserting itself in Naples, where a musical community had grown so active that it usurped leadership from Venice and lent its name to a new school of opera. This school is closely identified with the reformists, and it is not clear where Neapolitan opera ends and reform opera begins. They influenced each other. No one person or place devised the *da capo* aria, but Naples publicized it and the reformists certified it. The reformists separated serious from comic opera, and so did Naples: in the second decade of the 1700s, one Neopolitan theatre made a specialty of one-act comic operas sung in the local dialect. (Like the old *intermedi*, these slim pieces fit nicely between the acts of a serious play or opera, though reformist thinking frowned on such mixing.) Meanwhile, led by Allessandro Scarlatti, Neapolitan composers wrote either serious or comic, never both at once, helping to define two contrasting musical idioms that would further separate what had once been two fundamental and related operatic modes. Yes, *related*. Those who need proof that the sublime is only one step from the ridiculous have only to sit in on a performance of *L'Incoronazione di Poppea*.

Whether one calls it Neapolitan opera or *opera seria*—or, as most Europeans called it, "Italian opera"—this was the form that swept the West in the first half of the 1700s. Its influence was incalculable. Besides commercializing opera as a concert of costumed singers only nominally in their roles, *opera seria* confirmed dramatic and musical patterns still in use as much as two hundred years later, meanwhile edging comedy out of prominence for about fifty years. Obviously, it could not have felt so stilted to its public in the 1700s as it does to us—their spoken theatre, too, was stuffy and disjointed compared to ours—and the music must have redeemed a lot of crimes. It is also true that the better *opera seria* librettos, while flat as drama, were at times wonderfully poetic.

The librettists most associated with *opera seria* are Silvio Stampiglia, Apostolo Zeno, and Pietro Metastasio, in ascending order of importance. Stampiglia was a founder of the Arcadians, Zeno the most influential of the reformists at first, and Metastasio the greatest overall. They succeeded each other as Caesarean Poet at the Viennese court, thereby impressing the virtues of *opera seria* on what was then the musical center of the German subcontinent. Their period begins with the premiere in 1693 of *La Forza del Virtù* (The Power of Virtue), written by others but generally considered the first *opera seria*. Zeno more than anyone laid down the rules, but Metastasio's became the deathless verse of the genre, set over and over again by composers, a few of them as many as seventy times. Some musicians couldn't get enough of Metastasio, and took to writing several different versions of the same libretto. At one time or another, Handel, Gluck, Mozart, and Meyerbeer all "collaborated" with a Metastasian text, and such once essential composers as Johann Adolph Hasse, Niccolò Jommelli, and Tommaso Traetta virtually based their operatic output on Metastasio. Clearly, the man had something.

He was a fine poet. Connoisseurs enjoyed reading his verses for their verbal niceties alone, and no doubt *opera seria* would have run out of steam without the concise rightness of his lines pulling it on its candy-box excursions into the historical past. There aren't many really first-rate librettists in opera's history; the list might include only Busenello, Da Ponte, Wagner, Boito, Forzano, and von Hofmannsthal. Metastasio isn't one of them, but he wrote twenty-seven librettos—more than any of the great ones—which resulted in well over a thousand different operas performed from Petersburg to Lisbon.

Metastasio's life was a rags-to-riches romance. Found singing in the streets by one of the Arcadians, who adopted him and changed his last name from Trapassi to Metastasio (which means, roughly, "Transformatio"), educated and endowed, Metastasio became one of the great literary eminences of the eighteenth century. Though he made no history outside of the arts, he was intimate with those who did. Not surprisingly, there is an exaltation of epoch about his work; it is very post-Lully (and the Divine Right) but also very pre-Beethoven (and the Democratic Revolution). Metastasio's time was that of the illusory Enlightenment, when absolute monarchs traded ideas with *philosophes* at soirées but traded in war and repression in their state chambers. Because he hobnobbed with polite despots, Metastasio's operatic despots are unnaturally flexible (at least in the last scene, in time to bring about a *lieto fine*), though doctrinaire frontiers of duty, patriotism, and honor —i.e., Holy Roman stability—hem everybody in. Structure is everything in *opera seria*. The social code depicted, regardless of time and place, is structured. The operas are structured by acts, the acts by scenes, the scenes by recitative-and-aria, with an overture to open and an ensemble to close. How was art to breathe?

Only one element of anarchy subverted this structure, the star singer. Almost invariably Italian, the singers got their training in an age when careful physical preparation of the voice, instinctual musicianship, and solid grounding in repertory were taken for granted, when orchestras (except in France) were small and composers wrote for the voice instead of at it, when there was no jet lag and no language barrier because all opera (again except in France) was Italian. It was a golden age for singing, if not for music drama. Singers' vanity was the legend of that time, the big bad wolf that broke into Metastasio's brick house, ate all his pigs, and sat staring in a mirror for hours, trying on costumes. No matter what an opera was about, no matter who wrote it or who was in the audience, singers ruled.

For instance, while rehearsing Johann Adolph Hasse's setting of Metastasio's libretto *Demofoönte* in Dresden in 1748, the great poet himself encountered heavy weather in the person of the local prima donna, Faustina Bordoni. The issue concerned where Bordoni was going to stand in a certain scene. Metastasio wanted her placed according to character; Bordoni wanted to be placed according to pride. Hers. Because Molière had once worked in a theatre whose left stage door gave on a garden and whose right door gave on a courtyard, stage left was known throughout Europe as *coté jardin* (garden side) and stage right as *coté cour* (court side)—and for some reason the *jardin* traditionally belonged to the headliner. But Metastasio had taken great pains to lay out this particular scene's blocking to suit the dramatic situation, and he tried his considerable eloquence to its limits in an attempt to pry Bordoni out of the garden. He pointed out that as she was playing a princess disguised as a slave, realism of character demanded that she appear meek, unimportant in the stage picture. Nothing doing. Metastasio even appealed to the composer Hasse, who happened to be Bordoni's husband. Useless.

"A slave cannot occupy the *jardin!*" cried Metastasio, keening for his shattered poetry.

"A slave?" replies Bordoni. "Never! A *princess! Disguised* as a slave!"

"But everyone in the opera *thinks* you are a slave!"

Bordoni smiles; she has him now. "But everyone in the auditorium knows I am Bordoni."

It was like that everywhere. In another part of the forest, Handel attempted to implant an apprehension of musical integrity in Bordoni's rival, Francesca Cuzzoni, by offering to heave Cuzzoni out the window.

Most of this celebrity anarchy consisted only of posturing and threats. But then, so did *opera seria*. Handel's *Tamerlano* (1724) is typical; its look at Tamburlaine the conqueror and his prisoner King Bajazet is focused through a dreary politesse. The work was written for London, yet there is nothing of the savagery that Christopher Marlowe brought to the tale centuries earlier. In Nicola Haym's libretto, Tamburlaine intimidates and Bajazet scorns, Bajazet insults and Tamburlaine snarls. The worst thing that happens is Bajazet's suicide; he takes poison and has a moving death scene but—as *opera seria* requires—then "goes tottering to retire within the Scenes." And of course Tamburlaine forgives the survivors at the end. Even in an era that permitted Grub Street hacks to bowdlerize Elizabethan drama, this is very short weight after Marlowe's version: "Now, Bajazeth, abridge thy baneful days And beat thy brains out of thy conquered head," after which the captive smashes his skull against the bars of his cage.

The *pasticcio*, or pastiche, was thoroughly anarchic, a gleaning of bits from different works chopped and formed into an opera patty. (The word *pasticcio* means "pudding." It's close enough.) Because the aria opera consisted of separate numbers and stereotyped situations, it wasn't hard to pull numbers out or add numbers in. As a piece went from city to city, singers often created their own editions of it, omitting and including scenes at their pleasure. By the time a Hasse-Metastasio opera was given for the thirty-seventh time, it could easily represent the fortuitous collaboration of Hasse, Traetta, Galuppi, Bononcini, Graun, Handel, and Mattei for the music and Metastasio, Zeno, Salvi, Rolli, Goldoni, Marchi, and Stampiglia for the words. The composers themselves contributed to this helter-skelter, sometimes apportioning composing chores among three musicians. Despite the reformists' efforts to organize opera, the form is ultimately not a form but a world, an opera scene. As such it does not submit to organization. It contains too many dissents, conspiracies, accidents. Metastasio and his colleagues saw it as a parade—aim it properly, keep the road clear, and march it. Actually, opera is more of a riot.

Our modern urge toward fidelity to antique originals spares us the distortions of the pastiche, but we still have to effect some compromise with *opera seria* today. There are a composer's own revisions, those uncastable *castrato* parts, and the sheer plodding length of it all. Usually we unlink some arias from the chain, or shorten arias by snipping the middle section or the *da capo* repeat. Some performances retain the *da capos* but don't embellish them, which is absurd since they were meant to be embellished. As it happens, though, all these compromises were common even in *opera seria*'s prime; opera was more protean then than now, when everything is set down and only a composer (supposedly) has the right to rearrange his work.

For all of *opera seria*'s faults, few composers of the early 1700s resisted it, except in France. In Germany, opera had been launched in a polyglot muddle of Italian and French musicians, German musicians imitating both, and the infrequent instance of a German adapting an Italian work to a German style. (Heinrich Schütz, the greatest German composer of the century, set a German translation of Rinuccini's *Dafne* libretto in 1627, but we can only guess at its riches, as the score has vanished.) The disruption caused by the Thirty Years War of 1618–48, possibly the ugliest conflict in human history up to that time, was nearly fatal to German opera. But somehow the muddle became lively again in the late 1600s, and a true German continuity was promised in Hamburg, a free city which had managed to stay out of the fighting. There, a public theatre rose at the site of the old goose market in 1678, and Gänsemarkt opera found its champion in Reinhard Keiser, a wildly talented and prolific composer whose eclectic casts of characters and flexible *arioso* were not unlike the rich charades of the Venetian school. Keiser melded French and Italian styles with his own, but his subject matter leaned heavily to the German; mixed in with biblical and mythological entries is one called *Störtebecker und Joedge Michaels* (1701), on the life and loves of an outlaw.

So there was a German style in opera just as there were the French and various Italian styles. But there was no Paris in Germany to centralize the art. Politically Germany was even more of a patchwork than Italy, so divided that it was easy for the foreigner to conquer. By the time the reform librettists and Neapolitan composers were pushing the aria opera, many German composers crossed over to it without hesitation. Nice to settle down to something steady.

Even in democratic Hamburg, where Keiser's exuberant music theatre had given the folk a product of their own, Italian opera crept in with a young German whom Keiser had hired as second violinist in the opera orchestra, Georg Friedrich Händel. Keiser's German and Handel's Italian opera got into something of a contest when the newcomer made his first try, *Almira* (1705), though because the piece was as much German as Italian in style (it had a bilingual libretto), this was a confrontation of the old master and the upstart rather than of native and alien forces.

But Handel Latinized himself greatly by studying in Italy soon after *Almira*, and this was just about the time that *opera seria* became the mainstay of the German court capitals. Whether composed by Italian émigrés or German imitators, the Italian was the brand of opera being done—and if someone had had the idea of founding a real German opera, the important singers would simply have refused to learn parts that were not in Italian and did not give them their solos with *da capo* trimming. Thus Karl Heinrich Graun, the top-ranking composer in Berlin in the mid-1700s, wrote an *Adriano in Siria* (1745), an *Ifigenia in Aulide* (1748), a *Coriolano* (1749)—but never a German work. And when Graun's employer, Frederick the Great, collaborated with Graun on *Montezuma* (1755), Frederick wrote the libretto in French and had his court poet translate it into Italian. *Montezuma* is no vanity production—Frederick's picture of a brutally imperialistic Cortés is more sympathetic with the dialectic of our day than of Frederick's, and Graun was already beginning the subversion of the *da capo* aria that was to reclaim the pacing of opera as theatre. Yet to sing *Montezuma* in German would have been unthinkable.

In the nineteenth century, when numerous oppressed cultures roused themselves in liberation movements, these movements were to find opera a useful medium of popular incitement—not through propaganda, but through the simple inflammation of martial anthems or appeals to the heritage of father- and motherland. In Belgium, France, Italy, Germany, and Czechoslovakia, movements for freedom from local tyrants or foreign occupation turned to the idea of a national opera and found, to their astonishment, that national opera had to be invented overnight. Except on the popular stage, there were no precedents for a music theatre that absorbed folklore and history for its subjects, dialect or argot but at least language for its speech, ethnic atmosphere in its music, and a cultural attitude in its point of view. Why?

Because Italian cosmopolitanism subdued national impulses everywhere except in France. In other countries on the Continent the story was similar to that of Germany, where *opera seria* mopped up the field. Only England was different. While French opera resented foreign influence as a matter of policy and German opera welcomed it so warmly that it turned foreign itself, England was heterogeneous. The "new music" of the Florentines was known there, in both its recitative and its more songlike identity, and British travelers returned home with reports of the differing French and Italian formats and production technique. Moreover, the English had their native form, the court masque, a combination of spoken poetry, song, and dance for soloists and ensemble using a sustained theme but not equipped to delineate a plot.

The vital Elizabethan stage might have generated something comparable in music but for the intervention of the Puritan Revolution, which closed the public theatres and generally discouraged anything flamboyant, such as art. (Oddly, it had one good effect, in that limiting the use of music in church served to strengthen the growth of secular music.) Cromwell's regime institutionalized the Briton's congenital suspicion of aliens just when a sampling of alien opera would have been beneficial. At any rate, first stabs were had at opera even under Cromwell, in private performances. Some were masques stretching to tell a tale; others were copies of continental opera. Matthew Locke's *Cupid and Death* (1643) is an example of the former, *The Siege of Rhodes* (1656)—composed by five musicians (including Locke) to the words of William D'Avenant—of the latter.

So far, chancy but potential. The end of Cromwell's Commonwealth, however, saw the reopening of the theatres, and with the return of spoken drama, opera moved to the back burner. But Locke, for one, did not give up. He contributed to an English version of Lully's *comédie-ballet Psyché* (1673), and John Blow set what is probably the first legitimate English opera of which the music has survived, the pastorale *Venus and Adonis* (c. 1684), a mixture of French and Italian styles crisped in the sturdy cut of English song.

Blow's pupil Henry Purcell is the man who had it in him to launch a true English opera. Unfortunately, he just missed the calling, writing one superb hour-long English opera and then busying himself with masques and other incidental whingding. His pen flowed with overtures, songs, dances, interludes, and choruses—but all this was baggage,

not the flight itself. In work after work Purcell filled in *between* the
plot scenes instead of facing them head-on. In *The Fairy Queen* (1692),
some two hours' worth of musical vaudeville enlists such self-contained episodes as the tormenting of a drunken poet by the spirit world,
a comic flirtation, the solemn convention of Night, Mystery, Secrecy,
and Sleep with full retinue, and a parade of the four seasons—all this
somehow "related" to the plot of *A Midsummer Night's Dream*. That
is what *The Fairy Queen* claims to be, an adaptation of Shakespeare's
play (not Spenser's epic) with five extensive musicales closing each of
what was left of the five original acts. There were two casts, one for
the play part and one for the music—more like a *comédie-ballet* than an
opera.

The Fairy Queen's score is marvelous. The "four seasons" scene,
to pick one example, shows not only variety in the four solos but characterful invention, with spring pompous in her embellished line; summer a spry *castrato*, "smiling, wanton, fresh, and fair"; autumn a vain
tenor; and winter a bass dazed in decline. Grand music. But what has
it to do with *A Midsummer Night's Dream?* One searches the score for
some reference to Shakespeare's plot: nothing. The only item that
play and score have in common is the forest setting.

Works like this *Fairy Queen* were called "semi-operas." It was a
touchy genre. Some of the public wanted only the play, others only
the music. Still, it enjoyed a vogue in the 1690s, drawing contributions
from Purcell for *Dioclesian* (1690), *King Arthur; or, The British
Worthy* (1691)—with a text by John Dryden—*Timon of Athens*
(1694), *The Indian Queen* (1695), and *The Tempest* (1695). The
highly conditional state of semi-opera led Purcell to throw his weight
around here and tread lightly there. *King Arthur* is so fully composed
that it *might* be an opera, while *Timon of Athens* is more of a play
containing a one-act masque.

Altogether, Purcell had donated musical portions to more than
forty stage works by 1695, the year of his death. With him died English opera. But just before he embarked on his series of semi-operas he
had composed the first (and for two centuries the last) great English
music drama, *Dido and Aeneas* (1689). First performed by the student
body of Josiah Priest's School for Young Gentlewomen in Chelsea, this
remarkable artifact shows us what English opera might have been like
if someone had taken over for Purcell after his death. We get recitative
and aria, dances, and choruses as usual—but none of it is as usual: all of
it is distinctly British in aplomb, prance, and general cut of jib. In the
largely Italian context of Baroque opera, Nahum Tate's all-English
libretto stands out, of course. But it is the way Purcell set Tate's verses

that marks *Dido and Aeneas* for us as the classic sample of a British style in opera, as when Dido's courtiers reassure her doubting attraction to Aeneas in hearty chorus:

> Fear no danger to ensue;
> The Hero loves as well as you.

Dido is scarcely an hour long, yet filled with incidental charms. The interaction of the two principals is lightened by scenes for witches and sailors until, all charm put by, the composer spins out a moving solo for Dido's suicide, "When I am laid in earth," using the few words over and over as verbal-vocal components of a primarily musical structure. Three lines alone provision a scene of amazing emotional expansion, so canny is Purcell's use of them:

> When I am laid in earth,
> May my words create no trouble in thy breast;
> Remember me! but ah! forget my fate.

The Camerata's plan for music to serve the words has fallen away. Purcell shows us not the exception but the rule, one that the aria sequences of *opera seria* were to make permanently binding: that music does not just underline the words but exploits them, defining whole scenes in arrantly musical forms.

With Purcell's death English opera lost its direction. Foreigners sucked in, grabbing, and natives also essayed the foreign manner, most notably Thomas Clayton, an English musician reborn in Italy who either composed himself or (some said) borrowed Italian originals for *Arsinoe, Queen of Cyprus* (1705). Clayton went on to *Rosamond* (1707), with a libretto by the satirist Joseph Addison, but despite *Arsinoe*'s success, Clayton never really established himself. Indeed, no one man alien or local seemed able to replace the enterprising Purcell —in any language or style. In place of consistency there was novelty, and London's first taste of *bel canto* shows a typical sense of potluck, of opera as gadget. The work, Johann Jakob Greber's *Gli Amore Piacevole d'Ergasto* (1705), was Italian in form, composed by a German, and referred to by Londoners as *The Loves of Ergasto*.

Year by year *opera seria* inched its way in by virtue of first-rate *bel canto, castrati* and all. And yet, even as they acquired the taste for Italian opera, enjoying the singing during the performances and reading a translation of the librettos in some spare moment, Londoners had access to intermezzos *in English* between the acts, provided by managements not yet secure in their public's devotion to alien art. A major point here: an audience can appreciate a type of opera that by its very nature forecloses on the fundamental purpose of music theatre—the direct and complete communion of work and audience. Yet that audience can't give up that communication, and finds it in some alternative like these English intermezzos.*

No doubt if English singers had the technique for *bel canto*, the whole story would have been different. But there was a choice: great singing in Italian opera, or less great singing by natives in a native opera that had yet to be produced. The question was settled by Handel's coming to England in 1710.

Though he anglicized his name, Handel remained at base a German musician working in an Italian form. His output ran heavily to opera, opera written for London but obedient to the Italian star system. Because of this, there are those who accuse Handel of having killed English music. In fact, English music was already dead, and if there had been talent to revive it, Handel's genius would have been a challenge and an inspiration. As it was, while even Handel could not make *opera seria* stick, he did give his adopted countrymen one of their most vital forms, the oratorio.

We last saw Handel trying his operatic wings in Hamburg. In the meantime he had spent two years in Italy (as so many northern Europeans have had to, to release the sensuality in their logy *Schmerz*). In Rome, Handel touched base with the Arcadians, in Naples he studied composition, in Venice he witnessed the staging of opera for an aficionado public, his own *Agrippina* (1709). He gorged on knowhow. Fittingly, his first opera for England, *Rinaldo* (1711), did not so much open as explode.

The libretto for *Rinaldo*, taken from Tasso's *Gerusalemme Liberata*, was cooked up by Handel's first impresario, Aaron Hill, and—of course—translated into Italian, by Giacomo Rossi. For his part, Handel culled some two thirds of the music from his trunk. But there is no taste of the chowder. On the contrary, *Rinaldo* is a rousing adventure of crusaders versus infidels, true and false love, Christian faith and Eastern magic. The cast of the premiere did justice to the work, and its success laid the cornerstone for the palace of opera that Handel raised (of cardboard, it turned out) in England into the 1740s.

Despite Handel's extraordinary gifts and the care with which he cast his shows, his output of thirty-six operas for England had constant ups and downs in popular approval. There was, first, the economic angle. An opera company, the Royal Academy of Music, was formed

---

* Byron, in a footnote to *Don Juan*, cites an Englishwoman's opinion in this matter: "Rot your Italianos! for my part, I loves a simple ballat!"

around Handel, with shares sold to the public and full seasons to maintain. This meant singers to be hired, other composers enlisted—Handel can't do it alone—and a public to keep enchanted. One successful series of performances can be a gold mine and a personal triumph for those concerned. But the obligation to succeed regularly on an annual basis can lead to bankruptcy and humiliation.

There was the political angle. Whigs and Tories used their nights at the opera as an extension of their bickering. Since Handel had been court musician to George I when they were both still in Germany, the Tories expressed their disgust for the Hanoverian dynasty by rallying behind the Royal Academy's other major composer, Giovanni Battista Bononcini. Hating George I, they hated Handel. Naturally the Whigs sided with Handel; the feud was on. (Oddly, the Prince of Wales, later George II, misconstrued the conflict. He joined with the Tories to offend his father, whom he loathed, though the Tories' target was not only the King but all his issue as well. Apparently everyone was too embarrassed to tell the Prince he was on the wrong side.) Neither Handel nor Bononcini had any personal reason to support the feud, but one does get involved. The Academy tried to display its two star composers in a pastiche, *Muzio Scevola* (1721), in which each man would compose a different act; Whigs and Tories treated this as a Handel-Bononcini contest and prepared to cheer their favorite and greet their enemy in bad silence. *Opere serie* invariably had three acts, and with Bononcini setting the second and Handel the third, another composer was dropped in for the first, but interest followed the "battle" of the two giants so keenly that no one seems to have got the third man's name straight even at the time.

Muzio Scevola settled nothing. Both Bononcini and Handel showed fine form—which is to say, an able curate and Jeremiah each preached a sermon. Bononcini was not the hack that some have made him out to be; finesse was his forte, one neatly appropriate for the slender charm of the pastorale or comic romance rather than the jaw-breaking grandeur of *opera seria*. But Handel was the genius of the place, and none could top him. In the end, Londoners much preferred a feud between rival singers to one between composers, and they got to see just how such feuds work when Handel returned from one of his talent-scouting continental jaunts with a contract signed by the one and only Faustina Bordoni, supreme and terrible ruler of the *jardin*.

So there was the show-biz angle, too; of course there was. Besides Bordoni, Handel had bestowed upon London an awesome array of musicians, including not only the indispensable *castrati* but Francesca

Cuzzoni, less than Bordoni in terms of glamor and vocal agility, but most of them all for the seamless heart of her singing. If *bel canto* is anything, it is a *mutuality*, a coming together of text and music, singer and listener, a cohesion of intellect and sensibility. Cuzzoni apparently had it, but on the other hand there's nothing like novelty—and that was Bordoni.

With two volatile sopranos on his hands (not to count the *castrati*), Handel had to be very, very symmetrical with any opera that dared frame them both, and *Alessandro* (1726), the work in which Bordoni made her London debut, moves *very* carefully. It boasted perhaps the greatest cast of the era—the two women plus the *castrato* Senesino and the bass Giuseppe Maria Boschi. In all the excitement, who could resist taking some side in a Cuzzoni-Bordoni controversy? Certainly the two sopranos couldn't. They worked up to an onstage hair-pulling incident just in time for the climax of the following season, during Bononcini's *Astianatte* (1727). Yet despite the notoriety, the Academy could not sell enough tickets to stay in the black.

And there was the cultural angle. Alien music theatre that does not offer even the amenity of translation into the vernacular is a risky proposition of limited mutuality. As illustration of how theatre should operate, *The Beggar's Opera* (1728) opened a few months before the Academy folded forever. This extraordinarily idiomatic piece did not crush *opera seria* or Handel, but it reminded Londoners of what they had been missing in those Italian tales of haughty romance—namely, comic naturalism. A tale of thieves and trulls set to tunes in the popular idiom and performed in English, *The Beggar's Opera* appealed to all, instantly, requiring no tolerance for convention.

The Beggar's Opera belongs to the genre called ballad opera, a forerunner of modern musical comedy. Interspersed throughout the action are little songs, choruses, and dances, all more or less motivated by the plot though not terribly essential to it. John Gay wrote the libretto and Johann Christoph Pepusch arranged the music, folk and popular tunes plus one bit each from Purcell and Handel (a Crusaders' March from *Rinaldo*) to which Gay fit his own lyrics. Ironic that Handel should be included—purposeful irony. Gay's tone is satiric, his tale of love and intrigue among the criminal community intended as digs at contemporary sociopolitics and *opera seria* (even including a lampoon of the Cuzzoni-Bordoni business in the portrayal of two women who love Macheath, the robber hero). Where the *Rinaldo* march once accompanied lofty crusaders, Pepusch allotted it to a band of cutthroats chortling, "Let us take the road!" as they depart a tavern for an assortment of dirty deeds.

In Gay's eyes all men are thieves. Sings Mr. Peachum, a honcho of the underworld:

> The Statesman, because he's so great,
> Thinks his Trade as honest as mine.

The whole piece is so blackhearted behind its drollery that Bertolt Brecht, when he adapted it into his libretto for *The Threepenny Opera*, had only to impose a layer of Marxist misanthropy upon Gay's already quite dour original. Kurt Weill, Brecht's collaborator, even retained the tune of Gay's opening number, "Thro' All the Employments of Life," from which comes the couplet quoted above.

Gay's pastiche spoof, as cynical as *opera seria* was romantic, at first enjoyed a parochial triumph in London for the two authors and their producer, John Rich. (Some wag observed that the show "made Gay rich and Rich gay.") It was an urban rage, a pet of townies rather than the folk. Hogarthian was what it was. It inspired a sequel, *Polly*, published in 1729 but considered too dangerous to produce (and expurgated at that) till 1777. But soon enough *The Beggar's Opera* became an international triumph, beaming its satiric naturalism at other audiences who had also been stuffed with the fat of opera. Ballad opera was lean, a kind of purge. And, of course, there were to be other ballad operas, all profiting by the advantages of vernacular librettos, tunes in the popular idiom, and comic realism. Authors of such pieces had no problem deciding whether words or music should dominate—this was a fifty-fifty partnership. The public enjoyed the music and heard the words: complete music theatre.

Handel meantime persevered, though it grew increasingly clear that the English could make no real commitment to *opera seria*. Yet Handel was strong where *seria* was weak, in the continuity of aria piled on aria. Obviously this is *seria*'s critical flaw, because the forward motion of the plot, dragging itself through one solo after another, keeps working *around* the story's conflicts, setting them up in the recitatives but collapsing them in arias just when they need some connective tension. Handel even made recit musical, bringing the long-established *recitativo accompagnato* (instrumentally accompanied recit) to a new high of dramatic strength. Handel also wandered around opera's fixed position as he chose, getting into the supernatural, as in *Alcina* (1735), dance in *Ariodante* (1735), and even indulging a comic servant character in *Serse* (1738), an adaptation of a Venetian libretto originally written for Cavalli.

Yet the dowdy intransigence of the exit aria stumps even Handel's fierce flair. Take for example *Giulio Cesare* (1724), a look at Julius Caesar's Egyptian campaign with a pretty good libretto by Nicola Haym, an outstanding hit in its days and ours.* The two lead parts, Caesar (originally a *castrato*, now generally a bass-baritone) and Cleopatra (soprano), offer tremendous opportunities to singers with the right combination of vocal dexterity and personal magnetism. Cleopatra especially is a wonderfully rounded character, showing far greater depth than even the impressively "modern" Poppea of Monteverdi and Busenello. Musically the whole role lies in its arias, of course. She is confidently coy in "Non disperar" and all for the love game in "Tu la mia stella sei," when she intends to seduce Caesar to use him against her enemy Ptolemy. The seduction, "V'adoro, pupille," is ravishing. But the imperial hussy finds herself genuinely in love with the Roman, and Handel follows through with the moving "Se pietà di me non senti," showing a new Cleopatra praying for Caesar's safety instead of his worship. Even deeper truths are sifted in "Piangerò la sorte mia," when Ptolemy captures her and she gives way at first to a delectable despair, then to banshee fury as she vows to avenge herself on Ptolemy even after death.

Caesar, too, is richly drawn, perhaps most alluringly in his "Va tacito e nascosto," a "metaphor aria" in which he likens the oily Ptolemy to "the crafty hunter greedy for his prey"—and Handel heightens the simile by weaving a huntlike horn solo into the orchestral texture. Yet amid this inventive variety there is still the dogged layout of the arias. In Act II, a scene in a seraglio garden catches us up on the latest events in the subplot involving Cornelia and her son Sextus, just made widow and orphan by the odious Ptolemy. Not much happens. Both Ptolemy and his general Achilla make overtures to the aggrieved Cornelia; Achilla sings his aria and leaves and Ptolemy sings *his* aria and leaves. Then a minor character cheers Cornelia and Sextus with an opening for a revenge murder of Ptolemy; Cornelia sings *her* aria and leaves and Sextus sings *his* aria to close the scene. How much more incisive all this would be if each of these four principals did not claim a solo—and at that a solo with first part, middle section, and first part *da capo* with vocal decoration. Faced with this scene, Verdi or Gounod would have compressed all four voices into one tight quartet and got just as much said. But opera was much more elastic in their day.

It is interesting to compare Handel with Bononcini, as Londoners did during their trumped-up rivalry; any twenty minutes of Bononcini

---

* This was the work that made a star of Beverly Sills, helped force the current fashion for Handel, and lent the New York City Opera much of its éclat as a major American company, all virtually overnight in 1966.

shows why Handel was so revered by the generations of composers that succeeded him. (Until Mendelssohn and Schumann redisclosed the wonders of Bach in the 1820s and '30s, Handel was thought to have cut the pattern for creative genius in music.) The man really had power—obsession, ambivalence, woe, wonder, rage, and delight are no farther away than a swipe of his pen. Whereas even the best of Bononcini is never pointed enough, not sufficiently *opera*. *Griselda* (1722), often called Bononcini's masterpiece, is typical. Culled from the same source, Petrarch, that generated Chaucer's Clerk's Tale en route to Canterbury, *Griselda* is one of those "patient wife" stories. Indeed, Griselda is too patient; modern minds dislike the wimpy masochism of such patience as hers, dutiful to a husband's insanely cruel tests. (Chaucer, never taken in by the "virtues" of his age, disclaims any intention of teaching wives Griselda's self-denial; the aim is to teach persons to "be constant in adversitee." After all, he reminds us, "it were ful hard to fynde now-a-dayes In al a toun Griseldis thre or two.") In any case, Bononcini does not really bring his characters forward. His attractive musicality endows standard postures—a husband's regret, a wife's suffering, a daughter's innocence, a swain's sentimentality. Bononcini defines the genre but not the specific story.

How musical could opera get was the question, and even in Handel's time, when opera was very musical—though statically musical, lacking interior cohesion—the question had yet to be answered. Some major answers (and another reform) are to come in the next chapter, not only to the words-versus-music problem but to another one, equally relevant to opera's development: comedy versus serious drama. Obviously there is a difference between the two as theatrical forms, and there is also a difference between the kind of music that suits the comic and the kind that suits the serious. But this difference is not easy to pin down; composers will wrestle with the problem of tone and pace in comic opera from now on. *Opera seria* confronts *opera buffa* just as the music confronts the words. Which is to dominate? Or if the two must coexist, what's the right proportion?

These two conflicts form the basis of opera history, libretto versus music and the comic versus the serious. And the two conflicts are really two readings of the same conflict, because comedy is already a word-oriented form in that its naturalism keeps one alert and intellectual, always conscious of the work as presentation, while serious opera will increase its musical component, moving into human ur-myth to cast spells of romantic involvement on the listener. Comedy *is* words: meanings. Romantic (i.e., noncomic) opera is music: sensations.

More of this later. Meanwhile, we have seen opera developed in Italy in the early 1600s as a form of theatre in which music must "deliver" the text without making much extratextual commentary. We have seen audiences and composers both needing more music, eventually to raise up a dais for star singers and *bel canto* by the early 1700s. Except in France, Italian opera has conquered Europe as the story-concert of arias, overshadowing comedy and dragging the rhythm of theatre in a queue of vocal spots like charms bangling on a bracelet.

Now we come to revolution: comedy and music separately reassert themselves.

CHAPTER THREE

The Rise of Comedy and the Flight of Music

*It is to be hoped that some ge-
nius may arise, strong enough
. . . to impart to [opera] the
dignity and ethic spirit that it
now lacks . . . The opera must
be set on a different footing,
that it may no longer deserve
the scorn with which it is regarded by all the nations of Europe.*

—VOLTAIRE, *Mélanges Litteraires*

*There is too much music in mu-
sic drama.*

—BEAUMARCHAIS,
preface to *Tarare*

ONE OF THE MOST INVENTIVE OPERAS OF THE TWENTIETH CENTURY,
Richard Strauss' *Ariadne auf Naxos,* opens "backstage" in the house of
"the richest man in Vienna," where a last-minute emergency of scheduling requires that singers about to perform an *opera seria* on the
Ariadne legend and comedians who were to follow the opera with a
traditional farce merge their separate forces and share the stage. They
will have to create, in effect, an *opera seria* with comic interludes. Naturally, the *seria* people greet the order with consternation and disgust.
Naturally, the comedians take it with cynical tolerance. Noting the
opera's setting, the solitary isle on which Ariadne was abandoned by
Theseus, the farceurs' chief considers that their invasion of the higher
realms of *seria* cannot help but enliven *Ariadne*'s dour poise. "There's
nothing more tasteless than a desert island," he observes.

The excitable young composer of the opera can't understand such philistine complacency. "Ariadne on Naxos, sir!" he cries. "She is the symbol of human loneliness!" "Exactly why she needs some company," replies the jester.

The rapprochement of the comic and tragic—even under duress—was of course the last thing that the propounders of *opera seria* had in mind. But not even Metastasio could prevent an audience from enjoying a comic intermezzo between the acts of an *opera seria:* because art follows nature, and natural life isn't either serious or comic, but both. Sometimes, as in *Ariadne auf Naxos*, both at once. Opera had mixed the two modes in the days of Monteverdi and Cavalli and in some of Purcell's and Lully's pieces, and would remix them again in the work of Mozart. You can't keep a good idea down.

In the early 1700s, the international comic opera form was, of course, *opera buffa*. It involved humorous or sentimental characters usually drawn from the middle class, a certain amount of plot grinding, and less ponderous compositional techniques than informed *opera seria*. Vocal decoration was minimized, for instance, and ensembles were as common as arias, especially ensembles involving the entire cast in a commotion to bring down the house at the end of an act. There were one-act and evening-length *opere buffe*, the one-acters faithful replicas of the ancient *intermedi* and thus heirs to the rich *commedia dell'arte* tradition. A poor relation in the opera family, *opera buffa* never enjoyed the star singers or lavish decor that *opera seria* thrived on. But it set a tone for comic opera for nearly two hundred years after its inception in the early 1700s. The Neapolitans cut the die, and virtually no Neapolitan composer thought himself so fastidious as to write only *seria* or *buffa*. Allessandro Scarlatti, the great master of the Neapolitan school, wrote more than a hundred operas spanning the revolution from the delightfully chaotic Venetian opera to orderly *opera seria*. And toward the end of his career he wrote a *buffa, Il Trionfo dell'Onore* (The Triumph of Honor, 1718), without even having to shift gears.

As the respectable comic form in music theatre, *opera buffa* might have become the prominent form (as *opera seria* was the prominent serious form), but comedy is naturalistic by its very nature, and foreign comedy is unnatural. No matter where or when it is set or how realistic or fantastic its action, comic theatre invariably reflects a naturalism of the time and place of its audience (including revivals of ancient comedy). It didn't matter all that much that *opera seria* was sung—everywhere outside Italy—in a foreign tongue, for *opera seria* was something of a mad dream to begin with. But comedy, with its tales of old cuckolds and young wives, of hustlers and a scheme, of crazies falling in and out of baskets, relies on a kind of alienative intimacy to make its effect. It must address its public directly, so directly that one's sense of logic is never overthrown by the mystery of the theatre ritual. For comedy is logical, antiritual.

And comedy is bound to express itself, in music, in the popular idiom. We've seen something of this already in *The Beggar's Opera:* new lyrics put to pop tunes old and new. The genre in question is ballad opera, but this is merely a scholar's term for what Americans call musical comedy. Germans call it *Singspiel,* the French call it any number of things, and the Italians don't have a precise term for it, as their equivalent, the *commedia dell'arte,* has had a complex on-and-off relationship with its musical component.

In any case, the highfalutin excesses in opera often drove audiences to less luxurious art forms to clear the palette on a little naturalism. What they needed was not *opera buffa*—which is at heart a domesticated *opera seria*—but musical comedy in its various national styles. In France the tradition of such fare was old and pleasantly disreputable, a regular event of the annual city fairs. Paris held two in particular, the late-winter St. Germain Fair on the Left Bank and the late-summer St. Laurent on the Right. These huge commercial festivals ran for months at a time, and side by side with the booths set up for buying and selling stood earthy altars of entertainment. By Lully's time, the *drame forain* (fairground theatre) was already being referred to by set terms (*comédie en chansons,* or *comédie mêlée d'ariettes,* both meaning musical comedy), always a sign that the French intend to institutionalize a genre.

The impresarios of the fairgrounds drew heavily on the public domain, utilizing the timeless tropes of farce and sentiment and any old tunes that an actor could get by with. These were comedies more than musicals, and, anyway, *bel canto* would have marred their informal grain. But there was a hurdle to be leaped—the monopoly retained by the state companies, the Comédie-Française (for drama), the Académie Royale de Musique (for opera), and the Comédie-Italienne (for virtually what the fairgrounds musical comedy did, only with glitz). All Paris flocked to the fairs, and the official houses couldn't afford the competition. The Comédie-Italienne would have run the *drame forain* out of town if it hadn't offended Madame de Maintenon with too nice a caricature in *La Fausse Prude* (The Pretended Prude, 1697) and got run out of town first. But the other two companies tried to squash "*les forains*" with their royal patents. By the beginning of the eighteenth century the heat was on, the Comédie-Française claiming its monopoly on spoken dialogue, the Opéra claiming its monopoly on singing theatre.

The cheesy fairground gang showed their spunk, particularly in their resistance to the curmudgeonly "Romans" (as they called the Comédie-Française people because of the classical settings of Racine and Corneille). Forbidden to employ "dialogue," they let only one actor on stage at a time; there were a lot of entrances and exits, but the show went on, in monologue and pantomime. Forbidden to sing, they hoisted lyric sheets and posted claques, who led the audience in singing the numbers for the gagged actors. After all, the tunes were old friends, already known to the public—"vaudevilles," these tunes were called, and a show that utilized them was a *comédie-vaudeville*.*

By about 1715 the state houses and the *drame forain* had suspended hostilities, the latter buying a share in the royal monopoly, sweet and legal—and the fairground stage developed an all-inclusive designation, "*opéra comique*," perhaps the most ambiguous term the French have ever pulled off. Literally it means "comic opera." As a form it means a number of contradictory things, having evolved its aesthetics several times over the course of time. There has been one constant, however: the use of spoken dialogue (instead of the Italian recitative) between musical numbers.

Of course, back in its first heyday at the Paris fairgrounds, *opéra comique* actually was comic opera, but of a strongly vernacular sort— simple tunes, low fun, a touch of ribaldry, economical production, sentimentality in love and satire in everything else. In short, musical comedy. Despite the overall innocence of the aesthetic, these endeavors had an air of with-it cynicism—but that, too, is basic to comedy.

Opéra comique made its fortune on its librettos. These were something of a hodgepodge of leftover tropes from the medieval mystery plays and the *commedia dell'arte*, tricked out in retellings of fairy tales and spoofs of the latest ventures on the dignified Paris stages. But gradually a regularity of procedure gave birth to a style. Authors became famous writing for the fairs—Alain-Réné Lesage, Jacques-Phillipe d'Orneval, and especially Charles-Simon Favart.

Favart more than anyone developed the reigning style of *opéra comique* in the mid-1700s. He was a real thespian, not a scribbler; his purview took in not only theatre content but stage direction, design,

---

* Note the French predilection for coining terminology but applying it inconsistently. Here *vaudeville* denotes a popular tune adaptable to new lyrics. Later it came to mean an original melody sung by various characters to different lyrics, each character taking a verse. Still later it signified a variety show. This proves that the French are not a serious people.

casting, and everything else. He was part of a duo, the other half being Madame Favart, so-called (Marie-Justine-Benoîte Duronceray), who seconded her husband's efforts in writing and producing but also found time to be the toast of the fair as an actress. Though their private life flashed colors of scandal, on stage they emphasized sentimental rustic romances. "Thanks to you," Voltaire wrote to Favart in 1775, when he was the grand old master of his profession, "[*opéra comique*] has become the delight of all decent folk."

The Favarts influenced the French musical stage in the totality of their approach, even from their very much "off-Broadway" vantage. Lully had given French opera a form, Rameau invigorated it with music. But the continuity of *tragédie* into *opéra-ballet* was not holding up—the works lacked dramatic grip. *Opéra comique* taught vivid lessons in simple dramaturgy: let the material breathe. Opera was ceremonial, larger than life. *Opéra comique* was taken from life. Even its fairy-tale monsters and allegorical types accorded with a kind of perverted realism.

Opéra comique not only gave to opera; it also took from it, mounting precise burlesques of famous *tragédies*—both Lully and Rameau got the treatment. In a spirit exactly comparable to that of American "burlesque" in the Weber and Fields era and of Broadway revues of the 1920s and '30s, a spirit lately passed on to variety shows on American television, *opéra comique* opposed the gravity of opera with the lampoon. Instant heroism got the ax from Favart and company, and so did convention—the *poésie*, the machines, the glazed torpor of the chorus, the irrelevant to-and-fro of the dancers (Favart dubbed his burlesque of Rameau's ballet-heavy *Les Indes Galantes*, *Les Indes Dansantes*).

The musical organization was mediocre, but the theatricality was direct and expert. It had to be. *Tragédie* was a cultural institution. *Opéra comique* was pop art, pop but vital. Leclerc de la Bruère, the librettist of Rameau's *Dardanus* (1739), was so impressed with Favart's burlesque, *Arlequin-Dardanus* (1739—*opéra comique* had tempo!), that he proposed revising the original to absorb some of Favart's "improvements."

Musical comedy's parodistic element is significant, so much so that the spoof aspect of *opéra comique* eventually broke off to found its own genre, *opéra bouffe*—"comic opera"—when *opéra comique* had gone bourgeois. This is why a work such as Offenbach's *Orpheus in the Underworld* plays like a dinky parody of a serious Orpheus opera— it *is* a dinky parody. It is, as Offenbach put it, "*le genre primitif et gai*," all simplicity and reductive imitation. But until comedy won a legitimate chair in the operatic college, it held its classes irregularly, on the sidelines or on a rare sortie into the main halls such as Rameau's *Platée* (1745), which is in essence a musical comedy with an advanced score.

English ballad opera helped German *Singspiel* on its way. In 1743, while the latter was still in its formative stages, Charles Coffey's *The Devil to Pay; or, The Wives Metamorphos'd* (1731) enjoyed great success in Berlin, translated into German and recast with German characters and setting, though retaining its English tunes. The piece threatened to become a classic, so Johann Christian Standfuss supplied a wholly new score to a new translation by Christian Felix Weisse. As *Der Teufel Ist Los; oder, Die Verwandelten Weiber* (1752), the whilom ballad opera helped focus the related but separate genre of *Singspiel*.

Both ballad opera and *Singspiel* lean heavily on naturalistic comedy and simple melodies, but *Singspiel* was more fey and idyllic than ballad opera, and preferred new composition to arrangements of old tunes. English art is often gritty and brutal; a typical ballad opera wallowed in prurience and crime. *Singspiel* doted on true love and the rustic virtues, and couldn't wait for Romanticism to happen so it could discover forests, ruined castles, and family curses. As witness the trendsetting *Singspiel* of Adam Hiller: *Lottchen am Hofe* (Lottie at Court, 1767), *Die Jagd* (The Hunt, 1770), *Der Erntekrantz* (The Harvest Garland, 1771); and of Georg Benda: *Der Dorfjahrmarkt* (The Village Fair, 1775).

As will shortly be seen, *opéra comique* also helped inaugurate Romanticism in music theatre with passes at nature painting, ghostly apparitions, nick-of-time rescues, and the like. This is odd, for the most salient quality in musical comedy, whether French, German, English, or American, is its urge toward satire. Unlike opera, it is an entity invariably as verbal as musical, a profane art, alienative, nonspiritual, and antiromantic. But what happened was that both *opéra comique* and *Singspiel* fell under an Italian influence and began to lose touch with their verbal-naturalistic component. Anything Italian with music in it is always mainly musical—remember how quickly the Camerata's poetry-oriented *dramma in musica* was subverted by the *musica*. *Opera buffa* lacked satire, parody, and the moralist's bite that can illuminate our lives as intimately as tragedy. *Opera buffa*'s "realism" was pleasant, never taut, and its sentiment was always better nourished than its satire. True, at heart *opera buffa* looked back on the old *commedia*, and that is comedy at its meanest. But even as they inherited the stock characters, situations, and funny business (the *lazzi*, best translated as "shticks"), the makers of eighteenth-century *opera buffa* smoothed the edges and melted the hard core. Typically, the most celebrated of the *opera buffa* librettists was an Arcadian, Carlo Goldoni. Cultivated the Arcadians were, but comedy likes a dash of the vulgar.

Like Zeno and Metastasio an organizer of form, Goldoni tidied up the zesty Italian comic heritage, throwing out the "masks" (Harlequin, Colombine, Captain Horrible, and such), the improvisation, the lewdness, the absurdity, the fantasy . . . pardon me, the life. Of a certain kind of middle-class diversion Goldoni was certainly a fine craftsman. He was, for example, just the man to adapt Samuel Richardson's extremely sentimental *Pamela* (one of the century's most popular novels; they used to ring out the bells in French towns when the latest serial entry arrived, fresh from the pen). As *La Buona Figluola* (The Good Little Girl), Goldoni's *opera buffa* text on *Pamela* was set more than once, and no doubt helped instill in many impressionable hearts the value of being either good little girls or the good men who protect them. But Goldoni's was another operatic "reform" that gave short measure. *Opera buffa* was not as windy and scattered as *opera seria;* on the contrary, it was fleet and spare. But in developing a comic form in direct antithesis to the *commedia dell'arte* heritage, Goldoni impoverished *opera buffa*'s dramatic potential. He killed the *commedia*'s rich ambiguities and crowned its clichés. He made it chaste. In Venice, his home town, where traditional *commedia* ran from a lode of screwy brilliance, Goldoni practically wiped tradition off the stage with his bourgeois sobriety—though, on the contrary, his *spoken* plays showed a wild naturalism. As it happens, Goldoni was challenged by a fellow Venetian, Carlo Gozzi, who wiped tradition right back where it belonged in several flamboyant plays mixing farce and romance in the old style. Gozzi wrote no opera librettos, but he left his mark: Prokofyef's *The Love for Three Oranges*, Busoni's and Puccini's very different *Turandot*s, and Henze's *The King-Stag* are all based on Gozzi originals.

Opera buffa's importance lies in its music. The idiomatic musical aesthetic of musical comedy is both its strength and weakness—the vigor of its directness is offset by its often feeble musicality, which is why ballad opera quickly became moribund and *opéra comique* and *Singspiel* eventually increased their musical allotment. With *opera buffa* composed by gifted musicians, it was bound to overshadow the pastiche fortuities of the hack "arranger." So *opera buffa* was spry, droll, and deftly musical. And when it turned up in Paris—where music theatre was as dull as Lully or as "difficult" as Rameau or as thin as *opéra comique*—the wonder of it opened French ears very wide. And hell broke loose in Paris.

The *casus belli* was Giovanni Battista Pergolesi's *La Serva Padrona* (The Maid Turns Mistress, 1733), a comic intermezzo in the highly vocal, impulsive but beautifully judged Neapolitan style. Written to fill in between the acts of Pergolesi's full-length serious piece, *Il Prigionier Superbo* (The Arrogant Prisoner), *La Serva Padrona* amounted to *opera buffa*'s graduation exercise. It is sometimes cited as the first of its line; more exactly, it was the most resourceful example of a type already several decades old. It is like the tiniest jewel. Under an hour, it calls for three characters, one of whom is mute. The title really tells it all: Serpina, Oberto's servant, rules his bachelor household and ends as his wife after a series of arias and duets and a scene of comic disguise—lots of fun and plenty *lazzi*. The action, then, is basic, the music pleasing, and the piece so useful as theatre that until the recent rediscovery of Monteverdi and Cavalli it was the oldest work in the regular repertory.

An Italian troupe took it to Paris in 1746. It scored a mild success —Italian opera still wasn't going over well in Paris. (Cavalli had been so outraged by his experience there that when he returned to Venice he vowed never to write another opera.) But in 1752 another Italian troupe gave *La Serva Padrona* on the stage of the Académie Royale between the acts of Lully's *Acis et Galatée*, and war was promptly declared. One side upheld the French style (as laid down, of course, by the Italian Lully); the other side celebrated the incisive thrust of the Italian style. Pamphlets were distributed, letters written, politics brought in, and demonstrations made. No sooner had *La Serva Padrona* ended than the pro-Italians trouped out of the Académie en masse, leaving their opponents to suffer the remainder of Lully's fifty-six-year-old *tragédie* with a sinking heart—for much of what the pro-Italian faction claimed was true. Italian opera soared with life, wired for music from within. French opera dragged and declaimed, a play nervously beating time. The Académie hastily moved *La Serva Padrona* to the end of the program to keep a full house in session, but the point was made.

Or was it? The war, known as the *querelle*, or *guerre*, *des bouffons* (the war over comedy), purportedly fought out the virtues of Italian music theatre as opposed to those of French, and most of the fighters argued against or for French vocalism—the musicality of the language, the attack of the melody, even the quality of French singers' voices. But the true battle lines in the *querelle des bouffons* pitted the ponderous remoteness of *tragédie lyrique* (and *opera seria*, for that matter) against the populist informality of comedy.

The picture of an opera war may look dear to us, whose ideological conflicts run to weightier issues than art. But in fact the *querelle* had a political basis. The Encyclopedists (who had just put out their first volume in 1751) saw it as a chance to enlarge on their campaign to dislodge royal absolutism in cultural modes. Diderot had stated the function of the Encyclopedia as a catalyst of revolution—*"pour changer la façon commune de penser,"* to change public opinion. When Diderot, Grimm, and others of the *philosophes* joined the pro-Italian faction, they were really using an aesthetic argument against *tragédie* as a stick to beat royalism with.

The most outspoken of the pro-Italians was Jean-Jacques Rousseau, who plumed himself on his amateur status as a composer. Rousseau was an equalizer—"keep it simple" was his morality as well as his taste—and he hated Rameau's brilliant density even more than Lully's monotony. But Lully, Rousseau knew, was long gone and achieving the status of an antique; Rameau was very much alive. Even the normally anti-Rameau Encyclopedists had fallen all over themselves in admiration of Rameau's *Platée,* tricky music and all.

But was it *natural?* Rousseau asked. *Platée* was vital, yes, but did it have that essential quality of the Rousselian Utopia, *feeling?* To demonstrate feeling naturalism in opera, Rousseau wrote both words and music to his own intermezzo, *Le Devin du Village* (The Village Soothsayer, 1752), naturalism here referring as much to the artlessness of its melody as well as its amiable village setting. Staged at the Académie at the height of the *querelle, Le Devin du Village* enjoyed a smash success (Favart had a parody out a few months later, *Les Amours de Bastien et Bastienne*). It was if nothing else, natural.

But was it art? Historians are very polite about the piece. They respect it as a historical linchpin, call it "primitive" and leave it at that. Well, of course it's primitive. It wanted to be—disdain of expertise was Rousseau's credo. It's possibly the most boring opera ever written, but it has to have been a novelty placed next to Lully and Rameau on the stage of the Opéra. With the simultaneous eruption of *La Serva Padrona* and *Le Devin du Village* upon the ear of *le tout Paris,* the world of middle-class urban figures and right-hearted peasants—in music to match—enthralled a public who till then had mainly frequented the overdecorated world of heroic tragedy.

Rousseau completed his rout of French music in his famous *Lettre sur la Musique Française* in 1753, a comprehensive and raging dismissal of French music theatre past, present, and future. The language itself, he concluded, was unmusical. However, his side had won the *querelle* already, on stage at performances of *Le Devin du Village* and *La Ser-*

vante Maîtresse—for Pergolesi's intermezzo was shortly heard in French, with spoken dialogue to replace the recitatives. Technically, the French faction won the *querelle* by the expedient of the king's ordering the Italians and their artistically subversive repertory out of the country. But the Italian influence—the comic influence, the influence of naturalism in art both in subject matter and in approach—literally reinvented the French operatic stage. For while no one in the 1750s had any idea how to align *tragédie* with naturalism, numerous talents came forward to reestablish *opéra comique* along patently Italian lines.

An amusing sidelight of the *querelle* was *Les Troqueurs* (The Traders, 1753), a brief comedy about two men who swap girl friends. It was advertised as a translation of the very latest in Italian musico-dramatic enchantment. Needless to say, Paris adored the piece, upon which the authors identified themselves as Jean Joseph Vadé and Antoine Dauvergne. Frenchmen. They might have reengaged the *querelle* all over again but for the fact that virtually everybody was now willing to accept homegrown fare provided it was composed with some reference to the lithe musicality of *opera buffa*.

And so, moving from bucolic comedy into fairy tale, orientalia, and adventure melodrama, *opéra comique* developed a legitimate alternative to grandiose *tragédie*. It was even granted a permanent home in 1762, when it merged with and in effect swallowed up the Comédie-Italienne,* the resulting company headed by Favart and called, officially, the Opéra-Comique. Fire has leveled the original building and its successor, but a third edifice still stands in the same place, referred to as the Salle Favart by Parisians and the Opéra-Comique by everyone else.

Mindful of its Italian insemination, post-*querelle opéra comique* first bent to the efforts of a transplanted Neapolitan. Egidio Duni got his start at the Saint-Laurent Fair with *Le Peintre Amoureux de Son Modèle* (The Painter in Love with His Model, 1757), the libretto partly by Favart. The remainder of Duni's French career corresponded with the playing out of the rustic era, in such samples as Duni's *Les Deux Chasseurs et la Laitière* (The Two Hunters and the Milkmaid, 1763) and *Les Moissonneurs* (The Harvesters, 1768).

No single trend really dominated *opéra comique* even for a limited period, as the form still ran on the impetuously capricious energy that had fueled it when it was a mishmash of parodies with pastiche scores. Musical comedy is eager for novelty but just as eager for nostalgia—because people are similarly eager—and no era reveals an absolute in-

---

* The Comédie-Italienne, padlocked in the fracas over *La Fausse Prude*, had reopened in the meantime.

terest in village love over fairy tale, or oriental somesuch over medieval romance. *Opéra comique* drew it all together, in varying proportions of *tendresse* and farce, spectacle and informality, music and spoken dialogue.

Even more popular than Duni were the natural-born French composers André Danican Philidor and Pierre Alexandre Monsigny, and the Belgian André Grétry. Their works underline the wide scope of subject matter in *opéra comique*. Philidor, for instance, won favor for the rustic *Le Bûcheron* (The Woodcutter, 1763) but also for his adaptation of the romantic satire of Henry Fielding in *Tom Jones* (1765). Monsigny provided the usual country romance in *Rose et Colas* (1764) —an anticipation of the American musical *The Fantasticks*—but also managed to include some unusually low-comic scenes in *Le Déserteur* (1769). Michel-Jean Sedaine's *Déserteur* libretto thrilled pro-Italian veterans of the *querelle* with its emotional range: side by side with the conventional suspenses attendant upon the desertion of a soldier who mistakenly believes his fiancée unfaithful was a figure out of the Italian *buffo* tradition, a drunken cellmate of the recaptured deserter who cuts through the hero's despair with oblivious jesting. Such a blend of comedy and pathos led the Encyclopedist Baron Grimm to liken Sedaine to Shakespeare.

Grétry was the most important of these four founding composers of mature *opéra comique*, though his haphazard training rendered him a more inspired artist than a polished one. "One could drive a coach and four between the bass and the melody" ran a popular Grétry joke, but the man got the Rousselian feeling just right. His first success, *L'Ingénu; ou, Le Huron* (1768) is the opera that Rousseau himself should have written, for the "innocent" of the title is an American Indian, the "noble savage" so voguish among the French intelligentsia of the time. And this is no satire. *Le Huron*, as it is generally called, worshiped the barbaric avatar as its audience did, though its seriousness weighs in a mite heavily for the slight dramatic foundation of *opéra comique*. Ushering in an *ariette*, a curious Frenchwoman asks the Huron if he has ever been in love. "Yes," he replies, "with the lovely Abucadaba." After he sings his solo, the woman asks what became of Abucadaba. Says the Huron, "A bear ate her." In the end, the librettist, Jean-François Marmontel, arranged it to turn out that the Huron is actually the long-lost nephew of a Frenchman, which makes it nice for the love plot besides proving that one can be unspoiled and natural as well as French.

Grétry was the most adventurous of opera composers in terms of genre. He moved from fairy tale to adventure to farce with ease, though he preferred not to mix his modes in any given evening. A voluble theorist, he classified character types, instrumental colors, the moods of tonalities, and so on, receiving much credit from the Encyclopedists, though in fact everything that Grétry set down comprised basic musicodramatic technique and for that matter Grétry seldom used it as well as his colleagues. What he had was—well, his successor, Étienne Nicholas Méhul, put it nicely: "Grétry made spirit rather than music."

Grétry *felt* right. His farce *Les Deux Avares* (The Two Misers, 1770) is really quite funny and charming to watch, though on paper it looks dull. A tale of two old pennygrabbers in Smyrna keeping one's niece and the other's nephew apart (of course the young couple love as truly as young lovers can), *Les Deux Avares* was not stingy with the comedy, as in this exchange of the two misers. Gripon is off to lend two hundred ducats to a young debtor:

MARTIN: And at what interest?
GRIPON: Ah, virtually nothing: two percent.
MARTIN: Are you crazy? Two percent—
GRIPON: Per hour.

It's neck and neck between the farcical plot (the two men scheme to plunder a mufti's tomb) and the sweet love scenes of the young couple; farce wins out when, just as the lovers and the girl's maid are about to flee, the boy drops their valuables down a well and has to climb in after them, with the usual confusions. But all ends happily.

Turning to Arabian romance in *Zémire et Azor* (1771), a retelling of "Beauty and the Beast," Grétry shows how much more musical *opéra comique* was getting, in a tricky lead soprano part. Azor is the beast, Zémire the tender pretty whose love transforms him, and despite the bumblings of a comic servant, the lingering crudity of the old fairground is dispelled forever midway through Act III. Azor asks Zémire to sing for him, and she flips right into "La fauvette avec ses petits" (The warbler and her little ones), a wild coloratura showpiece complete with flute obbligato. Such convinced musicality lay way beyond the resources of early *opéra comique*.

Even at its most staid, though, *opéra comique* had heart and verve. Its audience made sure it did, as Grétry learned to his woe when he attempted an old-fashioned Ovidian pastorale *opéra-ballet*, *Céphale et Procris* (1773), a fiasco attended by angrily bewildered spectators. *Opéra comique* had broken with satiric musical comedy, but it could not successfully aspire to aristocratic pageant, either. It held to the midpoint between and thus gained the world's main stages, leaving its rougher but also more audacious days behind. It was important now, more important than its cousin forms in England and Germany, mainly because "comic opera" suffered from a drought of gifted composers and the average run of *Singspiel* was overshadowed by what Mozart, Beethoven, and Weber did for that form.

Having seen a popular music theatre set on its feet, we turn to the elite branch, *opera seria/tragédie lyrique*, to chart its fortunes in the late 1700s. Last seen still lumbered with the accoutrements of a court art, opera was now deeply into reform—reform of the hegemony of its star singers and of its convention of recitative-and-aria. No one, at first, challenged opera's subject matter—Ariosto, Homer, and history still provided the bases. But the contract between content and form was up for renewal.

The key transitional composers were Niccolò Jommelli and Tommaso Traetta. Now forgotten except by historians and seldom revived, they counted among the best known of their kind in the late-middle eighteenth century. By the time they came along, *opera seria* was decades old and felt it. While *opera buffa* had its ensembles for variety and character interaction and furthermore had picked up the habit of rattling off the recitative to get it said and done, *opera seria* still struck its marble poses.

Jommelli animated his recitative sections, defining them more musically. His arias, however, were among the most formal of their day, with lengthy orchestral introductions to and intervals between sections (the so-called *ritornello*, or refrain) and a near-absolute observance of the *da capo* repeat. But Jommelli was trying to bring the scenes *between* the solos into the musical framework.

Traetta went Jommelli one better, often replacing the *da capo* aria with the leaner *cavatina*. Traetta also showed a marked taste for librettos in the French style, with the *tragédie*'s emphasis on sensible dramaturgy. Thus he could combine the Italian musical elaboration with the more integrated verbal flow of the French.

That reform was needed was no secret. As early as 1720 the composer Benedetto Marcello had published *Il Teatro alla Moda* (The Fashionable Stage), a scathing satire of opera composition and production; as a composer he naturally reserved his most rabid sallies for the singers and those who catered to their regime. Oddly, Marcello seems not to have attempted any reformation in his own works. Far more influential among the elite was Francesco Algarotti, a literary man whose *Saggio Sopra l'Opera in Musica* (Essay on Opera), published in 1755, sparked possibilities in many a creator's head. Where Marcello ridiculed, Algarotti recommended, and he took the con-

servative line. The jarring shift of gears from recitative to aria just
wasn't working—why not return to the original operas, where action
(the recitative) and expression (the aria) were not polarized but har-
moniously blended? Algarotti made a beautiful comparison between
art and society: "it is impossible to preserve [both] from decay . . .
without making [both] return from time to time to original principles." The aria opera, in other words, was unconstitutional.

Right about now we need a savior to turn a reform, and now we
meet one, Christoph Willibald Gluck. This composer is the man who
refounded the primacy of poetry, who freed the orchestra of its accompanimental status, who made actors of singers and participants of
the chorus and dancing corps. Besides Gluck, there are three giants in
eighteenth-century opera, Rameau, Handel, and Mozart; all three were
incomparably finer musicians. Yet Gluck, in what he did for opera
that no one else did first, may well be the champion of the quartet.

It must be admitted that reform was a sometime thing in Gluck's
career. It came late, after some thirty-five *opere serie* and *opéras
comiques*, and once arrived it didn't stick with him, but came and went
depending, it seems, on the availability of reform-minded librettists.
Moreover, reform was not so exclusive that Gluck could not dip into
his trunk and reuse old material in a reform opera; whole swatches of
his most exquisite tapestries turn out to have been ripped from the
faded samples of his desultory years. But when Gluck was on, he was
a titan. Any hack can achieve pop success; any schemer can craft a
novelty. But to uproot custom and replace it with the art truths that
most people cannot live up to and therefore will not confront—yet to
win them over despite themselves . . . this takes genius.

We've seen some reform in opera already. The first operas aimed
to reform "unnatural" vocal music. The Metastasian libretto aimed to
reform the wanton plotting of Venetian opera. Lully's *tragédies*, not
specifically a reform, aimed to correct the freakish vocalism of Italian
opera. The rise of comedy in its various musical entities is also a sort
of reform, this one of the overposh in opera.

Gluck's reform, too, was a purge. Again the motto was "Back to
Greece," and classical subjects were favored—the timeless affair of
Orpheus, the poet in art, love, and death; the womanly heroism of
Alcestis; the awesome weight of action knocked down upon Orestes
and Iphigenia. This is potent material after the historical charades of
opera seria. But Gluck's reform focused not on what was shown but
how. Gluck redefined the relationship of music to drama in music
drama, phasing down the diversions and intensifying the essentials. He
let the arias find their own shape, as each situation required. He reno-

vated the recitative, bringing the orchestra in permanently for the dramatically fluent *recitativo accompagnato*. He developed the orchestra for psychological commentary, tamed the ballet, and used the chorus like a Greek. His was breathing, beautiful, awesome art.

Gluck's reform took off in about 1760, in Vienna—Metastasio country. Gluck himself had set several of Metastasio's librettos—he "has surprising fire," the Imperial poet noted of the young composer, "but he is mad." It sounds as if Gluck were already on his course, but in fact these early Gluck operas are humdrum. Still, the dramatist in him hungered to compose some real theatre, something elementally human and important, and he finally turned a corner in, of all things, a ballet, *Don Juan* (1761). Unlike the finicky court ballets of the time, *Don Juan* raged with an almost romantically glamorous doom, its music taking active issue with the events on stage.

In a way, *Don Juan* was Gluck's first reform opera; all he needed now was a reform-minded libretto. This was produced by Ranieri de' Calzabigi, an adventurer, polymath, and womanizer of the kind that help end and begin eras—in this case, the Classic and Romantic eras, respectively. Calzabigi, whose name turns up in several uncertifiable alternate spellings, was an admirer of Shakespeare (always a hailing point for the Romantic ideologue) and a foe of "cadenzas, *ritornelli*, and everything Gothic, barbarous, and extravagant that has been put into [Italian] music." Rather than hand Gluck the libretto and vanish, as was customary, Calzabigi *collaborated* with his composer, showing him the scheme of his design to encourage him to throw off *seria* convention in his music as he, Calzabigi, had done in his verses.

And Gluck did. Their first partnership was *Orfeo ed Euridice* (1762), put on in honor of the Emperor's name day. For a historical linchpin, it's embarrassingly unpretentious, a brief pastorale with a *deus ex machina*, Love, to spur Orpheus to seek Euridice in hell and to bring her back to life when he violates the legendary condition and looks back at her. But it was overnight reform. Gone were the *da capo* aria, the Muzak *ritornelli*, the lifeless recitative, all replaced by a mosaic of expressive recitative, arialike periods, dramatically relevant choruses, and dynamic orchestration. One embellishment lingered on: the Orfeo of the premiere was Gaetano Guadagni, a male contralto.*

But one can do just so much in a night. The material itself is what counts, for Calzabigi and Gluck killed the custom of passing one libretto around from composer to composer. One libretto, one score became the rule, at least partly because the two authors worked so well so

---

* *Castrati*, like women singers, sang in either high or low registers.

closely. It was Calzabigi's inspiration to open the action after the death
of Euridice, raising the curtain on her funeral, and Gluck handles the
scene with feeling nobility, splicing Orfeo's laments into the choral
threnody. Even more striking is Orfeo's scene with the Furies in hell,
pleading through his harp. Their zealous no!s became a byword of
musicodramatic tension to the extent that twenty-five years later
Mozart could borrow, spoof, and pay homage to them all at once in
the sextet, "Sola, sola in buio loco" in *Don Giovanni*. And for his practical in instrumental coloration, Gluck paints Orfeo's stunned first
experience of Elysium in a web of beatific delicacy, with humming
and trilling violins, a flute and a cello in echo duet, and a central melody of great breadth on the oboe.

Deeply reformist now, Gluck and Calzabigi prefaced the publication of their second collaboration, *Alceste* (1767), with a dedication
to the future Leopold II that amounts to an artistic manifesto. Lip
service is paid to the old business of "music serving the poetry"—but
it also serves that animates and intensifies. A more telling statement of
principle is Gluck's "I did not wish to arrest an actor in the greatest
heat of dialogue in order to wait for a tiresome *ritornello*, nor to hold
him up in the middle of a word on a vowel favorable to his voice, nor
to make display of [his vocal] agility," and so on. All the structure
of opera as it had been developed till then should follow the sense of
each specific opera, not the other way around. Content would inspire
form. This was not a new idea, but it was pretty much a new practice.
Gluck cut opera loose from its Baroque bonds, from the rationales for
expression, symmetry, harmony, elegance. The first of the Romantic
composers, Gluck for some unknown reason lived with the generalities
of his time (for what was the Enlightenment's "rationalism" but an
imposed universality disguised as humanism?) until one day for some
unknown reason he suddenly repudiated them.

Despite occasional backsliding, Gluck held to his new format
and took the public with him. Like *Orfeo ed Euridice*, *Alceste* was a
success, a work much more in the style of Gluck's Euripidean immensity than the modest *Orfeo*. Of course there are always those
glad to belittle art that wears its morals fervently. "For nine days
the theatre has been closed," observed one of *Alceste*'s first-nighters,
"and on the tenth it opens with a requiem." For their third and last
partnership, Gluck and Calzabigi tried something lighter. If *Orfeo*
was overwhelmingly simple and *Alceste* large and serious, *Paride ed
Elena* (1770) was large and simple. It's an odd piece, a revisionist look
at the elopement of Paris and Helen, viewed as the circumspect min-
gling of the barbaric Asian and the chaste Spartan (here only engaged

to Menelaus; what tact). *Paride ed Elena* calls for three lead parts—Love, as intermediary for Paris, is the third—and almost no action. (*Orfeo,* too, has only three leads and a chorus—a true Greek show—but it does have action and is less than half as long.) *Paride* is in some ways the most enterprising of Gluck's three Italian reform operas, but it did not go over and even today is seldom mentioned, let alone performed. Gluck thought it his most misunderstood and underrated creation.

Three reform works down; three to come, plus two reform revisions: Gluck came to Paris. Like Lully and Grétry before him, like Cherubini, Spontini, Meyerbeer, Offenbach, and Wagner after him, the foreigner needed Paris to propagandize for a new genre of music theatre. Anyway, the Gluckian opera was something like *tragédie lyrique* made Italian, the Racinesque libretto stimulated by music. Paris was the natural home for such artwork, far more so than any Italian town, suspicious of Gluck's "learned" approach, or than Vienna, which showed its unworthiness by rejecting *Paride ed Elena.* Besides, Calzabigi had gotten into one of his periodic scrapes and vanished. Gluck thought he could count on a royal ally in the Dauphine Marie-Antoinette, his singing pupil in her Austrian youth. Using as his agent François du Roullet, attaché to the French Embassy in Vienna, Gluck sent out diplomatic feelers pursuant to a reasonably glorious entry into French cultural life, and even began work—without commission—on a *tragédie d'après Racine, Iphigénie en Aulide,* libretto by du Roullet.

Paris needed Gluck badly. Under the pressure of the *querelle des bouffons,* French opera had collapsed utterly. True, there was *opéra comique;* there were Monsigny, Philidor, Grétry. But in the twenty-two years between the electrifying performances of *La Serva Padrona* and the première of *Iphigénie en Aulide* in 1774, the Opéra's backlist repertory of classics had simply dissolved work by work. By the time Gluck arrived in Paris, only Rameau's *Castor et Pollux* survived to remind the French of their great *tragédie* that was.

Paris was turbulent and hungry, all eyes on Gluck. Would he save the native opera? Replace it? How would he deal with the language? The French and Italian factions of the *querelle* mouthed rumors of the reform doings in Vienna, and musicians examined Gluckian scores (published in Paris, famed for the quality of its engraving) for signs. Even with Marie-Antoinette's blessings on him, Gluck was coming into a highly volatile situation.

Gluck was cautious. In early 1773 the *Mercure de France* published his open letter in which he assured one and all that a good language for opera was the language of a first-rate libretto, period. Du Roullet's *Iphigénie* looked fine; it had "all the energy needed to inspire me with good music." Gluck troubled to praise the counsel of that one-man *querelle* Jean-Jacques Rousseau himself, and attempted to assuage all factions by proposing "a music fit for all nations and to let the ridiculous distinctions of national music disappear."

A sensible proposal from a man born in Bavaria, raised in Bohemia, trained in Italy, influenced by the Viennese symphonists, and about to tackle French opera. And Gluck left little to chance. Du Roullet's text was fine indeed and Gluck's setting of it moving, thrilling, and very human, finding the musical language for the elemental in the story. The father-warrior Agamemnon, the mother Clytemnestre, the heroine Iphigénie, the lover-hero Achille, and the priest-politician Calchas all show amazing vitality both as characters in drama and as constituents of a musical design; as the coming Trojan War tugs on the action and the eager chorus clamors for Iphigénie to be sacrificed, words and music together actually seem to close in on the heroine, constricting in sound as well as movement. Thus Gluck relegated the obligatory ballet sections to the early scenes, before the conflict has begun to knot, and to the last scenes, after it has been resolved by a change of Olympian heart. Du Roullet even dispensed with the god and the machine, letting Calchas announce Diana's clemency and keeping the cast exclusively mortal. (It may sound clumsy, but it's better than Racine's ending, in which a "second" Iphigénie is substituted for the heroine, and it is certainly preferable to Wagner's revision of the piece, which plops the goddess into the scene in person, machine and all.)

Iphigénie en Aulide is a well-nigh flawless opera, and far more exciting than Gluck's three Italian reform works. None of those is perfect—*Orfeo* runs out of steam in its third act, anchored only by the hero's famous lament for his lover's second death, "Che farò senza Euridice?"; *Alceste* is paced somewhat sanctimoniously; and *Paride ed Elena*, despite its intriguing score, reduces to a five-act flirtation. *Iphigénie* shows the urgency of music in opera, the availability of melody, rhythm, and tonality for dramatic exactness. In his Achilles, Gluck composed a hero of extraordinary authority—at one point in Act II, he leads the chorus in a vibrant C Major apostrophe to Iphigénie, "Chantez, célébrez votre reine!," that must surely have been on Beethoven's mind when he wrote the finale to *Fidelio*. Sounds of such unencumbered virility simply had not been heard in opera before.

Gluck not only wrote a masterpiece; he also staged one. He demanded, and got, six months of rehearsal, and cast the roles with the best that Paris offered. Naturally, getting in on what promised to be the event of the decade was no small inducement to the singers. Wagner is often credited with inventing the *Gesamtkunstwerk*, the "unified artwork" of all talents in collaboration; in reality several theoreticians and creators tried the idea out first. Wagner only named it and publicized it. Here we find Gluck anticipating Wagner as a superdirector of the 1770s—but the road to coordinated art is paved with deadly reckonings. Like Faustina Bordoni and Francesca Cuzzoni in Italian opera, the French Sophie Arnould defended her perquisites with a lash for a tongue and temperament like a raw file. She found Gluck's vocal line talky and hissed for great arias. (Yet Arnould is known to have taken her calling seriously, studying acting with the tragedienne Clairon and respected by no less expert an ear than that of David Garrick, a revolutionary of the naturalistic style in theatre.) The ballet, too, had Gluck by the throat; trying to talk Vestris, the "god of the dance," out of parading around in *Iphigénie*, Gluck discovered, was like trying to fit Scylla for muzzles. Vestris danced.

Nevertheless, *Iphigénie*'s premiere in early 1774 was a tremendous success, and Gluck promptly followed it up with a revision of *Orfeo ed Euridice* as *Orfée*, the lead role rewritten for tenor and the score filled out with important new music (including a vicious Dance of the Furies culled from *Don Juan*). The production was another smash. Continuing to reform performance as well as composition, Gluck urged his tenor Orpheus, Joseph Legros, to cry out as if he were having his leg cut off in his lamenting exclamations in the opening scene. "It is inconceivable, Monsieur," Gluck complained. "You are always shouting when you ought to be singing, and now when for once it is a question of shouting, you cannot manage it!" But somehow Gluck dragged his singers along with him into his vision.

As king of Paris, Gluck was king of opera on an international scale. His suggestion that the "ridiculous distinctions of national music" be allowed to waste away, however, fell on closed ears. Seething at Gluck's revival of *tragédie*, the pro-Italian faction of the *querelle* regrouped for battle and sent for a champion, Niccolò Piccinni. This was a composer of moderately original but by this time rather settled gifts, who had made his mark with a setting of Goldoni's popular libretto for *La Buona Figluola*, the adaptation of *Pamela* referred to earlier. Piccinni's version (1760) was a delightful reading of Goldoni's text, a very succinct and sentimental comedy, and Piccinni's Italian vivacity seemed to some troublemakers the stuff on which a dream of a feud could be made.

Heaven knows Gluck had enemies who longed to humiliate him.

He was artistically bold; that's threatening. He was a proud man; that's impudent. And he was foreign; that's an outrage. To demonstrate what Gluck was up against, hear how even his prize singer could turn against him. He was at the home of Sophie Arnould, rehearsing her for his new French version of *Alceste*. Her lover, Prince d'Hénin, happened in and told Gluck, "In France, one stands up to salute a man of rank." "In Germany," replied Gluck, "one salutes men worthy of respect. Madame Arnould, if this is the way things go in your home, I prefer to leave." Out he went with the score of *Alceste*, which he presented to Rosalie Levasseur, till then considered secondary to Arnould. This new *Alceste* (1776) did not go over, partly through the intrigues of a group hostile to Gluck—and the story goes that it was Arnould who mobilized them. Later that same year, Piccinni arrived in Paris; a faction immediately formed around him, deeply heartened when they learned that the good maestro couldn't speak five words of French standing up. Here was a sure center for the vendetta of Italian music.

But Piccinni was not to challenge Gluck with operas sung in Italian, only French operas in Piccinni's naturally Italian style. Furthermore, he admired Gluck and Gluck admired back. As far as the two men were concerned, there was no feud, ever. But schemers at the Opéra hit on a way to strike one up: give the two composers the same libretto to set, each in his way. Delicious! And wouldn't one of Philippe Quinault's old Lully librettos make a dandy subject? Marie-Antoinette, who had been graduated from Dauphine to Queen and from Gluck's supporter to Piccinni's, gave her consent to the deal, and Jean-François Marmontel, a purveyor of *opéra comique* scripts who was insulted that Gluck had not chosen him as collaborator, revamped Quinault's *Roland* text and sent it off to Gluck and Piccinni. *Without* letting Gluck in on the scheme.

But Gluck found out in time. He burned what he had composed (or so he said; probably he put it right into his next opus) while Piccinni docilely finished his version. But how was the Italian to show what he could do unless he was permitted to work in his proper fields of *opera seria* and *buffa?* What an inefficient, not to say malicious, contest! Gluck ended the whole business by setting *another* Quinault libretto, that to *Armide et Renaud*, originally composed by Lully in 1686.

Using the text virtually straight from Quinault, Gluck proved how much his style of opera was rendered Lullian *tragédie*. But where Lully is inhibited in his recitative and pompous in his songlets and diversions, Gluck pulls the whole show together in a seamless fabric of solos, ensembles, choruses, and dances. For his source, Quinault had drawn on the eternal Armida and Rinaldo of Tasso's *Gerusalemme Liberata*. Handel's version, *Rinaldo*, emphasizes a bellicose chivalry; Gluck's *Armide* (1777) amounts to a five-act treatise on the ins and outs of love. Quinault deserves no little commendation for the durability of his verses, for they furnished Gluck with the basis for one of opera's great leading women, the eponymously pagan sorceress who would love to hate the Christian Renaud and ends up hating to love him. Her role lacks the Big Tunes that Gluck gave to his other title protagonists—the "Che farò" of *Orfeo*, the "Divinités du Styx" of *Alceste*—but shows a brilliant consistency of characterization through melody. Armide is not as sensual as Monteverdi's Poppea, nor as seductive as Handel's Cleopatra; Gluck composed her as a person too coiled ever to unwind. She is superb in anger, moving in distress—but never truly attractive. She wins our symapthies by falling victim to a most human snare: she loves in vain. Determined that this great character test the limit of what could be done in one opera, Gluck even added a few lines to the end of Quinault's Act III, wherein Armide conjures up Hatred and her demon suite to help her resist her attraction to Renaud. Quinault closed the act with Hatred's exorcism. Gluck closes with Armide alone, after the goblins have vanished, feeling from root to tip that the treatment isn't taking. To bring her terror home, the lower strings pound out an obsessive tremor on one note, and Gluck has Armide pray pathetically to a new demon for succor—demon Love.

At one blow, Gluck had connected himself to tradition and revolutionized the art, and no one knew it better than he. He grew more intransigent on the matter of casting and rehearsals, and threatened to withhold *Armide* from the Opéra if his conditions were not met. "I have composed it in such a way," he wrote, "that it will not age quickly." Indeed he had—the extraordinary final scene, in which the spurned Armide alternately mewls and rages, founded a custom of extraordinary final scenes for soprano solo that may be traced a century later to Brünnhilde's Immolation Scene.

Happily, the Opéra and Gluck came to terms. Rosalie Levasseur continued to displace Arnould as the soprano of the hour, and *Armide* triumphed despite the sincerest sabotages of the Piccinni claque. One of them, the odious Laharpe, hated Gluck so much he couldn't bear to hear *Armide*, though this didn't stop him from writing a hostile review. From another direction came criticism of a much friendlier sort: at the fairgrounds, an *Armide* parody was quickly mounted, written by the librettist of Gluck's *Orphée*, Pierre-Louis Moline. He called it *Madame Terrible*.

The ball lay in Piccinni's court, and was returned a few months after *Armide*'s premiere with the unveiling of his *Roland*. The Gluck circle thought it unimportant; the *piccinnistes* of course hailed it. They thought Piccinni's "musical" opera was confronting Gluck's "dramatic" opera—but Gluck's opera was dramatic *because of its music*. In that, Gluck was the most musical of all, as later generations came to realize.

For if the rise of comic-naturalistic forms was one of the two great events in eighteenth-century opera, the rise of a qualified musical absolutism was the other. Before and even during the Gluck era, reformers habitually accused opera of being "too musical." Algarotti, for one, revived the old notion that music theatre should be "recited in music—not preeminently sung." And Gluck himself claimed to subscribe to this apparent return to the thinking that first founded opera in Florence.

But this is wrong. Opera before Gluck was not too musical, it was simply overrun with irrelevant music. Beaumarchais' statement that "there is too much music in music drama" reflects a playwright's love of language and a progressive's contempt for convention. He might better have said, There is too much of the wrong kind of music—too much singing for singing's sake, too much divertissement from the ballet corps with no reference to the action, too much idle symmetry of ABA aria patterns. Fixed musical structures fix the drama they inhabit. Shouldn't each opera be different?

That was Gluck: each of his good ones was different. For his sixth reform piece, he continued the saga of Iphigenia, last seen just missing being sacrificed at Aulis. In *Iphigénie en Tauride* (1779) she is in Tauris, serving as high priestess to Diana and ineffective civilized role model to the indigenous barbaric Scythians. Going back to Euripides, the librettist Nicholas-François Guillard (reportedly assisted by Du Roullet) tendered Gluck a knot of sublime irony: two strangers have been stranded among the Scythians, who insist that Iphigenia slay them on the altar—but one of them is her long-lost brother Orestes. Where most of the operatic types we have met so far would have subsumed the confrontation in plotty intrigue, the Gluck-Guillard *Iphigénie* chases its destiny in a straight line of compulsion and vulnerability. Call it mythology, or history, or a hoax. In these hands it is very real, ethics of art teaching an ethics of life. The desperation of the matricide Oreste, the friendship of Orestes and Pylades, the expatriate loneliness of Iphigenia, and the resistance of all the Greeks to the local savages comprise the larger-than-real situations that our modern age has supplanted with the less regal dilemma of *Mother Courage* or *The Crucible* or *The [Old Lady's] Visit*. But if tragic beauty is now a matter of character rather than class, the ancient catastrophes are no less momentous. And, as psychology tells us, it is not necessary to commit blood murder to suffer guilt for it. True, the mindset of the age led *Iphigénie*'s authors to resolve their drama happily. But even as Diana descends on her cloud to absolve Orestes and send the Atreides home, the drama has already climaxed—Iphigenia recognizes her brother at the last minute and halts the sacrifice, and Orestes' friend kills the barbarian king. A human drama needs a human conclusion, and the apparition of Diana serves mainly as structural punctuation.

So brilliant that the anti-Gluck party didn't dare attack it, *Iphigénie en Tauride* completed Gluck's set of reform operas.* He returned to Vienna, heard Mozart's abundantly musical comedy, *The Abduction from the Seraglio*—it was the future and it worked in ways Gluck could admire but not emulate—rehearsed a German version of *Iphigénie en Tauride*, and died, his work over. After he had left Paris, the *piccinnistes* had the last word (they thought) with a second *Iphigénie en Tauride* (1781), set by their Italian ace to a different libretto. Inevitably Piccinni's *Iphigénie* sounded shallow by comparison; worse yet, at the premiere the prima donna had taken the precaution of uplifting the spirit of Italian song with that of French wine. It happens. Sophie Arnould, who never missed a chance to bring the ants to the picnic, loudly christened it "Iphigénie en Champagne."

Despite his sometimes sluggish melodic gift and lack of solid craft (it was said that Gluck knew less about counterpoint than Handel's cook†), Gluck reinvented opera as music theatre in which the music would at least express the text and would at most—at best—establish an emotional context for the drama on a line-by-line basis. A classic anecdote tells as much as analysis can: Gluck was taking the singers and orchestra through *Iphigénie en Tauride*'s first *Sitzprobe* ("sitting rehearsal," a full runthrough without staging or decor), and everything fell apart in Act II, during what might be called Orestes' mad scene.

---

* His last work, *Echo et Narcisse*, appeared just a few months after *Iphigénie*, not successfully; it seemed to combine the weakest aspects of *Orfeo ed Euridice* and *Paride ed Elena*.

† It was said by Handel, in fact, though the critic Donald Francis Tovey pointed out that Handel's cook, a trained singer much exposed to Handelian counterpoint, probably knew a good deal on the subject. The pianist and critic Charles Rosen resolved the discussion a few years ago: "It would be more reasonable to assume that Gluck no longer had a need for Handel's counterpoint."

He is alone, in prison, and though at first he calls upon the gods of this alien land to crush him and end his torment, a placid passage ensues and he goes to sleep. As he dreams, the ballet and chorus slip in to make a psychodrama of his guilt. Furies stalk him, a vision of Clytemnestra haunts him, and as he wakes in terror Iphigenia enters and the nightmare suddenly disperses. (A competent director should make of this moment a theatrical master stroke, as Iphigenia naturally resembles her mother Clytemnestra, thus convincing Orestes for a nasty moment that his dream is his reality.)

It was the placid passage that broke up the rehearsal. Guillard has Orestes say "Le calme rentre dans mon coeur" (My heart is calm again)—but Gluck set this to a restive viola part, obsessively scratching on one note. Hearing the singer invoke calm while they invoked worry, the violists figured they must be playing the wrong music and put down their bows. They were sensitive, these violists, but they were wrong. "He's lying," Gluck explained. "He killed his mother." And no doubt shaking their heads at Gluck's muddled gall, the singers and instrumentalists went on with opera's most notable early sortie into characterological ambivalence.

So. By the second half of the eighteenth century, heroic opera and comic opera had defined their separate forms. Did they influence each other?—did the one's musical penetration and the other's acute verbal realism ever cross over? Generally they did not. Though a very few composers sought to blend the ideal and the natural in music, the rise of Romanticism in the 1800s polarized the two. On the one hand, heroic opera blew up into Wagner's apolocalyptic mythopoeia; on the other, comedy thrived best under primitive conditions recalling those of the fairgrounds, in the parodistic musical comedies of Jacques Offenbach.

The years during and after Gluck's reform era comprised a golden age for *opera buffa*, but a static one. Convention was absolute and musicianship delightful but imitative; the Italian style established in Naples early in the century held firm and nobody minded. Domenico Cimarosa could let fly with a stream of *opera buffe* with virtually interchangeable parts: *Il Matrimonio per Raggiro* (Marriage by Trick, 1779), *Le Due Fidanzate* (The Two Fiancées, 1780), *Gli Sposi per Accidente* (Engaged by Accident, 1780), *La Sposa in Contrasto* (The Quarrelsome Wife, 1783), *I Matrimoni Impensati* (The Unexpected Marriages, 1784), *Il Marito Disperato* (The Desperate Husband, 1785), *Le Nozze Compite* (The Nuptials Fulfilled, 1786), and, best known of the set, *Il Matrimonio Segreto* (The Secret Marriage, 1792). Presumably the much married Cimarosa felt too expert on the subject of engagements and honeymoons not to expound upon them at length, but this is still rather much ado about one thing.

Even Joseph Haydn, the uncontested grandmaster of symphony and string quartet (almost raw when he met them and fully prepared when he retired) did nothing to restock the practiced situations. In *La Fedeltà Premiata* (Fidelity Rewarded, 1780), the customary two acts of recitative and exit arias culminating in lively finales are not broken up by a single duet or trio (there are a few choruses), no matter how much rapport is shared by two or three characters at a given point. And Haydn's *Orlando Paladino* (1782), another of the several operas from Ariosto's *Orlando Furioso*,* might almost pass for an *opera seria* but for the grotesque behavior of the knightly Orlando's braggart-coward of a squire, Pasquale. At least *opera buffa* gave Haydn's famous sense of humor a chance to use a few effects and wheezes, but for all his considerable charm these works don't show much initiative. His setting of Goldoni's classic libretto *Lo Speziale* (1768) is almost dull, and even his few *Singspiele* barely exploit the form's essential elasticity.

The similarity of the post-Baroque *opere buffe* did not irritate the public because most performance centers were still comparatively isolated. Cimarosa, for instance, spent a few years in Petersburg at the court of Catherine the Great, where his output might as well have been stamped For Russian Eyes Only; Haydn lived most of his adult life in the greasy Hungarian marsh where the Vienna-hating Prince Esterházy dwelled; and so on. Only a few cities on the order of Paris, London, and Vienna gave anything like international exposure, and even this was as nothing to the visibility provided by recordings or radio or television relays today—which is one reason why *opera seria* or *buffa* seems so much more conformist to us than it did to eighteenth-century audiences. Even as a rarity, any one performance goes much further nowadays.

Still, modern exhumations of *opera buffa* reveal works of winsome energy. A little-known British group, Opera da Camera ("Chamber Opera") colored in one of history's gray spots in 1974 with the English premiere of *Gli Equivoci* (The Misunderstandings, 1786), an adaptation of Shakespeare's *The Comedy of Errors* with a libretto by Mozart's collaborator Lorenzo da Ponte and music by Stephen Storace, half-Italian, half-English, born and bred in London, and the brother of Nancy Storace, the first Susanna in Mozart's *The Marriage of Figaro*. This "Shakespearean" *opera buffa* showed some real comic

---

* Vivaldi, Lully, and Handel all wrote versions.

organization in both words and music, with special care taken to display plot movement in ensembles instead of relegating it to recitative. The overture is commandeered to describe the sea storm that launches the action, and the finales of the two acts—roiling ensembles, of course—dig into the characterological conflict with imagination. Had Storace perhaps heard a little Gluck?

He may have, but if anyone influenced him it was not Gluck but Mozart, the giant of the years between Gluck and the start of the nineteenth century. The two great revolutions charted in this chapter are the rise of comedy and the revitalization of musicodramatic technique on a musical bias—but the man who brought both these revolutions to full flower was Mozart. His best operas are so rich, so natural when they are most heroic and so feeling when they are most satiric, that he is larger than any one aesthetic development, for he contains all developments himself. He deserves his own chapter.

CHAPTER FOUR

The Romantic Classicist: Mozart

> *When Mozart is merry, he never ceases to be noble . . . there is a supreme fineness in his merriment; he reaches it by intervals, because his soul is flexible and because, in a great artist, as in a perfect musical instrument, no string is lacking.*
>
> —HIPPOLYTE TAINE

THE CLICHÉS OF MUSIC THEATRE—PIETISTIC "RETURNS TO NATURE," vocal show, heroic attitudinizing, and fleering comedy—dominated Mozart's first operas. *Opera buffa*, *opera seria*, and pastorale, in legendary, historical, and timeless-modern settings—all these applied to his pen on commission, and all commissions were dutifully dispatched. But none of these early works attains more than apprentice-piece status, though isolated scenes show flashes of ingenuity.

In Wagner's day it was a commonplace that Mozart's approach to the composition of theatre scores was naïvely indiscriminate. But Mozart capped his career with four works of indisputable genius, *Le Nozze di Figaro, Don Giovanni, Così Fan Tutte,* and *Die Zauberflöte;* such masterpieces are not written by the instinct of a pure fool. The Wagner era's explanation was that top-flight collaborators guided the primitive Mozart with foolproof librettos.

A reading of the young Mozart's correspondence (to his father as well as to his librettists) illuminates this Romantic myopia; no composer of his time was more articulate in analyzing how opera works. Like Verdi, Mozart couldn't write the verses himself but knew *exactly*

what verses he wanted on a line-by-line basis; like Verdi he was forever demanding revisions: this motivation isn't clear; make this aria a
duet; the finale ends too quickly; that scene is wrong for this character;
make it *happen*.

Then why are Mozart's early operas so lackluster? Probably for
the same reason many first tries in art miss fire: it takes a while to
get the hang of it. Gluck's first operas were perfunctory, Rossini's and
Meyerbeer's imitative, Wagner's old forms looking for new ones,
Verdi's raw, Puccini's shrill or limp. And Mozart was writing operas
when he was twelve years old, a tall order even for a *Wunderkind*.
It is no insult to his talent to find his *opera buffa La Finta Semplice*
(The Girl Feigning Candor, 1768) ludicrous, his *opera seria Mitridate,
Rè di Ponto* (1770) almost wooden, and his Grecian pastorale *Ascanio
in Alba* (1771) moistly pretty—because another reason why Mozart's
first operas don't show more than glimmers of the awesome Mozart of
the later masterpieces is that the inherited idioms of the musical stage
constricted Mozart's wildly original talent. *Da capo* exit arias, dumpily
grandiose plots, pointless vocal dainties, and the segregation of the
heroic and the comic all kept Mozart down. Like Gluck, Mozart did
not work well within set convention—but where Gluck found his
personal style by rescoring French tragedy, Mozart synthesized his
form by combining the astute verbal art of the satirist with the
deeply musical commentary of the romantic. *Opera buffa*, at its best,
employed the former, *opera seria* the latter. Mozart had both, and his
trick was to use them not alternatively but simultaneously.

On the way to the completely Mozartean late works, he accepted
operatic format as he found it, struggling to express human character
in the attitudes—and a fluent kinetics in the stop-and-start scheme—
of *seria* and *buffa*. In *La Finta Giardiniera* (The Girl Posing as Gar-
dener, 1775), which gets better as its three acts go along, he lifted a
stereotyped libretto with music of surpassing resourcefulness. Rather
than impose the usual puppetlike adorability of *buffa* on the whole
charade, Mozart drew the comic characters in quasi-*seria* colors,
creating an unexpectedly deep-toned soundscape. In *Il Rè Pastore* (The
Shepherd King, 1775) he energized a tired Metastasian pastorale by
working some of the recitative into an orchestral accompaniment that
fired the action as the usual harpsichord recit never could. And while
he never abandoned the voice-oriented Italian thinking that all German
opera composers of his day respected, he eagerly sought a chance to
try his hand at opera in his own language that would bring in the
symphonic thinking of German music. A true German opera was

slowly coming into being, as in Anton Schweitzer's *Alceste* (1773) and Ignaz Holzbauer's *Günther von Schwarzburg* (1777). These isolated events heartened Mozart, if no other German composer, all the more.

As it happened, the young prodigy of Salzburg went Italian for his first important opera—an *opera seria*, in fact, still crazy after all these years. Mozart made it sane. Entitled *Idomeneo* (1781), it tells of a Cretan king who buys his safety in a sea storm by promising to sacrifice to Poseidon the first person he meets on land—his son, it turns out. Filling out the plot are two women in love with the son, lyrical Ilia and tempestuous Electra (yes, one wonders what she's doing on Crete). This ordinary story, resolved by the sea god's nick-of-time clemency, might easily have resulted in Mozart's thirteenth old-hat opera; but this time genius asserted itself in a score of surging dynamics, singing the poignant father-son relationship, the contrast of the two sopranos, and the subtle dovetailing of recit and aria (so as to float the action not number by number but act by act) to tell us more than words can. Because *Idomeneo* was adapted from a French libretto, there was much use of the chorus, for example to suffer (as offstage sailors) and to witness (as landlubbers) the typhoon that almost claims Idomeneo, thus getting the work's plot problem off to a vivid start.

Having invigorated a form that was almost extinct, Mozart now tackled the fresh German musical comedy, *Singspiel*. He had already made a first stab in this vein with the incomplete *Zaide*, just before *Idomeneo*.* Using a similar "escape from a harem" plot, but much more verve, Mozart now proposed a tone and shape for German opera in *Die Entführung aus dem Serail* (The Abduction from the Seraglio, 1782). *Zaide* is serious, but *Abduction* tacks to the comic, showing a tender heart in the main love story but otherwise delighting in devilry. A prime example of the "rescue opera" (rescues of Western women from Turkish harems being especially popular), *Abduction* presents a typical *Singspiel* lineup in its two tenor-soprano loving couples, one noble—they get all the big arias—and one of the servant class—they handle the prancy ditties—plus the Pasha (a speaking role) and his humorously malevolent custodian, Osmin, a low bass. Mozart is still rehearsing his comic and romantic materials; though the overall solution settles for fun, lumps of dewy love music bob about undissolved. And surely the heroine's big display piece, "Martern aller Arten"

---

* *Zaide* contains some intriguing experiments in "melodrama," dialogue spoken over orchestral intercourse, that opera never successfully assimilated.

(Tortures of all kinds), in which she spurns the Pasha's respectful
advances with spacious coloratura over special solo lines for flute, oboe,
violin, and cello, upholds the old fashion that Mozart was attempting
to dislodge. Today *The Abduction from the Seraglio* hangs behind the
"big four" in popularity, but in Mozart's lifetime it marched right out
in front, partly because numerous German and Austrian tastemakers
endorsed it as an authoritative novelty of German art.

Having raised some foundation, Mozart now wandered off and built
elsewhere. Precious years in this short life sailed by with much music
but no new opera from Mozart, with the exception of the one-act
Der Schauspieldirektor (The Impresario, 1786), a dishy skit on the
theatre world launched by an overture and topped off by musical
spoofs on the species prima donna and a finale. Two *opere buffe* were
begun and dropped partway through; the hoary contraption couldn't
hold Mozart's attention. He wanted something genuine to set, whether
comic or serious, German or Italian.

He got it with the international success of Beaumarchais' play *Le
Mariage de Figaro*. This examination of the class war was so revolutionary in outlook that certain cities banned its performance, but
everybody read and loved it. Even those scandalized by Beaumarchais'
disgust for the master class and its sycophants and his admiration for
the servants couldn't resist the sheer fun of the farce. *Le Mariage* is
a sequel to Beaumarchais' *Le Barbier de Séville*, showing what three
years of marriage has done to the earlier play's ardent young Count
Almaviva and his love, whose union was made possible by the intrigues
of the wily barber Figaro. *Le Barbier* is harmless fun, hip but basically
apolitical. *Le Mariage* is dangerous. The barber, now the Count's valet,
is not only wily but defiant. He dares to challenge the peaceful coexist-
ence of the "upstairs, downstairs" tradition. The plot twists intricately
around a premise as ripe for farce as for social manifesto: Can Figaro
marry and bed his intended before the Count gets his magisterial hands
on her? Interestingly, it is not the superb schemer Figaro who solves
the problem but the two leading women, Susanna and the Countess,
working together to shatter or at least compromise the *droit du
seigneur*.

Napoleon saw in *Le Mariage de Figaro* "the revolution already
happening," and Mozart seized a second revolutionary movement in
the opportunity to reinvent *opera buffa* with thematic and characterological profundity. For a libretto, he turned to Lorenzo da Ponte,
a voracious liver of life who somehow managed to cap a career as court
poet to Joseph II in Vienna by teaching Italian at Columbia University
in New York. Da Ponte's adaptation held true to the spirit of the

original; he dropped almost all of Beaumarchais' political exhortation*
but rebellion inheres in the plot. As *Le Nozze† di Figaro* (1786), the
original lost its anger but gained a kind of tactless delicacy, forgiving
even as it exposes. The Austrian composer's revolution plays as well
as the French playwright's, allowing the upstart Figaro and Susanna
to express themselves as deeply as the Count and Countess. This was
contrary to practice. Indeed, the patently sensual line of some of the
music suggests that the civil right most in demand is that to egalitarian
sexuality.

Is there a music for action? That is, as the aria and ensemble delve
into personality, what type of music is equipped to deal with narration? They were asking such questions then, and some sadly concluded that there wasn't a music for action, and that opera would
never come out right. The Camerata had insisted that solo voices
skimpily accompanied could deliver an entire piece in sung dialogue.
That didn't work. *Opera seria* and *buffa* relegated plot movement to
dry recitative. That made too much of aria and duet and too little
of the plot. Gluck's way out comprised setting librettos with very
little plot, building up to confrontational moments on emotional rather
than narrative energy—he cared more how people felt than what
they did.

Mozart found the music for action. He still uses recit, of course,
both in the dry keyboard style for fast goings-on and with orchestral
accompaniment for personal drama. But he also figured out how to
"orchestrate" any given moment in a piece. Before him, comic opera
only attempted this in the act finales and serious opera not even then.
This is why commentators make so much of *Figaro*'s second-act finale,
a twenty-minute sequence of scenes played on the surface for the
wacky shape of farce and in the interior for poignance and defiance.
A lot happens, and with each new episode Mozart appoints a change
in rhythm, melody, and mood while retaining plot suspense as well
as consistency in his separate characterizations. But more: he actually
states turns of plot in sound. For instance, the Count thinks he has
caught the Countess with his page boy, Cherubino, who has hidden
in the Countess' dressing room. The raging Count drags his wife away

---

* Some of this is excitingly radical. Says Figaro, thinking of his master: "What
have you done to deserve [your advantages]? You took the trouble to be born
. . . While as for me, good Lord! lost in the obscure crowd, I have had to employ more devices merely to exist than have been employed in the last hundred
years to govern all of Spain."
† *Nozze* here means "nuptials" rather than "marriage," and refers to the ruselike
ceremonies with which the Figaro side edges around the Count to the happy
ending: *Getting Figaro Married; or, The Aristocracy Foiled.*

to find a key, Susanna exchanges places with the boy, and the noble couple return, she pleading for mercy, he implacable. He opens the door—and out comes Susanna. How to define this moment in music? The Almavivas stunned in two different kinds of surprise (he thought he had the page dead to rights; she *knew* he did); and Susanna, the *serva padrona*, the smug mistress of the event playing dumb. What music would contain all this? Mozart's solution—an absurdly square little tune in the strings—covers the moment from every approach.

Only a moderate success at its Vienna premiere, *Le Nozze di Figaro* created a sensation in Prague, and it was there that Mozart and Da Ponte most impressively widened opera's generical boundaries. For all its heart and point, Figaro is technically a farce, brimming with slapstick and screwball riot. *Don Giovanni; ossia, Il Dissoluto Punito* (The Libertine Punished, 1787) does not classify easily. The posters that announced the premiere billed it as a *dramma giocoso* (comic play), and Mozart indexed it in his notebook as an *opera buffa;* furthermore, the Don Juan legend was routinely employed in the theatre as an excuse for nonstop drollery. A comedy, then? But by the time Mozart and Da Ponte finished their version of the Don, a cartoon heavy had been turned into an archetype of such broad appeal that endless speculation has failed to settle precisely who he is or what he represents.

The first known Don Juan play, *El Burlador de Sevilla y Convidado de Piedra* (The Playboy of Seville and the Stone Guest), dating from around 1610, was serious in intention, the work of a Spanish monk who wrote under the name Tirso de Molina. His is the essential Don Juan, a nobleman, a bon vivant, a blasphemer, and of course an insatiable seducer of women, irresistible but a plunderer. In a duel, he kills the father of one of his prey; a statue of the father comes to life and as the instrument of Christian justice drags Juan off to hell.

The tale reappeared in countless versions, its didactic frame intact but Juan's seductions a fertile source of disguise, mishap, and other comic paraphernalia. With no copyright laws to sort out ownership of characters, episodes, or lines, playwrights and librettists drew freely from each other, always retaining the identity of the profane voluptuary and the climactic retribution of the statue. Molière and Goldoni wrote notable versions (Goldoni dispensed with the supernatural scenes—his antihero is dispatched by lightning), and among numerous *opere buffe* on the subject was one with a libretto by Giovanni Bertati that Da Ponte seems to have referred to in planning his adaptation. He seems also to have been advised by his old friend and real-life Don Juan, Giacomo Casanova.

A classic moment of farce, in Act II of *Le Nozze di Figaro*, at Glyndebourne: the Count (Benjamin Luxon) has just found Cherubino (Frederica von Stade) hiding in a chair while alone with Susanna (Ileana Cotrubas). Basilio (John Fryatt) chortles; he loves trouble. Note the genuine dismay on Von Stade's lovely face. In Mozart, comedy has a feeling interior. *(Guy Gravett)*

The Magic Flute? No: its sequel, Peter von Winter's *Das Labyrinth*, revived in Munich in 1978 (sets and costumes by Jürgen Rose). *(Bayerische Staatsoper, München)*

In his memoirs Da Ponte recalls that while he saw *Don Giovanni* in its usual comic approach, Mozart saw it as a serious work. Maybe so; Da Ponte's memory has its lapses. But since it was Mozart's gift to bring out the ridiculous in the sublime and vice versa, in the end *Don Giovanni* is both comic and serious, a *seria* pretending to be a *buffa*—and vice versa. Like *Le Nozze di Figaro*, it has its masters and servants, though here they inhabit mutually exclusive spheres. On one hand are the grandees—Giovanni's castoff flame Donna Elvira; his first quarry in the opera (virtually at the top of the first scene), Donna Anna; her wimpy fiancé, Don Ottavio; and her father, who observes tradition by dueling with Giovanni and dying, to reappear at length as the statue with the iron grip who pulls the debaucher into the fiery pit. On the other hand are the rank and file—Giovanni's minion Leporello; another quarry, Zerlina; and her boy friend, Masetto. (The first four might have stepped out of the old aria opera, the second three derive from *commedia dell'arte*.)

Giovanni, of course, is a grandee, too, though he mingles with the peasants as easily as with the quality. It is his interactions with everybody that give the work its structure and tone. Giovanni is the sauce of the dish. The others are more substantial, meatier, but he gives the whole its savor. As proof of the charm with which the author imbues him, he is a rapist and killer who never shows remorse (not even at the Last Minute), yet everybody finds him fascinating. Elvira can't live without him. Anna spends the entire evening seeking vengeance against him, a very certain homage. Zerlina is obviously attracted to him. The men don't seem to like him (envy?), but Leporello both mocks and admires his master's success with women, and at one point even wears his clothes. We know how Freud scans such didoes.

Never mind that we never actually see Giovanni pull off a seduction for sure. (Anna says she fought him off, but who knows? And Zerlina's critical encounter with him occurs off-stage.) Da Ponte and Mozart clearly envisioned the character as a libertine deserving of punishment. Amidst all the romps and tumbles, between Anna's rage for justice and Elvira's approach-avoidance conflict, Mozart starts the evening off with a terrific blast of d minor, a silence, and an answering blast of A Major. The two opposing tonalities, articulated as stark, monumental shudders, anticipate the moment when the statue appears at Giovanni's door to close his mortal career; thus our crucial first glimpse of the opera's soundscape fills with the awesome inexorability of heavenly retribution.

A serious opera, then, as Da Ponte claims Mozart wanted? Not really. For all the terror of the statue's eruption into Giovanni's house, for all Donna Anna's aplomb and Donna Elvira's desperation, there remains the work's "other," *commedia* nature. Moreover, *Don Giovanni* ends not with the protagonist's death but with a satiric "moral epilogue" in which all the surviving characters survey the sulphurous remains of Giovanni's dining room, plan their immediate futures, and warn the audience, with classical exhortation but to music of cheeky raciness, that all evildoers end in ruin. It is as if there are two *Don Giovanni*s going on at once. One is the thrilling life and times of a dashing cad, as promised in the "statue" music, the other is a lampoon of these same thrills, as resolved in the epilogue. This is what makes Mozart so enthralling, the same operas over and over again so unendingly fresh: he sees the joke in the ideal and the honesty in the trivial, the attractiveness of villainy and the anger in "fun." The diversity amazes.

By this time, Mozart was so adept at filling out the silhouette of librettese with the eloquence of real-life feelings that the next collaboration with Da Ponte, *Così Fan Tutte; ossia, La Scuola degli Amanti* (All Women Do So; or, The School for Lovers, 1790), took more than a hundred years to find its niche in the repertory. People just couldn't understand why such a frivolous plot inspired a score of such spiritual transcendence.

Da Ponte started from scratch for once, inventing his tale, though the premise is a standard comic trope: two young men bet an old cynic that he cannot prove their sweethearts unfaithful, and they must themselves test the girls, each man taking the other's fiancée. There are only six players—the two couples, the old cynic, and the girls' comparably sardonic maidservant. Such is the extreme lunacy in the air that the elaborate charade succeeds in ungluing the girls' fidelity in only one day; and such is the beauty of the music that the ear wants to reject the farcical façade and find some other truth in the piece. But it is what it appears to be: what All Women Do is be delectable and weak, and Da Ponte hangs his entire text on that observation. What Mozart does, however, is find the ambiguity between the lines, the several truths that mock all pretensions, men's as well as women's.

As with *Figaro* and *Don Giovanni*, compositional technique makes an already keen libretto into sharpest art. *Figaro* is farce made sociopsychosensual; *Don Giovanni* is comic tragedy. *Così* is the first of the great ensemble operas, the last spade of earth turned over the coffin of *opera seria*'s soloism. Not that there are no arias in *Così*—but the use of duet, trio, quartet, quintet, and sextet makes one aware of how much an inventive musician can draw out of a concerted passage. Continuing his overhauling of the dry recitative between the musical numbers,

Mozart occasionally blurs the edges where the "talking" ends and the singing starts, and heightens the collaborative tone of this extremely conspiratorial piece by arranging a few of the recit lines for ensembles, too.

Mozart was now organizing his operas harmonically the way symphonies are organized, using a home key for the overture, finale, and certain numbers in between. *The Abduction from the Seraglio* may be termed an opera in C Major, *Idomeneo* and *Le Nozze di Figaro*, operas in D Major, *Don Giovanni*—keeping to its bimodal tone—an opera in D Major-d minor, and so on. As for the musical numbers, Mozart structured these as carefully as a symphonic movement, giving purely musical as well as textual penetration.

One would think a composer with all this expertise (quite aside from his endless fount of melody) would have been the toast of the German opera centers, but Mozart wasn't. Vienna especially seemed to prefer several rivals of no great account, mainly Antonio Salieri, who was said to have poisoned Mozart—Salieri even accused himself, babbling fey arcana on his deathbed. Partly to realize his dream of writing a one, true German opera and partly to win over the Viennese with their favorite form, the *Singspiel*, Mozart embarked on what was to be his last opera project, a fairy-tale rescue opera* with all the effects in place—exotic locale, scenic spectacle, flamboyant villainy and purest goodness, earthy comedy, children in cuddly animal get-ups, and assorted Oriental voodoo.

Sounds hot. But before completing this farewell to art, Mozart about-faced and set an ancient *opera seria*—by Metastasio, no less—refurbished by Caterino Mazzolà. Originally set down in 1734 and put to music by Gluck and Hasse among many others, *La Clemenza di Tito* (The Clemency of Titus, 1791) seems to have been a mistake for Mozart at this point in his life. He had advanced too well to tackle a croaking relic, even with Mazzolà's canny redivision of Metastasio's aria verses into duets, trios, and choral scenes. A lifeless tale of love intrigue, attempted regicide, and imperial forgiveness for the composer of the egalitarian *Figaro*, the chiaroscuro *Don Giovanni*, the wantonly ambivalent *Così Fan Tutte*? *Tito* was a festival piece (to honor the coronation of Leopold II of Bohemia), written to order for money; today it is usually heard more out of curiosity than admiration.

Returning to his *Singspiel*, Mozart immersed himself once more in his magical cosmos wherein love exercises a cutting edge and evil

---

* Fairy-rescue *Singspiele* were known by the classification *Zauberoper*, "magic opera."

has feelings. For this heartily German project Mozart worked not with an Italian scribe but a German—and his partner was less a writer than a man of the theatre, Emmanuel Schikaneder. An example of what used to be called the actor-manager (a combination of star player, stage director, and impresario), Schikaneder gloried in Hamlet and Lear but could turn with ease into a dialect comic. Naturally, he planned the casting around his own company, actors who could sing rather than real singers, which explains why the music is simpler than elsewhere in Mozart, folkish as often as "operatic." But then *Singspiel* is musical comedy, anyway, and customarily puts virtues of lightness and directness ahead of vocal *grandezza*.

There is a special exactness about this last opera of Mozart's that cuts it off from the progression he had worked out from *Figaro* to *Così*. Those were Italian works, owing much to orthodox Italian style. This new work, full of fantasy and a good-natured vulgarity, sought German policies for opera, using the German *Singspiel* form and the patterns of German song mixed in with those of Italian *canto*. This in itself was hardly daring, since the *Singspiel* was both established and thoroughly German. But Mozart being Mozart, he would write no mere *Singspiel*—he would write an opera using *Singspiel* dynamics.*

Drawing freely from a story he found in a collection of Eastern tales as well as from other stories and *Zauberopern* of the day, Schikaneder† based the action on a conflict between occult forces of good and evil. A good fairy sends a prince to rescue her daughter from the clutches of a malign wizard, giving him an enchanted flute that disarms all who hear it. For some reason that no one has explained, the authors changed their tack partway through the first act—the fairy turns out to be the evil force and the wizard a philosopher-king of luminous humanism. Without altering anything they had already written, Mozart and Schikaneder forged on, closing with the triumph of the goods but not bothering to clear up a host of inconsistencies created by the shift in plot. Subsidiary characters identified with the evil queen seem to have free access to the good prophet's domains, and though his humanist fraternity regard women as inferior to men, the princess whose rescue sparks the plot is clearly the peer of anyone else on stage for honesty, lovingkindness, and strength of will.

Taking the plot by itself, then, this piece would seem to be a typical chaotic *Zauberoper* of its time. But one thing sets the libretto

---

* For comparison, consider Gershwin's *Porgy and Bess*, a similarly hybrid work that employs the populist energy of musical comedy for the penetration of opera.
† It is often mooted, but never proved, that the real author of the libretto was Karl Ludwig Gieseke.

apart from its fellows: a deeply spiritual core that gradually transmutes the absurd action with a lesson in elemental human wisdom. It is a religious work, its belief being Freemasonry, the secret and quasi-egalitarian society that numbered among its members many of the most enlightened men of the late 1700s (including some prominent leaders of the American Revolution). Both Mozart and Schikaneder were Masons, and it is said that initiates of the secret sect recognize pertinent images or slogans in performance that others miss entirely. There are also more discernible references to the Masonic world view, as in that advice given to the young hero when he reaches what he thinks is enemy territory but which in fact is a holy City of Man: "Be steadfast, patient, and silent!"—three virtues of obvious appeal to Masonic thinking, risking prosecution to liberalize the world. But with or without the Masonic subtext, anyone may divine the opera's message of ecumenical outreach and education, told on three separate but interconnecting levels: the world of the Masonlike lodge of humanists; the heroic world of the prince, Tamino, and princess, Pamina, who pass the trials and join the sect; and the naturalistic world of the prince's companion, Papageno (after *Papagei*-parrot), a birdcatcher too clumsily appetitive to gain—or need to gain—the inner circle.

What makes *Die Zauberflöte* (The Magic Flute, 1791) so brilliant is Mozart's ability to portray these three levels in music that underlines both separateness and togetherness. The "Masons," the prince and princess, and the comic characters all sound different from each other, yet when they sing together they meet on the same plane. The point is that all the good characters, whatever their backgrounds, can understand each other. Only the wicked Queen of the Night, who understands nothing but herself, sings in an idiom that no one else shares, expressed in a pair of high-flying coloratura solos of convulsive arrogance that take the singer up to a high F (the highest note demanded—with no suggested lower option—in a repertory opera). Not exactly coincidentally, the singer who originally took this role, Mozart's sister-in-law Josepha Hofer, was one of the few real singers in Schikaneder's company.

Schikaneder played Papageno, larding the part with the universal rituals of comic improvisation. As much of the world as the Masons are above it, Papageno roots *Die Zauberflöte*, gives it belief; it is his relationship to the magic, the religion, and the fear and wonder in the story that guides our relationship to them. He is the Everyman figure disguised as Punch, Arlecchino, or Hans Wurst, a pancultural archetype whose utter reasonableness makes everything around him reasonable by association. Not exactly a winner, he nevertheless lands on his feet, grinning. One night during the run Mozart slipped backstage in the middle of a performance while Schikaneder-as-Papageno was "playing" the glockenspiel, the notes of course provided by a musician in the wings. Substituting for the musician, Mozart slyly added in a note or two when Schikaneder wasn't ready—and, Papageno to the life, Schikaneder incorporated the mishap into the scene, flirting with the dizzy instrument, glaring mock-angrily into the wings, and finally bringing down the house by walloping the glockenspiel in his hand and crying, "Hush up!" This sort of spontaneity belongs to the role as much as to the person who created it.

Die Zauberflöte seems to have scored a popular if not critical success, though years later it attracted the homage of German nationalists as an after-the-fact "foundation" of German opera. This it was not, as its unique blend of the spiritual and the earthly had no issue; no one else could develop, top, or even imitate Mozart's sophistication of humors.* This is why we speak of Gluck's reform and not Mozart's. Gluck could be enlarged upon, but Mozart, who spent so much time learning the operatic ropes, suddenly tied knots no one knew of and for years was almost unapproachable on an intellectual level. Indeed, the nineteenth century was to misread him completely. Those Romantics weren't as liberal as they promised to be.

---

* There were several attempts to write a sequel to Die Zauberflöte. Goethe, another Mason, started a libretto in which the Queen of the Night steals Pamina and Tamino's newborn son and hides him in the bowels of the earth, but he gave up work when Schikaneder himself produced Das Labyrinth; oder, Der Kampf mit den Elementen (1798), the music by Peter von Winter. The plot of this would-be sequel is even more scattered than that of Die Zauberflöte.

CHAPTER FIVE

Romanticism in Opera

More light!
—JOHANN WOLFGANG VON
GOETHE, last words

Poetry fettered fetters the human race.
—WILLIAM BLAKE, *Jerusalem*

I have no love for reasonable painting. There is in me an old leaven, some black depth that must be appeased. If I am not quivering and excited like a serpent in the hands of a soothsayer I am uninspired.
—EUGÈNE DELACROIX, *Journals*

Off with their wigs!
—Romantic partisans at the
world première of Hugo's
Hernani

NO QUESTION THAT THERE WAS A PERIOD IN MUSIC HISTORY WHOSE qualities have led us to identify it as Romantic and its operatic output as Romantic opera. But one theory holds that all opera is romantic to start with, no matter what the aesthetics of a given era may be. Opera is exotic, fantastic, self-dramatizing . . . and all that sounds like Romanticism.

But there is a specifically Romantic opera, not because it is more exotic, fantastic, or self-dramatizing than Baroque or Classical opera, but because the worldview that informs the manipulation of these qualities is a Romantic worldview, very different from the seriocomic la-di-da of the early Baroque (Cavalli, say), the magisterial resilience of the high Baroque (Handel and Rameau), the gravity of Classical tragedy (Gluck), or the brisk simplicity of *opera buffa*. If opera was already Romantic, the Romantic era made it more so, and we have come to that era now, moving from the *Sturm und Drang* of the late 1700s through Beethoven and Schubert into the holistics of Berlioz, Liszt, and Wagner.

Romanticism is a complex business, taking in personal psychology, revolutionary politics, a host of submovements in fiction, poetry, and drama, and computations in demographics that make English Romanticism very different from the French and German varieties. This development alone has produced many long books—even its minutiae are crucial—but we will try to slip into the epoch through its transitional works and pick up points as they come, rather than tote up the commentary all at once.

The *Sturm und Drang* (storm and stress) that so galvanized German letters (and even erupted into German symphony) did not at first affect opera to a great degree; there was no all-popular operatic version of the keynote Romantic work, Goethe's *The Sorrows of Young Werther* (1774), until the very end of the nineteenth century.* And the second wave of Romantic literature, the continental impact of Wordsworth, Byron, and other British poets in the early 1800s, did not wash into opera as powerfully as it did into the solo song. Still, there are signs of change: a tightening of structure, a blending of parts, extremes of pathos and ferocity. One notable example is found in the overture to Gluck's *Iphigénie en Tauride*, which opens calmly but quickly bursts into "storm music" that runs into the first scene. This might be called the *Macbeth* effect, using natural turbulence to describe human turbulence: heavy scenes, so to speak, calling up heavy weather.

The extraordinary sensuality of Mozart is another sign, especially in its comic contexts. We expect music of profound expressiveness in tragedy, music to involve us on an interior, an instinctual, level. But comedy is more alienative and intellectual; only a Romantic sensibility would be able to cast the spell of *sensual* intellect in comedy—and this Mozart does.

Atmospheric decor, too, inaugurated the new era, as when André Grétry's *Richard Cœur-de-Lion* (1784) unveils what was to become a staple of the Romantic scene shop, medieval chivalry. Grétry's *opéra comique* tells how the troubadour Blondel searches for his liege Richard, finds him incarcerated in a German fortress, and presides

---

* The durable *Werther* opera was Massenet's, in 1892, though there were earlier versions—Rodolphe Kreutzer's *opéra comique*, *Werther et Charlotte* (1792), for instance.

over his rescue. Grétry and his librettist, Michel-Jean Sedaine, carefully glaze their pan with blots of scenic color, class by class—the folk-festive peasants, weighty bourgeois, impetuous nobles. They hit upon one excellent device in a kind of motto theme for Blondel's search, an antique ballad, accompanied by solo violin and horn, that throws an opaquely ancient shadow over the whole work like the tower of a crumbling castle. This is one of the earliest uses of the *Leitmotiv* (a theme identified with a person, place, object, or idea) that was to obsess composers in the coming century. In *Richard-Cœur-de-Lion*'s Big Moment, the reunion of Blondel and his king, the two are separated by masonry, Richard high on the battlements of his prison and Blondel standing beneath him. Blondel signals his presence by launching this ballad, Richard continues it with a start of recognition, and the two complete it triumphantly; the picture might have been ripped out of a book of medieval tableaux.

It seems odd that *opéra comique*, with its emphasis on spoken dialogue, alienative comedy, and unpretentious showmanship, should be a vessel of Romantic infusion. But musical comedy is flexible; it can lean way over into the sentimental, the dramatic, or the satiric. Now, sensing vogue, it dealt heavily in dynastic curses, old hermits in wild places, and bands of brigands mooching around in the moonlight. Downplaying comedy and putting his all into music that lulls the mind and thrills the heart, Jean-François Lesueur composed the rescue opera *Le Caverne* (1793), inspired by Alain René Le Sage's trendy *Gil Blas*, and *Ossian; ou, Les Bardes* (1804), an almost intolerably Romantic piece that combined three of the era's fetishes, the middle ages, Scotland, and the supernatural.

Subject matter, too, tells us that the times were changing, especially in a new political awareness. The pastorale, in which nymphs and satyrs dallied, now turned to an idealization of rustic folklore based notably on a quasisociopolitical humanism, often merely cosmetic but at times truly felt. Suddenly the lonely solo of an anonymous fisher-man or milkmaid—heard, if possible, from a distance—constituted the apex of resonance, and the not fully evolved merry villager chorus was turning into something less functional than symbolic. They were the folk, even a people. The folk had feelings, but a people have history and a destiny. After the French Revolution began, in 1789, *opéra comique* became the preferred entertainment for its "popular" mu-sicology, and the rescue opera was particularly favored. While the Revolution was still in its moderate phase, Grétry's *Guillaume Tell* (1791) dealt with the overthrow of Austrian tyranny in Switzerland as led by William Tell (peaking in the scene in which Tell shoots the

apple off his son's head) and, a few years after the Directory dismantled the surviving radical wings of the Revolutionary government,
Pierre Gaveaux's *Léonore; ou, L'Amour Conjugal* (1798) looked back
at the Reign of Terror, telling how a woman infiltrates a jail disguised
as a man to save her imprisoned husband. J. N. Bouilly, Gaveaux's
librettist, adapted the tale from an incident that had occurred while
he was serving in an administrative position in Tours. He discreetly
moved the action to Spain, but billed the piece as a *"fait historique"*
(historical event), reminding his audience that this rescue opera of
the heroic woman and her liberty-loving husband provided a living
example of resistance to tyranny.

A splendid age. Freedom was no longer a concept to be debated
by Scholastics and authors of hieratic tragedies, but a promised—to
some, threatening—experience. The American colonies, having evolved
their cultural revolution of the middle class, fought a war of separation
from their mercantilist mother England, and the French had dissolved
one of Europe's most parasitic master classes. The industrial revolution,
still in its infancy, had yet to manifest that Invisible Hand which
remanded liberated individuals back into the slavery of mass production and consumption and electronic total media. It was that best of
times, one scaled to personal size. Court establishments and patronage
in opera and symphony gave way to impresario-mounted concerts
open to a wide public (more like Handel's London audiences than
like Lully's chic Parisians), and the solo recital of the charismatic
genius musician came into currency. No timeplace is ever Utopia, but
the early Romantic era had fewer defects than any other era known
in the West, and artists' imaginations ran to great possibilities of
brotherhood and private quest alike, using eighteenth-century reason
to find nineteenth-century feeling.

Could opera grow up to all this? Or would it go on distilling its
fantasy and watery idealism in folkish colors, demonology, and post-
card ruins? Opera, as the thoroughly elitist form of the Camerata, of
Lully, *opera seria*, and (somewhat) Gluck, held at first to its remote
nobility. This left a gap between opera and the more quickly Romanticized drama, poetry, and song. So the less penetratingly musical
but more demotic form of musical comedy—*opéra comique* and *Singspiel*, especially—moved in and had a heyday.

One might trace the rise of musical comedy from several per-
tinently Romantic touches in Mozart's *Singspiel, The Magic Flute*.
Its mysticism and fantasy are very fully conceived, as is its heroism, a
human heroism to retire forever the gods who in earlier days arranged
the happy endings: Classicism, with its Greco-Roman heraldry, was

officially terminated. It is Blondel the minstrel who frees Richard the Lion-hearted, Leonore who frees her husband Florestan, and musical comedy, rather than the musically more lavish opera, contained them.

Gaveaux' *Léonore* struck such a right note that other composers set the libretto; if Metastasio's *La Clemenza di Tito* formed the basic text of the high Baroque, the tale of Léonore became the idée fixe of the transition into Romanticism. Ferdinando Paër set Bouilly's libretto in an Italian translation as *Leonora* (1804), and Ludwig van Beethoven made the German version of this tale of resistance and liberation in 1805 for a Vienna occupied by Napoleon's soldiers. To distinguish his opera from Paër's, still making the rounds of the cultural capitals on the German axis, Beethoven's setting was called *Fidelio*, this being the alias Leonore uses when working in the prison where her husband is held. Joseph Sonnleitner's libretto followed Bouilly's closely; like *The Magic Flute*, it sets earthy characters (the jailer, his daughter, her unesteemed boy friend) side by side with more florid personalities (the imprisoned nobleman Florestan, his resolute wife, the prison governor who is about to kill Florestan after two years in solitary confinement, and the state minister who punishes the guilty and praises the righteous in the final scene). This slender social cross-section remained a feature of the various forms of musical comedy until the American type totally democratized it in the 1910s and '20s.

While Mozart wove his classes into a humanist tapestry, Beethoven is more attracted by the abstraction of freedom, and he segregates the jail staff from the more active participants in the drama. But since the plot takes some time to get going, Beethoven was faced with several numbers in a row dealing with the middle-class sentimental subplot (the jailer's daughter has a crush on the disguised "Fidelio"); literally nothing happened in his first act and not too much more in his second. Only in the third and final act did the central conflict of wife protecting husband from the villain really emerge, with its climax in the trumpet call that signals the arrival of the state minister, the reunion of Leonore and Florestan, the invasion of the full cast into the dungeon, and the exhilarating final chorus, thrill upon thrill.

Fidelio did not go over. The first act's sluggish pace blurred the definition of the music, and the French officers who made up the bulk of the audience were not much impressed with Beethoven's Germanic sound. He was prevailed upon to revise, and a horribly mutilated *Fidelio* came forth a year later, almost every number slashed for compression and a few dropped altogether. But the first two acts were wisely combined, putting some motion into the plot, and eight years later Beethoven overhauled the work a second time. This 1814 version is the one performed today, a cornerstone of the repertory and a constant "festival piece" whose message of brotherhood and liberty is no less vital for the problems mankind has had in maintaining either in regular quantity.

The two early versions of *Fidelio* are now referred to by the title Beethoven always preferred, *Leonore;* he wanted to emphasize not the transsexual disguise, the "Fidelio" device, but the woman beneath, the redemptive female archetype that has illuminated so many German dreams. Leonore is like a fierce Pamina, a pragmatic Senta (in Wagner's *The Flying Dutchman*), and to do her justice Beethoven wrote a part calling for stamina and punch seldom asked of sopranos at the time. Similarly, her husband Florestan, composed for tenor, is no standard-make hero. A man who has spent two years starving alone in darkness chained to stone must strike the ear out of an unimaginable horror, yet reflect the vigor of perseverance.

Obviously, Romantic opera could not sail along on the voice types that had served the Metastasio era. Orchestras grew bigger and louder, the accompaniment more "symphonic," the surge of drama more embracing. The hierarchy of the vocal typology had to shift. In Mozart's day a soprano was a soprano, going from Susanna to Donna Anna to Fiordiligi (in *Così Fan Tutte*) to Pamina with ease. Now such roles as Beethoven's Leonore separated the stronger from the lighter sopranos. The dramatic soprano took Anna and Fiordiligi and the lyric sang Susanna and Pamina. We notice too that the tenor, formerly favored only in France, was promoted to the roles once assigned as a rule to the *castrati*, whose fantastic timbre was declared obsolete by the sleek new ideals of Romanticism. The *castrato* had never fitted into any of the realistic or comic opera forms anyway; with these forms in the ascendance, he hung on only in Italy, where *opera seria* attempted to outrace its own extinction, failed, and vanished, taking the *castrato* with it.

Leonore and Florestan are two of the new era's choice prototypes. Other avatars specialized in world-weariness, mystical identity crises, and bouts with the devil; sometimes they belonged to the spirit world, which outfitted them with that charismatic attraction to and alienation from the mortal world that the German imagination especially found irresistible. Not all of these suited the erratic science of libretto writing, however, and composers, too, sometimes found the trickier ideological archons beyond reach of their talents. Ludwig Spohr attempted a *Faust* (1816), not so much after the provocative legend as dragging far behind it; and the viscerally Romantic opinion molder E. T. A. Hoffmann tried his amateur's hand on the legend of the chaste water nymph whose kiss is death in *Undine* (1816), only skimming the surface. The metaphysics of faerie were to bring out the best in composers, but only in the better composers.

Just to show that nothing in art is all one thing or another, some character types and subjects utterly appropriate to Baroque and Classical opera adjusted neatly to the change in climate. Étienne Méhul, one of several composers important in the Romantic transition who have since faded away, set in *Ariodant* (1799) the same tale (from Ariosto) that had served for Handel's *Ariodante* sixty-five years earlier. The difference lies in musical treatment. Méhul's Romantic orchestra assists in the narration as Handel's Baroque consort could not, Méhul's singers confront each other in ensemble where Handel's exchanged arias, and Méhul even supplied another instance of the early *Leitmotiv* in a "jealousy" theme associated with the villain whose revenge plot on the woman who spurned him sets the piece in motion. Méhul termed this theme the "*cri de fureur*" (cry of fury) and made it basic, in recurring variations, to the entire score. So the biggest difference between these two operas is the continuous musical involvement of the later work. In *opera seria* the stately structure suggested an author-to-audience resistance of emotion even as the story line indicated emotion; in Romantic opera the music really gets down with the action, *inhabits* it.

Subject matter does distinguish these new-style operas, however. The Romantic imagination luxuriated as much in certain locales, conditions, events, and effects as in certain types of character, and here too music found an expanded role to play in dressing the look or mood of a tale. Nothing seemed to elate the attuned listener more than a "folk song," or narrative ballad, or peasant dance, or some other touch of ethnic or historical color plunked into the scene to relate the ear to time and place. A medieval tale? Let bards thrum harps or a hunters' chorus entwine with horns. A foreign setting? Let some native exotic sound the simple folkish strain. Gioacchino Rossini, setting an adaptation of Shakespeare's *Othello* in 1816, turned a superb trick in the last act by musically crosscutting Desdemona's pathetic Willow Song with the offstage voice of a gondolier singing the words Dante gave to Francesca da Rimini in the *Inferno*, "Nessun maggior dolore che ricordarsi del tempo felice nella miseria" (No greater sorrow than to recall a happy time in a sad one).

Shakespeare generally joined Schiller and Goethe in vogue as source material for librettos, though the favorite by far was Sir Walter Scott. The appeal of the historical novel in the early 1800s cannot be exaggerated. These antiqued texts, savored both as documentary (of life as lived) and fantasy (of incredible feats, love beyond death, and the enchanted ecology of savage places), endowed the operatic scene with a host of new backgrounds, though the stories themselves were often compressed to resemble the love-and-honor intrigues of *opera seria*. The number of Scott operas in the first half of the nineteenth century is virtually uncountable, ranging from immediate flops to international successes still strong today. Rossini contributed *La Donna Del Lago* (The Lady of the Lake, 1819),* François Adrien Boieldieu greedily used both *The Monastery* and *Guy Mannering* for *La Dame Blanche* (The White Woman, 1825), while Heinrich Marschner produced perhaps the best of several *Ivanhoe* operas in *Der Templar und die Jüdin* (The Templar and the Jewess, 1829). Indeed, *Ivanhoe*, along with *Kenilworth* and *The Bride of Lammermoor*, proved the most fertile of the Scott sources; as late as 1891 *Ivanhoe* served Arthur Sullivan as the basis for his sole serious opera. *The Bride of Lammermoor* enjoyed a shorter but even wider fashion, turning up in some half-dozen adaptations (including *Bruden fra Lammermoor*, a Danish *Singspiel* with a libretto by Hans Christian Andersen), until Donizetti wrote *the* version in 1835.

With all this balladeering and folk prancing, aficionados of the German *Lied* might look for some carryover from the fine art of the song into opera, for the former's crystalline symbiosis of words and music surely set an example for opera. This was the era of the *Lied*, a Schubertian age among other ages, given to uniting verbal concepts with musical ones into tiny epics of intellectual and sensual imagery. Romantic symphonies sometimes followed dramatic programs (Franz Liszt made one out of *Faust*), and the tone poem would soon be devised to capture a given poem in musical depiction.

Perhaps Schubert wrote operas, then? He did, and in doing so demonstrated that opera is not simply a battery of songs. That "music for action," the operatic kinetics that keep Mozart's four masterpieces so fresh, is as much a part of composition as the Big Tunes. Schubert was the king of song, and when he troubled to, he could structure a symphony (his Ninth, for instance) on the Beethovenian plan. Melody and structure should make an opera, but in Schubert's case they didn't, not least because he failed to hold out for a topflight libretto. Schubert composed numerous *Singspiele* and one full-fledged opera; neither in

---

* Rossini's *Elisabetta, Regina d'Inghilterra* (Elizabeth, Queen of England, 1815) is sometimes added to the list of Scott descendants, though it predated the publication of *Kenilworth*, which it resembles, by six years. However, there is a little-known Rossini *Ivanhoé* (1826), a French pastiche with music drawn (by others) from earlier Rossini operas.

the former's spoken dialogue nor in the latter's recitative does the action ever quite get active, and the musical numbers themselves, though sometimes dazzling and never less than attractive, fail to engage the gears of conflict. Melody and structure need motion.

Schubert's one opera, *Alfonso und Estrella*, shows how music theatre with glorious music but off-center theatre doesn't work. With its love plot of prince and princess of hostile peoples; its ballad set piece, the Song of the Cloud Maiden (who lures hunters to their death); its Hitchcockian "macguffin" in the device of a jewelry chain of intense interest to the characters and none whatsoever to the audience; and its alternating country idylls and war scenes, *Alfonso und Estrella* hardly needed Schubert's helpful designation of it as a "Romantic Opera." What it did need was a text whose lines are not made up largely of song lyrics of consistent metre, each line repeated endlessly to fill out the musical shapes. This piece looked so limp on paper that, although Schubert finished it in 1822, it wasn't performed until 1854, and at that only because Liszt, music director at the Weimar court, insisted on staging it.

One facet of Romanticism that thrilled operagoers briefly was supernatural horror, a specialty of the German-speaking countries. As always with fads, its champions became extremely famous then and extremely forgotten later; Heinrich Marschner offers the case in point, with *Der Vampyr* (1828) and *Hans Heiling* (1833), both *Singspiele*. *Heiling* (which pulls the novel stunt of playing its overture after its prologue), is the better of the two for the creepy-crawly orchestral effects that lend *frisson* to the tale of a goblin prince who yearns for redemption in the arms of a mortal woman. Any resemblance to Wagner's *The Flying Dutchman* is somewhat more than coincidental, for, like a number of less well-known composers of the early 1800s, Marschner helped to energize high Romanticism by trying out new ideas that his successors would perfect, meanwhile rendering Marschner's imperfect original superfluous. (Similarly, Mercadante was improved upon and erased by Verdi, Adam by Offenbach, Spontini by Meyerbeer.) *Der Vampyr*, too, may have touched a Wagnerian nerve, for its vampire protagonist, Lord Ruthven, is one of the first antiheroes to grace opera in its post-*seria* days; Marschner's attempt to capture his vileness and humanity at once may well have inspired the interesting ambiguities in Wagner's Tannhäuser, Wotan, Gunther, Klingsor, and Amfortas.

The antihero as Romantic avatar fared better in poetry and drama —not to mention life—than in opera, where characters and situation had to suit the available musical technology or appeal incoherantly to the spectators. Certain characters, certain situations, just didn't feel musical. Trading in Metastasio's persons out of history for personages out of the historical novel and play, early nineteenth-century opera still preferred sopranos who loved and pined, tenors who loved and stormed, baritones who plotted or were misled, chorus members who just stood there in revelry or consternation (one often followed right on top of the other), and a narrative outlook that tied the ritual coils. True, everything now was defter, livelier, more intense, even demented. But opera was still getting its Romantic bearings, and if the dramatic scope of the music was wider, the plot material—vampires notwithstanding—was not always all that different from that of the previous century. It is no accident that such classics of the innovative Romantic spoken stage as Jacob Michael Reinhold Lenz' *The Soldiers* and Georg Büchner's *Woyzeck* and *Danton's Death* had to wait till the next century for operatic transformation.

In fact, nonmusical Romantic art so outstripped Romantic opera in originality that tastemakers had to reach back to Mozart's *Don Giovanni* to celebrate the all-basic operatic antihero. That *Don Giovanni* is as much satire as romance didn't faze them in the least. Having no sense of humor themselves, they did not so much ignore as suppress the comedy. They saw Giovanni as a Byronic clone, with all of Byron's reputed sexual radicalism and paradoxically pallid vigor, a man half devilry and half despair. Byron himself started a Don Juan epic in verse that is still one of the wittiest things around, but the reinvented Byronic Don Giovanni could not coexist with sardonic commentary. The Romantic's Giovanni was an idol of *Angst*, haunted and driven, cousin to Manfred, Faust, and Don Carlos, an icon in the ideology of doom. *Don Giovanni* as performed in the 1800s got very large and serious; the revisers even chopped off the sparkling moral epilogue in D Major to close with the d minor scene in which the Statue throws Giovanni into hell. To them *Don Giovanni* was a tragedy, and not till 1888—101 years later—did the axiomatically Romantic Don Juan turn up, in Richard Strauss' husky, gallant, dreamy, debonair, elegiacal, depressed, and transfigured tone poem after Nikolaus Lenau's verses.

Mozart's sneakily aggrandized *Don* Romantic *Giovanni* points up another facet of the era, the unhappy ending. For two hundred years, virtually every opera had resolved on a positive note; suddenly principals began dying of poison or consumption, throwing themselves off cliffs, or being led to the scaffold. Remember, it was an age that gloried in (and feared, surreptitiously) free will: with choice comes the possibility of grisly consequences. The spoken theatre forced the issue, raising up scores of heroes in the early 1800s whose uncompromisingly revolutionary politics destroyed them. But opera hung back. It wanted intimate, apolitical deaths. Beethoven, scoring the incidental music to Goethe's drama *Egmont* in 1810, caught the despair and triumph of the hero who has a vision of future liberty for mankind the night before his execution for sedition. The overture to the play at first seems about to close in limp resignation, then suddenly erupts in glory and strides to a grand finish screaming, "Live free or die!" But Beethoven, scoring the opera *Fidelio*, could not possibly have shown us Leonore failing to save her husband; that would have been too much for opera to bear in 1805.

Early Romantic opera not only could not tolerate any ambiguity in heroism, it also did not care for ambiguity in comedy. While *Don Giovanni* was carefully misunderstood and reinterpreted as the beautiful fall of a libertine, *Così fan Tutte* was not understood at all. Men testing their fiancées' fidelity—what an insult to womanhood! Beethoven declared himself shocked by it. Wagner decided it was a failure, and congratulated Mozart for failing. Ludicrous schemes "purified" it: new librettos were slipped in by dramatists of assumably greater probity than the disreputable Da Ponte, or editors arranged for the two girls' to be warned of the test by their servant, thus preserving their moral profile ("We knew it all along!").

Perhaps the best chance to see Romantic opera in its full flair may be taken in a look at the work of Carl Maria von Weber. One of the new era's pivotal figures, Weber fired off scattered bursts of Romantic intensity in his mainly Classical symphonies, concertos, and piano sonatas. But the stage brought out a true Romantic mechanic in him. The magic of the new style lay in narrative, in decor, in dramatic rataplan, and opera offered the ideal outlet for these diverse elements, besides presenting the Romantic with his favorite challenge, to find a conceptual unity in art.* Weber was attracted to the stage all his short life, but he failed to define his terrain for some years, trying out comic and fairy-tale *Singspiele* with little success until he settled in Dresden as conductor for life of the German opera house in 1817.

Dresden provided an unlikely laboratory for the man who more than anyone would work out the trajectory for a national German

---

* A little known but extremely typical sample of the Romantic urge toward artistic wholeness was Ignaz Franz Mosel's *Versuch einer Aesthetik des Dramatischen Tonsatzes* (Search for an Operatic Aesthetic), published in 1813. Mosel called for an organic collaboration in opera of poetry, music, singing, acting, and stagecraft, with myth as the most suitable subject. The anticipation of Wagnerian opera is remarkable.

opera. The city of Hasse and Bordoni, it reeked of *opera seria,* and Weber's appointment ranked lower than that of the conductor of Dresden's Italian opera company. Consequently, when Weber wrote the first of his three great operas, *Der Freischütz* (The Free-Shooter, 1821), he didn't even present it in Dresden, but carried it to Berlin, where it enjoyed the first of a quick series of wild smashes that was to make it, for a time, one of the most popular operas in the world.

Der Freischütz gathers together many of the characteristic Romantic ingredients, bonding them integrally in one folk-cultural horror piece in *Singspiel* form. The Free-shooter is a hunter who compacts with the devil for six bullets, five of which cannot fail to hit their mark—but the sixth flies for hell. Filling out the scene are the cliché pastoral figures of musical comedy, so beautifully limned in vocal line and orchestral character typing that their very ordinariness, their realism, startles. The weak hero, his fiancée, her pert sidekick (with the usual saucy aria about the kind of man she'd like to marry), the villain (a former free-shooter who tries to save himself by inveigling the hero into the unholy pact), the judicious Prince, and the pious hermit (who tells the tale's moral) offer nothing novel in dramaturgy. But Friedrich Kind's libretto was less a play calling for musical expansion than an excuse for Weber to detail the new "Romantic Opera" (as he termed it himself) in folk choruses (the girls are bridesmaids, the men hunters), arias friendly or passionate, a brilliant scene-setting overture, and, most famous of all, the ghastly Wolf's Glen episode in which the villain and the appalled hero cast the six magic bullets at midnight during an eclipse of the moon. Invisible spirits howl and chant, apparitions of "good" women haunt the hero, and a rota of demonic ectoplasm parades by while the bullets are calcined (the compound calls for, among other things, "powdered glass from a broken church window")—a black bear, four fiery wheels, the ghostly "wild pack," and a storm in full blow. To cap the scene, the villain goes into convulsions, the clock strikes one, the Black Huntsman himself appears, and the hero faints in terror.

If Weber's nature painting, folk quaintness, and nationalistic ethos made *Der Freischütz* the craze of its day, its nationalism eventually made it too parochial an experience for non-Germans, and it dropped out of the standard repertory as suddenly as it had entered. But it remains a landmark of cultural evolution. Its wholeness is amazing, considering the variety of its diversions—the Wolf's Glen scene, the opening and closing marksman's contests, the village dance and drinking song, the assorted Gothic calculus, the prankish *Gemütlichkeit*—but each set piece relates to and enhances the others with effortless rightness. It has that rare quality in popular art, authenticity.

Much of Weber passed on to Wagner: Weber's precise theatrical strokes, his selective instrumentation, his love of fantasy and horror, his amalgam of arts, and even the plot outline of the second of his three masterpieces, *Euryanthe* (1823). Admirers of *Lohengrin* will have no trouble sorting out *Euryanthe*'s principal characters and setting. There is the good couple: timorous heroine and her loving but not very tolerant knight. The bad couple: envious villainess and her knightly partner in crime, working to ruin the love story. Plus the grave king who hangs around mainly to fill in the bass line in ensembles, and the Holy Roman world of chivalry.

On closer inspection the resemblence is only superficial. *Lohengrin*'s libretto is sensible and psychologically intriguing. *Euryanthe*'s characters might be described as zombies of Romanticism but for the speed with which they pull unmotivated stunts on each other. Euryanthe is a "why" opera. Why do the characters speak as stodgily as possible and transmit essential plot information too quickly for anyone to hear? Why doesn't Euryanthe defend herself when the bad couple make her look unfaithful in front of the court and every man on stage turns against her in a second? Why are we expected to believe that the wilder places of medieval France were stocked with serpents, one of which attacks Euryanthe and her ex-fiancé, Adolar, who is planning to kill her for her assumed infidelity? Why did Weber set this nonsense in the first place?

There's always a reason. Having ratified German folk-horror *Singspiel* triumphantly in *Der Freischütz*, Weber had no intention of writing another one, though everyone was begging him to. Instead, he turned to the other fashionable genre, medieval romance. This one would not have the spoken dialogue of *Singspiel*, but would be a "real" opera of recitative, song, and dance, every word a vocal word. Structured to move with courtly leisure, *Euryanthe* really hones in on its principals, and the only flaw in the project was Weber's choice of librettist, Helmina von Chézy. A loony poet, she had trouble hammering out the details of exposition, with the result that neither the development nor the resolution of the story is entirely clear. Most disturbing of all are the occasional references to an Emma, who never appears but seems to exercise a strong pull on the action. She eventually turns out to be Adolar's late sister. (Weber, who had his own loony moments, had to be dissuaded from bringing Emma onstage, flitting spookily overhead.)

All this, ironically, Weber composed with genius intact, and *Euryanthe* ended up a master score wedded to an incomprehensible script. Attempts to revive it invariably fail—the goings-on are that silly —and other attempts to rewrite Von Chézy's text and revamp Weber's music to suit the rewriting are a despicable arrogance. Anyway, Weber wrote to point up Von Chézy's verses on a note-by-note basis; to alter those words in any way robs the music of its meaning.

Weber himself vastly preferred *Euryanthe* to *Der Freischütz*. The latter, after all, was something of a capstone in the *Singspiel* line, but *Euryanthe* promised to found a new type of German opera. Its influence was enormous, not only on Wagner, and helped affirm the new vocal condition of opera in its use of the high soprano and dramatic (i.e., robust) tenor for the nice couple and a darker soprano and dramatic baritone for the villains. This is, of course, exactly how Wagner laid out the counterpart roles in *Lohengrin*, but that is a minor homage. More significant is the adaptation of the *Euryanthe* voice—a strong, clear soprano—as the phonotype of the German opera heroine and of the Adolar voice—a sturdy, almost baritony tenor—as her vis-à-vis. Weber's form, too, set a tone for his successors, who pillaged medieval chronicle and legend for more such tales of nobility and baseness to set against a background of festive gatherings and romping peasants.

Having produced the best of one genre and the first of another, Weber returned to the old *Zauberoper* so much in style when Mozart and Schikaneder wrote the classic example, *The Magic Flute*. Weber's "magic [and rescue] opera" was *Oberon; or, The Elf-King's Oath* (1826), written for London to an English libretto by James Robinson Planché. This is a strange excursion for the proto-nationalist Weber, stranger yet when we realize that Planché's libretto is even more ludicrous than Von Chézy's for *Euryanthe*. But then rescue opera was always a little off the wall: the inconsistencies of *The Magic Flute* identify the genre better than the staid, steady crescendo of exaltation in *Fidelio* does.

Unlike those two classics, *Oberon*'s rescue carries no political or social exhortation. Planché cobbled his plot out of Christoph Martin Wieland, laced it up with a few figures out of Shakespeare, and sent it off to Weber on the Continent, act by act. There were some interesting constructions—a magic horn that Weber could conjure up out of the orchestra, no full-out love scene for the hero and heroine (they meet in a vision, and thereafter are too busy scrambling around in the rescue to duet), an unusually grand *scena* of several kinds of recitative and a wild-flying aria for the heroine—but mainly Planché had shuffled the trite diversions of magic and rescue and then dealt them out as they came. They included comic servants for the two leads, an abduction from the harem, virtue tested, Arabs, pirates, and knights, a storm at sea, the abstruse contortions of the spirit world, and of course the happy ending. No sooner had Planché's Act I arrived than Weber got nervous; even the best moments seemed wrong. Furthermore, the commission involved his journeying to England in full winter to conduct the performances,* a serious matter for the sickly composer. But the money was good and needed—and as for Planché's crazy libretto, Weber promised himself that after the premiere he would redo the whole work as a gala German opera, sung throughout like *Euryanthe*.

Tragically, the British trip proved fatal, and *Oberon* survives, barely, in its original form, usually translated into German. Most operagoers have heard of but not actually heard it, though for a very few years it was in demand everywhere. The world premiere production at Covent Garden was sincerely spectacular, offering Mary Ann Paton and John Braham as the leads and Lucia Elizabeth Vestris as the servant Fatima, all three among the best-loved singers in Britain; it got to New York a mere two years later; and in France, where *Der Freischütz* had created its most thorough sensation as *Robin des Bois* (The Forest Demon), businessmen looked forward to selling *Oberon* dresses, hats, and candies as they had sold *Robin* products. Everywhere *Oberon* went, it delighted with its score and deflated with its book. It is arguably Weber's best effort, his great enterprise in blending the vitality of Mozartean *buffo* with the new thrust of Romantic adventure. It would have reoriented German opera to tradition just when it most needed such reinforcement and would perhaps have fanned young imaginations. Nothing in opera captures the early nineteenth century's awe of, hunger for, and closeness to supernatural forces better than the "magic horn" theme that opens *Oberon*'s overture, a preview of the whole work spun out with dazzling symphonic control, leaping from wishful love to the dauntless enthusiasm of chivalry. The opening chorus, "Light as fairy foot can fall," luring us into Oberon's domain, similarly entrances, tiny as a pearl in a cowslip's ear. Then a bit of dialogue tells us that Oberon and Titania have sworn to stay apart until they have found a mortal couple of memorable constancy. Puck has just returned from a fruitless seach for such a couple, leading Oberon into a virile lament, dominated by woodwinds. So far, excellent. But suddenly Puck remembers a possibility, a French knight who must expiate an impolitic duel by sneaking up on the Caliph of Baghdad at banquet, kill the Caliph's left-hand guest, kiss

---

* We can get some sense of the pervasiveness of Romanticism in opera circa 1826 by reflecting that the first two operas that crossed Weber's path when he got to London were a *Rob Roy* and an *Aladdin*.

his daughter, and abduct her to France. One begins to worry, and sure enough, the rest of *Oberon* consists of great musical sections interspersed with a libretto so loco one almost wishes Von Chézy had written it instead of Planché. As with *Euryanthe*, interlopers have tried to reshape the piece, but as with *Euryanthe*, "improvements" only make it worse or cut music worth hearing. There is one instance of successful revision of Weber—Gustav Mahler's completion of the unfinished comedy *Die Drei Pintos* (The Three Pintos, 1888), filled out with little-known Weber material and not a revision so much as a completion.

Just as Romantic opera eventually proved itself less in what it did than in how it did it, Weber's folksiness, medievalism, and Gothic and fairy-tale devices appeal to us less than the urgency and charm of his music. *Oberon* has its "Turkish" march and story-book choruses, but the most ear-filling passages are the big arias allotted to the hero and heroine. His great solo, "From boyhood trained," launched by trumpet calls and stormy strings, combines the vocal flexibility and slow-gaited lyricism of *bel canto*, yet in a polished Teutonic strain; it catalogues his glories in armor only to reveal the ardent heart that longs for love. Her famous scene, "Ocean, thou mighty monster," is even grander, with its anxiety, then hope, then triumph mounting in apt musical sequences to the aria proper, a swooping finale fit for a Valkyrie, so stupendously "symphonic" that it really sounds more comfortable as played in the overture than it does as sung by the overworked soprano. Still, the piece is thrilling, the vocal climax of any *Oberon* performance, and a clear demonstration of the new dramatic boldness of Romantic opera.

For this is what happened to opera in the 1800s—an innovative validity of situation and character based on an expanding musical technology. Classical opera preferred *line;* Romantic opera prefers *tone.* And that's why the less pretentious genres came to the fore at this time, why the gala works of this transition—from *The Magic Flute* through *Fidelio* to *Der Freischütz*—stem from musical comedy: opera itself was too staid, too Classically statuesque, to negotiate the musical metamorphosis, and had to learn by imitating *opéra comique* and *Singspiel.* These less profoundly musical forms had something the era needed: alert dramatics.

Now we'll have to move back in time and see how the grander operatic forms fell in with the Romantic movement.

CHAPTER SIX

The Foundations of Grand Opera and Melodrama

*The ancient Romans, so they say,
Just spectacles and bread did own;
But for the French alive today
The spectacle's enough alone.*
—popular song of the French Revolution's Reign of Terror

One thing that no one thought of when Rossini appeared . . . is the point to which he is romantic. In him one finds those pathetic introductions and those passages which . . . summarize a whole situation for the soul and do it outside all the conventions.
—EUGÈNE DELACROIX

IF THE ROMANTIC HAPPENING TELLS HOW *opéra comique* AND *Singspiel* became musically articulate, it also tells how "serious opera" became dramatically revitalized. By the late eighteenth century the *dramma in musica* ailed badly. Both *opera seria* and *tragédie lyrique* were dying when Gluck produced his Italian and French reform operas—and who could follow Gluck? In the fifteen years following his retirement, only Mozart provided great operas, and these *sui generis* works were inimitable, part *opera buffa* and part something else neither comprehended nor fully appreciated. Suddenly, it seemed easier to follow Gluck than Mozart.

105

And this is about what happened. While Berlin and Vienna worked on *Singspiel* and Italy danced a last waltz with *opera seria,* Paris built on the Gluckian reverberation to assume operatic leadership. The contributors to the new movement in serious opera were Italians, but they lived in Paris and set French librettos. Most significant, they renovated the French tradition of declamatory song with Italian *canto,* slipping more and more into outright song until Rossini, the most Italian of Italian composers, finally Italianized the vocal resources of French opera almost completely. The result was an organic blending of French dramatic values with Italian musical values, and it cut the die for what we generally call "grand opera." This is a specific and frequently misapplied term; let's approach it as the Paris-based composers did, starting from Gluck to reach Rossini.

At first Gluck had no apparent heirs. His old rival Piccinni stayed on after him in Paris, seconded by other well-liked Italian masters such as Antonio Sacchini and Antonio Salieri. The French Revolution, a great time for theatre, brought out numerous "revolutionary" operas which came and, better, went; but when the smoke cleared, Luigi Cherubini began to trace a route back to Gluckian *tragédie* through his imposing use of *opéra comique* with *seria*-type characters, as in *Lodoïska* (1791), a rescue opera with a manically Romantic libretto made severe—Classical, even—by Cherubini's coldly tempered score.

Cherubini was the tyrant of French music. As head of the Paris Conservatoire, whose doors he guarded like a Cerberus, he set academic policy; as the most respected composer of Beethoven's era (an opinion held by Beethoven himself), he set a tone for the impressionable, measuring out sensuality with a teaspoon. Napoleon had hated him and kept him down, but after 1815 Cherubini rose high. He was rigorous and his grandeur demanded admiration, but only the most discerning ears found him moving. His lifelong involvement in opera was a marriage of inconvenience; he played the unbending husband to the public's neglectful wife. Yet his masterpiece, *Médée* (1797), stuns us with passion, pity, and horror. It is an extreme work in any age.

Despite its use of spoken dialogue (sometimes over shrewd orchestral underscoring), Cherubini's *Médée* looks back directly on Gluck's mighty Greek tragedies. The title role presented a stupendous challenge to Romanticism's barely invented dramatic soprano voice— too stupendous, maybe, because awful legends attached themselves to women who attempted it. The original Medea, Julie Scio, reportedly hurt her lungs fatally reaching for Cherubini's fiendish range of high and low notes and his no less daunting emotional range of pathos and viciousness. Margarethe Schick tried it and died insane. Anna Milder-

Hauptmann, Beethoven's first Leonore, hurdled the part without apparent penalty, but then, as Haydn once said, she fielded a voice "as big as a horse."

Big voices were not common then, and it may be that *Médée was* unsingable, given the resources of the time. But Cherubini saw *tragédie*'s potential too clearly to settle for the moderated intensities of Gluck's Alceste or Iphigénie. Here is a woman, Medea, who has betrayed her people for a man she needs so badly that when he throws her over for another she can settle accounts only by murdering her own—because they are his—children. Such ferocity called for a ferocious interplay of orchestra and voices. Perhaps not till Maria Callas revived the role in the 1950s did the piece play to an audience who could take it.

Unfortunately, the edition used in the Callas (and subsequent) stagings is not the opera Cherubini wrote. For a German performance in 1855, one Franz Lachner dummied up recitative for the original spoken text, adding nothing to the piece but time and ruining, among other scenes, the superb second-act finale, wherein Medea rages and worries in speech at the front of the stage while the chorus musically celebrates the wedding of Jason and Medea's successor in the background, until Medea at last explodes into song while the orchestra rumbles nastily. Too, the use of speech at Medea's first entrance gives one a feeling of edgy anticipation that Lachner's lifeless recitative dissipates. Yet it is Lachner's version, usually translated into Italian, that one hears today.

With a busy orchestra and chorus on hand to fill out the action, French opera followed through with Gluck's revolutions. The orchestra not only supported but added to the sung text with its own opinions, and the chorus layered the conflicts of the plot with its added pride, fury, sorrow, or sympathy. This would be part of the grandness in grand opera—size, expansion. (*Médée* already shows some of this in protracted musical structures that annoy with unnecessary repetition.) Switching over into all-musical opera, Cherubini exercised this new option of proportion in *Les Abencérages* (1813), a dry run for grand opera, ascetically tidy but indicative of what was to come in its picture of a political feud between the Zegris and the Abencerages in Renaissance Spain. The use of rival choruses gives a sense of real moment to the plot, making the love story between an Abencerage hero and a local princess almost secondary to the tide of historical intrigue.

Cherubini was late, however: what is often cited as the matrix of grand opera had already been produced by Gaspare Spontini—yet another Italian ingraining form in Paris. The generative opus was *La Vestale* (1807), a highly Gluckian piece that lacks Gluck's bounding vitality. Neither Étienne de Jouy's libretto nor Spontini's music offers much interior penetration; to know that the heroine is a vestal virgin who has broken her oath and fallen in love with a young Roman hero is to know all. Rather than fulfill the piece with Gluckian depth of *person*, the authors moved in the opposite direction—straight up—piling form upon form. *La Vestale* feels as if it were one-third procession, one-third ballet, and one-third tedious soprano aria.

The work is well constructed but slow and dull, some thirty years younger than Gluck's French operas but old-fashioned compared to them. Ancient Rome, the Christianlike pagans, the decorous dance sequences, the unseen *deus ex machina* whose flash of lightning rekindles the sacred fire that had gone out during the big love duet and thus pardons the heroine for the happy ending—it's all very well measured out but it's all too sacred and lacks fire. This so-called "first" grand opera is really more of a "last" *tragédie*, and points the way to grand opera only in the famous second-act finale, which foreshadows Meyerbeer's lurid finale imbroglios of plot twist and character conflict in which soloists, chorus, and orchestra all go at it full out. *La Vestale*'s second finale follows the love duet, during which the heroine lets the aforementioned sacred flame go out, a faux pas punishable by death. Though only the heroine and hero (and his confidant) know that the flame has died, menacing voices are immediately heard offstage: the chorus, exercising operatic instinct, simply converges on the temple to demand judgment on the luckless vestal, and the High Priest and Grand Vestal lead the crowd in fiery denunciations to Spontini's unpleasantly insistent Big Tune. But the composer does create an air of suspense for his curtain.

It turned out that Spontini felt more comfortable in less chilly settings, and he unbent somewhat for the more colorfully conceived text of *Fernand Cortez* (1809), with its heroine of an Indian girl converted to Catholicism and its real-live horses onstage, optional but strongly recommended. *Cortez* proved more successful than *La Vestale*, and the two together promised to establish Spontini as the supreme maestro of postrevolutionary French opera. Like Lully, he won imperial favor—Napoleon supported *Fernand Cortez* with gusto, hoping it would fan anti-Spanish hatred for the war he was just about to start against Spain. And yes, the score is quite rousing, though the plot is something of a make-do; when Spontini revised the work in 1817 he made the last act the first act, which doesn't say much for the logic of the original layout.

Spontini's contribution to the institutionalizing of a new opera genre lies as much in his approach to production as his personal talent. He ran tough but useful rehearsals in a time when lax performance discipline was thought to be a singer's perquisite. (Spontini so terrorized Dresden during his visit to stage *La Vestale* there in the 1840s that Wilhelmine Schröder-Devrient, who sang the title role, staged a sort of rival opera which may be called *La Finta Malata; or, The Prima Donna Feigns Illness to Send the Maestro Back to Paris.*) He was alert to the taste of his audience, placating it as he raised it. He never missed the chance to call for spectacle—loud sets, ballets, parades—and though in Germany he ran head-on into the *Freischütz* cult and saw how empty spectacle could look when set against the intimacy of *Singspiel,* he did instill a sense of format in his expansive historical epics.

Olimpie (1819), from Voltaire's tragedy on the mother of Alexander the Great, and *Agnes von Hohenstaufen* (1829) were Spontini's two best operas, excitingly musical, and a follow-up to Cherubini. *Agnes von Hohenstaufen,* for example, is in some ways a richer version of *Les Abencérages;* it codified the texture of grand opera in its sumptuous stream of solos and ensembles broken up by choral and dance diversions all building up to huge act finales. Cherubini is concise, Spontini complete—concision was not to be one of grand opera's qualities. *Agnes* lasts so long that the first act was premiered all by itself two years before the rest, and but for the helpful information of costumes and voice types, one can hardly tell who's who in the plot. Just for starters, there are two Philips and three Henrys. (One of the Philips is only mentioned, never seen. But still.)

While Cherubini and Spontini were anticipating the great French flowering of *grand opéra,* a third Italian was finding his very different road to the same form. But Gioacchino Rossini came to Paris late in his career, and his style rooted itself more firmly in Italian practices than theirs. *Opera seria* and *buffa* were his forms rather than *opéra comique* or *tragédie,* and the voice-hungry Venetians and Neapolitans provided his sounding board, not the drama-proud Parisians. In his lifetime—until he stopped writing operas halfway through it—Rossini was the most popular opera composer alive. Even when he was in eclipse his work held the stage, though he himself predicted that of his nearly forty stage works only *The Barber of Seville* and an act each of *Otello* and *Guillaume Tell* would survive. *The Barber* has endured. And if Rossini's *Otello* was superseded by Verdi's version and *Guillaume Tell* retired with the fading of grand opera, others of Rossini's output (the comedies particularly) hung on somehow, and a slow but steady Rossini revival launched in the 1950s has reinstated the music of this luxury-loving, sardonically witty, innovative "Swan of Pesaro." He is, once again, a giant.

He was the first giant to follow Mozart in Italian opera, but the line does not run directly from one to the other. Mozart "wrote" Italian while trying to find an outlet for his native voice; Rossini's native voice was Italian. Furthermore, whereas Mozart juggled the comic and the serious in works with, so to speak, two faces, Rossini invariably separated the two, though he was equally at home in either. His first opera was *seria*—*Demetrio e Polibio*, composed in 1808 but not performed till 1812—and his second was *buffa*, *La Cambiale di Matrimonio* (The Switched Marriage, 1810); thereafter he alternated the two irregularly. At first he showed no great insight in either genre, as likely to break into something unintentionally snappy in *seria* as lay the grand line on a comic heroine's little aria. Not that Rossini failed to construe the very different senses of pace and character in serious and comic opera: simply that as he wrote them, they had a bit in common. Thus when the perky Spanish-flavored overture originally written for *The Barber of Seville* got lost in some mishap, Rossini substituted an overture he had used for two earlier operas, *Aureliano in Palmira* and *Elisabetta, Regina d'Inghilterra*. That they were serious and *The Barber* comic didn't matter. The overture had always leaned a little to the prankish side in the first place.

Tancredi (1813), an *opera seria* premiered in Venice, brought Rossini his first fame, chiefly for its Big Tune, "Di tanti palpiti," which proved so catchy that a law was passed to keep the Venetians from making a pest of it with their whistling and humming. Taken from Tasso and Voltaire, *Tancredi* offers a perfect instance of *opera seria* in evolution. The subject, courtly love and war, is pure eighteenth century. But the use of ensemble and chorus and the dancing rhythms of the orchestra and the solo woodwind are up-to-date Rossini, and the title role of the knight beloved is scored for mezzo-soprano, a lushly Romantic touch. (In old-fashioned Dresden, a *castrato* was brought in for the part as if in Handel or Hasse.) Also, Rossini wrote out the melodic embellishments himself—composed them—rather than leave them to singers' chance concoctions. Most notable are the military passages and the passion of the love music; these characters are engaged in the action, not simply demonstrating it.

Rossini billed *Tancredi* as both "*opera seria*" and "*melodramma eroico*" (heroic opera), pointing up the transition from old opera to new. Feeling his way into the era, he even wrote an alternate sad ending (Tancredi dies) to replace the habitual *lieto fine*, helping to float the new taste for beautiful pathos. However, a dead Tancredi took all the fun out of the piece for the public, and the happy ending was generally used. Similarly, Rossini's first version of *Otello* (1816), a hamhanded adaptation with an ending faithful to Shakespeare, depressed audiences; they preferred a rewritten finale in which Desdemona and her husband make up. Not till the 1820s had the sad ending taken hold in *melodramma*, by which time it in turn became a convention.

While helping to bring *opera seria* into the more fluent and passionate 1880s, Rossini also tended to *opera buffa*. Here there was no renovation to make; it was enough to find a lively libretto, trick it up in playful music, and cast for verve. Rossini's comic genius added something to the recipe, a special "comic" sound in depicting the wicked joys of sporting and cheating. Amidst the elegant coloratura— which Rossini took as seriously in comedy as in romance—and the occasional lyrical idylls, these are very loony tunes, dryly self-aware. Finding his form in *L'Italiana in Algeri* (The Italian Girl in Algiers, 1813), Rossini reaffirmed it in *Il Turco in Italia* (The Turk in Italy, 1814), two studies in geographical culture shock.* Still performed today, these little wonders startle with their invention and idiosyncrasy. *L'Italiana* offers a classic instance of the frenetic Act I finale, when the plot machinery has gotten so oppressive that the principals have to line up along the stage apron to report on the noises that are banging away in their heads. Here the three women sing "din din din," the tenor goes "tac tac tac," the *buffo* figure (a fat, ridiculous bass) adds "cra cra cra," and the deepest male voice centers the harmony with a drumlike "bum." The Italian girl herself, in Algeria to find her lost fiancé, delivers the score's high point in "Pensa alla patria," a stirring address to her enslaved lover to consider "homeland, duty, honor." Her boyfriend is silent, but the chorus responds ardently, and she urges them to bravery in a quintessentially Rossinian soundscape, lightly pattering string chords and short choral notes under her vocal line, a simple tune deftly embellished. If *Il Turco in Italia* lacks *L'Italiana*'s dash, it does have a wonderful novelty in the character of "The Poet," who thinks he is writing the libretto as it unfolds and wanders in and out of the action, irritating the other characters with his exploitive omniscience.

No conscious reformer, Rossini couldn't help but affect opera for the better, if only by setting a high standard for composition. In turn,

---

* The traveler at loose ends among aliens was a favorite *buffa* situation in the late 1700s. Domenico Cimarosa managed to pull himself away from his serial examination of marital intrigue for a typical entry, *L'Italiana in Londra* (The Italian Girl in London, 1778).

opera affected him. Audacious librettists goaded him to dare, impresarios got ideas, singers with specialties contributed to his vocal bazaar. The most influential of the singers was Isabella Colbran, a striking Spanish woman with a sumptuous mezzo-soprano of polished agility. Rossini met Colbran when he moved to Naples under contract to the flamboyant director of the San Carlo, Domenico Barbaia. Colbran was Barbaia's mistress and prima donna; she became Rossini's, and eventually married him, leaving her stamp on most of his mature Italian operas in that their leading roles were cut to her measurements. She was nearing the end of her career when Rossini met her, and had lost her top notes, so necessity invented the Rossinian coloratura mezzo, a voice type so rarely encountered that many of Colbran's roles have had to be rescored upward to accommodate the coloratura canary, going *ping!* in high notes that Rossini never thought of. This practice suffered a refreshing humiliation about fifty years ago when the delightful Spanish mezzo Conchita Supervia revived some of these parts in their proper register with her signature "machine-gun" vibrato, and the modern urge toward authenticity has followed up with a whole school of genuine Rossini mezzos in a line from Giulietta Simionato on to Teresa Berganza, Marilyn Horne, and Frederica von Stade. The "Rossinian tenor," too, became a habit: a light voice capable not only of intricate coloratura but of sudden, bounding high notes often done in falsetto. There was even a "Rossini crescendo," a favorite device in the overtures, in which a tune would be repeated in an unchanging speed and texture while the orchestra got louder and louder.*

The mezzo, tenor, and crescendo are all in place in Rossini's most popular work, *Il Barbiere di Siviglia* (1816), based on Beaumarchais' play, the so-to-speak "prequel" to *The Marriage of Figaro*. It was already popular as an opera before Rossini tackled it, having been set by Giovanni Paisiello in 1782. There were French and German versions as well, but Paisiello's was the classic,† and a claque loyal to tradition made a disaster of Rossini's *Barber* on its first night at the Teatro Argentina in Rome. It seems incredible that a score of such exuberance and delicacy as Rossini's should have failed to please even a hostile au-

---

* In recent times Leonard Bernstein wrote a cute homage to the Rossini crescendo in the overture to his "comic operetta" *Candide*.

† As Paisiello's version was titled *Il Barbiere di Siviglia*, Rossini and his librettist Cesare Sterbini originally called theirs after its tenor hero: *Almaviva; o sia, L'Inutile Precauzione* (The Useless Precaution), to distinguish the two operas while showing respect for Paisiello. However, savvy producers advertised the Rossini as *Il Barbiere di Siviglia* to be sure to attract Beaumarchais' considerable public, and the younger work overshadowed the older so quickly that *Almaviva* became *Il Barbiere* by draft.

dience—and this after the composer had troubled to elaborate his style with a sly use of Spanish rhythms and a touch of bolero for the finale. But the work rose above fiasco to install itself in the international repertory with great speed. What is its charm? Why this one, of all Rossini's comedies? First, the usual *buffa* reasons: familiar plot (young lovers thwarted by her aged guardian, helped by debonair conniver; love triumphs) farced out to wiggy extremes; good (not Big) tunes; show-offy parts for all principals. Second, a show-biz reason: the continued practice of deleting and adding to suit singers' sense of celebrity established *The Barber* from the first as a flexible showcase for any vocalist with the muscle to fig a part out in solo delights.* The third reason is more general. Here, more than anywhere else, Rossini established a heuristics for comic play, a musical rationale for all the gabbling, squiggles, and facetiae that everyone had always taken for granted in *opera buffa*. Rossini made it all fresh. As serious opera was seeking to experience its characters and situations in sound, *agitato*, *estatico*, so was comedy finding a comparable route into its soul. Mozart, of course, had already found one such route—but Mozart was not, until relatively recently, an operagoer's idea of a *comic* genius; when Rossini produced *The Barber of Seville*, the two most frequently performed Mozart operas were the serious *La Clemenza di Tito* and the routinely comic *Die Entführung aus dem Serail*. No, it was Rossini whom they praised as the genius of comedy. Beethoven, when Rossini met him in Vienna, spoke for many others in urging him to forget *melodramma* altogether and give the world "plenty of *Barbers*."

But Rossini rose above his comic layer, presumably out of respect for Colbran's taste for heroic damozels. She was regal, melting, statuesque, delicately pained; she was Queen of England, Queen of Assyria, Othello's wife, Moses' niece; a Mohammedan conqueror loved her, the

---

* For more than a century nobody performed *The Barber* as written. The coming and going of extracurricular material reached a veritable bum's rush in the Lesson Scene, wherein Count Almaviva, disguised as a singing teacher, flirts with the heroine while her guardian dozes. Rossini wrote a lavish display piece for a Colbran-type voice, but the infiltration of high sopranos into the show led an assortment of prima donnas to replace Rossini's original with their trusty showpieces, regardless of relevance to the action. Big scenes, ditties, whole miniature concerts shoved in—everything from the endless mad scene from Donizetti's *Lucia di Lammermoor* to the dainty "waltz aria" from Gounod's *Roméo et Juliette*. Adelina Patti favored "Home, Sweet Home" and something called "The Echo Song." Marcella Sembrich preferred Proch's infinitely ridiculous Air and Variations. As late as 1943 at the Met, Bidu Sayão gave out with "Bel raggio lusinghier" from Rossini's *Semiramide*. The Rossini-Bellini-Donizetti craze of the 1950s commendably revived the one true lesson scene as Rossini set it, though occasionally a really fancy diva will direct a tongue-in-cheek return to tradition and throw the old party all over again.

Christian daughter of the Governor of Corinth; the King of Scotland doted on her, too, but she chose another. It was all seriously sentimental business, but in one year, 1817, Rossini consolidated his work in the fields of comedy and romance in two separate and very individual works, *La Cenerentola* (Cinderella) and *Armida*.

Cinderella was the only comic role that Rossini wrote for Colbran, and her taut line of take-offs, dives, and curlicues lives on in the highly decorated title role. All the parts are tricky, which is one reason why *La Cenerentola* has never rivaled the *Barber*'s popularity, though the heroine's joyful final rondo, with declamatory introduction, "Nacqui all'affanno" (Born to sorrow) and coloratura show stopper, "Non più mesta" (Sad no more), has enjoyed a life of its own as an encore piece. Modeling his libretto on Charles Perrault's fairy tale and pulling in bits from its other musical versions, Jacopo Ferretti emphasized farce over magic. The occult made Rossini nervous, even if he was to pull off a reasonably adept Apparition Scene in *Semiramide*. *Cenerentola* is all domestic comedy, true love, and prince-disguised-as-his-valet, with virtually all magic excised (Perrault's fairy godmother becomes a resourceful *philosophe* in Ferretti's reading). But then, *opera buffa* doesn't take well to the supernatural. It wallows in the testy stepmother and grotesque stepsisters, pushy in duet; in patter songs for the opportunist father and the wily valet, bubbly tunes chasing a wild spiel of Italian vowels and consonants in the standard first-act "What do we do now? We scream!" finale; in pathos and in goodness rewarded. Possibly the best of all Rossini's comedies, *La Cenerentola* closed his *buffa* series. It was not his last comedy, but it marked the prime peak of his comic style, that wonderful mandate for innocent mischief. The one composer universally thought supreme in comedy was kicking off those traces to find himself helping to sculpt the supreme style in romance.

The second of these two 1817 operas, *Armida*, shows this Romantic Rossini in action. Following up the refurbishing of *seria* launched with *Tancredi*, Rossini went all out on a libretto that didn't deserve it. The work of Giovanni Federico Schmitt, an industrious scribbler known mainly as the author of the standard Italian translation of *La Vestale*, *Armida* offers yet another rehash of the Tasso tale of the sorceress who temporarily enthralls a crusader. As portrayed by Quinault and set by Lully and Gluck, she was unending fascination; Schmitt encumbered her in mouthy banalities and archaic phrase structures. Worse yet, the impresario Barbaia had a spectacle in mind, and ordered Schmitt to include plenty of magical gala—just the sort of thing that Rossini distrusted. Furies abound; Armida and her knightly lover make one entrance on a chariot drawn by a flying dragon; and a "horrid forest" is transformed—"This is the realm of love," Armida gushes—into an "enchanted garden."

Rossini tried hard. He found a musical solution to the transformation, so strong that if the conductor and the designer can come to terms, the moment dazzles. He wrote a full ballet. He used every bit of Colbran's fading technique to bring the sorceress to life. He lavished love music of intense sensuality on the central couple. He wrote lead parts for no less than three Rossini tenors, since there were three such on hand in Naples for the premiere. And he wrote an ambitiously schizoid farewell for the abandoned Armida to close the show.

But he outwrote his public. Cries of "learned" and "too German" greeted the work, for which read "musically advanced": Rossini no longer wanted to dash off the songfest that Neapolitan audiences demanded. Besides, Colbran was unpopular now: the royalist faction adored her, so the liberal party denounced her. Stendhal, who wrote an inveigling and passionately unreliable biography of Rossini, observed that the anti-Colbran fever ran so hot that her detractors would have preferred her ouster to a democratic constitution.

One begins to feel that Rossini had outgrown Italy; still, he and Colbran hung on. Besides presenting a number of mostly unimportant operas on stages in Rome, Milan, and Venice, Rossini gave Naples further chances to see what could be done with *melodramma*. There was the craggy, muscular *Mosè in Egitto* (1818), an oratorio (staged, however, as was the custom in Italy, where Lent simply meant calling an opera by any other name). There was *Maometto II* (1820), a gleaning from Voltaire with a champion air of tragic grandeur. Best of this group was *Semiramide* (1823), outspokenly billed as a *"melodramma tragico"* and proof positive that *opera seria* was finished.

Wisely, Rossino launched *Semiramide* in Venice, where a less provincial public than that of Naples was amazed and thrilled at the wealth of musical point and dramatic heft, what with a Jocasta of a heroine and an Orestes of a hero. She is Queen of Assyria, he a war hero (a "trouser" role, sung by a mezzo-soprano), the object of her admiration but, unknown to her, her son. Making another of his several tries at convincing the spectators to accept an unhappy ending, Rossini and his librettist Gaetano Rossi retained the drastic conclusion of their source, Voltaire's play *Sémiramis;* the times were Romantic enough by 1823 to conceive of the queen's tragic death (when she comes between her son and his would-be murderer) as attractive and useful. It was Rossini's longest score to date, a full evening of exotic regalia with a musical integrity that confounds its dramatic silliness.

Rossini even yielded to the ultra-Romantic habit of quoting themes from the opera in the overture, thus making it a kind of tone poem introducing the action. Like Beethoven and Weber, Rossini became grander and more intense work by work.

Semiramide marks the finale of Rossini's Italian career, for at this point, as king of *melodramma* at the age of thirty-one, he visited London to enjoy being the rage at first hand, then settled in Paris to run the Théâtre-Italien, the local home for *melodramma*, staged idiomatically by Italian singers and staff. His salutatory entry, *Il Viaggio a Reims; o, L'Albergo del Giglio d'Oro* (The Trip to Rheims; or, The Inn of the Golden Lily, 1825), was a halfhearted three-hour one-acter, ill received and promptly withdrawn, though sung by an imposing cast headed by Giuditta Pasta. (*Semiramide* had closed Colbran's era.) Pasta was also on hand to send off Rossini's first non-Rossinian showcase of the latest in *melodramma*, Giacomo Meyerbeer's *Il Crociato in Egitto* (The Crusade in Egypt, 1824), for Rossini's bill of fare at the Théâtre-Italien. Meyerbeer, who was to succeed Rossini as the utter showman of French grand opera, was at this time fresh from having succeeded Rossini as a developer of *opera seria* into *melodramma*, and *Il Crociato* shows Italianate vocal writing that almost surpasses Rossini. There is, for example, the famous first-act trio, "Giovinetto cavalier" (The young knight), cautiously planned to be the prize of the piece for its luminously traced arabesques of soprano, *castrato*,* and mezzo-soprano, accompanied by flute, clarinet, English horn, French horn, violin, 'cello, double bass, and harp. Gaetano Rossi's libretto is a typical tangle of love and duty among Christians and infidels that Handel might have felt comfortable with, and there is nothing of the pyrotechnically theatrical that Meyerbeer was to be known for. *Il Crociato*'s main feature, in Paris, was that of all Rossini's offerings at the Italien: white-hot, sensual, full-cry singing, a feature of opera that the French still had not quite faced up to in their own product. The combined success of *Il Crociato* plus *La Cenerentola*, *La Donna del Lago*, *Otello*, *Semiramide*, and *Zelmira* (the entire repertory of Rossini's first full season), rendered the Italien aesthetically solvent and eradicated the bad taste of *Il Viaggio a Reims*.

As usual, Paris got an opera war going, with a pro-Rossini faction eyeballing a xenophobic French faction. Weber's *Der Freischütz* had hit town in its French version more or less synchronously with Ros-

---

* Giovanni-Battista Velluti, the castrato of *Il Crociato*'s premiere at La Fenice in Venice, is generally hailed as the last of opera's star *castrati*. Others outlived him, but the official line of international egomaniacal musicodramatic celebrity died with him in 1861.

Typical Rossinian first-act comic finale, here from Jean-Pierre Ponnelle's superb production of *L'Italiana in Algeri*: principals downstage, chorus upstage (holding heads to demonstrate the pains of fast plotting). Heroine Gwendolyn Hillebrew looks tired but luscious; the Bey of Algiers (Frederico Davià, to her right) seems about to pop from the excitement. *(Richard Braaten, Kennedy Center)*

Grand opera in the making in Rossini's *melodramma*, *Semiramide*: lush decor (note elephant), many extras, historical setting, and blockbuster star, Joan Sutherland. *(E. A. Teatro alla Scala)*

sini, and the French partisans overlooked its German origin to prefer it noisily to the Italian intruders. Weber himself stopped off on his way to stage *Oberon* in London, cheering the French faction with denunciations of Rossini, whose popularity had already annoyed Weber in German lands. But this *querelle* was soon over, for the vocal dynamite of Rossini's productions drowned out any academic dissension.

Heading his company were two of the most legendary singers of a generally legendary epoch, la Pasta and Giovanni Battista Rubini. Their prominence attests to the continued superiority of *bel canto*, though Pasta stood among the most progressive sopranos of her time, looking forward to a day when musicality of portrayal would count as much as musicality of vocalization, while Rubini seemed to have stepped out of the earliest days of *opera seria*. His tenor, as instrument, commanded an extraordinary top range, phenomenal breath control, and a natural elegance in phrasing. Rubini soaring high on a gilded tune must have been something to hear. But whereas Pasta tamed uneven vocal equipment to thrill through visual beauty and artistic commitment, Rubini was a doughy growth who wandered idly in and out of the scene waiting for Big Moments. He was the kind of singer about whom Italian-tenor jokes were invented. But when he put out, the heart trembled.

Rossini was not the ideal composer for either Pasta or Rubini. The soprano could not quite get her unruly voice around his tricky bravura, and the tenor—like the *castrati* of the old days—felt more comfortable in the intense slow passages that Rossini replaced with a more martial style. In Italy, Rossini had streamlined singing. He didn't simplify it, but he gave it punch and focus. Now, in France, he would give the already lean French declamation vocal expansion.

Obviously Rossini was in Paris not only to produce Italian but to write French. Wisely, he edged into the current, controlling as many of the variables as could be humanly directed. He studied French as language, hand picked the singers, pulled the Opéra's considerable resources into play, and, rather than start from scratch, rewrote an old work, *Maometto II*. Completely. With a new libretto that capitalized on the current Greek struggle for independence from Turkey by dealing with the same situation some centuries previously, *Maometto* underwent assimilation as *Le Siège de Corinthe* (1826), another possible "first" of the grand operas.* Combining French theatrical vigor with Italian musical vigor and blowing up the result with a world's end

---

* Cherubini and Spontini had first pointed the way, but their œuvre lacked an essential property of grand opera, sensational success.

of spectacle, grand opera marked the apex of opera as show biz. It had stars, it had topic, it had looks and style. It was very post-Napoleon Paris, politically leftist with a bourgeois heart. Its fascination for historical events gave it an air of infatuated documentary, but for all its calculation, Le Siège was very Romantic, deriving its patina osmotically from the association of the plot with the death of Byron at Missolonghi in 1824.

Le Siège a triumph, Rossini consolidated his hold on the Opéra with another major revision, that of the old Mosè in Egitto into Moïse et Pharaon; ou, Le Passage de la Mer Rouge (Moses and Pharaoh; or, The Passage Through the Red Sea, 1827). The Biblical setting is remote and the character of Moses ponderously epic, but the ballet, chorus, and decor filled out the big stage with a needed hustle, and the story served up yet another look at underdogs resisting despotism. Moïse enjoyed even greater success than Le Siège de Corinthe, and the new genre of grand opera was ratified by prompt imitation: Daniel-François-Esprit Auber's La Muette de Portici (The Mute Girl of Portici, 1828).

Based on a proletarian revolt against Spanish domination that had shaken Naples in 1647, La Muette acted as a model for grand opera, all the parts in place: five acts, with a ballet scene at the center; a host of principals caught up in historical turmoil; a chorus as given to artificial diversions (a wedding procession for pious splash, a "market square" chorus to raise an act curtain with suitable stir) as to mobocratic ravings; a libretto (partly, in this case) by the era's busiest wordsmith, Eugène Scribe; and a certain emptiness in the fifth act, when a full evening's worth of business is resolved, tragically, with startling efficiency. Perhaps because Auber normally expressed himself in the less pretentious opéra comique, La Muette is unusually concise for a grand opera,* but its dramaturgical flamboyance and musical drive is basic.

Auber was just the one to set this tale of a fisherman who leads a rebellion and is destroyed in its wake. Like Rossini, Auber employed virile rhythmic accompaniments to urge a scene forward, and he became celebrated for the plentitude of his barcarolles and marches; he also shows a pleasing tenderness in the Slumber Scene, "Du pauvre

---

* Length was a crucial feature, as the age loved luxury and grand opera comprised its official pageant. On the other hand, the curtain had to fall in time for commuters to catch the last suburban trains. This meant much overwriting at one's desk yet much cutting at rehearsals. La Muette contains about two and a half hours of music, but a more representative average would cite the four hours of Meyerbeer's Les Huguenots.

seul ami fidèle." There is nothing special in the way he "narrates" the text, and he is unquestionably more comfortable rousing the fishermen to their uprising than in dealing with the love plot, a triangle involving the son of the Spanish overlord, his Spanish fiancée, and the pathetic mute girl of the title, who offers the work's great novelty in that she must mime her part to music. (Ballerinas have played the role, but it is in fact an acting, not a dancing situation.) The protagonist is not the girl but her brother Masaniello, the leader of the rebellion (his prominence caused the piece to be called *Masaniello* more often than not), who fixes grand opera's politics at the start of Act IV, when his comrades have rounded up a number of Neapolitan power bosses. To a marquis, who proposes to buy him off, Masaniello says, "What can you offer me that isn't mine? This wealth is the fruit of our labors." So contagious is the spirit of revolution that the opera sparked a real-life one in 1830 in Brussels, when Belgium was under Dutch hegemony. A runaway success on its Paris premiere, *La Muette* quickly reached other stages—Antwerp and Budapest in its first year, Berlin, Vienna, London, Prague, and then Brussels in its second. Dutch authorities were nervous about Auber's inflammatory oomph, and after a few performances imposed a ban. Meanwhile, the July Revolution in Paris encouraged the Belgians, and public opinion screamed for *La Muette*. The ban was lifted, and the very next night *Masaniello* and his cohort sang not just to a post-card slice of Naples, but to all Belgium as well: "To arms!" Fighting broke out before the opera had ended, and within a few months Belgium proclaimed its independence, good-naturedly recognized by Louis Philippe of France and grudgingly accepted by the rest of Europe. The Dutch gave in.

It may seem amazing that the mainstream operatic type of the middle 1800s ran to the left of the road politically, but then it was only ceding to Romantic vogue: grand opera was less idealistic than *au courant*. And even in its quasilibertarian context, it remained artistically imperial, weighty with the self-importance of the Cultural Capital (Paris has always had a lot of New York in it). Now that most grand operas, like *La Muette*, have withdrawn into the niches of chronicle, they are mocked by writers who have not seen them staged or read the scores; when they are revived, with trumpeting huzzah, directors ignore the stage directions, singers fail to negotiate the difficult lines, designers fluff the spectacle, ballet persons wade bewildered through the divertissements, and conductors slash the structural inflations to peewee incoherence. And then everyone says, "Gee, it doesn't work." Even the classic grand opera jokes don't play fair. It's common to point out that, with the rebellion in disorder and Masaniello murdered by his own people, *La Muette* ends with the mute girl throwing herself from a balcony in downtown Naples into the crater of Vesuvius—"a distance," Edward J. Dent put it, "of some eight or nine miles." Wrong. The girl simply hurls herself off the high terrace: "into the abyss," the score reads (i.e., down to her death). Yet the joke has outlived the opera.

Vesuvius does take part in the finale, but only to steam, smoke, and erupt for a cataclysmic conclusion. This effect was thought so strategic to the work's fortunes that the French government sent stage technician Pierre Cicéri to Milan to see how La Scala's engineers brought off the final tableau of Giovanni Pacini's *L'Ultimo Giorno di Pompeia* (The Last Day of Pompeii, 1827). This was grand opera, then: a pseudohistorical gallimaufry of Romantic ethnopolitics, visual contraption, and a belief in almost nothing but the importance of being unique. It was *opera seria* merged with *tragédie*, refined and then expanded by Rossini, and naturally it was up to Rossini to execute the first all-around masterpiece in the form, *Guillaume Tell* (1829).

Again the subject is a patriotic struggle for autonomy, the Swiss against Austrian overlords. Unlike Grétry's *William Tell*, Rossini's derived from a literary source, Friedrich Schiller's play *Wilhelm Tell*, silghtly telescoped for the fit but faithfully restated by the Opéra's official poet (i.e., librettist), Étienne de Jouy. The writer was already an old hand at grand opera, having got in on the ground floor collaborating with Spontini on *La Vestale* and *Fernand Cortez*, and in *Guillaume Tell* he laid out one of the grandest of the grand, stuffed with ethnic genre pictures, manipulations of the natural world, and popular revolution. Thinking that De Jouy might have overdone it, Rossini passed the script along to Hippolyte Bis for cutting, though the finished product still sings in a somewhat scrambled word order, bowing to one of Romanticism's more dishonest devices, antiquing.

Guillaume Tell is stupendous. Bursting through the trappings of grand opera is a work of rude power and heartfelt beauty composed in a style totally unlike the Rossini of *Otello* or *Armida*. Feeling his way into a new style through his French versions of *Maometto II* and *Mosè in Egitto*, Rossini had not so much gallicized his technique as trimmed away the unnecessary vocal decoration of *melodramma*. One sees this most clearly in his last comic work, *Le Comte Ory* (1828), written for the Opéra a year before *Guillaume Tell*. *Le Comte Ory* owes nothing to the sound of French comic opera. One recognizes the autograph of the composer of *The Barber of Seville* and *La Cenerentola*, but the curves are tighter, the dimensions severe. The music has lost its quack, its silliness, and the characters appear more adult. *Count*

Ory's medieval plot deals with an amorous noble's attempt to seduce a faithful lady awaiting her husband's return from a crusade; disguised as a woman on holy pilgrimage, the seducer gets into her bedroom but no further, and the climactic scene in which his advances are resisted is played with ironic subtlety, in a decorous *adagio* rather the scampering doodle-doo of the younger Rossini. Similarly, the first-act finale, in which the count's first attempt to gain the lady's confidence is foiled, has none of the din-din and cra-cra of *L'Italiana in Algeri*. The vocal display endemic to the Italian mode is not stinted, but is drawn more integrally into the action. If there is no expressive call for it, Rossini leaves it alone.

When he first began composing for the Opéra, Rossini accommodated himself to French voices. Now, in *William Tell*, he was inventing voices that neither France nor Italy had in stock: clear of diction, finely tempered in emotional involvement, footsure in recitative and airborne in the grand line. The tenor lead, a young Swiss in love with an Austrian princess, is so heroic that even Adolphe Nourrit, Rossini's first choice for tenor leads, couldn't quite hack it, and by the second or third performance was already skipping an important scene in the fourth act. The Austrian princess, sympathetic to the Swiss people, is the soprano lead, Tell himself a baritone, and the vicious Gesler, *Gauleiter* for the Austrians, a bass. In all cases Rossini held out for the most adept singers, postponing the premiere when Laure Cinti-Damoreau, scheduled for the soprano part, became pregnant. As if sensing that this would be *the* work, Rossini took his time in composition— Rossini who once thought nothing of dashing off a complete opera in two weeks. But *William Tell* is two and a half times as long as the average Rossini opera, and conceived on a scale as deep emotionally as it is wide pictorially.

Schiller's play cried out for musical delineation, with its Alpine sound effects and folk songs, its climactic wonders of storm and sun, and its drastic standoff of oppressed people and oppressive army. But the incidental scores of dances, short solos, and act preludes guaranteed any play mounted by a first-class company were not sufficient to display the sheer raised fist of the piece. One had to hear the Swiss confront Gesler, hear what Tell thinks as he shoots the apple off his son's head, hear the joy of liberty won, not just in Schiller's poetry but in that ecstatic, other-directed poetry of music. If the 1800s saw the high point of play-into-opera, what Rossini did with Schiller's message must stand as one of the great reasons why.

That Rossini was at the height of his power as musical dramatist is not to be debated. The melody, as always, is almost unbelievable in its fecundity. The vitality and affection do not fail to rouse and touch. But more: there is an astonishing intelligence at work here. Romantic music craved unity in all things, especially the unity provided by a protean theme used throughout a work as a source of other themes; Rossini applies this sort of organization to *William Tell*, using as his basic building block a traditional *ranz des vaches* (cowherd's tune), variations of which turn up from scene to scene, now cheery, now skittish, now lowering, now exalted, and though Rossini does not attach this theme, in the style of Wagnerian *Leitmotiv*, to any one person or idea, it helps bind this immense score together.

Immense does not mean sprawling. Though Rossini does set the pace for grand opera, taking his time to say things and often repeating himself to round out a scene, *Guillaume Tell* moves with admirable clarity. There are diversions, of course. Act I is dominated by local-color scenes, amidst which an important duet between Tell and the tenor hero Arnold neatly strikes up the plot motives: Arnold loves his Austrian princess, Mathilde, but Tell insists that freedom fighting outranks courtship. By the time of the act's big choral finale—in which Tell rows a hunted Swiss patriot to safety while Austrian soldiers menace the Swiss and take Arnold's father hostage—the genre pictures have been retired and the love-or-duty conflict has taken over. Act II is the great one. After an opening hunting chorus, it moves from the private to the public in four superb scenes: Mathilde's aria, "Sombre forêt" (Somber forest), in which she deposits her Romantic-populist affidavit in an apostrophe to desert places, "I prefer you to the spendors of palaces"; Mathilde's duet with Arnold; a trio for Arnold, Tell, and another Swiss, in which the other two inform Arnold that the Austrians have killed his father, comfort him in the extraordinarily moving "Ses jours qu'ils ont osé proscrire" (His life, which they dared to end), and enlist him for the revolt; and an epic "gathering of the clans" in which warriors from three cantons arrive for the wapentake, one group in a march, one in a barcarolle, the third in a suspenseful passage for orchestra alone, and at last the three male choruses uniting in a rough-hewn, square-cut carmagnole. The whole business is held to a conspiratorial hush like an avalanche in pantomime, and Tell then launches the final chorus as the Swiss hoarsely edge around a shout and at last roar up a final "To arms!"

From that point on the work proceeds in the style to which grand opera was to accustom itself, the principals' personal lives constantly pushing back against the urgency of the chorus and its public concern —persons trapped in history. The apple-shooting scene caps the public-square festivities of the third act, and in the fourth and final act Arnold finds himself as a father-avenging leader of the resistance in the exhausting lyric-aria-followed-by-martial-aria-with-choral-backing that no tenor could bring off till Gilbert Duprez attempted the role eight years after the premiere with his pinging high C in chest voice (as opposed to the lightly shallow head-voice C applied up to then).* It remains only to purge the cantons of Gesler, and this Tell does in the climactic moment. To close the work, Rossini employs a last blissful variation of the *ranz des vaches* in an apotheosis of gently swirling orchestral figures over harp accompaniment, a nature picture of calm after storm as clouds disperse, the snow-capped mountains loom monumentally, a rainbow paints the mood, and the sun beams peace and beauty over a free people.

Sad to say, this masterpiece excited more enthusiasm from musicians than from the public. People thought it too loud, too long, and although it was repeated many times, each performance seemed to drop another scene. Finally whole acts vanished, until all that was left of *Guillaume Tell* at the Opéra was the second act, given by second-line singers as a curtain raiser for mixed-grill evenings of ballet and concert. A famous story finds Rossini meeting Duponchel, the Opéra director, in the street one day. "Well, for once you have no reason to complain about us, Maestro," says the impresario. "This evening we're giving Act II of *Guillaume Tell!*" "Really?" replies Rossini. "The whole thing?"

The most seditious of the grand operas because colonial tyranny was at the time a favorite step in the royalist's tango, *Guillaume Tell* traveled out of France in odd costume. Italian productions set it in Scotland or ancient Israel, and at Drury Lane in London it was completely made over as *Hofer; or, The Tell of the Tyrol*, music "arranged" by Henry Bishop; the nerve! Bizarrely, the first Viennese performances were not censored, though De Jouy and Bis depict the Austrians as thoroughly evil and debauched as well as imperialist. The Viennese seem to have taken no offense. "Long live the House of Hapsburg!" they cried at the finale.

---

* Rossini himself didn't care for Duprez' vibrant high notes, though popular interest in his Arnold reestablished *Guillaume Tell* in the Opéra's repertory; he likened Duprez' top C to "the squawk of a capon having its throat cut." Unwilling to hear Duprez in the theatre, the composer invited him to display his C at the home of a friend. Naturally, Duprez favored Rossini with Arnold's big scene, and Rossini later wrote, "I felt the same uneasiness that some people feel when a cannon is about to go off. At last the famous C exploded. *Corpo di bacco! What a din!*" Rossini rushed to a case of fine Venetian glass. "None of it appears to be broken," he reported. "It seems incredible." Duprez took this as a compliment.

In the end, *Guillaume Tell* did earn a respectful popularity, though most audiences never loved it the way Rossini's coprofessionals did. It more than any other work codified the grand opera style, but Rossini lived to see it elbowed aside by his successors, especially Meyerbeer. In fact, Rossini lived for another thirty-nine years and never wrote another opera—no one has ascertained why. Possibly he bore too strong a resentment of the upstarts who worked in "his" form to want to compete with them; this man was not stingy with contempt, either for colleagues he didn't respect or for the public that reveled in their output. Meyerbeer he particularly despised as a sell-out who capitalized on the Opéra's show-shop techniques. Then Meyerbeer's fabulous success was joined by that of Jacques Halévy; both men were Jewish, which kept the wags of Paris tuned to anti-Semitic *mots*. Rossini was such a wag. Approached by an Italian theatre begging for a new Rossini opera, he said, "I am waiting for the Jews to finish their Sabbath." He waited out the decades as a grandmaster raconteur and host, and people never stopped hoping that he might suddenly bring forth another sample of his genius. But *Tell* was the end of it after all. Another of Rossini's quips: "Retiring in time requires genius, too."

CHAPTER SEVEN

The Passing of Bel Canto

*The exceptional personage in
serious opera is the light soprano
who does not go mad . . . The
ordinary operatic heroine trusts
in the first act, is deceived in the
second, and goes mad in the
third. She is without character,
and is remembered not as an individual, but as a member of a
large and uninteresting class of
melodious lunatics.*
—H. SUTHERLAND EDWARDS

*All we contemporary com-
posers, without exception, are
so many pygmies beside this
great master [Rossini].*
—VINCENZO BELLINI

ROSSINI CAST A LONG SHADOW. IN ITALIAN *melodramma* HIS WERE THE
standard works by which young composers learned their practice, and
if French grand opera followed the flamboyant silliness of *La Muette
de Portici* more than it did the purer aesthetic of *Guillaume Tell*,
Rossini's masterpiece remained the example to which the most idealistic
composers aspired. Berlioz thought it one of the few operas not by
Berlioz to be worth hearing, Bellini saw it thirty times, and Donizetti
declared its second act was written by God.

But even as they followed the Rossinian road, the younger Italians
struggled to find their own way in *melodramma*. They were the heirs of
bel canto as well as of the Rossinian dialectic of music and drama, for
opera seria hung on in Italy long after it had died elsewhere—as late as
1838 Giovanni Pacini set one of Metastasio's texts, *Temistocle*. Rather
then pursue Rossini's adoption of French grandness, they concentrated

on the leaner, Italian-pure Rossini of *Otello* and *La Donna del Lago*, concise plots of love among the upper classes, prefering triangular intrigues and doting on Romantic tryst and elegy.

Today we term this the *bel canto* era, though *bel canto* dated back to the early 1700s and was now, circa 1830, approaching its twilight. The composers most prominent in what survives of that post-Rossinian repertory are Vincenzo Bellini and Gaetano Donizetti, with the older Saverio Mercadante coming in more and more these days for honorable mention and even an annual revival or two. Spending freely of hindsight, experienced operagoers can tell the three apart by their sound, but attempts to describe their autographs tend to bungle. Bellini, we are told, is lyrically plangent, Mercadante the most dramatic, and Donizetti something of a compromise with a pronounced light comic gift. But the distinctions don't really take. Bellini wrote what may be the most ferocious score of the era in *Norma;* Mercadante and Donizetti both borrowed heavily from the bank of the plaintive lyric when the situation required it; and all three of them had a habit of slipping into something comic quite accidentally.

Just consider the plots they dealt in. A veiled woman lurks about a woodsy lake, kindling violent passions in the young men of the vicinity, one of whom turns out to be her brother and another of whom kills himself on his wedding day; meanwhile she is revealed as the Queen of France and departs to mount the throne. Or: in Cromwell's England, a Puritan maid in love with a Cavalier believes he has abandoned her and gives way to a lacy madness till his imminent execution shocks her sensible; whereupon he is pardoned and they are reunited. Or: a Catholic novice falls for the mistress of the King of Spain, thinking her innocent, then rejects her when he learns of her past only to forgive her, at which point she impulsively dies for no particular reason, disguised as a monk, in his arms.* And this is not even to mention Donizetti's wide-eyed chronicles of British royal houses, from Alfred the Great to Elizabeth I.

Qua genre, the late *bel canto* operas have their ridiculous side, the almost obligatory final raving scene for soprano counting among the clunkier dithyrambs of the *dramma in musica*. But it is too easy to laugh; locked into these convention-bound works is a telling incisiveness of characterization and an elegant self-belief. If they seem to us pale when they are most earnest, it is at least partly because the pedagogical tradition that trained performers to spin out the grand line

---

* These sample plots belong to Bellini's *La Straniera* and *I Puritani*, and Donizetti's *La Favorite*, respectively.

has passed away—and holding that line is what endows these works with the surprise, guts, and melancholy they absolutely require. It is notable that when Maria Callas applied her amazing technique and temperament to these roles in the so-called *bel canto* revival of the 1950s, they stung with art truth, mad scenes and all.

The overall format owed much to Rossinian *melodramma*—which is to say the characters and situations of *opera seria* lived on, further Romanticized and musically remixed. The aria or some version of the solo scene still fascinated creators, performers, and spectators, but now the solo might take any number of forms: recitative and aria, aria-like recitative, or the extended *cavatina* and *cabaletta*, a slow aria followed by a livelier one, so that the character could relate the solo to a shift in or tightening of the action. Orchestral writing followed Rossini's lead in the use of solos or solo groups; the reedy keening of the wood- · winds and the bardic resonance of the harp were especially favored. Ballet and excessive spectacle were left to Paris and the Opéra to pro- vide—these were singers' operas—and there was very little *opera buffa*. Mercadante wrote few and Bellini none at all. Everything converged in lyric romance with a historical setting and conditions of power and passion in confrontation, resolved with beautiful suicides or marches to the scaffold. A lot of Scott, Hugo, "history," and titled noblewomen in trouble: Pia di Tolomei, Beatrice di Tenda, Maria di Rohan.

It was an age of heroines. In Paris the light Rossini tenor had evolved into the stronger grand opera tenor, but the Italian tenor hung back, consolidating his learned virtues of flexibility and expressiveness. No wonder the sopranos took the stage: they were the ones who made the dramatic commitment, who found the "theatre" in the grand line. Seeing how effective the best of them were, composers began to write specifically for that sort of actress-soprano, and symbiotically per- formers and creators devised a new category of voice, tensile and sizable as well as deft. Tenors, though they played opposite the so- pranos as love objects, were so to speak "soft theatre." The women provided the muscle.

Giuditta Pasta, for example. After singing Rossini in Paris, she really came into her own in the Bellini-Donizetti days, playing roles tailored to her mixture of *seria* control and *melodramma* punch. Her portrayals had a *center;* the great English actress Fanny Kemble saw Pasta in a revival of Johann Simon Mayr's *Medea in Corinto* (1813) and declared, "I have seen grace and majesty as perfect as I can conceive." Maria Malibran, on the other hand, had little of Pasta's concentration; sometimes she got so involved in what she was "doing" that she actually did it. Once, singing Rossini's Desdemona opposite Domenico Don-

zelli's Otello, she became so terrified in the murder scene that she began
edging away from Donzelli and finally raced all over the stage to avoid
being "strangled."

Mercadante, the oldest of these three late *bel canto* composers,
came along only a few years after Rossini. Wisely, the younger man
generally abstained from the comic genre that Rossini set so brilliantly,
preferring in his lighter moments what is called *opera semiseria*, involving a less overtly *buffo* style and stopping short of full tragic
nobility—middle-class romance, one might say. Mercadante's *Elisa e
Claudio* (1821) is a fair example; it seems to want to cut loose but
to know that it wouldn't bring it off, and instead of guffawing simply
bubbles decorously. Highly prolific—his output totals some sixty operas
—Mercadante took some time to find himself. For about two years in
the mid-1820s he was the most popular composer of *melodramma*—
Rossini had moved to Paris and Bellini and Donizetti had not yet broken
through to international success. Moreover, he was still composing after
Rossini retired and Bellini and Donizetti had died. Yet as soon as he
died, too, his works began to slip into obscurity while theirs lived on.

What Mercadante had was dramatic strength. It is a commonplace
that his narrative pulse anticipates Verdi's, and Mercadante is exciting,
though seldom as fleet and unified as Verdi. In *Il Giuramento* (The
Oath, 1837), he made one of the great essays in balanced characterization, bringing all his principals forward instead of just the soprano and
tenor. Gluck and Mozart had already done this, but it was a novelty
in *melodramma*. He swept through what was left of the old *seria* cardboard like a whirlwind, deemphasizing the solo scene for vigorous ensembles. It is usual in opera for characters not to get along, but in
Mercadante they come on fighting and often end that way; in his
version of *La Vestale* (1839), the heroine is buried alive, and his *Medea*
(1851), based on the libretto that Mayr used, is updated for finesse of
violence. In Mayr's *Medea in Corinto*, the betrayed heroine sings to
the gods, "Avenge for pity's sake the offense to my marriage bed." In
Mercadante's *Medea*, at the same point, she instead plans a monstrous
revenge: "What extreme act could be written in heaven's eternal
book?"

Unfortunately, Mercadante lacks an essential ingredient of late *bel
canto melodramma*, Big Tunes. Obviously, singers' opera is also "music
opera," a vehicle for stars only insofar as a great feeling melody shows
off a great feeling voice, and *melodramma*'s aesthetic evolved entirely
on the purity of Romantic song. The art of embellishment was still
vital, but now it filled out rather than decorated, weaving a melodic
line into a languishing or vaulting web of sound that, in the right mouth,

came off as anything but artificial. And embellishments, high or low notes, and vocal coloration were all only a part of it. Even the long-disdained recitative came alive in this era, for *melodramma* dwelled exclusively in lyricism, deep, sweet, pale, and surpassingly dramatic for all its loopy arabesques. *Melodramma* grew so attuned to the art of song that the orchestral solos used to set up the atmosphere of a scene would be applauded if the player showed virtuoso involvement in the line.*

The line, the line—just a sequence of notes. But late *bel canto* made it the calculus of opera, and no one demonstrates how well this worked more than Vincenzo Bellini. A gifted musician, he scored sparingly, exposing the melodies to the utmost. This accounts for the occasional feeling of banality about his work; over, say, a rum-ti-tum accompaniment, a voice may be doubled by flute and clarinet. The effect is chaste, austere, and puts a terrific amount of weight on the *canto*. Later on in the century, more sophisticated scoring technique would bolster a weak tune with strongly characterized accompaniment—late Wagner, to some ears, is almost nothing but accompaniment, the line obscured in total music. But *melodramma* required a genius for song.

Bellini had it. As early as his third opera, *Il Pirata* (The Pirate, 1827), he asserted the new style, showing how an adept of Rossini could utterly feature the singer yet narrate with fierceness. Not even Mercadante was this vigorous; and no one of the day manipulated the dramatic and lyric possibilities of recitative as precisely as Bellini. Singers' opera? They'd better be actors as well. The pirate of *Il Pirata*, Gualtiero, is a noble ruined by politics who turns corsair to prey on his foes. Worse, his love Imogene has been compelled to marry Gualtiero's archenemy Ernesto. Basing his text on Charles Maturin's absurdly rabid play, *Bertram; or, The Castle of St. Aldobrand*, Felice Romani limited the action to Gualtiero's accidental return to Imogene and the ensuing triangle, resolved by Gualtiero's murder of Ernesto, his trial and death sentence, and Imogene's mad scene and presumed imminent empathetic death. Thus the entire work turns on the confrontation of tenor and soprano lovers, of soprano and baritone husband, and the tenor-baritone feud: hopes, suspicions, fury, despair. A great first-act finale brings all this into play, first in a chorus-backed quintet in which the principals enter one by one, moving from a taut a minor into a climactic A Major, then a hectic closing led off by the soprano in which

---

* The playing in the Italian provincial houses and even in some of the larger cities could be pretty scrappy, which is one reason why Italian composers exploited the orchestra long after the French and Germans did. A major force in the ascendancy of La Scala among Italian theatres was the high competence of its orchestra.

the conflict is pounded home. This last section resounds with Rossinian practice, including the irresistible Rossini crescendo, yet Bellini shows his individual mettle in the tangy combination of rhythmic energy and vocal benison. Given a lead soprano who can accommodate the top line and a reasonably masterful conductor to hold it all together, the finale brings down the house.

Romani served as Bellini's regular librettist. All but the last of his ten operas bear Romani's byline, and Romani contributed significantly to *melodramma*'s development. He was an enthusiastic adapter, seldom original, and the regrettable prolixity of nineteenth-century drama made his task primarily one of condensation. Some plays, though innately musical, did not cut well. This *Bertram*, for instance, contains far more action than *melodramma* could handle, and although it is Bellini's longest opera, *Il Pirata* still makes very little sense to anyone who has not read the "argument" in which Romani sums up the details of Gualtiero, Imogene, and Ernesto's industrious past.

Romani did even less well in streamlining the source of Bellini's next opera, *La Straniera* (The Stranger, 1829), based on a French novel of unforgivable intricacy; but he hit on a bright conciseness in *I Capuleti e i Montecchi* (The Capulets and the Montagues, 1830) by returning to the lean Italian versions of *Romeo and Juliet* rather than Shakespeare's ample package with its many principals, secondary parts, and juicy bits. The Bellini opera centers on the two lovers and Tybalt, a triangle backed up by Capulet, Friar Laurence, and choruses of the two warring families. At that, this comprised a tightened version of Romani's libretto for Nicola Vaccai's *Giulietta e Romeo* (1825). Rather than take in any characterful Veronese panorama (as grand opera would have done) or pausing for incidental vignettes, *I Capuleti e i Montecchi* concentrates on the tragic poetry of the love story, regularly intruded on by the bellicose faceoff of Guelphs and Ghibellines. If its martial strains are often rudimentary, the love music is a treasury of inspirations on copacetic melancholy. Here, more than ever before, the mutuality of *bel canto* engages the ear. Given that almost every opera so far has a love plot, it is astonishing that not till Bellini was romantic pathos so beautifully invested—as here, in the tremendously effective blending of soprano (Juliet) and mezzo-soprano (Romeo, a trouser role).* One is all the more astonished to report, then, that for some years after the premiere it was customary to substitute Vaccai's setting of the tomb

---

* Some modern productions cast Romeo as a tenor, which is productive for drama but antiseptically incorrect for *bel canto* style. Middle High Romanticism saw no artificiality in a woman's playing Romeo; on the contrary, it added to the visual, pre-pre-Raphaelite *frisson*.

scene for Bellini's. Vaccai's finale earned its popularity for Romeo's Big
Tune, "Ah! se tu dormi, svegliati" (Ah! if you're sleeping, awaken),
bigger than anything in Bellini's finale, but Bellini's is far superior for
consistency of atmosphere, wonderfully unnerving in the moment
when Juliet comes to life just after Romeo poisons himself, and he
realizes in a flash how close they came to slipping through the needle's
eye alive.

Unlike his contemporaries, Bellini was not a fast worker. He preferred to compose one opera a year, meticulously—and charged extra
for his extra time. Like most of his contemporaries, he saw no opening
for *commedia* in *bel canto;* that much of Rossini's heritage lay dormant.
The closest Bellini ever came to comedy was a *semiseria* piece, the
delectable *La Sonnambula* (The Sleepwalker, 1831). Where Rossini
deployed the snicker, Bellini tenders the sigh. Tactful in the recits,
ardent in the tunes, and admitting of infectious embellishments (his own
in the first verse of an aria and the singer's in the second, as in the
da capo of *opera seria*) Bellini softened his style for this tale of a girl
whose fiancé jilts her when she is caught in a man's room. She herself
doesn't know how she got there: she's an undiscovered sleepwalker, and
all is made whole again when the entire cast catches her in the act.
Unconscious, she treads a fragile wooden bridge that threatens to
collapse and drop her into the path of a water wheel. The strings
shudder and the chorus can scarcely open its collective mouth—a single
cry will kill her! But she makes it across, murmuring free associatively,
and Bellini guides our response by quoting pathetically from earlier
scenes in the opera. This is *semiseria*'s equivalent of the mad scene,
tidily affecting instead of desperate. The soprano enjoys one of the
most grateful solo spots of the age, the ultrasensitive cavatina "Ah!
non credea mirarti" (Ah! I didn't think I would see you so soon dead,
dear flower . . .), followed, after she awakens ("Where am I?"), by
the sprightly *cabaletta*, "Ah! non giunge uman pensiero" (Ah! Human
thought cannot imagine the happiness that fills me . . .). A smart soprano will stick to Bellini's embellishments the first time through, then
elaborate with stupendous little curls, folds, and presses in the second
verse, as Callas did in the famous La Scala production under Leonard
Bernstein in 1955. To hear Bellini brought off with that command of
extravagance is to understand the style.

La Sonnambula (and Callas, for that matter) brings Pasta back
into the picture, for this singer (often compared to Callas for the
precision, the Classicism, of her intensity) created the lead roles in
La Sonnambula and Bellini's following opus, *Norma* (1831). *Norma* is
the late *bel canto* masterpiece and the great argument for the integrity

of the singers' opera. It is almost nothing but singing after its tempestuous overture: its militant chants of Druids resisting Roman oppression; its stalwart-voiced but vacillating tenor, the Roman Pollione, telling of his dream (aria) in which his Druid wife Norma took terrible vengeance because he has abandoned her for another Druid, Adalgisa, and then (*cabaletta*) invoking the protection of love, *canto vibrato;* Norma herself, spinning out the endless Bellinian line in the quintessential "Casta diva" (Chaste goddess); Adalgisa regretting her guilty love for Pollione in recit that melts imperceptibly into song; Adalgisa's confession to Norma that she loves a foreigner and Norma's forgiveness . . . until Pollione appears and Norma realizes that the two women are sharing the one man, a moment that Bellini crafts to fulfill coloratura as an engine of dramatic expression in a dangerous paroxysm of runs and turns. And so *Norma* proceeds, painstakingly stoked for vocal fire, a landmark in the development of dramatic singing and singing drama.

Bellini is supposed to be the most pallid of the Romantic melodists, the man who introduced the languishing line generally called "Chopinesque." But he had energy, a wildness, even—and it is precisely the broad emotional range of Alexandre Soumet's play, *Norma; or, L'Infanticide*, that attracted Bellini in the first place. Opera is not just concert. What a part for Pasta, he must have thought, a Medea-like Druid priestess caught between the collapse of her private life and the insurgence of her tyrannized people.* Rising to the occasion, Romani suppressed Soumet's finale, in which the heroine enjoys a mad scene, kills one of her two children, and jumps off a cliff with the other. Mad scenes were the thing in late *bel canto* opera, but this one is so impassioned throughout that any further outbursts would not conclude but explode it, and the authors pull back for a Classical resolution, a measured and statuesque finale in which Norma prepares to expiate her sin in self-immolation and her errant husband, struck with admiration, joins her in death.

A hostile claque led by the mistress of the second-rate composer Giovanni Pacini cast a pall over *Norma*'s La Scala premiere; later performances revealed the piece to unbiased ears and it quickly gained ground, especially when Pasta was available to sing the lead. Its influence on what followed in Italian opera was enormous, especially in the development of the dramatic (i.e., strong in both lung power and endurance) voice. There were not many of these at the time; there

---

* For once, Bellini moved with great speed, getting his *Norma* onstage a mere eight months after the premiere of Soumet's drama.

didn't need to be. Most Italian theatres were not large, and the bigger ones were built for height rather than depth, so voices did not have to penetrate the abysses of the great modern auditoriums of America. Most orchestras and choruses were smallish too. The vocal texture sounded almost intimate—again, the mutuality of *bel canto*. Even writing his big works for big Paris, Rossini never forced the voice. But *Norma* required more in sheer spirit than *melodramma* normally supplied, and Bellini released that spirit in vocal lines of grand vigor and breadth. In Bellini's lifetime, two of the work's three lead parts were just castable—the ecstatic, feral, and at last cathartically tranquil Norma, soprano, and the forceful Pollione, tenor. Compared to them, the much lighter second soprano, Adalgisa, was easy pickings. Today a revised tradition places even stronger voices in these roles, making the work just *un*castable—Normas lean to Wagnerian tonnage, Polliones fall in from the ranks of heroic "Italian" tenors, and Adalgisa is regularly assigned to a dramatic mezzo-soprano for a better blend when the two women sing together. But such heavy instruments lack the flexibility for coloratura.

Bellini's last two operas are more lyrical than *Norma*, as if by way of repentence for having pushed *bel canto* so far. *Beatrice di Tenda* (1833) is underrated, *I Puritani* (1835) overrated; the latter also bears perhaps the silliest libretto of the century. Yet it is vastly more fun than *Beatrice*, which is too much like too many other late *bel canto* operas on love and death (with concluding scene for star soprano) among the Renaissance nobility. *I Puritani*, however, is a work of parts. It is typical: a study in the extremes of lyricism and militancy that bind the mandate of Bellinian opera. It is cyclic: the composer wrote it for Paris, and there came under the tutelage of Rossini, whose fingerprints analysts have found hither and yon in the score. It is historic: the four original stars, soprano Guilia Grisi (also the first Adalgisa in *Norma*), tenor Giovanni Battista Rubini, highish bass Antonio Tamburini, and deep bass Luigi Lablache entered the annals as the "Puritani Quartet." And *I Puritani* is ridiculous: it not only observes all of late *bel canto*'s most asinine conventions, but goes out of its way to make no sense— two mad scenes, for example.

I Puritani marked the only time Bellini didn't work with Felice Romani. They had quarreled, at base because of Romani's frustration at the opera librettist's increasingly second-rate status. He himself was preeminent—everybody said so—but while the music was on, it was all Bellini's tunes and the singers' voices. They might easily have sung do-re-mi for all the public seemed to care. So Bellini turned, in his last opera, to an expatriate Italian count, Carlo Pepoli, a poet but no dramatist; and *I Puritani* ends up, in terms of theatre, a wacky piffle. But in music theatre it is the composer's form rather than the textual content that makes the art, and in these terms of music theatre *I Puritani* turns —when a suitable cast can be assembled*—into dynamite. Sensing that Pepoli was not the man for the job, Bellini had admonished him on the praxis that Romani so resented: "Engrave on your mind in indelible letters: in opera it is the singing that moves to tears, that arouses terror, that inspires death."

If Bellini provided the best, the most authoritative singing line of his day, his coeval Gaetano Donizetti turned out melody of a less distinct glow but a comparable—at times superior—dramatic charge. Bellini, with his ten operas (plus one aborted attempt at an adaptation of Victor Hugo's arch-Romantic play *Hernani*), could select from his muse. Prolific Donizetti drained his. Italian theatres survived mainly on neither classics nor even recent hits but on brand-new works, and Donizetti supplied most of them, seventy-five or so in all. Some are a lot better than others.

His first international hit, *Anna Bolena* (1830), fixes Donizetti for us. Loosely inspired by events connected with Henry VIII's liquidation of Anne Boleyn, it offers one of the era's least foolish librettos (by Romani) and one of its most imposing scores. The tenor, Anne's old flame still hoping to throw off a few sparks, is a luckluster part. But bass Henry makes a dashing tyrant, mezzo-soprano Giovanna (Jane) Seymour, torn between affection for Anne and hunger for power, comes off beautifully dimensioned, and soprano Anne rings with precise fire, a truly noble woman rising above shabby treatment. At the end, she goes to the block in a superbly developed solo finale quite unlike the usual solo. Sandwiched between her fragile aria and tempestuous *cabaletta* ("Iniquitous couple!" she rails at Henry and Seymour) is a quartet for her and her three partners in "crime" (Henry has dumped her on a pretext), the tune remarkably like that of "Home, Sweet Home."

Even at his most delicate, Donizetti never attained the limpid Bellinian nocturne, but the rhythmic pulse of his confrontations screams with theatre, and he could build a finale like nobody's business. *Anna Bolena*'s first-act finale is a knockout: the tenor has been vainly plead-

---

* This suitable cast is hard to find. Rubini's voice claimed high notes and technique not in the modern lyric tenor's kit, and a number of wrenching accommodations must regear the part in current revivals. Among few others, Giuseppi di Stefano, Nicolai Gedda, and Luciano Pavarotti have distinguished themselves in the role since the "*bel canto* revival" began, but all three made some compromise with the score as written. Anyway, they are outnumbered by less able tenors who excruciate Bellini's tender line.

ing with Anne to dally with him as of old when the king suddenly bustles in. Things look grim until one of the minor characters accidentally produces circumstantial evidence against Anne, and her subsequent plea, filled out by the others, leads to some heated exchanges. "Hear me," she begs her vicious husband, and he says, approximately, "Tell it to the judge." There follows a great line of recitative, Anna's "Guidici! ad Anna! Guidici!" (Judges! Of Anne Boleyn? *Judges?*), and we're off, led by Anne in a wild tempo with intent accents on the off-beats. The others join in, backed by the chorus, and after a dazzling moment in which Anne, Jane Seymour, and the tenor engage in a fast counterpoint of three different florid lines, Donizetti pulls off a *stretta* ("tightening"—the speeded-up final section) as Anne and her fellow victims of a monarch's no-fault morality are led away to prison.

For fifty years *Anna Bolena* remained one of Donizetti's most popular works, but by the 1900s it was just an entry in the indexes. Then the famous La Scala revival of 1957, with Callas, Giulietta Simionato, Gianni Raimondi, and Nicola Rossi-Lemeni, conducted by Gianandrea Gavazzeni, brought it back with a bang, much credit due to the carefully ancient polish of Luchino Visconti's staging and Nicola Benois' sets. This *Anna Bolena* marked the apex of the period of *riesumazione* (exhumation) of the Rossini, Bellini, and Donizetti œuvre; the first two composers had already enjoyed international priority all over again, while the Donizetti third of the revival was happening more slowly. Even today, every year or so, another Donizetti gem turns up prominently. One such is *Lucrezia Borgia* (1833), based on Victor Hugo's play and unusual in that there is no conventional love plot: the two women singers play the tenor's mother (Lucrezia) and best friend (Orsini, a trouser role). However, as the tenor admires the heroine without knowing who she is and as her husband suspects them of illicit courtship, the soprano-tenor scenes sound like lovers' duets, the baritone husband rages with conventional jealousy, and Italian opera waited till Verdi's *Macbeth* to produce a Romantic opera without a romance.

Only one of Donizetti's noncomic operas survived the passing of the *bel canto* era as a constant repertory favorite, yet even this one needed a certain rediscovery in the matter of performance practice. This was *Lucia di Lammermoor* (1835), the pride of the Walter Scott opera canon—not the most interesting, but filled with the sweetmeats of the Romantic candy box: a storm, scenes in a tower and a tomb, and nonstop droopings and swoopings. Donizetti and his librettist, Salvatore Cammarano, made nothing of the ethnohistorical naturalism that Scott specialized in, but then this is opera lean, honing in on the principals in their ecstasies of sundered troths and family pride. Other than the heady coloration of the kilt and whatever Scotch mist the designer can provide on the backcloths, there is no local color; the music turns immediately to the story—Lucy must marry for convenience, suffering the disgust of her true love Edgar and consequent madness and death—and stays with it till the final curtain, resting briefly for two "party choruses."*

The certain province of coloratura sopranos, who tended to view the four-principal work as their personal charade, *Lucia di Lammermoor* fell into overuse and superficiality, and only when the *riesumazione* recreated the true Donizetti idiom did the opera really come back to life. Even in Donizetti's own time, less than superb singers were turning the purposive drama into a vocal act. "Ornament takes up all the room there is in this music," Delacroix wrote after hearing *Lucia*. "You get nothing but festoons and astragals . . . It is designed just to tickle the ear for a moment." Actually it isn't at all. The *riesumazione* reaffirmed Donizetti's dramatic point, the great citation here being the 1954 La Scala revival with Callas, Giuseppe di Stefano, Rolando Panerai, and Giuseppe Modesti conducted by Herbert von Karajan. Even that production failed to restore whole scenes of the full score that had been lopped away by the uninterest of sopranos and audiences alike in any scene not featuring the soprano, but this cast's commitment was something new in *Lucia*. It was especially welcome in the lengthy mad scene, a *locus classicus* of the type. The deranged Lucy has stabbed her inconvenient husband and now floats onstage in a bloodstained nightgown to reminisce and hallucinate in what is for the time an intelligently molded musical montage. A paradox of these late *bel canto* mad scenes is that while the heroine has presumably lost her mind, she must get this across to the audience in vocal acrobatics calling for absolute technical concentration. The madness obtains in dreamy or dramatic atmosphere, not in musical chaos—there was no musical chaos in Donizetti's day. A gifted soprano such as Callas or her illustrious successors in the part, Renata Scotto and Joan Sutherland, can make these vocal

---

* These jubilant curtain raisers form the least strategic section in mid-nineteenth-century Italian opera, there merely to generate a minimal flash for the social scenes. "Hello, we're festive party guests awaiting the action" is pretty much the level of words and music. These bits become controversial in the stereo era, when record producers decided that opera on disc ought to comprise an experiential rendering of rather than an audio supplement to theatre performances. The sound effect grew into an art, and a novelty was added to the inventory of operatic devices, the Party Noise. London Records (Decca in England) proved the most ambitious. Some of their efforts in this line sounded like the screams of the doomed in an avalanche.

decorations the equivalent to the infatuated precision of the thoroughly mad. Callas swayed and pined; Scotto took little steps and lurked; Sutherland ran in and out of chorus groupings like Lillian Gish in a wood; and all three sang the dickens out of it, climaxing in the indispensable high E Flat that, like so many high notes heard in these operas, is not to be found in the score.*

Donizetti felt at home with royal tribulations, especially British; his fire burned white for queens in distress. *Maria Stuarda* (1835) offers two queens, Mary Stuart and Elizabeth I, in a libretto based on Schiller's extremely popular play. Schiller, of course, was one of Romanticism's founding fathers, and his dramas did yeoman service on the musical stage during these years. Three Italian composers (Mercadante among them) preceded Donizetti's with Mary Stuart operas, though it did not adapt as easily as *Wilhelm Tell*. In Donizetti's version it lost much of its incisive detail work to the insecure ministrations of an amateur, teenage librettist, Giuseppe Bardari—but the challenge of creating the two quasi-legendary rivals brought out the best in the composer. Elizabeth is proud, vain, vicious, and has all the power; Mary is proud, beautiful, loving, and has nothing but doom. Their conflict, mainly political in Schiller and exclusively amatory in Donizetti, so fascinated the composer that he created what amounts to two protagonists, but he guides our attention by giving Act I to Elizabeth, Act II to the two women's momentous meeting, and the last two-thirds of Act III to Mary. Furthermore, the music tells us immediately which of the two deserves our sympathy. Elizabeth's line is taut, always on the verge of vindictive fury; Mary's is always gracile. Obviously, this is a top-flight prima donnas' opera, and later operatic usage suggests that

---

* The final high note in *Lucia*'s mad scene has undone many a singer and, one time at least, a few innocent bystanders as well. In a performance in Philadelphia in the 1960s, one Tina Garfi came to grief on the E Flat and fell to her knees, begging the maestro for another chance. Not at the note itself—the whole scene. To anxious buzzing in the auditorium, Garfi recommenced the marathon. And behind her, choristers quietly began to crumple in exhaustion. Such destabilization of the suspension of disbelief does not run counter to *bel canto* style. For all of Callas', Scotto's, and Sutherland's tries at mad realism, the *bel canto* public received this art half in and half out of the opera, as it were: simultaneously engaged in action and appreciative of the singer's aplomb. No one knew this better than Callas, who portrayed Lucia while the opera was on and Callas-as-Lucia when the music stopped. Thus the critic Desmond Shawe-Taylor, who caught the Scala *Lucia* on tour in Berlin, noted that ten minutes of curtain calls did not drain all the Lucia out of Callas, with "her air of wondering simplicity, her flawless miming of unworthiness, her subtle variation in the tempo of successive appearances and in the depth of successive curtseys, and her elaborate byplay with the roses which fell from the gallery."

Mary be the soprano and Elizabeth a mezzo. But the lower-ranged soprano hadn't yet acclimatized itself to lead roles in the 1830s, and Donizetti originally wrote for two sopranos. Then a restaging of the piece in Milan with Maria Malibran led Donizetti to recompose Elizabeth to suit Malibran's voice, and nowadays we expect to hear the darker Briton contend in voice color as well as action with a lighter Scot. The great moment is the second-act confrontation, in which Mary must humble herself to obtain Elizabeth's pardon. Donizetti tries something interesting here which compares favorably with a similar moment in *Lucia di Lammermoor*. In both cases the action is halted for a sextet while the characters, all in asides, express their fear or rage in lines that both blend into and stand out from the overall texture. The *Lucia* sextet caps a climactic turn of plot—Edgar's irruption into the marriage ceremony, just after Lucy has pledged herself to another. But the *Maria Stuarda* sextet precedes the climax: Mary and Elizabeth have just come face to face (as in Schiller but not in history) and, before anything can happen, Donizetti aggravates the suspense in a musical freeze-frame, Elizabeth contemptuous, Mary and her confidante atremble, one mean courtier sneering, and two nice courtiers apprehensive. The number over, Donizetti launches the Dialogue of the Two Queens to skittish violin figures: Elizabeth heckles her enemy and Mary struggles to maintain her composure. At last she breaks, and in gallant recitative lays the English queen out to filth:

> Wanton daughter of Boleyn,
> *You* speak of dishonor?
> Lying, disgraceful harlot,
> I blush for you.
> The English throne is profaned,
> Vile bastard, under your foot!

This leads inevitably to the massed finale and, in the final act, a big solo scene for Mary as she is marched to execution.

With so many operas dedicated to the love triangles that rock a nation, all holding pretty much to the same format, Donizetti can suffer from overexposure and eventually the *reisumazione* may run out of steam. Already there have been complaints, as when the New York City Opera mounted a Donizetti British cycle for Beverly Sills, taking in not only *Anna Bolena* and *Maria Stuarda* but *Roberto Devereux* (1837), about the further love adventures of Elizabeth I and musicodramatically the most advanced of the three. Are we possibly getting too much Donizetti and Bellini, it was asked, when other archeological expeditions are moving so slowly? The question blew into a controversy in the late 1970s when American audiences were treated to a number of revivals of one of Donizetti's late works, *La Favorite* (1840).

Note the spelling. This is a French opera; like Rossini, Donizetti had gone to Paris, in 1839, to cap his career with new works and revisions of old ones. There was a *Lucie de Lammermoor* (surprisingly different from the original), a *Les Martyrs* (a grand-opera version of his *melodramma Poliuto*, written for Naples in 1838 but banned by the censor), and, among other things, a work for the Opéra, partly based on a score planned for another Parisian house that had suddenly gone bankrupt. Overhauled as *La Favorite*, the new work told of royal immorality against a religious background in relatively old Spain. It is not one of Donizetti's stronger works; its highlights rise quite high, but in between is a great deal of fill and nonsense. The interest of such Italian mezzos as Gabriella Besanzoni, Ebe Stignani, Fedora Barbieri, and Giulietta Simionato—in the Italian version, *La Favorita*—kept it fitfully alive, and a lyric tenor with an ample *legato* (suave, integrated singing, the creamy top of *bel canto*) shows off well in it. But perhaps the piece's confused origin and the gala cetera of grand opera's processions and ballet held Donizetti down. In any case, the rash of American *Favorita*s in the late 1970s marked for some the saturation point in Donizetti, despite absolutely first-rate vocalism from Shirley Verrett, Alfredo Kraus, and Luciano Pavarotti in various performances.

But it may be that Donizetti deserves more time than Rossini and Bellini. Rossini, in his Paris works, is untouchable, and Bellini holds the palm in *canto*. Still, it is Donizetti who ran the most consistent campaign toward integrated music theatre in pre-Verdian *melodramma*, and it is notable that Verdi himself was more deeply affected by Donizetti (and Mercadante, for that matter) than by Rossini or Bellini.

Further to Donizetti's credit, he alone kept *opera buffa* alive in this ultra-Romantic age. Not only did *Don Giovanni* and *Così Fan Tutte* lead on to nothing—even *L'Italiana in Algeri* and *La Cenerentola* excited no successful imitation. The whole genre might have died out but for Donizetti, and his output yields a few classics. *L'Elisir d'Amore* (The Love Potion, 1832), the earliest, is quite probably the best. Based on Auber and Scribe's *Le Philtre* (The Potion, 1831), which had been produced at the Opéra with a cast of *Guillaume Tell* veterans, *L'Elisir d'Amore* gives off at first sniff fumes of cliché. The soprano is a sophisticated landowner, the tenor a bumpkin who loves her in vain, the baritone a Miles Gloriosus who has won her heart, and the bass a quack peddling a liquid cure-all. Tenor quaffs quack's elixir, panics when elixir doesn't work, joins the army to buy another bottle—and so on. Rossini could have made it work with nimble heehaw, and this Donizetti does. But he does more: he invests the two leads with music of moving intimacy. Though he had only two weeks in which to lure, plead, and threaten a text out of the sluggish Romani *and* set the text, Donizetti found time for the evolving of an aesthetic, and insisted over Romani's skepticism that the last act needed something warm from the tenor. This ultimately panned out as the opera's hit tune, "Una furtiva lagrima" (A furtive tear), cast to contain the young swain's thrilled realization that the soprano at last loves him back in music of a moonstruck paleness. (Too many tenors turn the aria into a bleating lament; it is anything but.)

There was, of course, no Italian counterpart to musical comedy in the 1830s. *Commedia dell'arte* was moribund, and thus there was no outlet for the spoof component of old *opéra comique* or ballad opera. Other nations maintained their parodistic theatre, however, and it was W. S. Gilbert who wrote the best-known burlesque of *L'Elisir d'Amore: Dulcamara; or, The Little Duck and the Great Quack* (1866). Gilbert also arranged a *Norma* parody, *The Pretty Druidess* (1869), in which the Gauls raise money to repel the Romans by holding a community bazaar. Sings Gilbert's Norma:

> Though people are easily shocked or awed
> By commonplace robbers—all applaud
> That fidgety, finicky, flimsy fraud,
> A Family Fancy Fair!

Nothing in *opera buffa* approaches that level of commentative parody, but Donizetti did attempt to connect back to the *intermedio* in *Il Campanello di Notte* (The Night Bell, 1836), a one-acter in which the baritone hero wrecks the wedding night of the soprano he loves and the *buffo* bass apothecary who got her, by ringing the latter's night bell in a variety of disguises. The work is simple and utterly winning, but it calls for a baritone of finished comic gifts. For one of his impersonations he must pull off a convincing French accent; for another, as a singer facing a debut in—yes—*Il Campanello* with a sore voice (a touch of Pirandello there), he spoofs a tenor's vanity with falsetto high notes. As the work is too "insignificant" for stars to bother with, it is usually staged for amateurs or second-raters and thus falls flat.

A French item dating from Donizetti's Paris years, *La Fille du Régiment* (The Daughter of the Regiment, 1840), is an *opéra comique*, with spoken dialogue, very slim plot, and a lead soprano part of extreme appeal to stars with a yen to play the tomboy. "Nightingales" favor it—Jenny Lind, Henriette Sontag, Adelina Patti, Marcella Sembrich, Toti dal Monte, Lily Pons, and Joan Sutherland have strutted through it with glad cries; as *L'Elisir d'Amore* belongs to the tenor, *La Fille* favors the soprano. A more balanced vocal distribution graces *Linda di Chamounix* (1842), a rare foray into the *semiseria*. Like Bellini's *semiseria* opus *La Sonnambula*, it goes in for pastoral sweetness, but unlike the latter it combines the lightest *buffo* elements with the darker nobility of *bel canto*, not entirely well.

Some listeners consider *Don Pasquale* (1840) to be Donizetti's comic masterpiece, even his best opera altogether, though he himself rated a last grand opera, *Dom Sébastien* (1843), as his greatest endeavor. Again we see how recreative talent influences composition: Donizetti had at his disposal for *Don Pasquale* three of the "Puritani Quartet"—Grisi, Tamburini, and Lablache—with a new tenor, Mario, replacing Rubini, and parceled out the duties so broadly that one weak link in the chain can ruin the whole evening. *Don Pasquale* is a paragon of the ensemble opera; the four singers *are* the show. These four deserved to be. Grisi, one of the first of the great Absolutely Guaranteed Last Farewell Performance singers, excelled in both the fiery and the flirty. She was no blissed-out canary; as the heroine who pretends to marry an old man with the aim of making his life so miserable that he'll be glad to farm her out to his young nephew, she payed heavy coin in vocal agility and comic mummery alike. Mario was a rarity, an aristocrat singer (his full name was Giovanni Matteo Maria di Candia, shortened to protect the family rep) and a natural. He rose to the top on the basis of a gorgeous God-given instrument and good instincts. If Tamburini seems the most unusual of the four—his somewhat bass-baritone voice suited no existing category at the time—Lablache took the prize for prodigy, being the champion all-around acting and singing bass of his day in both tragedy and farce. Adoring, goading, and dodging Grisi, the three played, respectively, the ardent nephew, the conniving doctor, and the sad old codger himself, Don Pasquale.

What makes the work so vital after so many years? Its heart. The libretto itself is total *commedia*, biased in favor of young love and cruelly intolerant of old, yet the music is openly human, taking no sides, or all sides. One of *commedia*'s givens holds that the old man in search of a wife deserves the worst from plotting young people, yet there is a fine moment here when a "quarrel" duet after the fake marriage results in the soprano's slapping the old man. *Commedia* invites us to laugh at the comedown; Donizetti excites our sympathies—not only for the ill-treated Pasquale but for the likable soprano forced to play the shrew. It's unusually feeling for a farce.

Still, it's a truth that comedy of any kind stood secondary in the interests of the era, always ready for another go-round with the sort of characters that had peopled opera (meaning "serious," meaning Romantic, opera) since just after Monteverdi's day, still doing pretty much what they did then. Mercadante writes *I Due Illustre Rivali* (The Two Noble Rivals, 1838), about a queen and a princess in love with the same man. Except for a Romantic touch which finds the princess attending her own very premature funeral, the plot might easily have served Cavalli.

So the general look of noncomic Italian opera had not changed all that much in two hundred years. What had changed was the use of the musical components that make up a score, and they had changed because Rossini changed them: the use of chorus and orchestra, the new structures of aria and ensemble, the dramatic finales, the solo scenes. The merging of *opera seria* with *tragédie*, launched by Spontini, was completed by Rossini and followed by the Italian composers who followed him, in his Franco-Italian style if not to Paris in person. Just as Italian *canto* enriched grand opera, the French flair for theatre came back and enriched *melodramma*.

CHAPTER EIGHT

Grand Opera and Opéra Comique

High C's from every type of chest, bass drums, snare drums, organs, military bands, antique trumpets, tubas as big as locomotive smokestacks, bells, cannon, horses, cardinals under a canopy . . . orgies of priests and naked women . . . the rocking of the heavens and the end of the world, interspersed with a few dull cavatinas here and there and a large claque thrown in. —BERLIOZ, on grand opera

WITH PARIS ESTABLISHED AS THE INTERNATIONAL OPERA CAPITAL AND grand opera its choice form, it became clear that the master of grand opera would rule opera entire, and composers of all nations flocked to test their gifts at the Paris Opéra. A German named Jakob Liebmann Beer, his name amended with that of a philanthropic grandfather and Italianized to Giacomo Meyerbeer, bore the name of the age. No other composer has ever been as popular as Meyerbeer was in his lifetime, and no other very popular composer has been so reviled as Meyerbeer since his death.

The arguments against Meyerbeer hold that his four classic grand operas are meretricious colossi, so sensationalized for popular approval as to own nothing of value behind the gaudy façade. Eugène Scribe, the most active librettist of the French musical theatre at the time, comes in for the same criticism, for Scribe cut the canvas on which Meyerbeer painted. A showy canvas, it is said, oversized, overdecorated, and overdramatized, yet always banal, shallow, stupid. Scribe writes a libretto like a fanfare and Meyerbeer sets it for a hundred brasses. It's noise without psychology, it is said. It has no artistic idealism. Wagner summed it up for everyone in analyzing the Meyerbeer-Scribe format as "effects without causes." And the proof? Around 1910 Meyerbeer lost the only thing he had ever really had a fix on—fashion—and his operas began to disappear. By 1940 almost nobody was doing them at all.

But if Scribe was a mere formula technician, an acrylic of librettists, Meyerbeer was a genius of sometimes clumsy talents. Too often his tunes start big but fail to develop, causing arias especially to dwindle away after strong starts, and his musical differentiation of character is naïve. But he had vision and his operas are stunners. When Meyerbeer is on, he has the swagger, the punch, the sentiment, the violence, the bitter contrasts of the status quo and the noble misfit that grand opera had been working up to since Gluck. He was an innovative orchestrator, a brilliant stage director, and a gallant respecter of singers' individual gifts. Even as they berated him, composers and librettists stole from Meyerbeer for fifty years.

After Meyerbeer had completed two distinct creative periods in German *opera seria* and Rossinian *melodramma*, culminating in *Il Crociato in Egitto*, he came to Paris during the consolidation of the Opéra's new format in Auber's *La Muette de Portici* and Rossini's *Guillaume Tell* and took the cake with his even grander entry, *Robert le Diable* (Robert the Devil, 1831). Scribe, who as coauthor of *La Muette* had kept the action crazy but tight, let himself go this time with total craziness and extraneous diversions of all kinds, but Meyerbeer responded with his most consistent score. There is little here to match the greatest pages of the later works, but the whole four-hour business sounds one fancy, clarion summons all its own.

Robert the Devil's protagonist is something of a Don Juan, though unlike Mozart and Da Ponte's libertine he is not an amoralist but simply a Romantic hero gone wrong, capable of redemption in the fifth act. Robert, the Duke of Normandy, misled by a demon who turns out to be his father, keeps jeopardizing both his soul and his engagement to the soprano, the Princess of Sicily, with irresponsible stunts. He gambles away all he owns, he fails to show up at a tournament of the Princess' suitors, he dallies (in the big third-act ballet) with the ghosts of debauched nuns. Only the exposure of his father by Robert's sisterlike friend saves Robert's soul and allows for a last spectacle: the interior of the cathedral of Palermo, with an antiphonal double chorus of churchgoers and invisible spirits solemnizing the pantomimed wedding of tenor and soprano.

Robert the Devil won an immense *réclame*, and Rossini for one was dismayed: hadn't Meyerbeer borrowed the *format* of *Guillaume Tell* while ignoring Tell's absolute integrity of action? Hadn't Meyerbeer husked Rossini's masterpiece? With the possible exception of the dance numbers, nothing occurs in *Guillaume Tell* that doesn't belong there; *Robert the Devil* glories in accessories. Furthermore, the supernatural plays an important part in the proceedings, a sure sign to Rossini of triviality. These were bourgeois operas, written for Paris' swelling middle-class rich to tell of nobles and commoners at odds and thus make the audience feel better at not belonging to either group. Politically, however, Scribe was not unadventurous, and all four of his librettos for Meyerbeer's grand operas expose or at least touch on the follies of organized Christianity—*Robert* in its defrocked nuns, *Les Huguenots* and *Le Prophète* in depictions of late Rennaissance sectarian wars, and *L'Africaine* in an appearance by the Portuguese Inquisition. Still, Rossini felt that his time had passed in only two years —*Robert the Devil* even drafted *Guillaume Tell*'s original soprano (Laure Cinti-Damoreau), tenor (Adolphe Nourrit), and second bass (Nicholas Levasseur).

Compared to Rossini's masterpiece, *Robert* does look overblown and nugatory, a two-ton frisbee. Meyerbeer's was an eclectic's touch. The Opéra has installed an organ? Let's have a church scene. The technical staff has found another way to deploy gas light to create a mist in the air? We can use that in the ruined cloister scene. There's a tournament in the second act? We can slip another ballet in there, as a kind of appetizer for the big one in the third act—and there, as chief defrocked nun, let's get the formidable Marie Taglioni. The tone of that act is a little too macabre, though—let's make the second tenor a comic character, so he can sing a funny duet with the demon; that'll be sure to go over.

And so on. But the odd fact is that, all together, everything works, in the theatrical sense. Indeed, the public found *Robert the Devil* endlessly enchanting; *Guillaume Tell* they had found endless. Why *not* have a church scene? Scribe's theme is the battle of good and evil forces for a mortal soul—what identifies the community of good more efficiently than a church choir? Why not take advantage of technological developments in stagecraft? All theatre is illusion. And doesn't the use of dance in the tournament scene help capture the athletic energy of the medieval jousting field? Why not let Taglioni dance in the central ballet number—is there something "genuine" in not using a star? And as for making the second tenor a comic, *Robert the Devil* had originally been planned as an *opéra comique*, so this is a matter of genre convention. It not only doesn't weaken the show but, in the comic duet, helps point up the demon's debonair depravity. Meyerbeer's errors are lapses of judgment or talent, not proofs of a low attitude. Is it a crime for opera to be theatrical? Yes: when the work has no conviction other than the wish to succeed. But Wagner, Meyerbeer's most outspoken critic, discerned the paradox of this theatricality when conducting *Robert the Devil* in Würzberg. His personal scorn for the music warred with his involuntary admiration of its power to affect the audience.

Meyerbeer outdid himself with his second grand opera, *Les Huguenots* (1836), depicting the strife between Catholics and Protestants that culminated in the St. Bartholomew's Day Massacre in 1572. As always in grand opera, "history" is made intimate in the amorous and prideful intrigues of a few principals; here Scribe provides a Romeo-and-Juliet couple who, through a misunderstanding that makes him think her unfaithful, aggravate the trouble and thus cause the Massacre (and, gloriously, die in it). The defects and virtues of Meyerbeer's format are more pronounced here than in *Robert le Diable*, with silly sensation, time-consuming dance and ceremonial, sharp contrasts in action, music, and even décor, constant musicodramatic climaxes, sly orchestral detail—including a long aria mostly accompanied by the antique *viola d'amore*—and a few scenes that count among the most imposing in opera. *Les Huguenots* is Meyerbeer clumsy and Meyerbeer inspired. A chorus of bathing women fills the eye instead of the ear, and for a prelude Meyerbeer attempts an academic *fugato* treatment of "A Mighty Fortress Is Our God" that has to be heard not to be believed. Other numbers are neatly decorative but unimportant—the entrance aria of the page Urbain (a trouser role that set a style for page boys sung by sopranos in tights), "Nobles seigneurs, Salut!," for instance—and the page's second aria, "Non, vous n'avez jamais," composed for the contralto Marietta Alboni for a Covent Garden production and including among its deep-voiced delights an F below middle C. But the eerily sacramental and barbaric Benediction of the Swords is smashing opera, though it is surpassed immediately after by the two lovers' incredible *grand duo*, interrupted by the tolling bells that signal the start of the massacre. Scribe, too, worked hard for art truth, binding his huge five-act text in the omnipresent menace of the religious contest. Even in Act III, when a Parisian street scene promises the usual ballet foo-foo, the authors include in their diversions an a cappella rataplan for Protestant soldiers and an answering chorus of Catholic women in prayer, then sound the two simultaneously.

It was inevitable that grand opera's rage for hugeness inflate its conventions beyond reason, but perhaps the prime beneficiary was the Big Duet, for lead tenor and soprano as a rule, to force the love plot to a summit of passion and belief. *Les Huguenots* calls for two lead sopranos.* One is Queen Marguerite de Valois (a coloratura lyric), the other Valentine (a dramatic voice for weight more than agility), daughter of a Catholic noble. The tenor, Raoul de Nangis, sings duets with both, and though he truly loves only Valentine, the authors manage to touch on two types of romance. In Act II, when the Queen hopes to arrange a religious truce by uniting the Protestant Raoul with the Catholic Valentine, Raoul is treated as the amorous knight and the Queen as the coquettish but basically uninterested fairy godmother. The real action occurs in Act IV, just before the Catholics crush the Protestants with a bloody "Dieu le veut!" (God wills it). This is no time for courtly love, and Meyerbeer plans his *grand duo* on a tension of love and duty amplified on a moment-to-moment basis. He wrote in the book of classics this time: the tunes are superbly developed, the sections joined through the silences by mounting horror and rapture, character in action very, very right. "O Heaven! Where are you going?" asks Valentine. "To help my comrades," Raoul answers. She pleads with him, even blocks his way, and at last confesses that she loves him. Now, some seven minutes into the scene, comes the Big Tune, "Tu l'as dit" (You have admitted it), Raoul's high-flying line imitated after each phrase by trembling 'cellos. The tension derives not only from the impending massacre and our anxiety for the two lovers, but from the sensual grip of the tenor voice pushed to its limits. When Valentine takes over for the 'cellos, dovetailing her lines with his, the sheer sensation is almost too much to bear. But then the bells toll—for thee and thine, Raoul—and he attempts to drag himself away. Meyerbeer shifts from hysteria to crazed calm in perfect proportion, keeping the music flowing in tune with the event until Raoul at last leaps from the balcony to alarm his fellows, Valentine screams and faints, the curtain falls, and the public goes beserk. Even

---

* *Les Huguenots* boasts a third principal soprano if one counts the page, a secondary role but one usually entrusted to a star. Then, besides the tenor, there are two lead basses and a secondary baritone, and they also go to stars. This made performances of *Les Huguenots* the preeminent celebrity collection in opera; Met stagings in the 1890s were dubbed "nights of the seven stars" and the ticket prices boosted accordingly. A sample Met cast: Nellie Melba, Lillian Nordica, Sofia Scalchi, Jean de Reszke, Victor Maurel, Edouard de Reszke, and Pol Plançon.

Wagner was stunned with admiration—and, when she heard a replay of the scene taped at the 1962 La Scala revival, the celebrated New York aficionada Lois Kirschenbaum fell across four chairs.

Obviously Meyerbeer was writing for singers who could pursue their music through the drama; the increasing lack of highly trained singing actors is one reason why this music dropped from view in the early 1900s. At the premiere of *Les Huguenots* Valentine was sung by Marie-Cornélie Falcon, who enjoyed one of the shortest major careers ever, six years. Like a number of peculiarly French sopranos, she had strength but a curtailed top range (rather like Gluck's Armide, Clytemnestre, and Iphigénie), and since her day the French mezzoish soprano has been termed the *falcon*. However, her partner, Adolphe Nourrit, must have felt even more overextended meeting Raoul's exhausting obligations than he felt as Arnold in *Guillaume Tell*. Alas for him, only a year after *Les Huguenots* his successor Gilbert Duprez burst upon the scene with his overwhelming high notes in chest voice (Nourrit used the delicate "head voice" for top notes), and Nourrit promptly quit the capital in despair; he toured provincial towns and Italy for a bit and then, in Naples, threw himself out of a window to his death.

As of *Les Huguenots*, Meyerbeer was compared to Beethoven, to Mozart; they called him a Goethe of music theatre. Only German musicians held back. Meyerbeer's old friend Carl Maria von Weber had reviled him as a traitor to the cause of German opera some years before, and now Robert Schumann said, "In *Il Crociato* I still counted Meyerbeer among musicians; in *Robert le Diable* I began to have my doubts; in *Les Huguenots* I place him at once among Franconi's circus people." In other words, the further Meyerbeer had pulled away from the clarity of Rossini, the more he had debased his art. But German music was carrying on a love-hate affair with *bel canto* anyway; the intellectual North envied the South's sensuality yet disdained its lack of "discipline" and *Angst*. The Italians didn't read enough Schiller. It would have been unseemly to attack Rossini, retired but still very much alive and respected, so they made Meyerbeer their scapegoat, some of them out of honest disgust for his showmanship, some out of resentment at having to borrow from him or because he had personally interceded for them with some publisher or impresario, and some—Wagner in particular—simply because they could not tolerate knowing that the epoch's emblematically successful composer of opera was Jewish.

There was a lot of Rossini in Meyerbeer, the comic Rossini especially, but then there was a lot of Rossini in *opéra comique* now, and the smaller, informal genre was increasingly sharing its charms with grander opera. If Bellini and Donizetti could compose their *opere semiserie*, why shouldn't grand opera, too, accumulate a touch of the *bouffe?* Meyerbeer himself composed two *opéras comiques*, not well. The first of them started off as a piece for Berlin (whither Meyerbeer had adjourned as Friedrich Wilhelm IV's music director), a *Singspiel* entitled *Ein Feldlager in Schlesien* (A Military Camp in Schlesien, 1844) designed to capture a sense of life in the time of Friedrick the Great. Restaged as *Vielka* in Vienna for Jenny Lind, it was melted down and reforged for Paris as *L'Étoile du Nord* (The North Star, 1854), now capturing several extremely fictional episodes in the life of Peter the Great. In grand opera, Meyerbeer has sweep; in *comique* he is a butterfingers. He tried again in *Le Pardon de Ploërmel* (The Pilgrimage of Ploërmel, 1859), for once deserting Scribe in hopes of achieving the *gai primitif*. But *Dinorah*—as the piece is usually called, after its heroine, an idiot—ended up with a pygmy sweep of pseudofolkish Breton "primitivism" that only slows the action. *L'Étoile du Nord* peaks in a once-famous mad scene for coloratura soprano and two flutes; *Dinorah* enters dizzy (with her pet goat, Bellah), gets dizzier, and reaches an apex of dizziness in the notorious Shadow Song, "Ombre légère" (Light shadow), during which she dances with her shadow.

Meyerbeer's field, then, was opera at its grandest. But his next big one, *Le Prophète* (1849), though acceding to the standard organizational plan, offers a bizarre departure: the protagonist is neither tenor nor soprano but contralto, the first of the great mother roles in Romantic opera. Indeed, the nominal protagonist of the piece, a radicalized peasant who leads a heretical uprising and crowns himself King of Münster,* is a far from heroic character, and the soprano he loves gets left out of almost every important scene—no *grand duo* for her. But his mother, Fidès, is another story altogether. From a humble, loving peasant she becomes—when she believes her son dead—a beggar and the Prophet's outspoken foe, and it is she who provides the work's greatest single event: her confrontation with the gilded Prophet, passing in full convoy into the cathedral. He is, of course, her son; but he claims not to know her. "Who is this woman?" he inquires. "Who am I?" she answers, her voice trembling. "Who am I?" she asks indignantly. And "I? Who am I?" she asks, collapsing into tears.

---

* Scribe based his text on the Dutch Anabaptist revolt of 1530; the real-life prophet, called John of Leyden, actually held the city of Münster as his kingdom for a year, taking unto himself a number of wives. Needless to say, the sensational possibilities in messianic debauchery were not lost on the authors, who prepared a Choosing of the Queens scene in which the prophet selected his consorts. The number was cut during rehearsals for the premiere.

She was Pauline Viardot, one of the most spectacular women of her day, and the reason for the unusual nature of *Le Prophète*. Born into a noted musical family (her father was the tenor and composer Manuel García, the original Almaviva in Rossini's *The Barber of Seville*, and her sister was Maria Malibran), Viardot was a finished pianist, an informed musician who encouraged and advised Berlioz, Gounod, Massenet, and Turgyenyef among others, an inspired actress, a brilliant linguist, a publicizer of Russian music (then almost unknown in the West), a portraitist, and a composer. She had one disadvantage: everyone compared her unfavorably to her sister Malibran, whose singular beauty and early death had Romanticized her career into legend just when Pauline was making her debut. At first a soprano, her voice began to crash in early on, and she switched to contralto roles; if *Le Prophète* was the right work at the right time, Pauline Viardot was the right sound, technique, characterization, and, in truth, person for *Le Prophète*.

How did Meyerbeer conclude his career? Always a meticulous creator, quick to compose but eternally reshaping, adding, and cutting, he died before editing *L'Africaine* (1865), the product of twenty-seven years of on-and-off labor. The musicologist François Joseph Fétis pored over Meyerbeer's manuscript—he found almost enough for two operas—and settled on a performing edition for the premiere. If only Meyerbeer had lived to smooth over the brusque joints and rewrite the vulgarities, what an opera this would be. It is in some ways the most honest of grand operas, the least concerned with pictorial and vocal display and the most dedicated to character. It is almost Gluckian in the portrayal of its most interesting principals, two natives of a non-European country caught up in European imperialistic exploration. Just where they are natives is not clear. Originally the Europeans were Spaniards and the natives Africans (thus the title, The African Woman), but somewhere along the route the Spanish turned into Portuguese, the lead tenor (and the opera's title) became *Vasco da Gama*, and the natives now hailed from India. But the opera world was expecting *L'Africaine*. Rather than lose a prepromoted title, Fétis located the third-world scenes "on an isle on the east coast of Africa"—Madagascar?—allowing both for the original name and for the natives' Hindu rituals.

Meyerbeer starts the piece in top form. After the most promising of all his orchestral preambles, he takes us to the council hall of the Admiralty in Lisbon, where the plot is laid out in the usual desperate terms of public history pressing against private love: noble Inès (light soprano) loves Vasco (tenor), who served with Diaz in the East and now hopes to attempt a second voyage himself, having brought back with him two Easterners, the white-hating Nélusko (baritone) and Sélika (dramatic soprano), the African queen hopelessly in love with Vasco. The weighty Don Pédro (bass), however, wants both Inès and the glory of piloting a Portuguese ship to spiceland.

It's the usual Scribean writ—which of the two women will Vasco end up with? How can Vasco neutralize Don Pédro? And what of Nélusko, who of course completes the circle by hopelessly loving Sélika? Also usual is the potential for decorative splendor—Act III is set on Pédro's ship, which smashes onto a reef and is boarded by a troop of Sélika's compatriots, and Acts IV and V disclose the beauties of fairyland, the last set presenting a promontory dominated by a huge tree whose blossoms give off a hallucinatory poison, with the sea in the distance. But for once everything that is seen and heard actually belongs to the action. The ballet and ceremonial scenes in the African acts establish the primitive character of the place and people. This is not sociology, not history, but an epic of individuality struggling against the pressures of establishmentarianism (the Inquisition in Portugal; the tribal taboos in "Africa"). *L'Africaine* has the commitment that *Robert le Diable*, *Les Huguenots*, and *Le Prophète* in part lacked. Sélika is the work's eponymous heroine and the most sympathetic character, but Vasco's enduring love affair with historical necessity is what makes the show roll. His defiance of the Church-state authorities, his push to and awe of the "new world" and desperation to carry news of his discovery back to Portugal apply concept to the freewheeling grand opera form—a concept ultimately flubbed in that *L'Africaine* ends not with Vasco's triumphant escape with Inès but with Sélika's lengthy, silly death scene (by those poisonous blossoms) and Nélusko's lament over her corpse.

A renewed interest in Meyerbeer is now bringing grand opera back to life. The singers have been found, directors are trying hard, conductors are enthusiastic. But only the biggest companies can handle the elephantine in style; the going has been slow and the reception mixed. *Les Huguenots* launched the Meyerbeer revival in 1962 at La Scala, heavily cut and in Italian but cast for rare strength with Joan Sutherland, Giulietta Simionato, Fiorenza Cossotto, Franco Corelli, Vladimiro Ganzarolli, Giorgio Tozzi, and Nicolai Ghiaurov, and excitingly conducted by Gianandrea Gavazzeni. The production was flatly lavish—painted backcloths and a stand-still chorus—but Sutherland's confident coloratura, Ghiaurov's colorfully plain-living Huguenot, and the astonishing forthrightness of Simionato and Corelli in the *grand duo* made this a major event. Then came *Le Prophète* in West

Berlin in 1966, in Bohumil Herlishka's bizarre contemporary interpretation, more a commentary on the grand-opera style than a presentation of a grand opera. Sandra Warfield and James McCracken did not do justice to Fidès and the Prophet. Two years later, at the Florence May Festival, *Robert le Diable* affirmed the escalating fascination with Meyerbeer in an austerely intriguing production designed by Josef Svoboda and staged by Margherita Wallmann. Between the first and second dress rehearsals, however, something like an hour of music was stripped away, though the cast headed by Renata Scotto and Boris Christoff varied from competent to superb.

Competent is not enough—these works want *stupendous*. Vocal brilliance and scenic trickery—an overall refulgence of sound and sight —are virtually written into them. Not surprisingly, the best of the modern Meyerbeer resuscitations depended on an all-out effort, San Francisco's *L'Africaine* in 1972 with Shirley Verrett, Evelyn Mandac, Placido Domingo, and Norman Mittelmann, conducted by Jean Perisson. This *Africaine* completed the set of Meyerbeer's four grand operas, and found the right approach at last, being neither "antique" nor obtrusively "modern." Not that Meyerbeer does not adapt to the prevalent postwar tradition of neoexpressionist or neorealist rethinking: *Le Prophète* turned up at the Metropolitan Opera in 1977 in an almost convincingly simple production memorable for Marilyn Horne's titanic Fidès. The problem is that Meyerbeer is if nothing else picturesque. John Dexter staged and Peter Wexler designed this *Prophète* for an evening of sombre; it didn't quite come off. (Another problem was McCracken's continuing difficulties with the title role, and Renata Scotto's wonderfully crazy girlfriend actually upset the balance in the dramatis personae by giving too much structure to a vapid part.)

It will be interesting to see if others of Meyerbeer's age are brought back with him—interesting, too, to see how other composers dealt with Scribe's librettos. There is, for instance, Auber's *Gustave III* (1833), on the same plot as that of Verdi's *Un Ballo in Maschera* and once celebrated for the contrast of dynamics in the masked-ball finale, in which the assassination of an enlightened king impends amidst exuberant dance music. Better known than *Gustave III* is Jacques Halévy's *La Juive* (The Jewess, 1835), which deals with anti-Semitism in fifteenth-century Constance. Halévy's tenor lead is an odd one, Eléazar, a Jewish patriarch; for once, the vocal line had to be sung with the weight of years as well as the metal of heroism. A second, lyric tenor handles the love interest, divided between a Christian princess (the coloratura soprano) and the patriarch's daughter, Rachel (the dramatic soprano), and the bass line goes to a cardinal whose only daughter disappeared years before. It develops that the patriarch knows the cardinal's daughter's whereabouts, and at the grisly end, when the Jewish family is to be boiled in oil, the patriarch waits till Rachel is thrown into the caldron, then tells the cardinal, "*There* is your daughter." Typical Scribe. But Halévy, himself Jewish, endowed the tale with smashing engagement. The tenor Adolphe Nourrit, too, became fascinated by the possibilities in the role of Eléazar; it was he who talked Halévy into making the patriarch the first tenor, and apparently Nourritt wrote the words to Eléazar's famous aria of ethnoreligious exhortation, "Rachel! Quand du Seigneur" (Rachel, when the Lord entrusted you to me) and its fiery *cabaletta* (after the crowd outside has howled for the execution), "Dieu m'éclaire" (God inspire me), for some ears the sole ingenuous scene in all grand opera.*

If grand opera was rarely ingenuous, *opéra comique* was almost invariably so by its very nature, and, unlike Italy, France still did a land-office business in comic opera. *Opéra comique* had lost its satirical character, however, and now thought of itself as the "lighter" version of opera: smaller in scope, less drastic in plot, less noble in breeding, and easy on the ear. Auber, much more comfortable here than in grand opera, describes *the* style while citing his own: "When I write for the theatre, my only ambition is to compose music which is transparent, simple to understand, and amusing to the public." Occasionally an ambitious librettist or composer would impose greater responsibility on the form—a deeper reach in the music, or more gritty characters. Because many composers wrote both for the Opéra and the smaller stages that favored *comique*, the two forms began some casual dialogue. The natural lightness of *comique* crept into Meyerbeer; Halévy's ambition fired Auber; and of course Scribe wrote for everybody. Inevitably there would be a crossover of aesthetics.

Auber proves it himself. His best-known *comique*, *Fra Diavolo* (1830), is all farce and sentiment limned in cute but empty tones. Diavolo is a dashing brigand, and the people caught up in his exploits include his comic subalterns, a loving young couple, and a pair of ridiculous British tourists, Lord and Lady Allcash. (In them, at least, *comique* retained its old edge of burlesque.) *Opéra comique* is busy: the plot includes flirtation, comical (and limited) voyeurism,† disguise,

---

* It is touching to note that in our own day, when revivals of *La Juive* had flagged to nothing, Richard Tucker craved to sing Eléazar, but his home company, the Met, was then in its Bing years and fearful of novelty. Tucker finally got to perform the role in New Orleans just before his death, and regarded it as the capstone of his career.

† It's nothing, really. A pretty soubrette undresses for bed while Diavolo and his two bravos gawk at her in hiding. Mendelssohn was scandalized.

and various sudden comings and goings. *Opéra comique* is artless: the sparkling tunes are so clearly cut and the rhythms so footsure that the dullest ear has a good time on first hearing; but how many more times would one care to hear music so facilely digested? *Opéra comique* is obliging: originally Diavolo was killed, but audiences found this a little fanatic for musical comedy, and an alternative ending (invariably used) shows him eluding justice and singing a reprise of his once-famous theme song.

That was the transparent Auber, repeatedly successful in such events as *Le Cheval de Bronze* (The Bronze Horse, 1835), *Le Domino Noir* (The Black Mask, 1837), and *Les Diamants de la Couronne* (The Crown Jewels, 1841). Not all of his many *opéras comiques* were as frivolous as *Le Domino Noir*, in which the heroine is a nun who spends her evenings prancing at masked balls,* and not all were so transparent, either. In *Manon Lescaut* (1856), Auber and Scribe turned Prévost's sentimentally naturalistic novel into an *opéra comique* of unusually fine-grained passion. Scribe ignored Prévost's plot entirely, and Auber made little attempt to musicalize Manon's oddly attractive super-ficiality. This is less an adaptation than an exploitation, filled with di-versions. Manon's illiterate friend Marguerite pops in with a note from her boyfriend asking Manon to read it for her, and *voilà*, a Letter Duet. In Louisiana, Scribe provides "local color" with a slave girl who sings in pidgin French. And in a restaurant, to raise money for the bill, Manon sings "The new Bourbonnaise that all Paris adores," once known as the Laughing Song. Still, this first of several Manon operas builds to a moving finale, set in the remote wastes of Louisiana where Manon dies of exhaustion in her lover's arms, and almost grand-operatic in conception, orchestration, and lyrical intentness.

Auber was the exceptional *opéra comique* composer in that his fellow musicians really admired him. Call him a lightweight and you'd hear from Rossini and Wagner. Halévy, too, had a knack for the needed transparency. In the same year he thrilled the soul with *La Juive*, he complementarily chucked the chin with *L'Éclair* (The Flash). *Opéra comique* is exotic: *L'Éclair* scampered over to Colonial Boston, and Halévy's *Jaguarita l'Indienne* (1855) pictured a war be-tween Dutch settlers and the "Anakotaw" Indians. Those who liked their musicals a bit recherché delighted in *Jaguarita*'s Mama-Jumbo, a halfbreed buffalo hunter, and those who love a love plot above all could enjoy real *grands duos*, for Halévy didn't ease up on style for

---

* Not to mention that the heroine of *Les Diamants de la Couronne* doubles as the chief of a band of highwaypersons and Queen of Portugal. She's selling off the crown jewels to keep Portugal solvent.

comique and gave all his audiences the same amounts of vocal display. (The role of Jaguarita calls for the kind of singer who would almost certainly go on to the big coloratura parts in *Les Huguenots, Guillaume Tell, La Muette de Portici,* and so on.)

Still, *opéra comique* is simple, and stayed that way. The work of Adolphe Adam is definitive in its amiable ordinariness; Adam proved as successful as Auber and Halévy but much less special, and everyone knew it, and nobody minded. His classic score is not even opera but ballet; *Giselle* (1841) is the definitive statement of the pathetic-jilted-maid-handsome-prince-haunted-forest-dance-of-death Romantic thrillers. If Auber was transparent, Adam was a ripple of air around a sylph's *plié,* with a feckless charm that could never outlast its little era. Of his *Le Postillon du Longjumeau* (1836), once a universal favorite, nothing remains now but Nicolai Gedda's debonair rendition of the hero's "Mes amis, écoutez l'histoire" (My friends, listen to the story of the postilion . . .), with its exposed high D.

At the base of opera and *opéra comique* alike lay the great French dramatic tradition. No matter what country a Parisian composer came from and no matter what genre he wrote in, he had to reach a public that took theatre for granted—theatre in all its aspects from tragedy to farce, with all the dynamics of plot, language, theme, and showmanship. So however composers might approach the text from a strictly musical standpoint, the theatricality—the life of the piece—was vital, and vitality means flux. Elsewhere in Europe forms took hold and held on for epochs; in France forms were always shifting, borrowing from each other (thus the ambiguity in the term *opéra comique*). But there could be too much shifting, for the public allowed itself to be led by philistines, morons, and invidious journalists, and Hector Berlioz, the greatest French composer in this time, struggled against great opposition to take a place in the opera world.

The most ideological of the Romantic composers, Berlioz theorized feeling and imagination into a diligent hysteria of aesthetic revolution; it inspired and damned him. But his persistence in the face of incomprehension, half-praise, and hostility eventually made him almost a success. His symphonic pieces were much more popular than his operas. But he had such a *sui generis* attitude about form that some of his symphonies *are* operas. This revolution doesn't classify easily.

Berlioz held that music that appeals to the imagination has no public because the public lacks imagination—so he built the necessary imagination into his music. Not everything in Berlioz is music theatre, but all his music is dramatic, has a theme, descriptive effects, and even, almost, visuals. His first was no mere but a *Fantastic* symphony, using movements as a poet uses cantos: to tour an opium-induced hallucination haunted by the character of a beautiful, unapproachable woman. Assigning her a *Lietmotiv* so we can identify—see—her appearances, Berlioz applies grotesque rhythm and scoring to her tune in the last movement to turn her into a hag and thus exorcize her from his consciousness with ridicule.*

The *Symphonie Fantastique* is strictly an orchestral work, for all its subtextual imagination; but this was 1830 and Berlioz had hardly begun. As the exorcism didn't take, he wrote a sequel a year later, *Lélio; or, The Return to Life.* This time he employed an actor to close the gap between the creator's vision and the public's lack of it. Assisted by soloists and chorus, the actor continues the attempted rite of transcendance, now hoping to drive the woman from his mind through nostalgic potpourri and affirmation of his questing art. *Lélio's* musical numbers all came from Berlioz' trunk and provide a checklist of Romantic conventions: a tenor solo with piano accompaniment on Goethe's poem "The Fisherman"; choruses of ghosts and brigands; a Song of Joy, lovingly languishing; an intermezzo featuring harp and clarinet; a grand Fantasia on Shakespeare's *The Tempest.* And at the last moment there is the glorious shiver of the possessed as the *Leitmotiv* of the Beloved from the *Symphonie Fantastique* echoes in the first violins. "Again!" sighs Lélio, shuffling out of sight. "Again and forever . . ."

Lélio is not quite a stage work—more of a monologue-cum-concert. But clearly Berlioz was not thinking in conventional terms about anything, and he was bound to raise many hackles when he got to opera proper. His sound was definitely peculiar. Though he understood perfectly the way what was left of *bel canto* worked, its old symbiosis of verbal and musical idea, his quasinaturalistic sense of melody led him up all sorts of byways in developing a tune. Shudders, squalls, moans, and chuckles decorate his line, and his orchestration advanced far beyond what the ear was used to in mood color. Detractors noted with disgust that one could not play Berlioz comfortably on the piano (even Beethoven's redoubtable nine symphonies adapted fairly well to the salon recital), as if working the orchestra as a huge keyboard constituted the height of scoring technique. The Romantic nineteenth

---

* Psychology enters the picture here. The *Symphonie Fantastique* is semiautobiographical, the woman who obsessed Berlioz being Harriet Smithson, an Irish actress of disputed gifts whose connection to opera comprises a flop engagement in the title role of Auber's *La Muette de Portici* and the somewhat meatier role of Mrs. Hector Berlioz. One wonders if the household chatter chez Berlioz ever got around to Harriet's opinion of the *Symphonie Fantastique.*

century doted on originals, but Berlioz was too different, overvogue. His autograph took in both the fleet shrillness of *opéra comique* and the weightier grandstanding of opera. But, to dish a phrase, would it play in Paris?

Berlioz' first opera, *Benvenuto Cellini* (1838), didn't play, except for four performances at the Opéra undermined by Duprez' inability to fill the title role, by an unsympathetic conductor, and by prejudiced audiences. A tricky work, somewhat stop-and-start but dashing and lyrical when it's moving, *Benvenuto Cellini* is one of Berlioz' most personally delineative documents, the sculptor and the composer sharing an affidavit on confidence, passion, and self-defense against philistines. Berlioz had considered other subjects for his operatic debut—a medieval saga, Scott, *Hamlet*. But any Romantic might have tackled such. Berlioz wanted something closer to himself, something to rise logically through the hero's second act aria, "La gloire était ma seule idole" (Glory was my only idol) to build to the climactic scene in which Cellini must cast a statue of Perseus—or die. "Seul pour lutter," he sings, launching his great solo just before the casting—"Alone in battle, alone with my courage, and all Rome watching me! Rome!"

Berlioz originally wrote *Benvenuto Cellini* as an *opéra comique*, then set the dialogue to music when the Opéra took it over. It's no grand opera, nor is it an *opéra comique*, if the terms applies to what Auber and Adam were up to. Its music has the spunk of the snap genius who *knows* and does it, without regard for how the public will deal with it. This piece is almost schizophrenic, leaping from the most outrageous farce to the most serious melodrama to the most affecting romance. It's like one big carnival, with mad scrambles and guffaws and sudden pensive hushes; Léon de Wailly and Auguste Barbier's libretto owed nothing to the orderly Scribe. But more extreme yet, Berlioz was the first French composer since the *guerre des bouffons* who really wrote French, without the slightest Italian influence. His line sounds more like Gluck's than like Rossini's, but it basically sounds like no one else's. A freelance critic of wit and imagination, he once anticipated the general reaction to his kind of vocal writing and performance in picturing the Parisian resistance to anything but sweet-pickled *bel canto*: "How ridiculous is Madame Branchu in the role of Clytemnestra [in Gluck's *Iphigénie en Aulide*]! Why, she does not add a single note to her part, not even in the aria of Jove and his thunderbolts, though on the first verse a twelve-note roulade would admirably depict lightning and on the second a little *martellato* would prettily stress the crushing of the Greeks."

After all, Meyerbeer, Auber, the other composers and the singers who served them supplied the roulades and the martellato ("hammered," notes sharply accented). Why not Berlioz? Because Berlioz was that toughest of artists, the unavailable man. He set standards, wouldn't meet those set by others. And his next musicodramatic event reaffirmed the unique collation of the sumptuous and the wacky in his sound and furthermore defied classification. Depending on how one views it, it's a symphony that should be staged or an opera that can't be: the "dramatic legend" La Damnation de Faust (1846). Berlioz had to defray the expenses of the premiere and the French were not at first impressed, but this is one of his most accessible pieces and it soon established itself all over Europe. It has a libretto, mostly by Berlioz and partly adapted from Gérard de Nerval's translation of Part I of Goethe's Faust; it has orchestral sections that importune the ballet corps; it has a beginning, middle, and end, in that order; it has roles for Faust (high tenor), Marguerite (mezzo-soprano), Méphistophélès (baritone or bass), plus a second bass to handle the Song of the Rat; it can be staged, and often is. But what is it?

"Scenes from an opera" describes it best. Unlike the Faust musicales of other composers, who cover a little more plot but fewer ideas, The Damnation of Faust does not purport to be a linear narrative "after" Goethe's huge drama, but rather a selection of its more adaptable moments, designed to suggest the original's spirit. Begun at the start of Berlioz' career—opus 1—as Eight Scenes from Faust, it was expanded and reworked into the present full-length opera-dance-concert, and now stands as an incisive extrapolation of the personae, atmosphere, and vision of Goethe's epic—Faust's communion with nature, Marguerite's dazed despair, the Devil's cynicism, the raucous university students, square-cut peasants, frothy phantoms, incomprehensible fiends, and an added attraction that somehow feels just right, the traditional Hungarian Rákóczy March.

Théophile Gautier named Berlioz as the musical third of the supreme triumvirate of French Romantic art (he cited Hugo and Delacroix for literature and painting), and already one can see that besides embracing the occult dynamics of the Romantic ideology, Berlioz upheld to the nth the solitary quest of the Romantic revolutionary. The motto of French Romantic opera might well have read "Don't make waves," for if grand opera's interest in popular uprisings actually sparked one in Belgium, it merely entertained in Paris. At the premiere of Hugo's play Hernani in 1830 starchy traditionalists and the flamboyant avant-garde fought a battle for supremacy, but there was no such controversy in opera. Everything that was performed fit the grooves cut by Rossini, Auber, Meyerbeer, and Scribe. Everything that didn't wasn't performed.

This is why Berlioz, so attracted to the dramatic in music that all his music is *about* something, wrote so few operas: why compose when there is so little likelihood of being heard? Look at *Benvenuto Cellini* —a few hesitant performances at the Opéra in 1838, further failed productions at Weimar (under Liszt) and Covent Garden in the early 1850s, and then silence until long after Berlioz' death. Even so, in the 1850s, Berlioz conceived a project so like (yet unlike) the Opéra's typical monster show that he began work on it without commission, sometimes thinking that the finished work would be too genuine for the gaudy Opéra to contemplate and sometimes thinking that it would be too splendid for the Opéra to resist. And indeed: both of the above. The Opéra agreed to do it, but couldn't do it—and, it began to seem, wouldn't. Only part of the piece was performed in Berlioz' lifetime, by a second-rate theatre that wasn't able to do it justice, and until recently it was savaged by critics. It's too long, they said; too silly; too boring; depressing; pretentious; poor Berlioz. None of the above: it's about four hours of music (shorter than comparable Meyerbeer or Wagner), profound, absorbing, exhilarating, and epic. The *Aeneid* is its source, *Les Troyens* (The Trojans) its title, and it is one of the four or five greatest operas ever.

The return to a classical subject after so many years of pseudo-historical melodrama is significant. Romantic opera had yet to reach its arcane mytho-Christian summit in the Wagnerian theatre, but Berlioz was already, to a point, pulling out of the movement, showing what grand opera should have been all along in a work balanced between heroic turbulence and transcendent nobility, *grands duos*, ballet diversions, spectacle and all. Again there is a strong sense of Gluck about the piece, especially in the writing for the two lead sopranos; again Berlioz sounds even more like the only French composer who learned nothing or little from Rossini. Berlioz wrote his own libretto, and from the first the enormous idealism of the project enthralled him —"my great beast of an opera," he called it. Cadging quiet times for composition between variously outraging and placating the kingpins of the Parisian musical community and writing the journalism with which he earned his living (reviews, Berlioz noted, of "recitals by beginners . . . revivals of antiquated operas, first performances of antiquated operas"), he found himself inadvertently summing up two hundred and fifty years of opera history. Everything superb that music had figured out how to bring off is in *Les Troyens*, though Berlioz couldn't possibly have heard it all himself. The uncluttered pathos of Monteverdi's Orfèo and the sensuality of his Poppea, the magnificence

of Handel's warrior kings and queens, the librettistic clarity of Quinault, the tragic grandeur of Gluck's antiquity, the choral expansion of
Spontini, and the historic "moments" of Scribe all registered with Berlioz' Shakespearean ear for detail and counterpoint. And, holding to a
Classical purity of mode, Berlioz restrains his sense of the grotesque.
There were comic shades in his portraits of Benvenuto Cellini and
Faust, even in his extraordinarily lyrical "dramatic symphony" *Roméo
et Juliette* (1839). But he painted his Trojan fresco with the tact of
the archivist.

In typical grand opera we see individuals victimized by history. In
Les Troyens some are crushed by it but others make it themselves.
Berlioz' protagonist Aeneas, goaded on by cries of "Italy!" from gods,
ghosts, wood spirits, and his own men, seeks a new land to regenerate
the seed of fallen Troy. On his journey he dallies with Dido, Queen
of Carthage, becoming first her victorious general, then her lover. But
destiny drags him away, and we close with Dido's grudging suicide,
ruined by her vision, in her last moment among the living, of the Rome
that is to be. This is a subject for pageant, and the result is not so much
long as big. But the spaciousness belongs to the theme, puts a face on
the interior motion of the whole. From the opening scene of Trojans
pouring through the city gates to celebrate the assumed Greek departure, through the staggering display of the Trojan Horse wheeled
into the town as Cassandra agonizes, on to the spectacle of Dido and
her citizens on holiday, speeding into the famous ballet sequence called
The Royal Hunt and Storm and to abandoned Dido's touching farewell, *Les Troyens* stretches the facilities of the theatre not for diversion
but to comprehend epic.

Perhaps the work's most striking quality is the tension it fastens
from scene to scene, building on each succeeding event a majesty of
time and place that, till then, was thought unapproachable in the theatre. *Le Prophète*, perhaps the biggest of Meyerbeer's grand operas in
physical and spiritual scope, is continually fragmenting itself in character scenes, obligatory amusements, and spectacle. *Les Troyens* never
slackens, though it, too, offers great variety of action. Near the end
of the evening Berlioz presents the Trojan fleet at port in Carthage
at night. A sailor high up in the rigging sings softly of the isolation of
the wanderer, two sentries glumly second his thoughts, and Trojan
chiefs rush in to prepare for a sudden withdrawal while an unseen
ghost chorus beats out the motto of the quest, "Italy! Italy! Italy!" The
message has dogged Aeneas through the opera; now it closes in on all
the characters. "We have withstood the Olympian command too long!"
the chiefs cry. "We must go!" Slipping into their tents, they abandon

Les Huguenots, Act II, at La Scala, 1962, with Fiorenza Cossotto, (Urbain), Franco Corelli (Raoul), and Joan Sutherland (the Queen). Note old-fashioned approach. This production rode on voice, voice, and then lots more voice. *(E. A. Teatro alla Scala)*

Les Troyens at La Scala, 1959: grand opera transformed from discovaudeville into austere epic. In the finale, Dido (Giulietta Simionato, center) prepares to mount her funeral pyre. *(E. A. Teatro alla Scala)*

the stage to the two sentries, who further define the encircling tension by seeing it through their everyman's eyes. "They're crazy with their Italy," says one. "We've got a good life here." "Good wine," says the other. "Tasty venison." They have compliant women and a new home: why leave? The music gallumphs in a quiet march halfway between grouchy and plaintive, filling in for the whole world of people tossed by time, and only now does Berlioz snap his trap closed. Aeneas has his big scene, and still the ghosts haunt him: "No more delay! Not a day! Not an hour!" Morning dawns as Aeneas calls his men to action, and even Dido herself, ranting on the docks, cannot hold him. Aeneas and the Trojans have taken up the Italy! cry themselves: the hero loves Dido, but serves destiny above all. He goes.

The opera might have ended there, but Berlioz can keep us in suspense for a last act, devoted entirely to Dido's grief. It may seem curious that what has to this point been a saga suddenly dwindles into the almost trivial tale of a woman spurned—but it does not dwindle. Indeed, Berlioz now draws us upward from the tumult of the Trojan adventure to the eerie, still despair of one person. The conclusion fits the ambition of the epic, for Dido is after all Aeneas' counterpart: we first saw her at the celebration of the seven-year founding of Carthage, having fled a wrecked Tyre as Aeneas fled Troy. They are equals: except that his story continues and hers is finished. In a beautifully woven texture of solo, ensemble, and chorus, Dido expires, blown away in the wind of change that sweeps through lifetimes, history, myth. It is unbearably grand and real at once. And it can be done.

At first it was done in bits. Berlioz, torn between admiration for his Cassandra and empathy for his Dido, was only to hear the latter on stage. An early plan to assign both parts to Pauline Viardot, dissolved in the Opéra's hemming and hawing, bore accidental fruit when the premiere of the Met's first staging in 1973 found the Cassandra, Shirley Verrett, also deputizing for the indisposed Dido, Christa Ludwig.* In the eleven decades between the inadequate 1863 premiere of the Dido portion as *Les Troyens à Carthage*† at the Théâtre-Lyrique and the Met's ambitious but somewhat wrongheaded production (it looked as if it had been designed by Henri Bendel), *Les Troyens* had

---

* Verrett, who will surely be spoken of in hushed tones in years to come, was tremendous in her *tour de deux forces*, but in truth a Cassandra-Dido is not right for the work. They are two different women, not two incarnations of a type; anyway, no singer should be put through this sort of marathon.

† The Cassandra portion is called *La Prise de Troie* (The Fall of Troy). Actually these are misleading divisions. *Les Troyens* does not have two "parts": two parts have been injudiciously imposed upon it.

at last been perceived. "If only I could live another hundred years," the composer had said, "then at least I would be appreciated." And just as the entire Berlioz œuvre had finally entered the list of classics, mainly through the assimilation provided by stereo recording, so had *Les Troyens* finally made it to the stages of the great houses. Unfortunately, it is too expensive to keep on regular call, like a *Rigoletto* or *Carmen*, and is subject to compromises. The world premiere of the complete work took place in little Karlsruhe on two successive nights in 1890 (in German), and later mountings suffered cuts, poor casting, or production problems (such as a flimsy or even invisible Horse). Probably more people love it in its platonic essence than through a true theatre experience—but this is a testament to its power, if in reverse. Even when it's not working, through recreative fault, *Les Troyens* still hypnotizes. It is simply very, very great music.

Les Troyens would have made a fitting conclusion to Berlioz' career, the Romantic mellowing out at the *envoi*, but another opera followed the composition of *The Trojans*, an adaptation of *Much Ado About Nothing* called *Béatrice et Bénédict* (1862). This ebullient *opéra comique* stripped away most of Shakespeare's plot to center not on Hero and Claudio but on the two who graduate from quarrels into love. The dialogue, Berlioz' own modification of the original, is also stripped to a minimum, and the result yields a very light evening of nocturnes, dances, and chorale. There is a little excitement (when the two leads discover their mutual affection) and a little farce (from an added character, a pedantic musician), but all modes of emotion are twirled on a pinwheel of agile lyricism, to create an unexpectedly consistent atmosphere. *Béatrice et Bénédict*, then, is as small as *Les Troyens* is grand; together, the two make one of opera's oddest pairs of last works.

In grand opera and *opéra comique*, the symbiosis of the musical and the theatrical in opera continues strong. Just as vernacular musical comedy proved more flexible than full-cry opera when Romantics first breathed the conflictive airs of social liberation and spiritual engulfment—needing *William Tell* yet admiring Goethe's *Faust*—so did musical comedy still inspire the drama in opera. Similarly, opera mustered musical comedy's musical campaign, inspiring the expressive potential in the lighter composers by its own example. "Music has wings," Berlioz said, "that the walls of a theatre will not allow to unfold." Music theatre had to free itself of all constraints—of conventions, of public apathy to experimentation, of show-biz harassments. It must be protean, capable of assuming any form that content requires. Meyerbeer and Scribe propounded a classless human nobility. Auber and Scribe propounded verve and piquancy. Berlioz, bigger than them all, and the most Shakespearean in an age that read Shakespeare but feared his rich honesty, let novelty and imagination propound a piquant nobility until he separated the two in his last two operas, leaving a model of grand opera in *Les Troyens* and of *opéra comique* in *Béatrice et Bénédict* just when the forms were ready for transition. For years his imagination kept him from writing what everyone else was writing. And at the end, when he wrote what they wrote, he surpassed them so outrageously that they still couldn't face up to him. It is up to us, today, to do that.

CHAPTER NINE

Midcentury Styles: Early, Middle, and Late Nationalism

What an opera you can make out of our national tunes! Show me a people who have more songs!

—NICOLAI GOGOL, article in *The Contemporary*

BY THE MIDDLE OF THE NINETEENTH CENTURY, OPERA AS SOCIAL AND cultural institution had changed remarkably from what it had been before the Romantics seized the stage. Just as the material of opera no longer centered exclusively on mythical or noble archetypes, so did the audience now show a democratic layered effect, taking in the dwindling aristocracy, the new middle class, the organized art communities in the capital cities, and cognoscenti of all classes.

A multiplicity of theatres assisted opera's expansion, enabling creators and public to nurture the resources of serious ("grand") and comic (vernacular) music theatre on separate stages. True, this nurtured uniformity, even stagnation. But it also undercut the old one-state, one-theatre, court approach to the lively art. On the other hand, the court-sponsored theatres of the 1600s and 1700s gave an ambitious musician free rein; the theatres of the 1800s, run by impresarios, had to answer to the box office. We noted Handel's problems in London, when he was running one of the few public theatres in the eighteenth century, and Berlioz' career certainly shows how commercialized opera tends to hamstring genius. The public wanted new works, always new works—but not necessarily new ideas. We find a sameness of format in Donizetti and Bellini, in Meyerbeer, in the *opéra comique* of the Auber years—they were the successful composers—and a questing variety in Rossini and Berlioz—who, respectively, retired rather than submit to commercial mediocrity and was simply neglected off the stage.

Production technique had changed remarkably. Reports that have come down to us about singers of the 1700s stress vocal quality and "deportment," for by its nature *opera seria* militated against in-depth characterization or ensemble engagement. It is the 1800s that first spoke of great acting in opera—Malibran and Lablache, for example—of the intelligence, poetry, and realism used as leverage to raise a flat role into a feeling person. It is also the 1800s that saw the profusion of the multidimensional roles that demand great acting. Not that Baroque and Classical opera do not challenge the singing actor; consider Monteverdi's Penelope and Poppea, Rameau's Thésée, Handel's Cleopatra, Gluck's Oreste and Armide. But the sophistication of Romantic opera, plus its frank theatricality, gave even second-rate composers an emotional palette of immense variety to paint from. Auber, for instance, was no master of the distinctive melody that individualizes character or event, and Scribe, as they say, ran a libretto factory. Yet there is much more personality in *Le Philtre* or *Manon Lescaut* than in the average *opera buffa* of the Goldoni years. Opera was widening its dramatic base, shaking loose from attitudes. It was, to its credit, wild to loot the French and German stage of adaptable properties, and the special effects that artificialized grand opera ultimately contributed to the revolution in stage technology late in the century. Every device, no matter how exploited, improved opera as theatre.

But was it improving as *vocal* theatre? Old-timers, especially of the Italian school, thought not. The amateur musician Edmond Michotte left us one expert opinion on the state of the art in 1858 in his essay, *"Une Soirée Chez Rossini à Beau-Séjour,"** in which the long-dormant maestro expounds on the truth of *bel canto*. Rossini defines it as a homogeneity of three elements, the voice, technique, and style, and goes on to deplore the collapse of discipline. Singers were impatient, now, of education, ignorant of tradition. "For example, my concierge's daughter. She is eighteen, and aspires to learn singing so as to go into the theatre. One won't ever be able to remove from her head the idea that at the end of one year she will be totally prepared to make a

---

* "An Evening With Rossini" contains one of the most famous quotations in all opera. Asked for his opinion of the elite among sopranos, Rossini replied, "The greatest was Colbran, who became my first wife. But the unique was Malibran."

debut in *Les Huguenots!*"

The decline of classical *bel canto* came about mainly through the growing internationalism of the opera world, the sharing of works, singers, customs, novelties. Out of the fixed centers of the old days— London, Paris, Vienna, Petersburg, Milan, Dresden—each with its certain musicians, poets, singers, and repertory, opera had created a circuit of theatres, each equally friendly to new pieces and the great singers. Lully *was* Paris; Cavalli, Venice; Handel, London. Now the latest Donizetti or Meyerbeer entry might turn up in any number of cities, one after the other, each production imposing the composer's style upon that of the house. Thus ingrained habits began to rub away under the friction of ever shifting casts and repertory: incessant travel cut into singers' study time and vigor, commercial demands drafted singers for careers before they were ready, and cosmopolitan casts destroyed the local stage usages that in the aggregate comprise a national style. The loss of stylistic identity can cripple a work in performance—as will be clear to anyone who has seen Auber's deft and traipsy *Fra Diavolo* done by a German troupe, with all the mugging and bottom pinching that Germans find indispensable in comic opera. Yet *Fra Diavolo* in its German translation and approach was more popular than the authentic *Diavolo* back home in France.

This brings us to the question of national opera, a rubric often used as a catchall for the operatic equivalent of "significant others" (i.e., the Slavs, Spain, Finland, and so on), but a topic referred to in great seriousness by French, Italian, and German theorists as well. We've already seen a great deal of national footwork in the conflict of operatic forms—French *opéra comique* as opposed to German *Singspiel* as opposed to ballad opera, for example, or Handelian *opera seria* versus Handelian (English) oratorio, not to mention the *guerre des bouffons*. So let us consider where opera stands at the mid-century mark on a country-by-country basis.

We haven't heard from England for quite some time now, mainly because there hasn't been much to talk about. Covent Garden proved a magnet for international singing stars, and many a fabled production was mounted there, but it seems to have pulled out of the competition to introduce new works by major continental composers after Weber's *Oberon* in 1826. Worse yet, the Britishers' preference for static oratorio over story opera left a gap in their musical history which composers were struggling to close throughout the 1800s. Their efforts were rhythmically hearty but dramatically feeble, at least to modern ears; they opted for a succession of musical numbers with strong tunes rather than the "character" and "action" music developed by Gluck,

Mozart, and their successors. Thus, while the early and middle Romantic opera of France, Italy, and Germany may be revived today to the public's surprised delight, English opera of the same period mostly inspires tactful hem-hems. William Vincent Wallace's *Maritana* (1845) and Julius Benedict's *The Lily of Killarney* (1862), kept alive in the English outback by amateur and touring companies through the 1930s, seem old-fashioned even for their day, too ready to take refuge in a ballad when something gutsier is needed. Oddly, though Victorian London gloried in the Italian style to the point of hearing French or German works in that language, little Italian influence is discernible in these scores. Indeed, Edward Loder's popular *The Night Dancers* (1846) went back to *Oberon* for its references.

Perhaps the classic entry here is Michael William Balfe's *The Bohemian Girl* (1843), set to a terrible libretto by Alfred Bunn about an Austrian count's daughter, stolen from him in infancy, and her love for a Polish fugitive; a medallion sets things to rights at the end. Balfe clearly knew his Bellini and Donizetti, and his ensembles and finales show signs of life. But when he gets to the Big Tune, he is all nondramatic English ballad—in this case, the soprano's "I dreamt that I dwelt in marble halls." Bunn didn't trouble himself much about the motivation for this number. The heroine and hero enter. She says, "Where have I been wandering in my sleep and what curious noise awoke me from its pleasant dream? Ah, Thaddeus, would you not like to know my dream? Well, I will tell you." And off we go. Bunn served Balfe better in the finale, which bears a striking resemblance to the finale of *La Sonnambula*, very hot in London at the time through Malibran's ministrations. As in Bellini, the heroine celebrates the happy ending in a lively solo with oompah bass and choral interjections, and if Bellini's "Ah! non giunge!" gives the soprano far more room for proclamatory coloratura, Balfe's "Oh, what full delight" does evoke a charmingly juvenile effervescence.

The English problem lay in refounding operatic traditions. The eastern European countries had to start from scratch. There had been no Purcell, no Arne in Czechoslovakia, Russia, Poland, and Hungary: political and cultural imperialism had neutralized any possibility of a national operatic movement. Mikhail Glinka might have come out of nowhere with his *Zhizn za Tsarya* (Life For the Tsar, 1836),* hailed

---

* Glinka intended to name the piece *Ivan Susanin* after its hero, who sacrifices himself to save the young Russian emperor from the Poles. But after Tsar Nicolai I enjoyed a dress rehearsal, Glinka changed the title to emphasize the subject's devotion to the ruler, first hitting on the Polish threat—"Death to the Tsar"—and then on Ivan's motivation—*Life for the Tsar*. The Soviets had the

as the first nationalist Russian opera, Russian in story, melody, feeling. There had been operas written to Russian texts or on Russian subjects, but not till Glinka did all the potential aspects of a Russianness in opera coalesce so aptly. Even more influential, though always more admired by musicians than enjoyed by the public, was Glinka's second and last opera, *Ruslan i Lyudmila* (1842). Where *Life For the Tsar* looked back on Russia's history, *Ruslan* moved into legend. A rescue opera tapped from Pushkin, it cut the die for the fairy-tale pieces that were to be the pride of Russian music theatre, introducing an Oriental savor into both tunes and harmony. Lyudmila is a princess stolen away and put to sleep by a wicked magician, and Ruslan one of three knights who attempt to free her; as he is her true love and has the aid of a good magician, it is Ruslan who eventually brings her back to life, via a magic ring. This promising tale unfortunately turned into a heavy and at times immobile libretto, so despite Glinka's melodic gift and alluring Eastern coloration, the work has made few friends outside its native borders. (Even in Russia it is regarded more as a duty than a delight.)

But at least Glinka had broken the ground. After him came the equally trend-setting Alyeksandr Dargomizhsky, whose work in pointing recitative lyrically and dramatically inspired others as much as Glinka's story-book arabesques did. Somewhat in *Rusalka* (The Water Nymph, 1856) and supremely in *Kamyeni Gost* (The Stone Guest), begun in 1865 and performed posthumously in 1872, Dargomizhsky entrusted the recitative with the characterological and melodic information that most composers leave entirely to the arias and ensembles of continuous musical flow. *The Stone Guest*, which offers only a few moments of outright operatic "singing," connects back to opera's first days among the Hellenic aesthetes of the Camerata. It is, however, a vastly livelier project than their pastorales, based as it is on Pushkin's version of the Don Juan story; here Donna Anna accedes to Juan's advances, and the statue who conducts him to hell commemorates not her father but her husband.

In what is now Czechoslovakia similar artistic developments led to the foundation of a national opera in the work of Bedřich Smetana. It was some battle: the land was overrun with colonialist Austrians, and many artists and intellectuals—Smetana among them—spoke German rather than a "native" tongue. When Smetana wrote his first two operas, in 1866, he set Karel Sabina's Czech librettos a little clumsily,

---

libretto rewritten to omit all mention of the Tsar (the threat is now a simple Polish invasion of the homeland) and the indexes have returned the work to its original title.

getting his accents wrong. But this was a minor flaw in a thrilling experiment, for if the historical *Braniboři v Čechách* (The Brandenburgers in Bohemia) has never become famous, *Prodaná Nevěsta* (The Bartered Bride) a few months later turned out to be one of the classic examples of national opera, a folk comedy of village love, village business, and village farce. Smetana does not quote folk tunes; rather, he synthesizes the folk sound with his own inventions, burnishing his line with the rhythmic authenticity of the living language that makes the Western translator's job so tricky. Originally a musical comedy, with spoken dialogue, *The Bartered Bride* was revised, accents corrected and recitatives filled in, and has traveled the globe as the essential Czech opera. But Smetana's later and less well known operas are no less national, and there is sweet sentiment to be had in the comedy *Hubička* (The Kiss, 1876) and nobility afire in the legendary-historical *Dalibor* (1868) and *Libuše* (1881). The last two vie for place as Smetana's masterpiece; the former, with its parallels to *Fidelio*, may one day overtake *The Bartered Bride*.*

In Germany, where Wagner was trying to cadge a hearing for even his more orthodox work (Liszt directed *Lohengrin*'s premiere at Weimar in 1850), the mid-1800s saw the stabilization of the materials that were used to launch the Romantic era in the first place—medievalism, the supernatural, obsession, nature play, folkstuff, and so on. The *Singspiel*, in which form *The Magic Flute, Fidelio,* and *Der Freischütz* solemnized the birth of Romanticism, continued strong, and Gustav Albert Lortzing's fourteen *Singspiele* count among the most German operas ever composed, as witness their total failure to attract an ear in other countries. (It seems, however, that many Germans didn't like them much either when they were new.) Rustically hearty, elephantine in sentiment and comedy, they never rise above the nationalistic style with any individuality. But if one likes the hamhanded mid-nineteenth-century Teutonic approach to *"komische Oper,"* one will take to Lortzing. Usually his own librettist, he had a sharp sense of theatre, and found his métier early on in *Zar und Zimmermann* (Tsar and Carpenter, 1837), in which Peter the Great and another Russian also named Peter, both working as shipbuilders in the Netherlands, are mistaken for each other by everyone else in the cast. Lortzing drafted another historical personage for operatic fiction in *Hans Sachs* (1840), which finds the protagonist more youthful than he is in Wagner's *Die Meistersinger:* in this one, he gets the girl. Unlike Wagner, Lortzing

---

* Other eastern European nations also hang their operatic traditions on one generative work, Hungary on Ferenc Erkel's *Hunyady László* (1844) and Poland on Stanislaw Moniuszko's *Halka* (1847).

doesn't use Sachs and the German musical tradition of which he was a part as a pretext for a thesis on Germanic art—Lortzing is always simple, all for laying out a story with a few nice tunes. His is a Biedermeier mind with a slight Romantic tic, though he did try his hand at one Romantische *Zauberoper* in *Undine* (1845), further adventures of the archetypal water nymph and the mortal who dies to love her. Yet even here, Lortzing held on to the *Singspiel* format in spoken dialogue and droll servant characters. He produced his most fully realized effort in an out-and-out comedy, *Der Wildschütz* (The Poacher, 1842), a score of sophisticated folksiness and unexpected elegance.

As bumptious but not as gifted as Lortzing were Otto Nicolai and Friedrich von Flotow, both of whom achieved international success for one work each, Nicolai's Falstaff opus *Die Lustigen Weiber von Windsor* (The Merry Wives of Windsor, 1849) and Flotow's drearily lyrical farce of love-in-disguise, *Martha* (1847). Sadly, the comic gem of this era, Peter Cornelius' *Der Barbier von Bagdad* (1858), has never shared their popularity, though it deserves to erase them from memory. A romantic farce, composed to glide from number to number without a break, *The Barber of Baghdad* offers a novel barber: instead of the usual Mr. Fix-it of wry commentary and slick conspiracies, we get a blowhard moron who makes a mess of everything he touches. Cornelius' sleek Oriental palette is a relief after the decades of Lortzing's big-bellied, foot-clomping burghers, and his tune trove goes deep enough to allow the bungling barber to lead off the grandly graceful finale (built on refrains of the Arabian salute, "Salamaleikum") without losing sight of his character.

One last item detains us in the comic arena, Wagner's early opera *Das Liebesverbot* (The Ban on Love, 1836), based on Shakespeare's dark comedy *Measure for Measure*. The following chapter will discuss Wagner in his glory as a Prometheus of evolution in composition, conceptual exhortation of the soul, and stagecraft; but he got off to a weakly derivative start filching procedures from Marschner, Weber, Meyerbeer, Auber, Bellini, and others. Yet looking backward from his mature achievements, one can hear the individuality. A first opera in the gruesome *Hans Heiling* genre, *Die Hochzeit* (The Wedding), was abandoned midway in 1833, when Wagner was twenty; a few months later he completed *Die Feen* (The Fairies), loosely based on Gozzi's *La Donna Serpente*, often ridiculous, and not performed till after Wagner's death. At least *Das Liebesverbot* is a work of some consequence, though its underrehearsed premiere at Magdeburg consigned it to oblivion overnight. Pulling away from the German Romanticism of *Die Feen*, Wagner wired *Das Liebesverbot* into Italian currents, in search of the same lightness and directness that the pro-Italian faction of Paris' *guerre des bouffons* had remarked with such enthusiasm. There is lively choral writing, strong if simplistic characterizations, a decent stab at *buffo* sparkle, and a few telling uses of the *Leitmotiv* that was to become the basic component of the Wagnerian score. Unfortunately, Wagner's libretto scants Shakespeare's brilliant interface of comedy and horror. Shakespeare's "ban on love" deals with the resumption of sumptuary laws in Vienna by an outwardly austere but secretly sensual deputy ruler, who throws a variety of farcical and romantic characters into dismay until he—and the "propriety" of man judging man—is unmasked. Wagner reset the action in Palermo to underline the *commedia* aspect of the whole, but failed to match the highjinks with the horror; he enjoys preaching against hypocrisy but ends in trivializing Shakespeare's theme. *Measure for Measure* is Christian parable, *Das Liebesverbot* a happy-go-lucky charade on sexual liberation. Still, it's an amusingly rebellious piece, and an essay in international opera that this extremely nationalist composer had to get under his belt before he could find his native voice: an exorcism.

German comedy, in any case, was thriving. Serious German opera, now in active competition with *Singspiel*, depended on the excitement and insight of strong musical delineation. Robert Schumann's *Genoveva* (1850) typifies German-Romantic opera at the mid-century mark. Some detritus of folk coloring and the supernatural hangs around, but the piece focuses on character and conflict. Based on the life of one of Europe's most beloved saints, *Genoveva* tells of a noblewoman framed on an adultery charge by the man she spurned and the sorceress who loves him. Pious to a fault, the good wife prays more than defends herself, though ultimately, for reasons that are not made clear, she is saved. The opera held the stage for decades but had faded away by 1900; it deserves revival for the depth of Schumann's psychology. Concurrently with Wagner, he expanded the use of the *Leitmotiv* to inform the listener of the plot's interior motion, of who is undergoing what thought or feeling (in the orchestra) while the action proceeds (in the vocal parts). This use of the *Leitmotiv* enriched opera incalculably. It is one of the century's great innovations, for though it was not unknown to earlier eras, it was used very sparingly when used at all. One thing had not changed in opera since Cavalli's time: accused heroines were still not hunkering down to cases and defending themselves adequately when falsely accused of some abrogation of the sexist double standard. Genoveva is not as irritatingly silent as Weber's Euryanthe, the prize ninny of the early 1800s, but in the year of *Genoveva's* premiere, Wagner unveiled the very empress of tongue-tied defendants in Elsa, the heroine of *Lohengrin*. It seems that Gluck's industrious Armide and Beethoven's intrepid Leonore had few successors: though the soprano had wrested center stage from the outcast *castrato*, she somehow could not stand up to tenors or baritones in terms of plot initiative.

We move to Paris, still the center of Western opera in the midst of the Meyerbeer epoch. A change was in the air, however: grand opera was about to become less tumultuous, smaller and more lyrical. It really had no choice in the matter, for it had grown too expensive and unwieldy a proposition to mount without some guarantee of success. Only Meyerbeer had consistently brought it off—and that but four times in thirty-five years. A new monster that flopped could empty the Opéra for a season while the tired successes of the past were thrown into the breach and Paris waited for the next huge do. A bellwether for the shift in style was Charles Gounod's first entry, *Sapho* (1851), written for Pauline Viardot and the Opéra's grand stage but shorn of spectacle and diversions. The plot is nonsense, a love triangle involving the poetess; her (male*) lover, a revolutionary schemer; and another woman, who takes Sapho's lover from her by threatening to expose the scheme. All of this appears to function mainly as an excuse for Sapho's solo finale, "O ma lyre immortelle," a pleasant change from Scribe's crazed finales—and note the return to a Greek subject after decades of post-classical "history."

Not that Gounod was a reformer. But perhaps grand opera was too extreme a form to be the one that every serious opera composer had to work in. Couldn't there be a middle line between the totalism of grand and the leanness of *opéra comique?* The two masters of French opera in the late and post-Meyerbeer years, Gounod and Ambroise Thomas, tended to that middle possibility. Earlier, grand opera borrowed from *comique* but remained grand; *comique* borrowed from grand yet stayed lean. Gounod and Thomas devised a hybrid which is sometimes called "lyric opera," varying in size from medium large to small, regarding dance and "effects" as optional, respecting the legitimacy of great singing without calling for incessant virtuosity, and favoring adaptations from literature. Both Gounod and Thomas got started when Meyerbeer was top, and they did nothing to cut down his fashion. But their best work proved as popular as his and even outlasted it. One influence lyric opera did close down, that of Rossini. Their lyric opera, though a melding of forms that Rossini had intro-

---

* The Sappho of tradition was a lesbian; the word derives from her home, Lesbos. Those who giggle at the idea of an operatic lesbian might consider that Cavalli pulled it off a number of times.

duced, represented a suppression of the more Rossinian elements. After years of foreign direction, French opera was French again, for the first time in two hundred years.*

"Lyric" is the right word for Gounod and Thomas, for tunes flow out of them with a spontaneity that Meyerbeer never knew. Their output shows variety, reaching farce, romantic comedy, and intimate and public tragedy; and they wrote for stages large and small. Gounod's *Le Médecin Malgré Lui* (The Doctor in Spite of Himself, 1858) holds true to Molière; Jules Barbier and Michel Carré's libretto incorporates much of the original dialogue between the musical sections and Gounod salutes Molière's (i.e., Lully's) era by opening his work with the old "French overture" devised by Lully. Thomas' *Le Caïd* (1849) bids farewell to the Rossinian comic style by way of lampooning it with a fond look backward at the Europeans-trapped-in-the-East plot once so basic to *opera buffa*. Gounod's careful Molière and Thomas' spoof of the Italian spirit that moistened the dry patter of *comique* are, in their way, as nationalistic as anything by Glinka and Smetana. But the French took their opera for granted now and weren't arguing it the way they had done in the days of *querelles* and *guerres*.

They certainly took Thomas for granted. This talented but quiet man, who eventually succeeded Auber as the chief of the world-important Conservatoire and who morosely inhabited the glittering Parisian beau monde flubbing countless opportunities for *bons mots* or even basic grace, wrote countless *opéras comiques* before *Le Caïd* and the immediately following *Le Songe d'une Nuit d'Été* (The Summer Night's Dream, 1850) brought him forward. (*Le Songe* sounds like a version of *A Midsummer Night's Dream* but isn't; the cast includes Shakespeare, Falstaff, and Queen Elizabeth I.) Not till 1866 did he find the ideal condition for his dance rhythms and delicate vocal writing, *Mignon*, shredded out of minor episodes in Goethe's novel *Wilhelm Meister's Apprenticeship*. Castigated in Germany for its desecration of the original, *Mignon* enjoyed a fine career everywhere else for the pathos of its gamine gypsy heroine, the coloratura pertness of its second female lead, the actress Philine, and its assorted Romantic flavorings. Here was another jaunt for Barbier and Carré, two of the busiest scribes in opera history; not only Germans have condemned them for their inane libretto. It is not good Goethe, but then neither is *Wilhelm Meister's Apprenticeship*. Their text works as theatre, and

---

* If Lully founded French opera, then French opera was never French. But before Lully there were Perrin and Cambert, native if not favorite sons.

the authors were smart enough to fill the evening with ballads and reverielike solos that slow the action but turn a key into the Italophile *fatigue du nord* that sparked the novel, especially effective in Mignon's famous "Connais-tu le pays?" (Do you know that land where the orange tree grows? . . .), a translation of Goethe's lyric, "Kennst du das Land?" Completely wrong for Goethe but right for *opéra comique* is Philine's "Je suis Titania," a zap of scales and high notes sung upon the actress' triumph as Titania in *A Midsummer Night's Dream*, for which Thomas may have entertained a fetish (in the libretto as Barbier and Carré wrote it, she plays Juliet). The Paris premiere featured the ravishing and girlish Mignon of Marie-Célestine Galli-Marié, but this was no star vehicle: the work itself is what went over, time after time, most frequently in an expanded version with recitatives instead of dialogue and—in Germany, to placate Goethe's compatriots— a special sad ending in which Mignon dies to conform with the original.

Barbier and Carré also raided Shakespeare for Thomas, in a grand opera that took him six years to complete. *Hamlet* (1868) had an immediate success too, though Shakespeare is served even worse than Goethe. Outrages multiply: a drinking song for Hamlet, a setting of "To be or not to be" so monotonous that virtually every company suppressed it, a ballet called the Spring Festival, and a happy ending— Hamlet lives. There are novelties as well, such as the use of a saxophone to feed the anxiety of the "Murder of Gonzago" play-within-a-play, and a baritone rather than the expected tenor as Hamlet. Only one moment in the whole work casts a Shakespearean spell, Ophelia's eerie mad scene. And even this takes too long to climax what is already an undeservedly long role.

So Thomas rose like a comet, though his striking and ambitious *Françoise de Rimini* (1882) failed at the peak. It was different with Gounod. He established himself in short order and then underwent a steady descent with one failure after another. He too let Barbier and Carré embezzle the auras of Goethe and Shakespeare for him. *Faust* (1859) they gave him, and *Roméo et Juliette* (1867), each a lyric-opera treasury of Victorian Big Tunes, the kind that trawled the globe in pianoforte "arrangements," palm-court medleys, and music boxes. *Faust!* The epic of narrative, poetry, and ideology an opera? Even Meyerbeer, the grandest of all, felt unworthy of the task when it was suggested to him. But Meyerbeer was German and idealistic and lacked arrogance, all of which gave him a stake in protecting the integrity of Goethe's masterpiece. Let it be, he said. Hadn't it been travestied enough in the music halls and burlesque? Hadn't Berlioz already attempted it in a kind of opera? But understand the age: it craved adaptations, especially from Romantic shoguns; it needed, perversely, to tame wild Romanticism on middle-class opera stages; and all it saw in the sprawling *Faust* was the love story of Faust and Margarethe. So, disencumbering the material of its philosophical and religious elaboration, its mythic premises, its aspiring attempt to state what lesser men than Goethe were content to feel, Barbier tricked up the Gretchen-Faust soap opera for Gounod—basing it on Carré's play *Faust et Marguerite* —retaining the Devil, Gretchen's brother and neighbor, and some supernatural, bourgeois, and pastoral choral diversions, while Gounod made his characteristic "lyric" entailments on the grand in opera. Predictably, the result was the song heard 'round the world. Predictably too, it was Queen Victoria's idea of a splendid operatic outing. At a command performance of some scenes at Windsor Castle, a spectator noted that her "face lighted up and her lips parted with a transient smile of recognition whenever some well-known phrase occurred." Truly, *Faust* is an authentic relic of pan-European Victoriana. Till fairly recently it turned up everywhere on a regular basis—though German houses billed it as *Margarethe* after its heroine. Goethe's *Faust* is *Faust*. Gounod's *Faust* is about this girl and this man and this devil who helps the man destroy the girl.

Gounod's tunes, the lyric in his "lyric opera," should not be talked down to; not all composers have such a gift. Ferruccio Busoni, for instance, who wrote a vastly more intelligent *Faust* opera (not after Goethe, by the way) in the 1920s, seldom got his pen around a champion vocal melody. Gounod's *Faust* overflows with numbers that excerpt well for sheer musical valence but also do justice to situation and character. What other opera contains so many hits? The brother's "Avant de quitter ces lieux," a farewell as he marches off to war (added to the score for an English performance in 1864); the devil's Song of the Golden Calf; the choral Kermesse Waltz, once a favorite subject for virtuoso piano turns; the young suitor's "Faites-lui mes aveux" as he leaves a bouquet for Marguerite; Faust's apostrophe to Marguerite's cottage, "Salut! demeure chaste et pure"; her tour de force of folkish ballad about the King of Thulé followed at once by the Jewel Song; the lovers' nocturne duet; the Soldiers' Chorus, announcing the return of the brother, who learns to his horror that Marguerite is pregnant; the Devil's Serenade in mockery of her dilemma; and the concluding Prison Scene in which Marguerite dies and is received by a heavenly choir. These are long-loved highlights, but most of the score is as good; for once, Gounod really hit it big. He had managed again to clear the hurdles of grandeur without overextending himself. Though Meyerbeer's *L'Africaine* and Verdi's *Don*

Carlos were yet to come, genuinely grand opera could number its days, and *Faust*'s precise portability is one of the reasons why. It was conceived as an *opéra comique*—recitatives and a ballet sequence (a witches' Sabbath) were added later. Gounod freed French opera from its too long relished pomposity, yet sounded "important" when a scene called for it. There are moments of a distinctly Meyerbeerean flavor—the Chorale of the Swords in the Kermesse scene, in which the folk repulse the Devil with improvised crosses, and the Duel Trio, in which the heroine's brother battles Faust and falls. But Gounod is compact where Meyerbeer sits heavy. Even the vocal casting represents a revolution of sorts in that Marguerite is a lyric rather than a dramatic soprano or *falcon* and Faust a tenor of more sweetness than heft. Only the Devil, a bass with plenty of *buffo* gaming, recalls the Rossinian bass introduced into grand opera in the devil character in *Robert le Diable*. Berlioz cited Marguerite's timorous, gently surging "Il m'aime!" (He loves me) monologue at the close of the love duet as a stroke of genius —what a dainty way to close what in many another hand might have had to be a slambang grand duo. They call *Faust* "pretty"; this is unfair. The rightness of the music rises above the libretto's vandalism. Even that lump of a Soldiers' Chorus (known in lowbrow circles as "My father ki-illed a kangaroo") has a swagger and chic that mark it as French trying, not seriously, to pass for German.

Unfortunately, Gounod's muse flitted in and out unreliably. In *La Reine de Saba* (The Queen of Sheba, 1862), which flopped dismally but which he bitterly loved, a really stupid text (Barbier and Carré again) stumped him. Yet even here Gounod has resonance, as in a big aria for his hero, an architect and sculptor, "Inspirez-moi, race divine." The scene begins with drastic recitative: "Weakness of the human race! What is our work? . . . a temple for pride, scarcely worthy of a man!" In the opera's prelude and this recit, Gounod has defined his hero's mystical sense of vocation in a four-note theme, used sparingly. Now, as the aria proper commences, the hero builds his song on this theme, giving it a swing and a rhapsodic concentration that equals anything in *Faust*.

Gounod's solid sense of melody came to life again in *Roméo et Juliette* (1867), a grandish opera bound together by the title couple's four duets. This once all-popular work now sells even fewer tickets than *Faust*; perhaps it is too terminally Victorian, too dully beauteous. The heroine's dashing little entrance song strikes the right note, but a bit later Gounod assigns her a redundant waltz aria, particularly redundant after the comparable Jewel Song in *Faust* and yet another waltz aria in *Mireille* (1864). Coloratura waltzes counted as a Gounod specialty, or perhaps they were demanded by the militantly flighty Marie Miolan-Carvalho, wife of an important impresario and the creator of Marguerite, Mireille, and Juliette. However, these waltz numbers are all interchangeable in terms of character and furthermore lack dignity. (The rumor that one may sing that *Mireille* waltz to the accompaniment of Juliette's waltz and vice versa is unfounded. But *se non è vero, è ben trovato.**)

Adaptations from Goethe and Shakespeare began to share the French operatic stage with exotic subjects like Gounod's *Queen of Sheba*, with a slight touch of the Hindu, the Moorish, the Oriental in the orchestration. *Opéra comique* in particular took to the practice, as with Félicien David's *Lalla-Roukh* (1862), set in Kashmir and Samarkand, or Georges Bizet's *Les Pêcheurs de Perles* (The Pearl Fishers, 1863), set in Ceylon. David didn't trouble much about ethnic color. Hearing *Lalla-Roukh*'s academically symphonic overture, one would never expect the curtain to rise on an Eastern chorus citing the "tent" and the "silken carpet" under the direction of characters named Kaboul and Bakbara. Bizet, however, controlled a very poetry of instrumental timbre, and his poor unloved tale of two friends in rivalry over a virgin priestess tenders to the willing ear ingenious quaint effects. And just wait—it is Bizet who will, some chapters hence, turn *opéra comique* from a frivolous "family entertainment" into music theatre of sensuality and bite.

There is no one mid-century style, then—but opera is coming to believe in tradition and destiny. Rossini's sweeping dismissal of late *bel canto* singing, the nationalist schools in eastern Europe, the schedule juggling of city impresarios caught between the public's thirst for novelty and their nostalgia for the great roles and Big Tunes of old— all this pointed to a gathering sense of identity. For too long creators and recreators alike took little notice of their calling as a stock of work. It was a métier, a commerce, living entirely in the present, heedless of ancient inheritance as art. A whole museum lay ready to be opened, but who would endow it? At one of Rossini's Paris soirées, Prince Poniatowski asked Marietta Alboni to sing "Ah! quel giorno ognor rammento" from *Semiramide*, but when she agreed with pleasure and went over to the piano, Rossini matter-of-factly admitted that he probably couldn't get through the scene from memory and didn't even have a score of his own opera on hand. He didn't have *any* of his scores around, neither manuscript nor any publication. When someone registered surprise, the composer likened the preservation of his scores

---

* "If it's not true, it might as well be."

to the saving of old matchboxes and worn-out slippers.

Perhaps Rossini was only being waggish; apparently he accompanied Alboni in the aria without disaster. The attitude typifies his generation, but luckily this *laissez-mourir* about the past was changing by the middle of the century. A growing historical sensibility would eventually lead to the German Handel and Verdi revivals of the early 1900s, the Italian rediscovery of Monteverdi's stage works, and the full scale exhumation business of the post-World War II era—Cavalli, Lully, Rameau, Haydn, Meyerbeer, late *bel canto*, and other genres once again plugged into the electricity of live performance. These discoveries are not exclusively the work of nationalist true believers, either. It was Thomas Beecham and the Covent Garden management who raised up *Les Troyens*, Raymond Leppard who made the most successful performing editions of Monteverdi and Cavalli. Still, we look to the French to reclaim Lully and Rameau on stage with their ballet style and their natural affinity for the classic French stage out of which *tragédie lyrique* was synthesized; or to the Italians to fulfill Mercadante, Bellini, and Donizetti with their collective memory for the tracings of *bel canto*.

The beginning of nationalist exhumation may be dated from Felix Mendelssohn's performance in Berlin of Bach's St. Matthew Passion in 1829, a revelation that brought an all-but-forgotten composer back into currency and resulted in the publication of a complete Bach edition starting in 1850. In opera, the counterpart event occured in Paris in 1859, a production of Gluck's *Orpheus* opera prepared by Hector Berlioz for the Théâtre-Lyrique and starring Pauline Viardot.

What exactly are we to call this version? Musically it leans toward the original *Orfeo ed Euridice*, but Berlioz retained Moline's French text and some of the new music Gluck wrote for the French revision while rejecting both the Italian *castrato* and the French tenor heroes by recasting the lead for Viardot's by then degenerated contralto. So it is neither strictly *Orfeo* nor *Orphée;* whatever the proper title, it marked a historic attempt to blast sloppy performing traditions with authenticity. After all, the days when composers produced their operas —and so personally filled in on points of interpretation that weren't written into a score—were long gone. Berlioz put the Gluck back into a work that had been reorchestrated, rearranged, amended, and otherwise intruded upon by singers, conductors, and ballet masters. The impresario who commissioned the production, Léon Carvalho (husband of the soprano who created all those Gounod heroines), urged Berlioz to trick up the score with the addenda of the show shop. Use *Iphigénie en Aulide*'s overture! Quick, a chorus from *Armide!* But no. Berlioz, referring to the repulsively ersatz French *Freischütz* that F. H. Castil-Blaze had arranged, swore to discharge his office "without Castilblazade of any kind." He not only retrieved the notes that Gluck had written but set down new cadenzas and coached the cast in Gluckian plastique. (He also, reluctantly, decided to reorchestrate one number, but couldn't bring himself to do it and entrusted Camille Saint-Saëns with the task.)

The purified *Orpheus* enjoyed a sensation. As Berlioz' latter-day biographer, Jacques Barzun, reports, "[the historian Jules] Michelet was transported and Dickens reduced to tears. Flaubert went repeatedly and would go to nothing else." And surely the glory of the experience was Viardot, whose poise and transfiguring eloquence directly connected to Gluck's Classicism. Some suggested that her deteriorated instrument actually added to the pathos of the role, and helped complete the illusion that she was not Viardot but a Greek poet. The critic Henry Chorley was stunned by the naturalness of her portrayal—"the wondrous thrill of ecstasy which spoke in every fibre of the frame, in the lip quivering with a smile of rapture too great to bear, in the eye humid with delight, as it had been wet with grief, at the moment of recognition and of granted prayer."

The renovated *Orpheus* inspired similar mountings of Gluck's operas in Paris. It did not make the world yearn for operatic disinterment—that would come later—but it did impress upon experts and general public alike the validity of reexamining the past to find the root meanings of the present. This *Orpheus* succeeded not only on the merits of work and performance, but in comparison to the often artificial character of what was new since Gluck. On the other hand, one of the newest, Richard Wagner, had only just come to Paris to intrigue for an Opéra staging of his *Tannhäuser* and to introduce, in a series of concerts, samples of what he was calling "the music of the future." While opera had to reexperience its past, it also had to give thought to what directions it might take next. Wagner's plan was not to build on anything that had come before him, however—not even Gluck or Mozart. Wagner wanted to start over from scratch.

CHAPTER TEN

Apocalypse Now: Wagner

*First of all, Bayreuth is almost
unattainable . . .*
—GRACE M. TILTON, on attending
the first Bayreuth Festival, 1876

*With the Greeks the perfect
work of art, the drama, was the
abstract and epitome of all that
was expressible in the Grecian
nature. It was the nation itself—
in intimate connection with its
own history—that stood mir-
rored in its artwork, that com-
muned with itself and, within
the span of a few hours, feasted
its eyes with its own noblest essence.*
—RICHARD WAGNER,
The Music of the Future

*Goethe once set himself the
question, "What . . . [is] the
fate of romanticists?" His answer was: "To choke over the
rumination of moral and religious absurdities." In short:*
Parsifal.
—FRIEDRICH NIETZSCHE,
The Case of Wagner

IN SOME WAYS THE MOST ORIGINAL OF ALL OPERA COMPOSERS, RICHARD
Wagner launched his career on a secondhand output of mixed German
and Italian rudiments. For his third stage work, a breakthrough more
in reputation than in style, he tried the French mode. Trapped on the

outskirts of the opera scene in small-town posts, Wagner sought a way into the limelight by writing a grand opera, one *so* grand that only a major company could pull it off: *Rienzi* (1842). Many of the grand-opera pieces are in place: historical setting and subject, spectacle in decor and processions, ballet, dramatic tenor hero with democratic politics, chorus used as a force in the action, and so on. The Wagnerian conductor Hans von Bülow declared it Meyerbeer's best opera.

Rienzi is rather Meyerbeerean in overall effect, though scene by scene it seems less Meyerbeerean than proto-Wagnerian. The Weberisch and Italianate vocal decorations have begun to disappear, the ceremonial scenes bear a briskness all their own, and the concentration on three principals (the demagogue Rienzi, his sister, and the aristocrat who loves her) and one plot (Rienzi's rise and fall) offer unity to a sloppy form. However, essential characteristics of the mature Wagnerian opus (such as the protean *Leitmotiv* germs, the mytho-Christian dialectic, the pronounced sensuality) are not even hinted at: this is still first-period Wagner, the journeyman in training. *Rienzi* came to light in Dresden with great success, despite its great length; yet, though it remained a fixture in the local repertory, it did not catch the international eye that Wagner craved.

Still, he had got the last of tradition out of his system and could now concentrate on finding his style. No more would he base operas on plays or historical novels (like everyone else), and he would increasingly lose the ability to tolerate conventions (such as the French taste for ballet) or even technical limitations (such as singers' stamina or spectators' intellectual engagement). As others had before him, he pointed to the Greek stage—not, for once, for its natural aesthetic, but for its sacramental communion. The Greeks, Wagner insisted, raised up a theatre as a kind of religious mystery, on familiar tales out of the culture's mythology. Knowing the stories, the public did not so much treat itself to "entertainment" as take part in an archetypal imagery of its collective spirit.

No number of successful *Rienzi*s, then, could satisfy Wagner; he had to go back to the Greek plan and reinvent opera whole. For the first subject of his second period, experimentation, he chose a tale that looks and acts like a timeless legend, that of the "Flying Dutchman"— though in fact the notion of a ghost sea captain doomed to sail the ocean till he finds redemption in the arms of a faithful woman appears to be a product of Romantic balladeers rather than of the folk imagination. Certainly the wanderer alienated from society in quest of salvation paints an ageless picture, and of course the redemptive woman is basic to Germanic myth. Wagner was to make it an obsession of both his art and his life. "But [this woman] is no longer the home-tending Penelope that Ulysses courted in days of old," Wagner wrote, "but the quintessence of womankind—and yet the still unmanifest, the longed-for, dreamt-of, the infinitely womanly woman . . . the Woman of the Future."

In any case, *Der Fliegende Holländer* (The Flying Dutchman, 1843), like *Rienzi* first produced in Dresden, shows how fully Wagner had reorganized his thinking. For the first time we meet the truly symphonic opera, in which the all-basic melody that Wagner identified with Rossinian opera (in all its outgrowths, presumably) now cedes leadership to the commentative orchestral web, woven to fill out the sung text on the psychological level. The "number opera," with its clear-cut divisions of overture, opening scene, aria with chorus, duet or trio, and finale (or some such combination, with recitatives connecting the numbers), begins to fade into "through composition," one organic whole of nonstop music. (The two-and-a-half-hour *Flying Dutchman* is written to be played in one act, with orchestral intermezzos connecting the three different scenes; many houses stage it in three acts, however.) Seduced into a spiritual oneness with the work, the audience is both lulled by the music's power and "informed" of the music's message. One achieves a fellowship in the mythopoetic universality of the drama. To this end, the famous *Leitmotive* (literally "leading themes") guide one through the sound; they are the strands of the web, and they change their form or combine with other *Leitmotive* to illuminate the action, often telling us what the characters know but aren't saying or even what the characters don't know. In the *Flying Dutchman*, *Leitmotive* symbolize—among other persons and things—the protagonist, the roiling sea he endlessly courses, his longing for death, the simpler toil of the human seacoast world he can visit once every seven years, and the redemption he at last gains in the selfless devotion of Senta, the heroine. Not every measure of the score involves the use of a *Leitmotiv*, of course, and there is a great deal of purely melodic singing besides the declamatory passages. But one cannot deny that Wagner has broken new ground here. Suddenly vocal melody is not the basic form of communication: it shares the "story" with representational themes.

The third of Wagner's Dresden operas, *Tannhäuser* (1845), also deals with a hero in search of spiritual release against a supernatural background. But here there are two influential women, the blonde and dark ladies: Elisabeth, chaste and forgiving, and Venus, archon of conscienceless sensuality. Between them stands Tannhäuser, a poet and musician; we see the two women entirely from the male viewpoint, as savior and temptress (true mythic archetypes, they seem to have no other function in life than as lessons on Tannhäuser's way to self-knowledge). The opera unfolds far more complexly than *The Flying Dutchman*, moving from Venus' kingdom to pastoral simplicity into the world of courtly love and on to a plane of Christian sin and salvation. The *Dutchman* is compactly tumultuous, always close to the turbulent waters of the hero's quest, whereas *Tannhäuser* retrieves the contrasts and luxurious gait of grand opera. Much of it is dull. It lacks the play of *Leitmotive* that add so much to the Wagnerian adventure, and tenders a song context, modeled on a famous real-life tournament of minnesingers (troubadours) held at the Wartburg in Thuringia in 1207, that slogs along until Tannhäuser compulsively breaks into a hymn to Venus and scandalizes the court. But Wagner had to write the piece if only to explicate further the theory of self-abnegation that was eventually to inspire his two most ambitious projects, *Der Ring des Nibelungen* and *Parsifal*.

Another reason for *Tannhäuser* was its adaptatibility, as quasi-grand opera, to the major theatres that continued to resist *Rienzi*. Wagner's arrival in Paris in the year of Berlioz' *Orpheus* revival promised a *Tannhäuser* at the Opéra if the green-room maneuverings of diplomats and artsy hangers-on should have issue, and they did: Paris saw *Tannhäuser* in 1861. But Wagner had developed considerably in the sixteen years since the Dresden premiere; in particular his advanced harmonies enabled him to limn in sound what only lunatics and lovers had heard before in the madder music of their minds. Clearly an Opéra debut with all Europe looking on called for a revision—what did *Tannhäuser* need? A ballet, of course, said the Opéra management, right in the middle of the evening to accommodate latecomers. Wagner shrugged; they'll get their ballet.* What *Tannhäuser* really needed was a more definitive characterization of the love goddess and her hedonist gallimaufry in the Venusberg. Having completed the sensual *Tristan und Isolde* two years earlier (it had not yet been staged), Wagner easily remedied Venus' and Elisabeth's relative similarity in soprano sound, tightening the former's range to that of a soaring mezzo-soprano, adding in a few new lines, and totally rewriting her part in melody and accompaniment. In the Dresden version, Venus comes off as a mildly

---

* Dance was not obligatory in a given work provided its length allowed for the inclusion of a separate ballet on the same bill. Gounod's *Sapho*, for example, had no ballet but was short enough to double up with one; *Tannhäuser* was too long, and had to compromise.

unconventional hausfrau, a kind of "other half" of Elisabeth as the
bifocal projection of Wagner/Tannhäuser's sexual worldview.* But
in the Paris version Venus comes alive as a force of libidinous persuasion, and makes the work's either-or burn with suspense. The ballet
that Wagner added for Paris, a bacchanale, also helps establish the
voluptuousness of the Venusberg scene. But this comes at the very
front of the show, a dangerous spot for ballet in Parisian grand opera,
and certain latecomers led by the aristocratically vulgar Jockey Club
punished the outrage by making a shambles of the second and third
performances.† The opera was withdrawn at Wagner's request.

A fourth opera completes this middle period of Wagner's still-
evolving maturity, *Lohengrin* (1850). If *Tannhäuser* is longer and
grander than *The Flying Dutchman*, *Lohengrin* is longer and grander
yet, and marks Wagner's peace with and emancipation from the operatic forms of his day. Marschner, Bellini, Weber, and Meyerbeer all
donated to the works mentioned so far; *Lohengrin*, despite its resemblance to Weber's *Euryanthe*, shows Wagner come at last into his style.
Lohengrin's subject passes through such Romantic tidbits as the supernatural and the solitary, redemptive wanderer to plumb some meaning
at last: how magical *is* salvation? Who may seek it? The libretto's
source, too, is ultra-Wagnerian, a medieval tale touching on history but
rooted in legend. Lohengrin, a knight of unknown origin and exceptional grace under pressure, defends the innocent Elsa von Brabant from
a plot organized by Friedrich von Telramund and his evil wife (the real
instigator), Ortrud. The bads discredited, Lohengrin takes Elsa as his
bride, warning her never to ask him who he is. Of course she does,
prompted by the bads, and Lohengrin departs forever after identifying
himself as one of an occult Christian order guarding the Holy Grail—
and the son, by the way, of Parsifal, whom Wagner was to deal with
in his last opera in terms of such piety and manly beauty as to make
Lohengrin look like a pizza waitress by comparison.‡

Unity, here, is all. Though the opera is immense, it seems to have
been struck off of one molecule of vision, like a sheet of glass. The
other-worldly knight, the good Belgians and Germans, and the bad

---

* Birgit Nilsson brought this home in the mid-1960s at the Met, singing both parts
in the Dresden edition. A valiant stunt, it only underlined the blunt sameness in
the two roles and the overall "so what?" that the Dresden version prompts.
† Some of the disturbance was political, reflecting anti-German sentiment, especially aimed at Princess von Metternich, wife of the Austrian ambassador, who
had agitated fiercely for *Tannhäuser*. During an intermission she got so exercised
arguing the work's merits that she broke her fan.
‡ Trivia collectors will want to note Lohengrin's mother's name, not mentioned
anywhere in Wagner but cited in one of his sources, Wolfram von Eschenbach's
Parzifal—Kondwiramuir. She sounds Irish.

couple, distinguished in musical terms, occupy the opera's dramatic space in effortless confluence, separating only for the three act preludes, the first given over to the Grail in luminous haze of stationary strings, the second to the bads in oily brasses, the third to the Lohengrin-Elsa wedding in joyful noise. The symphonic motion spills through an entire act in one multicolored movement, erasing any echo of the number opera that preceded Wagner and began to disappear directly after him, and the table of *Leitmotive* is complex, using harmony to suggest the difference between Lohengrin's sacramentally burnished selflessness (in strong, basic sound constructions) and the bads' malevolent ambition (in unruly, almost foundationless sounds that "lie" to the Western ear). Wagner was to refine and expand his sound vastly after this, but even so *Lohengrin* finds him at the start of his seniority as opera theorist, librettist, and composer. He had yet to implant himself in international chronicle, however. His friend (and future father-in-law) Franz Liszt staged the piece in his little court theatre at Weimar with an orchestra numbering fewer than forty players, and Wagner couldn't even attend, as he was waiting out a political exile in Switzerland. At least the composer was spared the skimpy production and firstnighters' incomprehension—and Weimar, a cultural capital, was an awfully conspicuous place in which to flop.

Wagner did not give up. His head buzzed with projects, all building on the legendary and sociospiritual aspects typified in *Lohengrin*. Lovers, warriors, kings, slaves, and monsters haunted him with their potential for his new Greek theatre in which the public would shut itself away from daily life and undergo a ritual of encounter with the hopes and demons of subliminal truth. So convinced was he already that within a few years of *Lohengrin's* premiere he had conceived all the operas that were to follow—some three decades' and twenty-eight hours' worth of music drama. It's hard to decide exactly what order the remaining operas fall into except by date of performance. *Der Ring des Nibelungen*, for example, was not completed until 1874, but Wagner had the libretto published privately as early as 1853.

Wagner's third period of confident revolutionary innovation begins with his invitation in 1864 to become court composer to "mad" King Ludwig II of Bavaria. Munich's public probably would not be any more receptive than that of Weimar and Paris had, but at least a major theatre would be put at his disposal. With Wagner, everything, including life, is larger than life, and rather than adapt to the resources in Munich, he promptly staged the unstageable: the erotoparanoid, drugagonzo romance, *Tristan und Isolde* (1865).

The love plot had always been the most basic single factor in the opera libretto, but Wagner exploded this particular love plot in poetry and music of a dazzling sensual honesty, as if the whole piece were a study in orgasmic representation. It is, of course, much more than that, because Wagner exploits the situation with his characteristic fascination for the stimulating nuance. His lovers, adulterers by the technicality that Tristan brought Isolde from Ireland to Cornwall to marry his uncle, King Mark, speak as no operatic lovers spoke before, commencing their famous duet in Act II with riddles on the horror of day-life and the transfiguration of night-death. There is a great deal of talk in *Tristan* and little action: in Act I the pair accidentally drink a love potion (Isolde had meant to poison them both), in Act II they are discovered in tryst, and in Act III the wounded Tristan raves, dies, and is eulogized by Isolde, who then (it seems; Wagner's directions are ambiguous) dies on his body. On one level, there is no action in the opera at all, merely a metaphorical poem on love, with Act I the anticipation, Act II consummation, and Act III exhaustion.

This is highly profane mysticism for a proposed sacred theatre of mythic communion, but Wagner brings it off through the cosmic neuroticism of the sound of it. It *feels* like what it is. *Tristan* is without question his most Wagnerian project to date, with *Leitmotive* slipping in and out of the orchestral texture in ceaseless variations of themselves, growing from one idea into another as the two lovers grow. *Tristan* sighted the land's end of the Romantic continent with the medieval legend, the magic, the folklike touches (a sailor opens Act I with an unaccompanied song, and a shepherd pipes, courtesy of the English horn, in Act III), the gathering sweep of the musical structures, and the big, dramatic voices. The difference between Wagner and everyone else is that he conceived his operas in an organic onenesss that threatened to engulf the impressionable. It felt *too* much; it never rested. No wonder *Tristan* shocked in 1865; it had been fifteen years since the last Wagner premiere (*Lohengrin*), and the public had scarcely had a chance to get used to the *old* Wagner. *Tristan*, with its blatantly sexual love-death, was an unparalleled outrage. Somehow Wagner did find a cast to sing it, and the orchestra played, though it was all Greek to them. And King Ludwig, at least, enjoyed the three performances of the premiere production. But *Tristan* was very seldom performed thereafter, and only in Germany, until the Wagner cult began to pick up steam in the 1880s. Even then, not everyone accepted *Tristan* as Wagner meant them to—how could a Victorian public do that? As Denis de Rougemont explains it, the assimilation of *Tristan und Isolde* "was facilitated by the frivolousness of the ordinary theatregoing public, by its clumsy sentimentality and—frankly—its wonderful ability not to hear what is being sung."

As culmination of Romantic opera, Wagner's stage works belonged more to their own era than to any utopian Hellenic theatre. Like the Florentines and Venetians of the 1600s, Wagner called his pieces music dramas, and like some of the noncreative commentators we have passed along the way here, he saw the "art work of the future" as tending to a fusion of the arts, ruled by poetry, but with music, song, dance, and decor all in on the collaboration. There is a flaw: how can poetry be king when the orchestra is so busy, at times even more "melodic" than the voices? Good question. But Wagner wrote so much theory that some of it was bound to read a little cockeyed. If anything, his *Gesamtkunstwerk* ("work of all the arts") is overrun with (orchestral) music, the importance of poetry depending on such variables as singers' diction and one's knowledge of German.

Did Wagner generate a wholly new type of music theatre, or did he simply revise existing forms? According to the ardent Wagnerite George Bernard Shaw, "[Wagner's] music is no more reformed opera than a cathedral is a reformed stone-quarry." Wagner himself reckoned that if his operas had any precedent it was Beethoven's Ninth Symphony, with its shattering dimensions, developmental majesty, and ecumenical message. And it is true that from *Tristan* on, his operas do not parse as successors of any kind to anything. The *Gesamtkunstwerk* theory was old when Wagner was born, and much of the material he used was simply Romantic opera stuff multiplied to the nth degree—not least the "*auteur* theory" of one man, one opera: librettist, composer, producer all incarnated in one genius. But in the end, his unique conflation of allegory and ecstasy was something new. *Le Nozze di Figaro* is perfect naturalism; *Fidelio* perfect idealism. That much opera already had to its credit. But in Wagner, the imagination soars into primal imaginings of unutterable prescience.

Comedy and the everyday was not beyond Wagner; in this field, too, he transmits elemental truths. Casting legend aside, he borrowed history and song tradition to examine German nationalism while lecturing the public on the necessary regeneration of art in the jolly, fiery, and pensive *Die Meistersinger von Nürnberg* (1868). The mastersingers of the title represent the rising middle classes, aspiring culturally and economically but not forgetful of their roots in the folk. Their pastime, singing, has become an elitist vocation, bound on all sides by an aesthetic code. Into their midst comes a young knight, and he too can sing, but he is self-taught and bows to no rules. He also furnishes half the love interest, opposite the vivacious daughter of one of the masters. The huge work concentrates a good deal of action into a twenty-four-hour period, and hanging over it all is a song contest, to be judged by The People, with the daughter as the prize. Only a master can enter, and the knight's audition for the guild fails because of his arrogant "modernism." It looks as if the girl must be handed over to his rival, the town clerk, an obnoxious pedant; she has the option of declining, but in that case must remain unmarried for life.

Clearly this is a parable on the "artwork of the future." Wagner is the knight, with his sensuality, truth, and heterodox style; the pedant stands for Wagner's enemies, the envious critics (he was originally going to call the character Hans Lick, after Eduard Hanslick, the tyrant of Viennese music journalism). But Wagner allots himself a second alter ego, Hans Sachs, the most beloved of the masters and the most concerned with the course of art and life in his timeplace. If the knight is Wagner as hero, Sachs is Wagner as philosopher-king, showing the young iconoclast how his fresh approach, when observant of tradition and discipline, keeps art vital. The art revolution does not destroy the past, but renews it. With Sachs' coaching, the knight unveils a "prize song" and wins the girl as the citizens of Nürnberg hail their great cobbler, poet, and mastersinger Hans Sachs.

Quite a change from the arcane love mystery of the immobile *Tristan und Isolde*. But Wagner is practicing as he preaches, submerging in fundamentals before he extends himself even further from C Major and basic counterpoint. There is little of either in *Tristan* but tons of both in *Die Meistersinger*—academic chorales, pompous marches, parodies of authentic mastersinger devices, a colossal fugue for a late-night riot, and, just to remind us of Wagner's revolutionary standard, the brandishing of a few bars of *Tristan* to accompany Sachs' mention of the couple.

Die Meistersinger is steeped in nationalism. Wagner's librettos last longer and "talk" more than others, but then they say more. Verdi, in the next chapter, will teach the value of what he called *la parola scenica*, the "theatrical word" that encapsulates the emotion of the moment. Verdi seeks leanness, speed; Wagner expounds. In *Die Meistersinger* he needs to develop the sense of German destiny not only in the cut of its music but in the conceptual apprehension of its artists. "Beware!" Sachs cries just before the final chorus. "Evil tricks threaten us: if the German people and culture should degenerate . . . alien mists and alien rubbish they will plant in Germany, and no one would know any more what is German and true."

This sounded great to the Nazis, who took it as a fiat for National Socialism's racist program. Hitler compared the original Nazi party to Siegfried, and Goebbels heard in *Die Walküre* the "marching of the

Steel Helmet troops." In fact, Wagner's politics would have dismayed them. A veteran of Dresden's insurrection of 1849, a close friend of Mikhail Bakunin and other volatile and deadly serious anarchists, Wagner was anything but a fascist. If he belonged to any party, it was that of opportunism. He excoriated "Jews in music" when he was down and they were up; later, as emperor of Bayreuth, he entrusted the premiere of his last opera to Hermann Levi and production rights to all his operas to Angelo Neumann—both Jewish. Similarly, he hated luxury-livers when he was left out but donned silk dressing gowns when he had made it. When it felt right, he exulted in "the German spirit"; at other times he touted a Christian ecumenism over patriotism. Like any politician, he simply needed to get elected.

One significant component of his worldview can be traced sociopolitically: his obsession with self-denial. Senta, Elisabeth, and Lohengrin have it, Tannhäuser learns it and is "saved" (fatally), *Tristan and Isolde* both don't have it (because they hunger so fiercely) and do (because their love transmutes into transcendence), but that work is a great lie—Wagner won't admit that his hero and heroine are the two most selfish people in opera, because Wagner was the most selfish person in the opera world, who built his œuvre on studies in selflessness.

Der Ring des Nibelungen (The Ring of the Nibelungs, 1876), the paragon of Wagnerian music drama, turns entirely on a denial of the will. Borrowing the apocalyptic cosmology of Norse legend, Wagner combined two major and numerous minor sagas to confront the inextricably doomed order of the despotic gods with a new order of anticorporate youth: power is overthrown by love. This sounds simple, but the *Ring* is a thrillingly complex work ranging from the heavens to human earth to the underground of the Dwarf Home, taking in a "hide helmet" that can change the wearer's features or transport him anywhere in a flash, potions of oblivion and recollection, a sleepy dragon on his hoard, mermaids, Valkyries, and of course the ring, forged of gold that can only serve him who renounces love and whose magic is such that who bears it can rule the world—but whose magic is also such that the bearer must be consumed by his own magic. Power corrupts.

Starting with world creation and closing with world's end, Wagner manages to include not only characters and situations basic to Germanic myth but more universal images—the deluge, the virgin sleeping on an unapproachable height, the young hero of unknown origin who redeems humanity through martyrdom. So much goes on in the *Ring* that even a Wagnerian-length evening could not contain it.

Having conceived the project as an opera called *Siegfrieds Tod* (Siegfried's Death), after the climactic event that claims the epic hero and clears the way for a destruction of the impure old society and the commencement of the new, Wagner realized that the all-important meeting of the hero and Brünnhilde, which changes man's earthly career from love of power to humanism, needed not just to be mentioned but seen, and he wrote *Der Junge Siegfried* (Young Siegfried) to precede *Siegfrieds Tod*. But Wagner still had his people telling of events that needed showing: how the gold was stolen from the Rhine and made into the ring, how the ring became cursed, how Wotan (Odin), the king of the gods, learned to "will what is necessary" (i.e., his own downfall), how in an attempt to forestall the inevitable Wotan conceived a boy and a girl of a mortal woman and how the young couple incestuously conceive Siegfried, and how the ring becomes tragically mixed up in the personal loves of all of the above. So now Wagner saw that the whole business was going to occupy four nights at the opera: a two-and-a-half-hour prelude of gods, giants, dwarfs, and nixies, *Das Rheingold* (The Gold in the Rhine); and then three big works increasingly given over to the mortal sphere, *Die Walküre* (The Valkyrie) and the retitled *Siegfried* and *Götterdämmerung* (Twilight of the Gods).

Now Wagner shows everything essential, but some events are still lacking. In accordance with the dimensions of epic, he constantly has characters reporting to other characters on what we have not seen, as well as on what we have. In *Das Rheingold*, Loge the mercurial fire spirit tells the assembled gods how Alberich, king of darkness and Wotan's opposite, courted the Rhine Maidens and, rebuffed, forswore love and stole the gold—though we have just witnessed this in the preceding scene. In *Die Walküre*, Siegmund tells his long-lost sister and her husband about his childhood, news to us. Later in *Die Walküre*, when his plans go awry, Wotan despairingly reviews all the action to that point in conversation with Brünnhilde. And so it goes, each new climax in the plot prompting a new survey by some character, and each survey both adding to the saga and keeping its subplots firmly in our minds, so that by *Götterdämmerung*, more than half of the libretto comprises this epic synergism, pulling all the parts together as calamity nears: to root us at the center of things, of the world. Comparably epic is the vastly expanded use of the *Leitmotiv*, which now forms the absolute material of the orchestral texture. Virtually every moment of the *Ring* is made of a *Leitmotiv*, either a development of a *Leitmotiv* or a variation that in turn becomes a new *Leitmotiv* with a new meaning. Every one of the *Ring*'s hundred or so "leading themes" may be traced back to one generative cell, the first thing heard in the work. "Thing" is just the word, as at first it is more of a deep, toneless hum than a melody. Expanding the hum into a tune, Wagner employs the most primal harmonic relationships to suggest primal movement, the hum of life in the first flow of water. Gradually, the music "flows" into a simplistic rising melody, associated with the Rhine River and, by extension, with the natural world that human ambition disrupts and pollutes. Nothing is static in life; nothing is static in the *Ring*: this "water" theme, transposed to the minor key, takes on a new significance as the motto of Erda, Mother Earth, gloomy and wise. By still another variation, the theme is "reversed," its now falling spill symbolizing the end of the gods, the reversion of all things in nature back into matter and nothing. Applying this process of variation, Wagner makes of that first water theme *all* the *Ring* themes, and all the music that the *Ring* contains. This is no specialist's stunt, but an attempt to build opera on a musical conception, distilling information even as it is imparted. This organic integration of thought and sound is what makes this tautly sprawled, self-hating and human-loving, exhilarating and corrupt masterpiece endlessly fascinating. Again and again one hears new ideas in it, sees supposed inconsistencies vindicated, responds to new facets of character, notes old fashion crumble as certain of the *Leitmotive* do in *Götterdämmerung*, anticipating the fall of the power bosses and the cyclic rebirth of spirituality. Transformation is art's great topic; it is what the *Ring* is about as concept and also how the *Ring* happens as art. Many opera buffs enjoy it strictly as a spectacle of love, magic, and murder; never bothering to learn what sort of world would succeed Wotan's, they don't understand why Wagner retained those talky narratives, and they look upon Brünnhilde's Immolation Scene as the latest in a long line of solo soprano finales. But sociopolitical interpretation is endemic to the *Ring*. Wagner himself pointed the way in many writings on the work, on politics, on opera. Whether one hears it or not, it's there.

Perhaps it's hard to hear because its subject is self-denial, but its sound, largely, is affirmative and energetic. No one in opera is more exuberant than Siegfried, no one more self-possessed than Brünnhilde. Like Tristan and Isolde, they are unlikely subjects for Wagner's lesson on selflessness, and we wonder if, somehow, Wagner the librettist is attempting to impose a ridiculously naïve solution—*love;* what's love, anyway?—on a problem that Wagner the composer describes with great sophistication.

It is this Wagnerian ambivalence that turned Friedrich Nietzsche, once Wagner's most enthusiastic ally, into Wagner's most articulate critic. At first the philosopher hailed Wagner's revival of the Dionysian theatre rite, seeing the mystical communion of myth and mob as invigorating and, incidentally, a chance to see his own theories put into practice. But with the *Ring*, Nietzsche saw in Wagner a megalomaniac grinning through the Christian prophet's magnanimous mask. What good, Nietzsche asked, can possibly come of denying one's selfhood? This is not vigor but decay. "The artist of decadence," he called Wagner. "Is Wagner a man at all? Is he not rather a disease? Everything he touches he contaminates. *He has made music sick.*"

If the message of the *Ring* is defeatist, its music proved a fountainhead to generations of composers. They caught Wagner's vitality, not his decay. In France particularly, the spell of Wagner's symphonic riot and his legendary universals of psychopathic obsession enthralled many, and while most critics assailed the signs of creeping Wagnerism they thought they heard in obtrusive *Leitmotive* or too big an orchestra, musicians digested and imitated. England, too, enjoyed a Wagner vogue, but few composers succumbed; English Wagnerism was an amateur's cult. At first the faithful had to journey to Germany to hear in person what they had read in the printed score. *Lohengrin* reached London in 1868, *The Flying Dutchman* in 1876, the *Ring*, *Die Meistersinger*, and *Tristan* in 1882; Paris heard *Lohengrin* in 1887 (in French). What to do till the whole canon turns up locally? Form societies, publish articles, play the published scores on the home piano, and compose spinoffs. In the latter area, the French shone.

César Franck's *Hulda* (1882), Ernest Reyer's *Sigurd* (1883), Edouard Lalo's *Le Roi d'Ys* (The King of Ys, 1888), Ernest Chausson's *Le Roi Arthus* (King Arthur, 1903), among others, all shared some Wagnerian derivation in subject and sound. Reyer's huge opus was the most bizarrely transethnic Wagnerian event, a retelling of the last act of *Siegfried* and much of *Götterdämmerung* in endearingly French terms (including one short ballet turn for Valkyries, elves, nixies, and the three norns), with a few *Leitmotive* stiffly resisting any variation. *Sigurd* offers much that is sumptuous and moving; Brunehilde's awakening scene, "Salut! splendeur du jour!.," misses Wagner's miraculous stillness, but in the grand opera context really blows the roof off. Naturally, it is a German who takes the palm for Most Slavishly Authentic—August Bungert, who projected two *Ring*-like cycles on the *Iliad* and the *Odyssey* to be called *Homerische Welt* (Homeric World); Bungert completed only *Die Odysee*, performed work by work at intervals around the turn of the century. Still, it was a Frenchman, Emmanuel Chabrier, who wrote the best of this repertory, *Gwendoline* (1886), a compact blend of *The Flying Dutchman* and *Tristan und Isolde* set in a Saxon seacoast village in the eighth century. Enthusiastically neglected since its very first days—it even had trouble getting a hearing in France, despite numerous stagings in Germany—it cries for revival, with its superb overture of intense *Leitmotive*, Gwendoline's Senta-like ballad of "the red-haired barbarians" (the invading Danes), her charming Spinning Song, and her transfigured immolation in the company of the Danish chief Harald, true unto death.

It was one thing to borrow Wagner's legendary material and *Leitmotive;* living up to the *Gesamtkunstwerk* was another. Wagner specifically hoped to destroy opera as it was, not to share with it, and it was part of his plan to write works not feasible given opera's technology. When he composed the *Ring*, he called for a platoon of voices, a rota of stage tricks, and the indulgence of audiences never before assembled, turned, or begged. Even with Ludwig ready to foot the bill, it seemed impossible to hope for a production. And where would the singers be found to live these parts as mythical beasts and beauties, quite aside from the hurdles in vocal stamina that Wagner had been erecting since *Tristan?** Encouraging Wagner, Liszt likened the composition of the *Ring* to the program that "the Cathedral Chapter of Seville gave to their architect for the construction of the Cathedral: 'Build us such a temple that future generations will say the Chapter was crazy to undertake anything so extraordinary.' And yet, there stands the Cathedral!"

Wagner's new type of opera obviously couldn't fit into the type of theatre that would house, say, *Le Prophète* or *La Cenerentola*—the resources backstage and the attitude in the auditorium would have to be totally different. At Ludwig's insistence, Wagner allowed the Munich court opera to stage *Das Rheingold* and *Die Walküre* in 1869 and 1870, before the rest of the *Ring* was ready, but this was not even a stopgap. Rather, it was a humiliation, laying his prize piece before the people of what he called "a hotbed of priestly-political intrigue." Already Wagner was planning for a rural place, isolated for the contemplation of the art ritual, active in the summer when specialists could be gathered from all over the music world; there would be specialists in spectating as well as singing, playing, and producing. In 1870 he rediscovered Bayreuth, a small town with a lovely Baroque theatre that boasted the deepest (but nothing like the widest) stage in Germany, and which luckily lay on Bavarian soil (and thus within Ludwig's domain). The theatre, designed by Giuseppe Galli di Bibiena, of the

---

* Someone once asked Kirsten Flagstad if there were a secret to the singing of Wagner's heroines. "Yes," she replied. "Always wear comfortable shoes."

famous Bologna-based family of architects and artists, would not serve. But Bayreuth was the place all right, and on a hill overlooking the town Wagner raised his temple. The exterior looks clumsy from the side, like the House of Seven Gables about to devour the Albert Hall, but the point of the construction is the interior, where the audience views the opera as if entering a dream. All reminders of the real world, all bars to the mystical oneness of the *Gesamtkunstwerk*, are obliterated: no lights in the auditorium while the art is on, a partly covered orchestra pit with the players and conductors out of sight (and Wagner's voluminous orchestration salubriously handicapped), the seats arranged in a fan shape, like a Greek amphitheatre in one rising set of tiers—no boxes, no balconies. And in August of 1876, the first summer music festival in modern Europe—the forerunner of today's Glyndebourne, Aix-en-Provence, and Santa Fe—staged the first complete *Ring* cycle. Ludwig, who more than anyone else had made it possible for Wagner to write and produce in style, did not attend. He had seen the whole four nights of it by himself at a dress rehearsal the week before.

Though by now the *Ring* has found its way into every Western opera house that calls itself major, Bayreuth still sets the vogue for *Ring* stagings. At first everyone felt bound to realize Wagner's original productions as much as possible, with the absurdly detailed flats and wing pieces, the paper wood, the leaves gristly with paint, the cumbersome arrangements for flying Valkyries and swimming Rhine maidens and, of course, the dragon that Siegfried slays. (Wagner had to send to England for that piece, to a firm in London renowned for theatrical reptiles.) Imitation wasn't all that difficult, if the budget allowed, for Wagner could not revolutionize acting, scene design, and lighting technology as he could musical composition. Remember, the breakthroughs in the development of modern acting ensemble and realistic or suggestive stage illusionism occurred *after* Wagner, around 1900. It was Adolphe Appia who first managed to gear design with electric lighting to evoke the "sense" of the action in the look of the stage, and as his work influenced Wagner's son Siegfried (who introduced the cyclorama) in the 1920s, so did the rest of the world accommodate the new *Ring* style of pliant, shadowy post-art nouveau delicacy. And after World War II Wagner's grandsons Wieland and Wolfgang repatterned the façade with nonrepresentational decor—swirling mists, great bursts of light, towering natural rubble veiled in the distance—thus depending to a great degree on the intensity of the cast. The Bayreuth look continues to change: for the centennial in 1976 Patrice Chéreau staged a weird commentative production in Vic-

How not to stage *Tristan und Isolde*: Director Gian Carlo Menotti and designer Luigi Samaritani played the piece in Spoleto, 1968, as if it were *Pelléas et Mélisande*. King Mark (Malcolm Smith) surprises the lovers (Claude Heater, Klara Barlow) in tryst while Tristan's sidekick Kurwenal (Antonin Svorc) looks on. Heater made a handsome, muscular hero and Barlow has the pre-Raphaelite look down cold, but *art nouveau* does not suit the music. *(Spoleto Festival)*

Changing styles at Bayreuth: above, Brünnhilde swears on Hagen's spear in *Götterdämmerung*, Act II, in 1952; below, the same moment in 1976. *(Festspielleitung Bayreuth)*

torian dress, though the commentary was hard to follow and many reasonable onlookers thought it a rotten escapade.

It is amusing to trace the different guises that Wagner's *Ring* machinery has taken over the years. Take the dragon, for instance. In the composer's lifetime a well-intentioned but asininely literal realization belched silly smoke; Fritz Lang's silent film *Siegfried* disclosed a remarkably slinky monster worked by a dozen men inside and under the body; one postwar Bayreuth mounting merely suggested the animal with multiple sets of eyes lurking in the darkness; Herbert von Karajan's Salzburg production in the 1960s slyly animated what had previously appeared to be the floor of a forest and what then looked like a rug doing a grouchy dance; and the Chéreau *Ring* brought on a great rubber squeeze toy.

As there are different solutions to the *Ring*'s peculiar staging problems, so are there different interpretations of the work itself. In *The Perfect Wagnerite* (1898) George Bernard Shaw gave it a Marxist reading (Alberich's king-enslaved Nibelheim is a sweatshop, Valhalla a villa, and Siegfried a "born anarchist") that collapses in a snit when Shaw gets to *Götterdämmerung* and finds that his allegory is not Wagner's. Often as enlightening as the interpretations are the spoofs. Shaw is Johnny on the spot here as well ("Siegfried inherits from Wotan a mania for autobiography . . . [he] tells the Rhine Maidens as much of [his life] as they will listen to, and then keeps telling it to his hunting companions until they kill him"), as was Claude Debussy ("From one angle, it's very serious, but we also have to contend with dragons singing, birds giving valuable advice, bears, a horse, and two crows—all intervening in a charming fashion"), and Anna Russell, not the first but certainly the most popular *Ring* analyst to assess the romance of Brünnhilde and Siegfried: "Well, then they fall in love, and he gives her the ring . . . She's his aunt, by the way." Of course what makes the jokes so swank is that they don't have to exaggerate—the Ring *is* extreme.

And *Parsifal* (1882), Wagner's final opera, is even more so. Much smaller than the *Ring* in scope, it still makes for a long, slow evening. A lot that we have grown used to in Wagner is here—the Christian wonder, ambition versus transcendence, sensuality versus chastity, woman as temptation and redemption, and so on. But for once the music actually internalizes the self-denial preached in the libretto, convincing as never before in Wagner. *Parsifal* is ecclesiastical where the *Ring* is barbaric; closed and intimate where the *Ring* stretches to fit the world; arcane rite draining itself of earthly will. Virginia Woolf,

who like Nietzsche became a lapsed Wagnerian, wrote of *Parsifal* that
"the music has reached a place not yet visited by sound . . . the Grail
seems to burn through all superincumbences . . . one is fired with
emotion and yet possessed with tranquility at the same time."

The Holy Grail glows at *Parsifal*'s center, surrounded—admired,
hated, or ignored—by a collection of archetypes such as might have
peopled a medieval miracle play: the good man susceptible to sin
(Amfortas), the arrogant lieutenant turned to evil in envy (Klingsor),
the Magdalene figure (Kundry), the wise old man powerless to help
(Gurnemanz), the raw youth who turns out to be the only character
capable of understanding and improving the human condition, the
ascetic initiates of the mystery who guard the Grail. Drawing mainly
from von Eschenbach's *Parzival*, Wagner made this musical legend the
ultimate of its kind. One could mistake the *Ring* for an "action" piece,
a Norse western; but *Parsifal* moves too hieratically to be misread. It is
notorious for Gurnemanz' endless lectures, and its choral scenes in the
hall of the Grail belong to a highly remote brand of tension building
that many listeners do not respond to. Perhaps the sole moment of
visible motion in the whole evening occurs in Act II, when a magic
garden materializes, filled with winsome flower maidens to tempt the
hero. Like the *Ring*, *Parsifal* had Bayreuth written all over it; at the
premiere there, the eager group of French devotés included Léo Delibes,
a composer of light ballet and opera scores. What did Delibes think of
this remarkable work? Well, he loved the second act because—this only
sounds right in French—"Il y avait des petites femmes, et que les petites femmes, c'est toujours amusant" (There were little cuties, and
little cuties are always fun).

Indeed, Bayreuth was more or less, as an American visitor put it in
1876, unattainable: Bayreuth as Wagner's revolution in the public's
relationship with opera. For despite the many specific imitations and
despite the enormous influence Wagner exercised in sheer musical technique (certain moments in *Parsifal* anticipate the radical harmonies of
the twentieth century, and the breathless Wagnerian "symphony"
changed forever the number-by-number format so essential till his
time), Wagner's mythic rituals marked the beginning of nothing: the
line ended with *Parsifal*. There were to be no other Bayreuths, no
successful attempts to continue the music theatre festival on these
stupendous lines.* The tools and materials with which Wagner built
his stage—yes, these entered the public domain of composers and libret-

---

* True, August Bungert pleaded for a special theatre to house his *Odyssey*
tetralogy, but no one except Bungert thought this useful or even amusing.

tists, and his shadow hung over everyone for years. But as Wagner's operas began to be heard everywhere, from *Rienzi* to *Parsifal,** they somehow managed to fit in between the *Prophètes* and *Cenerentola*s without loss of resonance. Wagner suddenly seemed less exotic. Was it a theatre revolution, after all? Yes. But its effect lay not so much in what it was itself as in what it lent to what came after. It was as if, when the barricades were pulled down, everyone went right back to the old society . . . but regarded it with new eyes.

---

* The composer intended *Parsifal* to be the exclusive property of the Bayreuth festival, but the Met challenged the monopoly in 1903 and successfully defended its rival production in court, opening the way for other *Parsifal*s.

CHAPTER ELEVEN

The Precise Romantic:
Verdi

*Three things are required in the
art of operatic music: voice,
voice, and voice.*

—GIUSEPPE VERDI

I detest pointless things.

—GIUSEPPE VERDI

UNLIKE GLUCK, BERLIOZ, AND WAGNER, VERDI WORKED ENTIRELY
within the canons of contemporary taste, almost immediately falling
into a very personal style that he ceaselessly but very gradually evolved
over the course of twenty-seven operas into a consummation of Italian
music theatre. He went his own way, but argued that the public knows
good opera at first hearing, so while he was no panderer, he was no
idealist either. He just kept getting better and better at what he did.

He arrived on the scene, after Bellini's death and during Donizetti's
last years, with pedestrian assaults on *melodramma* and *opera buffa* in
Oberto, Conte di San Bonifacio (1839) and *Un Giorno di Regno* (King
For a Day, 1840). But with his third work he set the new Verdian tone
for raw, aggressive *canto* in a Biblical piece that rocks with power,
Nabucodonosor (Nebuchadnezzar, 1842). If *Oberto* was humdrum
Donizetti and *Un Giorno di Regno* sparkless Rossini, *Nabucco* (as it
is called) unveils a composer whose obsession with good theatre would
remake *melodramma*'s conventions so accidentally—it seems—that by
the time his career is over one suddenly notices that the conventions
have vanished.

Certainly they are all in place in *Nabucco*, with its atmospheric
overture, its scene-setting opening chorus, its aria and (embellished)

cabaletta constructions, its massed finales with their faster, *stretta* conclusions, its adaptational source in the French theatre, and its observance of the singers available for the La Scala premiere in the casting of the characters. But there is more in this set of friezes on power politics in Jerusalem and Babylon: a sense of musicodramatic unity that pulls all the ends into the center, a virile dash, and a patriotism that communicates "Italy!" through the mouths of Nebuchadnezzar's Jewish captives. Some critics have linked Verdi's expansive use of the chorus (which caught on among his colleagues) with the Italian nationist movement called the *Risorgimento* (Resurgence). Italy was a beleaguered agglomeration of segregated kingdoms at the time, some of them under foreign domination, and the unmistakably nationalist exhortation in Verdi's sound and in his librettist's verses contributed much to his early success. Like so many others in this century, he saw opera as a national vehicle for the laments of conquered peoples, an institution in which politics and tragedy blended right in with song, effortless Romanticism.

But like few others Verdi pushed his collaborators fiercely, demanding the utmost in concision and clarity. The custom of transforming the garrulous plays of the era into opera librettos tested the most gifted poet—how to shred all that information into a few pages of poetry?—and in the end Verdi set his share of silly or incoherent texts. Too, such concision sometimes robbed the characters of everything but their most intense moments; Otto Nicolai, who had first dibs on Temistocle Solera's *Nabucco* libretto, rejected it as nothing but "rage, invective, bloodshed, and murder." And that applies even more to Verdi's next opus, *I Lombardi alla Prima Crociata* (The Lombards on the First Crusade, 1843), a story so busy that it needs an explanatory first act that confuses more than it explains. But *melodramma* could not tolerate an original libretto conceived for opera's special requirements: everything was adaptation. *Opera buffa* texts did not necessarily rely on existing properties, but then every *opera buffa* plot already belonged to tradition: the old bachelor takes a wife, the lovesick bumpkin courts the wily soubrette, the boyfriends test their girls.

So Verdi must borrow his subjects—but at least let him borrow from authors of power in idea and image, the true Romance of Schiller, Voltaire, Byron, Hugo, with Shakespeare hanging over them all, the champion Romantic of another time. Hugo's aesthetically revolutionary play *Hernani* provided the basis for Verdi's next opera, *Ernani* (1844), his best so far. Bellini had tackled this play, but interference from the censor discouraged him; Verdi, too, was to outrage authoritarian taboos from Venice to Palermo, with his incessant *libertà* and *patria*, his subversives and assassins. *Ernani* has some of this, but what one most notices is Verdi's spreading confidence in the graceful line—*bel canto*, sort of—to match his native vigor. In the heroine's "Ernani, involami" and the baritone's "Oh, de' verd' anni miei" Verdi reaches that plateau of vocal expansion that Italian opera must have. His lines are short, more like Donizetti's than Bellini's. But this only adds to his strength.

Ernani, Verdi's fifth opera, shows the format that the composer was to use unchanged for the next dozen or so operas, and he seems to have found the same sets of characters fascinating enough to set each clone individually, so that works with similar plot premises don't sound alike. (This is not always true of Donizetti.) Thus we hail a virtual parade of jealous tenors, unloved baritone wooers, frantic sopranos caught between the two, looming basses holding tenors to impetuous tragic oaths, mobs hailing a leader, national anthems, fidgety conspiratorial scuttlebutt, and clumsy but likeable *banda** music for ceremonial or party scenes. Verdi is lean to the point of brusqueness; his dramatic instinct is very, very sure, but at this point in his career he is suspicious of that amplitude and diversion that built grand opera big. Verdi gets on with it, cuts in and cuts out, point, point, point. His momentum has a shape, an allure that enthralls the ear. Too often in *melodramma* the action comes to a dead stop as each separate number sets in, and the recitative must then start up the gears all over again. But when Verdi's numbers end, one leans forward, aroused: what happens next? He is impatient with recit, racing through plot business to crash headlong into character.

Hugo hated Verdi's *Ernani*—all his masterstrokes sheared away in what amounts to a synopsis of the original. But the loss of nifty wordplay notwithstanding, the drama reduced to *melodramma* nicely; what its Romantic extremism loses in verbal detail it gains in musical definition. There is even a touch of *Leitmotiv* (only a year after the premiere of *The Flying Dutchman*) in a grim tune referring to the horn that the tenor presents to the bass, his rival in love, promising to kill himself the next time he hears it. But Verdi was never to employ this device except as dramatic punctuation, such as quoting signature themes for sentimental or ironic purposes. Many years after *Ernani*, when he

---

* The "band" represents another of *melodramma*'s conventions, a wind consort (separate from the pit orchestra) that played marches onstage. The quality varied from theatre to theatre; smart composers writing for a company with a poor *banda* would delete its business at the premiere and add it in at a revival for a more decently outfitted house. Verdi thought the *banda* a "provincialism," but it lent needed color to certain scenes, and he used it as late as 1871, in *Aida*.

finally got his first taste of Wagner, he was partly impressed but never influenced.

Byron and Schiller provisioned Verdi's next two pieces, *I Due Foscari* (The Two Foscaris, 1844) and *Giovanna d'Arco* (Joan of Arc, 1845), though Solera insisted that his *Giovanna* libretto owed nothing or so to Schiller's play *Die Jungfrau von Orleans*. (There were other versions of the life of The Maid; Solera may well have copped bits from each.) *Giovanna d'Arco*, heard in Rome as *Orietta di Lesbo* because Joan had not yet been canonized and was thus technically a heretic, offers one of Verdi's most distinctive heroines; her role contrasts remarkably with the rest of the opera, generally a dull effort with a baritone father who betrays and then rescues her, the loving tenor who is also Charles VII of France, and competing choruses of angels and demons for Joan's visions. This is rather concentrated even for Verdi: there is almost nothing else in the work but these three principals, a bit of back and forth between the French and the invading English, and Charles' coronation at Rheims. Still, as the ongoing Verdi rediscovery drags these pieces out of obscurity, we note that even when melodic inspiration flags, they work with wonderful honesty as theatre. That unity, again—the absolute rightness of tone that centers a work, gives its parts drive and guts that composers of greater refinement could have used far more than a Tune. The most ordinary tune, in Verdi, does not bore: placement and tone disarm all critique in smashing involvement. Thus in *Attila* (1846), the Hun's war parley with a Roman general yields a moment that regularly had Italian audiences screaming glad, when the Roman states his deal: "You will have the world—let me have Italy." The tune is in no way special, yet, drawing on the hope of nationalistic unification as a spur, Verdi makes the line tremendous. One doesn't have to love or admire it. One *undergoes* it as if one were there.

The earliest exceptional Verdi opera was *Macbeth* (1847), and that partly because it is heard today in a revision made for Paris in 1865. Yet even passages from the presumably unpolished Verdi of 1847 amaze with their intent subtleties. Verdi loved his Shakespeare, so rather than fold the play into *melodramma*, Verdi changed *melodramma* to fit the play. This was the *"opera senza amore,"* the opera without a love plot—without even a principal tenor, Macbeth being a baritone—and perhaps the first *melodramma* that tried to duplicate the coloration of the spoken theatre, with its sudden shifts of tone, its word wrenching, its shouts and whispers. Standard vocal talent would not do, as Verdi pointed out when Eugenia Tadolini was suggested for Lady Macbeth: "Tadolini is a fine figure of a woman, and I would like Lady Macbeth to look ugly and malignant. Tadolini sings to perfection, and I would rather that Lady didn't sing at all. Tadolini has a marvelous voice, clear, limpid, and strong, and I would rather that Lady's voice were rough, hollow, stifled."

Macbeth did not totally reinvent *melodramma*: Lady Macbeth leads the company in a drinking song at the banquet in which Macbeth rages at Banquo's ghost, and the witches, who assume great importance in the opera, at times sound a little too carefree to be true. But Verdi's daring here far outweighs his routine. For instance, the two leads take a duet just before the murder of King Duncan. The scene begins with Macbeth's recitative modeled on "Is this a dagger that I see before me?" and Verdi instills the sense of hectic fear in a fresco of song and declamation, refusing to settle into any regular rhythmic structure. The moment is confused and jagged, only temporarily decisive, and on this note Macbeth creeps out to do the job. Lady Macbeth now appears, to give her line about the owl and his good night in response to a lamenting English horn and bassoon—typical venturesome scoring in this opera, which constantly evokes Shakespeare's nightmarish story in "supernatural" orchestration. Now Macbeth returns—"All is finished!"—and the duet proper commences, restless and suffocated. The two must not sing, Verdi directs, except for a few phrases; everything is *sotto voce*, dark, with little coloratura outbursts from Lady Macbeth that presage her coming madness (which Verdi scores later, in the Sleepwalking Scene, for a mood of eerily twitching calm). As the duet proceeds in its contrasting movements, one theme seems to become, so to speak, into another—Lady Macbeth's mad little decorations turn up, for example, at the end of the duet in slightly different form—and the scene ends as the two slip out in a hush. "Come," she says. "Come! Come! Come!" And the astonishing thing is that this marvelous essay in theatrical exactness dates from the 1847 original, and was only touched up for 1865.

Verdi had a terrible time getting the libretto he wanted out of his partner, the agreeable but limited Francesco Maria Piave; the composer's exasperated reproaches of the writer's first, second, or third drafts count among the most insulting dispatches to pass through the operatic mail. At length, Andrea Maffei assisted Piave. Maffei then stepped in solo on *I Masnadieri* (The Robbers, 1847), from a play of Schiller's somewhat miscellaneously rebellious youth, *Die Räuber*. With this work Verdi went international for the first time: a premiere in what may have been the world capital of Italian opera then, London —and with Jenny Lind and Luigi Lablache in the cast. The piece did not go over and remains one of the least favorite among those who fancy Verdi's less renowned works. But he had better luck in Paris later that year when the Opéra mounted a French revision of *I Lombardi* blown up to grand opera proportions and titled *Jérusalem;* if the result is less fun than *I Lombardi*, it is a finer opera.

We should consider Verdi the democrat. Romanticism emphasized the individual in a time when relatively oppressive monarchies were the rule, and Verdi inclined by nature to what the censors looked upon as dangerous subjects. But life was dangerous: while still in Paris, Verdi saw northern Italy involved in a series of battles to oust foreign and local overlordism. Obviously the arts would deal as far as they were permitted to with the question of freedom, and in Verdi opera had its most convinced anti-imperialist. This should color his operas for us today no less than it did for his contempories; to know that a wailing tableau of dispossessed Scots in *Macbeth* spoke to Italians of their own plight, or that when Joan of Arc falls in battle Verdi's people translated her into an Italian martyr, is to understand how vital opera was as art and idea, as communication. It nurtured morale and reminded the despots and monarchists who naturally attended opera of the fist ready to smash them at the first chance. For that alone it was worth the trouble.

This gives us a context in which to perceive Verdi's three operas of 1849–50, *La Battaglia di Legnano, Luisa Miller,* and *Stiffelio,* for all three turn on some aspect of Verdi's nationalist populism. *The Battle of Legnano* is generally written off as a jingoistic piece of little musical value, inspiriting while the fighting is on and hollow thereafter, but in fact this tale of a love triangle viewed against the Italian resistance to Barbarossa is a first-rate theatre piece whose quality of tune may disappoint but whose musical electricity, never. Its chorus work is impressive (as one would expect of a patriotic essay), especially one scene, entirely Verdi's idea, in which envoys from Milan attempt to talk the citizens of Como out of their traditional feud to unite against the invader, to learn to their horror that Como has compacted with the German emperor—who promptly turns up in person.

Luisa Miller is by far the prize of the trio. Here the issue is the corruption of power. The opera's source, a play by Schiller, defines its scope: *Kabale und Liebe* (Intrigue and Love). The love is felt by a middle-class father and daughter and the young aristocrat who loves her, and the intrigue is provided by the nobles and their sycophants—intrigue to gain power by force and retain it through blackmail. Even the young count, whose tenor line falls so gratefully upon the ear, is not above an underhand gambit. Only the father and daughter are honest, and between their simple convictions and the tenor's impetuosity, the opera centers itself beautifully on character, on love and its many versions more than on intrigue. This comes to a head in the last and best of the three acts, almost totally given over to the three principals and the tragic impasse of caste and passion. A fretful, scarcely bearable tenderness binds father and daughter in their duet, bitterness exhausts daughter and lover in their confrontation, and a final trio brings in despair and death, all in Verdi's topmost form. Indeed, throughout the opera striking innovations in technique endow Verdi's customary incisiveness with an elegance that makes one realize how far he had come since *Nabucco* and *Ernani.* Critics point to *Luisa Miller*'s overture for its full-scale but economical developmental construction, using only one theme, in minor- and major-key versions.

Stiffelio is an odd case, an almost totally neglected work of great power. Here the plot premise is truly revolutionary for an Italian opera: a Protestant minister discovers his wife in adultery and, rather than apply the usual remedy—revenge—pardons her. Even before the public had a chance to deal with this, censorship hacked at the text, reducing the strongest lines to vapidity, and though *Stiffelio* was performed, Verdi so resigned himself to the impossibility of hearing the piece as conceived that he later recast it as *Aroldo* (1857), with the same plot in a more secular setting in medieval England. Both versions entice, but it is *Stiffelio* that shows—as did *Macbeth*—that Verdi's reorganization of *melodramma* came out of his valuing good theatre over "good" opera. And the former, Verdi proved, invents the latter, anyway. His operas were at least "good" (i.e., musically sensitive), and when they weren't they were better. His antiheroic bass hero Attila (the most admirable figure in that opera by far, including the saintly prelate* who turns him back from Rome in a few lines of *arioso*), his sometimes acting rather than singing Macbeths, his forgiving cuckold Stiffelio (an unusual tenor role, an old man instead of the usual boiling youth), his now-and-again experimental harmony and orchestration and his subordinating the *cabalette* and *strette* to dramatic exigency, all make for operas excitingly different from those of his contemporaries.

Somewhere around here Verdi's middle period begins, perhaps with *La Battaglia di Legnano* or *Luisa Miller* or perhaps with the next three works, basic to world repertory: *Rigoletto* (1851), *Il Trovatore* (The Troubadour, 1853), and *La Traviata* (The Sinner, 1853). With a French polish acquired in his lengthy stay in Paris that helped dress

---

* Technically "an ancient Roman" at the insistence of the censors; history tells us this was Pope Leo I.

the occasional blunt outburst in subtle colors—and despite an increased vigilance from the censors, ordered not to let anything slip past them that might encourage further outbreaks of the rebel spirit of 1848— Verdi now assumed the leadership in an otherwise floundering art, tackling bold subjects head-on. He taught flexibility of form: unusual content calls for unusual procedure.

Rigoletto, Trovatore, and *Traviata* demonstrate Verdi's progressive dialectic of tradition and innovation. Derived, like almost all of Verdi's operas, from the spoken stage, they are three very different types of opera, the first a psychological melodrama touched with black comedy, the second an old-fashioned chivalric thriller, and the third a contemporary romance. All are rich in Tunes, but each sounds different—especially noteworthy in that the blatant *Trovatore* and the intimate *Traviata* were virtually concurrent projects. Perhaps the stories themselves aren't all that different. All three devolve on a woman caught between two men, though Gilda's vise comprises a protective father and a licentious duke, Leonora contends with a more conventional set of rivals, and Violetta's "other man" is a bit player of little interest, what is known in opera as a *comprimario*. But it isn't stories that matter here; it's the approach, the quality of opinion in vocal line and orchestral exegesis: what Italians term the *tinta*.

Vocally, all three works show Verdi in his element between 1800 and 1900. Wagner's superheroes and -heroines would nail up *bel canto*'s coffin with their triumph of lung power over verbal clarity and decorative finesse, but Wagner was not to be heard in Italy for some time yet, and Verdi was writing for the same singers who dealt with the considerably florid scores of Mercadante, Bellini, and Donizetti—indeed, the first of these was still living and active. Verdi admitted the effectiveness of coloratura, but limited it to the women's parts; the men had little more to negotiate than the ritual *cadenza* ("cadence") at the close of an aria or duet. But while Verdi made use of the tenor in both his lyric and dramatic versions,* he regularly subjected the baritone to murderous exposure at the top of his range, more or less inventing a voice called "the Verdi baritone."

Rigoletto, the hunchback who shows an invidious misanthropy on the job as jester to the Duke of Mantua and a tender heart at home with his daughter, may be the classic Verdi baritone part, though one

---

* The difference in type is considerable. *Rigoletto's* tenors toss off "La donna è mobile" (Woman is fickle) like cavalier larks, but *Trovatore* tenors must belt out the weighty "Di quella pira" (The hideous flame of that pire . . .") as the roc might roar, unto and including a high C that—as so often in these cases— tradition, not Verdi, composed.

of his least typical. Like Attila, he is far from likeable. Yet one cannot hate him, for if the Hun has a warrior's nobility, Rigoletto has vulnerability. *Trovatore*'s and *Traviata*'s baritones, a spurned lover and a well-mannered middle-class father respectively, function along standard lines. But Rigoletto dominates his opera as his model, Triboulet, dominates Rigoletto's source, Hugo's play *Le Roi S'Amuse* (The King Enjoys Himself), considered so sensualistic—though it criticizes unbridled sensuality—that the government closed it after one performance in 1832 and it was not given again in Paris for fifty years. Because Hugo focused on the depredations of the court of François I, it is generally thought that *Le Roi S'Amuse* presents another example of antiroyalist exhortation put down by royalists; actually Hugo's illustrative depravity offended more than his politics. In one notorious scene Hugo had the heroine lock herself in a room to escape the king, who then pulled out a key and chortled hideously as he made his way inside. More offensive yet was Triboulet himself, goading his master on to seductions and rape without conscience. But Triboulet is undone. At the play's center lies a curse laid on him by the father of one of the king's victims, and the rest of the drama amounts to a working out of that curse to an exact irony: Triboulet's own daughter is ravished by the king—and then murdered, inadvertently, in Triboulet's revenge plot.

With his urge toward the immediate, Verdi made the curse the center of *Rigoletto*,* setting it as a *Leitmotiv* that figures prominently in the orchestral prelude and several times in the action proper. *Rigoletto* was originally to be called *La Maledizione* (The Curse); it was also originally forbidden by the military governor of Venetia, though a few minor changes, including a promise to omit the scene with the key, smoothed the way and *Rigoletto* triumphed in Venice.† The Tunes helped—"La donna è mobile" was heard everywhere, much as *Tancredi*'s "Di tanti palpiti" had been thirty-eight years before—but Julien Budden, Verdi's most detailed analyst, emphasizes *Rigoletto*'s Shakespearean juxtaposition of the comic with the serious. The protagonist is a jester, after all, and a nasty one, so his manner at court is different from his person elsewhere, the who that he "really" is. Yet

---

* The name is not a transposition of the French, but a new word derived from *rigolo*, "comic." Ergo, Rigoletto: "Funnyman." The assassin he hires, who betrays him and completes the curse, also bears a generic name, Sparafucile: "Shootagun."
† As with many other of Verdi's operas, censorship problems dogged *Rigoletto* even after the premiere; it came to light in other cities in textual revisions under such titles as *Clara di Perth, Lionello,* and *Viscardello.*

the curse, hurled at the harlequin, smashes the man. Verdi's unity never bound a work more tautly. Budden suggests that the *King Lear* project that Verdi was never to see through might have been sublimated in *Rigoletto*.

The composer's gift for condensation is also typified in these three contrasting masterpieces of "early middle" Verdi. *Rigoletto* features a stunning recitative scene for the protagonist, "Pari siamo" (We are equals), in which he compares himself to the hired murderer Sparafucile and goes on to look at his life in its essences. The number, which never breaks more than momentarily into song, carries the structural importance of an aria yet tells more than a host of arias could. Its succinct, almost free-associative panorama is a triumph of compression for Verdi and his librettist, Piave, bound in its opening and closing by the refrain of the curse theme and taking us from the dank duet with the assassin to the brighter plane of Rigoletto's relasionship with his daughter, who comes running out to meet him as the monologue ends. See how much the authors have contained, as in this sample:

> *O rabbia! Esser difforme!*
> *O rabbia! Esser buffone!*
> *Non dover, non poter altro che ridere!*
> *Il retaggio d'ogni uom m'è tolto—il pianto.*
> (O fury! To be a freak!
> O fury! To be a buffoon!
> No duty, no power but to laugh!
> Denied the heritage of every man—tears.)

Il Trovatore's musicodramatic condensation comes off less well, for here Verdi and Cammarano are reducing a windy Spanish drama inflated with secrets and coincidence. The Spanish liked their theatre spacious, but Italians, Verdi believed, liked brevity; anyway, *he* did. So much happens in *Trovatore* and so fast does it move that it has earned classic status for its incoherance—but this is nonsense. It has one of the clearest librettos of its kind, as any Italian can tell you after one unprepared hearing. But its action depends on something that happened years before, set out in a strophic narrative in the first scene —and this sort of thing never tells well when one must depend on a synopsis. *Trovatore* is incomprehensible to lazy foreigners; to those who speak the language of its performance, it may abound in craziness, but of a highly lucid kind.

It does race along. There was much discussion, during composition, about the final moments, in which the tale's unraveled ends are tied up in a prison scene. The soprano just dead of suicide and the baritone Count di Luna in power, he orders his rival in war and, till a second before, love, to the scaffold. Little does he know that the tenor, the eponymous troubadour, is actually his long-lost brother. The fourth principal, a mezzo-soprano somewhat reminiscent of Viardot's mother role in *Le Prophète*, is the tenor's foster mother, a gypsy torn between an obsession for vengeance on the baritone's family and love for her son, and the opera races to its conclusion so swiftly that she can scarcely wrestle with her ambivalence before the tenor has been beheaded and she, willy-nilly, reveals the baritone's ghastly fratricide:

COUNT:	(Dragging her to a window) See!
AZUCENA:	Heaven!
COUNT:	He is dead.
AZUCENA:	He was your brother!
COUNT:	He! What horror!
AZUCENA:	Oh, Mother, you are avenged!
COUNT:	And I still live!

And the music doesn't dally, either. Many listeners wonder how the tenor, who has been taken away moments before the above excerpt, can be dispatched in so little time. Cammarano had provided a more thorough finale, but Verdi made his own abridgment, citing his *parola scenica* in the use of the one word "avenged"—which, he swore, does it all. As Azucena's mother started the whole thing when the Count's father had her burned at the stake for witchcraft, so Azucena finishes it with her last line.

La Traviata is more like *Rigoletto* in its pacing, tight but unhurried, and intriguing gaps in the story line between each of its three acts tell more than they omit. In Act I we see the protagonist, Violetta Valery, reject one swain's tender love for an open field of pleasure; in Act II we find her and her suitor living together in bliss till the young man's father persuades her to leave him, whereupon the rejected lover rejects her, paying her off for her "services" by throwing a wad of bills at her in public; in Act III we discover Violetta dying of consumption, reconciled with her lover only to die as they plan their future. To pull this distended love affair's three parts together—the aborted flirtation, the true love and separation, and the aborted reconciliation—Verdi opens the work with a dimly ethereal violin plaint that reaches painfully upward and falls back again, ceding to a simple tune of greath warmth that is decorated on its repeat with flighty violin figures. It seems to be a character study of Violetta, the beautiful soul balanced by the coquette. But when Verdi restates the ethereal music in the prelude to the last act, we realize that it is Violetta's death music. The opera becomes a fatalistic study in decline, and the Act I prelude is not so much a characterization as a preview of the action: The Death and Love of Violetta Valery. This view has inspired a number of directors to stage the first two acts as a flashback, with Violetta recalling the events from her deathbed during the opera's prelude and the story picked up again in time present at the start of Act III. It can be very effective.

The delineation of character in these three operas is similarly various. In *Rigoletto*, Piave kept Hugo's excellent models in mind and fed the composer the basis for truly unusual people in the schizoid jester, his infantile but determined daughter, and the hedonist Duke. *Trovatore*'s Cammarano, however, collaborated with Verdi on what was a throwback to Verdi's youth in both text and music. Piave again, in *Traviata*, had a real challenge, for its source, Dumas' play *La Dame aux Camélias*, was a "modern" play, dealing with Parisian society as it was at the time: and in opera only comedy dared be contemporary. To instill the sense of the soirée in two party scenes, Piave and Verdi introduce an assortment of *comprimari*, best friends, "protectors," and hangers-on. There is no cloak-and-dagger in *Traviata*,* none of *Rigoletto*'s foot-padding or *Trovatore*'s battles and oaths. *Traviata* is intimate, liberated, up to date. Unlike the other two, it failed on its first performance, in Venice, and it is a cliché of opera journalism that the contemporary decor was a chief cause. In truth, contemporary decor was such an outlandish notion that the management of La Fenice refused to entertain it, and set the time back to circa 1700. No one has satisfactorily explained the original *Traviata* fiasco—for once, it had nothing to do with a hostile faction—but a year later, in another theatre in the same city, *Traviata* made a hit with a few minor revisions, a superior cast, and, again, an antique look. No matter what period is imposed on it, *Traviata* remains a startlingly modern piece for 1853 simply in terms of its action. And no matter where one begins to time Verdi's middle period, we are now dealing with a bold and innovative creator.

Next, it was back to Paris in person for another shot at the Opéra, this time working with—perhaps "around" is a better word—the honcho librettist himself, Eugène Scribe. Scribe and one of his many collaborators, Charles Duveyrier, palmed off on Verdi a text called *Le Duc*

---

* There is a duel—in response to the money-throwing incident—but this typically occurs during the break between Acts II and III, and one gets the impression that it's to be taken as something of an anachronism.

d'Albe, which Halévy had rejected and Donizetti only partly set. Changing the subject from a failed Flemish uprising against Spanish tyranny to a successful Sicilian uprising against the French, the writers handed Verdi the verses for what was to be his most underrated work, *Les Vêpres Siciliennes* (The Sicilian Vespers, 1855), an exciting expansion of *melodramma* exploiting some of grand opera's conventions—ballet, very *grand duo*, and so on. It was Verdi's first long opera: long-lined, not long-winded. He harassed the sloppy Scribe incessantly for revisions, and seems in the end not to have got them, for the bass role of Jean Procida, the figure who should stand central in the piece—the catalyst for the bloody riot which the entire evening anticipates on an almost moment-to-moment basis—never quite comes alive. He is an agitator, period. The other characters have greater interest—the baritone French governor Guy de Montfort; the soprano Hélène, sworn to Sicilian revenge against the hated French; and the tenor, a Sicilian patriot, Henri, caught between two different kinds of loyalty when the governor turns out to be his father. Verdi had dealt with situations like this in the past, but he never created a woman richer than Hélène, and he wrote her into one of the great tours de force, a barbarian noblewoman who loves as violently as she hates.

An Italian version (several, and in the usual varying titles) was duly made up, but even as *I Vespri Siciliani* this wonderfully inventive work has not enjoyed its due. One reason is a bad press. Idiot critics more comfortable with gossip than analysis have traditionally announced that Verdi, the utter Italian, couldn't deal with an alien language or form. In fact, Verdi's three Paris operas, *Jérusalem, Les Vêpres*, and *Don Carlos*, all prove his capacity and—since the second is better and the third best—growth in French grand opera. We may chuckle at the gaucheness of his *banda* party music, but this has nothing to do with the quality of Verdi's Paris ballet scores (including one for *Il Trovatore*, a big success as *Le Trouvère* in 1857), which observe the received graces. Indeed, Verdi's approach to grand opera should have given a lift to the form, which was tottering by the 1850s. There weren't enough Meyerbeers to hold it steady—and Meyerbeer never had Verdi's focusing, nonstop relevance in the first place. While composing *Les Vêpres*, Verdi attended the opening of Meyerbeer's *opéra comique L'Étoile du Nord* and was shocked at the public's raptures for a work that to him made no sense. "And this same public," he wrote, "even after twenty-five or thirty years, hasn't even managed to understand *Guillaume Tell*, so it's performed in a stunted, mutilated version . . . in a *mise-en-scène* unworthy of it. And this is the first theatre in the world."

By this time Verdi had logged so much time playing the practical against the ideal in *melodramma* that he was working in a kind of magic: every piece is superb, different, more advanced in technique, popular, and each sings in its own peculiar *tinta*. He had grandmaster clout now, composing at a slower rate and demanding The Works from the companies he wrote for. Only seven operas remain, and the single one of them that may have been less than superb—*Simon Boccanegra* (1857)—was put to rights twenty-four years later in a revision. The problem here originates with the source, a play by the same Antonio García Gutiérrez whose *El Trovador* supplied the chaotic goings on in *Il Trovatore*. Gutiérrez' *Simón Bocanegra* is if anything even less well centered. It has the same two men-one woman, aristocrats-versus-commoners, and stolen-baby themes, plus the confusing two-generation time span. But while *Trovatore* wraps a series of love trysts and battles in a revenge plot, *Boccanegra* subsumes its "operatic" matter in a dour yet strangely hopeful look at the social progress of modern man. Boccanegra is a pirate who becomes doge of fourteenth-century Genoa, torn as all Italian cities were by the Guelph-Ghibelline feuds, and while there is a love story (involving Boccanegra's daughter and his worst political enemy), the opera's general effect overwhelmingly tends to the political—thus its reputation as a piece filled with dark male voices complaining and conspiring. "It's sad," Verdi admitted. "It's sad because it has to be, but it's gripping." So much so that despite himself he overhauled it completely at a time when he had all but retired, ravishing the black and brutal score with the autumnal surpassing of a quarter-century's wisdom. *Macbeth* grew up in revision; *Simon Boccanegra* was reincarnated, aided particularly by Arrigo Boito's textual emendations. In a scene original with the second version, Boito gave Verdi what must count as the essential Verdian politics when Boccanegra, crying "Fratricides!," throws himself between the warring factions in a climactic solo, "Plebe! Patrizi!" (Plebes! Patricians! People of a ferocious history!). The Genoese are heirs of hatred and think only of shattering brotherhood in blood. Boccanegra weeps for them, for the beauty of life that they ignore, mounting from a dry *declamato* to the beginning of a full-scale ensemble passage:

> *E vo gridando: pace!*
> *E vo gridando: amor!*
> (And I cry: peace!
> And I cry: love!)

One constant held true the length of Verdi's career, the challenge of finding suitable subjects, and one subject eternally fascinated him, *King Lear*. For a while, in the mid-1850s, it looked as if *Il Re Lear* might come about after all for San Carlo in Naples, with a baritone Lear, a contralto Fool (despite Verdi's distaste for trouser parts), and a Gilda-like Cordelia. The project got as far as a finished libretto (by Antonio Somma), but, as before and after, Verdi held back, and instead he set a text adapted from Scribe's for Auber's *Gustave III*.* A simple love triangle interlaced with assassination, the story was set in Sweden, borrowing history for the culminating regicide at a masked ball but filling in otherwise with operatic attitudes. Paris in 1833, when *Gustave III* premiered, tolerated what Italian censors usually banned, and eventually a compromise was reached by which the action was moved from Sweden to late-seventeenth-century Boston. It doesn't quite work, though Verdi came to prefer the New World scene to the original.

As *Un Ballo in Maschera* (1859), the piece occupies a comfortable niche in the repertory somewhere between *Rigoletto* and *Ernani* in popularity. As always in his maturity, Verdi tries something new—but this is exactly why the Bostonian location doesn't sit well. The novelty obtains in the character of the lead tenor—Riccardo, the King's governor of Boston—an elegant, carefree blade like the Duke in *Rigoletto*, but admirable also for a generous nature. Carefree? Riccardo is reckless. Told that some of his subjects are planning to kill him, he gets impatient, waves it away; his idea of statesmanship is a late-night drop-in at the hut of a black witch, everyone in costume. Showing up in fisherman's clothes, he sings a sensuous barcarolle. And when the witch backs up the report of the potential assassination by predicting that a friend will kill him, he jokes it away—though he is in fact in love with his best friend's wife. Everyone else onstage gets uneasy, but Riccardo laughs it off.† Verdi even doubles the character's frivolous side with the use of an elfin page, Oscar—a trouser role possibly modeled on the page in *Les Huguenots*—who adds to the work's piquancy and supplies a pretty soprano line in ensembles. Now all this gaming is musically enticing, but it feels preposterous in colonial

---

* The plot also saw service under Mercadante and Cammarano as *Il Reggente* (The Ruler) in 1843.
† Some tenor, no one knows precisely who—sprinkled giggles between the notes in this number, "È scherzo od è follia" (It's a joke or folly), founding another of opera's unwritten traditions and making the aria a Laughing Song. Who started it? Some say Alessandro Bonci; some say Caruso. If done well, it adds to Riccardo's presence as a madcap, but if Verdi had wanted giggles he would have written giggles.

Boston, where they were hanging witches, not disporting in their lairs. Riccardo, as character, is a great achievement, but everything about him and his court would have been anathema in Boston. On the other hand, no one complains about the incongruously Latinate slant in the many late *bel canto* Scott adaptations; why hold Verdi responsible for a realism of setting that his predecessors would have thought irrelevant? There's an answer: Verdi has become so sophisticated in his manipulation of form to the demands of content that his work must be judged by his own high standards, not by the routines of his era.

His next work, *La Forza del Destino* (The Force of Destiny, 1862), has the distinction of being Verdi's least unified piece; the light and dark that face off so neatly in *Un Ballo in Maschera* here seem to be running in opposite directions, as if two operas were going on at once in alternate acts. Or so the complaint goes. Many find *Forza's* riches irritatingly dense and scream for cuts, more cuts, whole scenes dropped. But Verdi is seeking a Shakespearean density in a *melodramma* with tons of grand-opera-style diversions. Surely, then, this is a Paris opera? No, a Russian commission—the tsarist capital still preferred Italians in Italian opera to any version of a local product (including Glinka and Dargomizhsky) and Verdi, grousing all the way, journeyed to Petersburg himself to see it through. In a way, the trip took seven years, for not till Verdi revised the opera for La Scala in 1869, ending the boycott of that house that he had maintained since *Giovanna d'Arco* in 1845, did *La Forza* play to his satisfaction.

The revision changes the original only slightly—a big overture in place of a little prelude, shifts in scene order, an understated finale to replace a violent one. Still, the rearrangement does not appease those who miss the old Verdi of the tight, fleet *melodramma* of three of four principals and a healthy but not obtrusive chorus. Here the three principals (two ill-fated lovers and the woman's brother who wants to kill them both) contend with numerous secondary roles and a wildly active chorus of real people—peasants, soldiers, buoyant camp followers, whining raw recruits, dull pilgrims, cranky charity cases having a row in a soup line. For the old Verdi is gone: the new Verdi has seen grand opera. It's not spectacle that he wants, but fullness. With its sprawling, coincidental plot (a Spanish source again), constant interplay of the private and the public, and blending of *buffo* elements into a romance, *La Forza* might have been written for Paris—and it nearly underwent another revision for the Opéra, until an entirely new work was decided on, the stupendous *Don Carlos* (1867).

There can't have been a less suitable figure in all history for the romantic hero treatment than Carlos II of Spain. Sickly, stupid, sadistic, and mad from the fanatic Hapsburg interbreeding, he was rumored to be impotent, though on the other hand he was given to molesting women in the streets as well as the palace backstairs. Nor was he anything to look at. But some of this was unknown and some forgiven when Friedrich Schiller did the research for his play *Don Carlos*, fired by the revolutionary spirit of the Flemish people (ruled at the time as a Spanish province), with which Carlos seems to have had some vague connection. Schiller's great play, a study in religious and state tyranny peopled by real-life sixteenth-century Spanish figures highly romanticized, provided the basis for Verdi's third Paris opera, the libretto begun by Joseph Méry and finished by Camille du Locle. In Schiller and Verdi, handsome, idealistic prince Carlos loves the French princess Elisabeth de Valois—but she is married to his father, Philip II. Moreover, Carlos has a proud and dangerous would-be lover in Eboli, one of the Queen's ladies. Meanwhile, Carlos' stalwart friend Rodrigo attracts the king's admiration and protection, though both he and the prince have secretly allied themselves with the Flemish. Thus what might ordinarily have served as a love triangle actually opposes love and power (broadly, worldly vanity) to humanist republicanism (in the "Flemish Question"), and the text maintains this tension, using as its two spokesmen two second bass parts, the Grand Inquisitor and an anonymous Friar who turns out to be, lo, the opera's surprise ending. Obviously the Inquisitor sits with worldly vanity; he grasps for power under the lie of godly transcendence, and Verdi demanded that he be played as horribly ancient and blind: obsolete, closed to human truth. The Friar, however, stands for the renunciation of power. He first appears during a funeral service for Carlos I, who as Holy Roman Emperor Charles V ruled an epoch of enormous upheaval and finally retired to a cloister (and turned up as the baritone lead in *Ernani*). Now, a chorus of monks intones, he is "nothing but silent dust." The Friar draws the lesson: he hoped to rule the world, and forgot God. But heavenly morality, the free hope of all men, must conquer; and while the Spanish Church-state sifts for and crushes heresy, the hero finds his truth not in the love plot but in political activism. In the final scene, he meets with Elizabeth not to dally with her but to bid a last farewell and make common cause with the Flemish.

Don Carlos stands as a consummation of middle-period Verdi, bringing his characteristic qualities to a new high of development. There is, first of all, the composer's democratic beliefs. Second, there is his canny manipulation of operatic convention for thematic and personal depth. Eboli's colorful genre piece, the Veil Song, is not just a vocal diversion: it displays her fire and vivacity, plus supplying some useful Moorish hues for the canvas. Or take the auto-da-fé scene, a Meyerbeerean ceremonial here employed as a ghoulish exposure of ecclesiastical and statist totalism. Third, there is the motivic organization, Verdi's special unity of sound by which all the opera's parts accord with a this-time-only style. Fourth, there is Verdi's evolution of the set piece to conform to situation rather than the exigencies of the singer's opera. Big Tunes there are in plenty, and endless opportunity for the gifted voice; but the drama comes first, and we find all the old structures that served Bellini and Donizetti so well refined beyond recognition. Thus for her big aria in the last scene, "Toi qui sus le néant" (You who understood the vanity of earthly life . . .), addressed to the tomb of Carlos I, Elisabeth restates the work's ideological premise in a passage of outright song, shifts to recit in conveying plot information, reminisces on earlier happiness to episodic reprises of themes heard earlier, then restates her song to a more urgent accompaniment.

The opera's ending has always troubled people. Surprising Carlos and the Queen at their farewell, the King and the Inquisitor put the pair under arrest, when suddenly the Friar materializes in crown and royal mantle. Everyone recognizes him as Carlos I, and draws back in terror as he pulls the bewildered Prince into the sanctuary of the cloister while the curtain falls. The public, too, is bewildered. *Is* it Charles V, presumed dead till this moment, or just a friar in Charles' robes? Even Verdi, it appears, wasn't too sure what his librettists were driving at, and stage directors have tried alternative solutions to clear up the ambiguity. Actually, the ending is right as written. It may look a little flaky, but in music and text it reprises the Friar's message about God and his eternal sphere outlasting mortal vanity. When the opera began, Carlos was struggling between the two; when it ends, he has learned to comprehend God. The Friar's intervention acts as an ideological apotheosis, a mystical charade to cap the work's theme: the renunciation of material power.

These final few moments are the least of *Don Carlos'* problems, anyway, as there is a confusion of edition that has yet to be sorted out. There are many *Don Carlos*es: the original, a gigantic French grand opera in five acts (which has never been performed complete because of its length); a shortened version of the same (which was heard at the premiere in 1867); a vastly compact and recomposed reduction in Italian with the first, so-called Fontainebleau, act shorn off, dating from a La Scala production in 1884; a compromise version in which the Fontainebleau act of 1867 is joined to the rest of the piece in its 1884 revision; and possible other compromises that pick from Verdi's

French and Italian settings of individual scenes. Even the smallest *Don Carlos* is still considerably longer than most of Verdi's operas, but compressing it does it a disservice: it was conceived to go grand and feels right only when it is let do so. The famous and for some unknown reason consistently overrated production that inaugurated Rudolf Bing's tenure at the Met attempted to scale the work down in thrift-shop decor and dowdy post-card poses; for a more authentic (if Italian) *Don Carlos* one had to apply to the equally famous and rightly celebrated Covent Garden staging of 1958, designed and produced by Luchino Visconti for breadth.* When the Met was hauling out its putrid *Don Carlos* to cast it with just about anyone available, Covent Garden upheld a high standard, though buffs look back fondly on the first-night cast as unstoppably together: Gré Brouwenstijn as Élisabeth, Fedora Barbieri as Eboli, Jon Vickers as Carlo, Tito Gobbi as Rodrigo, Boris Christoff as Philip, Marco Stefanoni as the Inquisitor, Joseph Rouleau as the Friar, and Ava June as the Heavenly Voice, with Carlo Maria Giulini conducting.

Verdi's opera tally had reached twenty-four, and he was growing less and less fiery about his calling. Du Locle pestered him from Paris with possibilities, but Verdi kept declining, even citing the confining conventions of grand opera—which he himself had so smoothly defeated in *Don Carlos*—as deleterious to his style. "I believe in inspiration," he wrote Du Locle, while the French "believe in construction." Yet Verdi remained *the* maestro, literally unrivaled. A sense of his contemporaries' vapidity may be gleaned by examining the list of contributors to a Requiem Mass projected in 1868 to honor the recently deceased Rossini, each movement to be composed by a different man. Besides Verdi, the names are ghosts of no acquaintance (the most famous of them are Enrico Petrella and Federico Ricci, which must set a new low in fame): Verdi *was* Italian opera.

How could he think of retiring? He ceased to after seeing Du Locle's treatment of a story by the Egyptologist Auguste Mariette, a saga of love and war in the days of the Pharaohs. This, obviously, was to be *Aida*,† commissioned on exorbitant terms as part of the Egyptian

---

* One admits that Visconti's auto-da-fé looks awfully threadbare for grand opera, but the rest of the sets are really smashing, and the production was still shipshape more than twenty years later. Covent Garden can be slow to replace productions; it held on to its first *Bohème* decor for something like sixty years.
† Charles Osbourne reveals some rather close parallels between the *Aida* libretto and two earlier works, Racine's play *Bajazet* and especially one of Metastasio's less well known texts, *Nitteti*, first set in 1756 by Niccolò Conforti. Presumably Du Locle referred to his predecessors in the ancient manner while adapting Mariette's tale.

Khedive's burst of internationalism attendant on the opening of the Suez Canal. (Contrary to legend, *Aida* missed the opening of both the canal and the Khedive's new opera house, following both events by two years.) Du Locle wrote the words, but Verdi decided to set them in Italian translation, running his usual roughshod over the translator, Antonio Ghislanzoni, and dashing *Aida* off in four months, incidentally taking in his (and Italy's) first taste of live, complete Wagner in a *Lohengrin* at Bologna.

Aida (1871) promptly drew charges of "Wagnerism!" from a number of critics, but as Charles Osbourne sagely points out, "Verdi was his own Wagner." He was too alert himself to the lure of renewal to need advice from others, and *Aida* adheres to the late-middle Verdi format of swift-moving *melodramma* expanded—sensibly, pointedly—to grand opera proportions. Ballet and ceremonial play an important role here, for though at base *Aida* tells an old tale of triangular love, it shivers at the hugeness of history, and political rather than romantic intrigue prompts the tragic dénouement. In some ways it is a throw-back; but most of Aida's part constitutes a step forward in subtlety, and the use of a pseudo-Egyptian *tinta* opens up a luxurious chamber in Verdi's house of melody. "That Meyerbeero-Wagneroid bore!" Vincent D'Indy called it, though his own *Fervaal* (1897) owes a great deal to *Parsifal* and, for that matter, could have used some Meyerbeerean revving up while he was making *hommages*. Anyway, not every spectacular opera is Meyerbeerean; Meyerbeer would never have composed so tight a pageant as the gathering of the King and his guard, the high priest and his followers, and the court to hear a messenger's report on the Ethiopian war. Aida, her lover Radamès, and her rival Amneris have just concluded a raging trio; quite suddenly, with Verdian directness and to a churning accompaniment, the stage fills with people, the King speaks briefly, the Messenger delivers his bad news concisely, Radamès is named to head the defensive campaign against the Ethiopians, and a majestic chorus with solo interjections closes the event, capped by Amneris, the Egyptian princess, who cries to Radamès, "Ritorna vincitor!" (Return a conqueror!). The crowd echoes her cry, and leaves. Then, for a brilliant stroke of theatre, Aida alone launches an aria with those same words, ironically twisted—for she, a slave among Egyptians, is in reality the Ethiopian princess, and her lover can only return as the conqueror of her people. Nothing in Meyerbeer is so tautly defined; but D'Indy's insult shows how large a shadow the king of grand opera cast. Like Wagner's style, Meyerbeer's counts as one of the obsessions of the century.

In the end, Verdi did for his native form what Rossini had done—

infused it with the solid theatre thinking of the French forms. But where Rossini's internationalism also reached out to Italianize French singing, Verdi led the movement of the era *away* from *bel canto*. Wagner, too, sought a cleaner line, but his clung too tenaciously to the symphonic "accompaniment"; few composers wanted their characters to sound like Wagner's.

After *Aida*, it looked like the end for Verdi. He superintended a few revivals and produced the Requiem Mass in memory of Alessandro Manzoni, a *Risorgimento* hero and author of the classic Italian novel, *I Promessi Sposi* (The Fiancés). But Verdi resisted all pleas for another opera. His work had been on the boards for over thirty years: where was the younger generation? Filippo Marchetti typifies the second rank with his *Ruy Blas* (1869), based on a provocative subject that Verdi himself had often considered; but Marchetti's was the sort of piece that peaks in its *grand duo*—stirring, but twice-told. A distinctive but erratic talent lodged in Amilcare Ponchielli, who got the honor of composing the operatic adaptation of *I Promessi Sposi* (1856). Though *Il Figluolo Prodigo* (The Prodigal Son, 1880) is said to be his masterpiece, his only popular entry was *La Gioconda* (The Merry Girl, 1876), a sappy and chaotic cloak-and-dagger romance set in—all over, in fact—Venice. Big-Tuned arias and ensembles, the glitter potential in a scene plot that moves from the courtyard of the Ducal Palace out into the lagoon back into town to the Ca D'Oro (two views) and finishes on the Giudecca, and the charm of the Dance of the Hours ballet have forgiven *La Gioconda* its ludicrously involved story line. *La Forza*, too, depends on the crucially fortuitous meetings of its principals, but there coincidence is the point, the coincidence of macabre destiny that can't be evaded. In *La Gioconda* coincidence is a librettist's convenience. All the more surprising, then, that the culprit, Tobia Gorrio, was the anagrammatic pseudonym of Arrigo Boito, librettist for Verdi's last two operas, by common consent the two stand-out texts in Italian opera in that time. *La Gioconda*'s heroine is a street singer (with a blind mother) who loves a pirate (in vain) and is loved by a police spy (in vain) and who turns up, act after act, in the most unlikely places but at *just* the right moment to pull off a strategic stunt. When, in the final act, she is discovered sitting disconsolately in the ruined palace where she makes her home, one is amazed to learn that such a mobile woman has a home at all.

Boito was a composer as well. A founding member of the flamboyant avant garde group known as the Scapigliatura (roughly, "The Mess"), he dedicated himself to artistic revolution, and tackled nothing less than Goethe's *Faust* in *Mefistofele*. Musically and textually, the

Les Vêpres Siciliennes, Act III. Note how little the massed finale had changed from Rossini's day: the principals still stand apart downstage singing separate lines while the chorus comments more generally. Here at La Scala, 1970 (with Renata Scotto, Gianni Raimondi, Piero Cappucilli, and Ruggero Raimondi under Gianandrea Gavazzeni), Giorgio de Lullo updated the action to the 1800s; Pier Luigi Pizzi's designs, at least, impressed—"once accepted," wrote Peter Hoffer in *Opera* magazine, "that everybody looked like a cross between Ibsen and Turgenev." *(E. A. Teatro alla Scala)*

Boito's *Mefistofele*, designed by Nicola Benois for La Scala. *(E. A. Teatro alla Scala)*

piece is imposingly experimental. Its title role, the devil, is a sort of *buffo* villain; its love duet finds the heroine asking Faust if he believes in religion; it juxtaposes the crudest high spirits with the most incantatory ecstasy; its prologue, set in heaven, pits soaring, giddy, pious, and bumptious passages against each other, bound by titanic brass flourishes both onstage and in the pit; and it is the first of the *Faust* operas really to investigate the Romantic's primal quest for cosmological-existential meaning. The original *Mefistofele*, in 1868, provoked one of La Scala's more famous first-night riots; a shortened version with added lyrical passages in 1875 reclaimed it, and it has since hovered on the outskirts of the active repertory, given an extra boost in America because of the popular New York City Opera production featuring Norman Treigle's oleaginous Mephistopheles.

Those close to Verdi hoped that the volatile but extremely gifted Boito might lure him out of retirement with a choice libretto. Verdi's publisher, Giulio Ricordi, and the composer and conductor Franco Faccio, a former *scapigliato*, served as agents. To the point was the excellent text Boito had run up for Faccio's *Amleto* (1865), an adaptation of *Hamlet* that preserves the great lines yet holds to a fluidly operatic shape. As an earnest of good faith, Boito undertook the thankless job of revising the *Simon Boccanegra* libretto; meanwhile the subject for the new Verdi-Boito opera had already been chosen: *Othello*.

This is symbolic: Verdi's *Otello* superseded Rossini's version just as Verdi's *melodramma* replaced Rossini's. The later man's vocal writing, his orchestra, his tempo, and his view of love-and-duty had become the standard approach. Not surprisingly, the new *Otello* (1887) was hailed as the paradigm of modern *opera seria*, and the following Verdi-Boito collaboration, *Falstaff* (1893), Verdi's farewell to art, was likewise taken as the exemplary modern *opera buffa*. When *Otello* debuted at La Scala, there had not been a new Verdi opera for sixteen years—and the reception was explosively positive. Incredibly, the man had not run out of melody; he seemed rather to have sharpened his sense of Tune so that each new line sounded like a distillation of all Verdi, a replenished absolute of causes and effects. Still his own Wagner, he improved his own terrain only, the things *he* admired—Shakespearean poetry, character as fate, love and power and nation and despair. In a time when all Europe was buying the *Leitmotiv* in quantity, Verdi used it (as he had always done) sparingly, for reminiscent irony, in the music associated with the kiss shared by Otello and Desdemona in bliss, which returns in the same form at the close of the tragedy to accompany Boito's equivalent for "I kiss'd thee ere I kill'ed thee; no way but this, killing myself, to die upon a kiss."

For his part, Boito did what almost no librettist before him had done in this age of play adaptations. He conveyed the full value of the original in the strait reincarnation of opera, so that Shakespeare loses none of his pungency, beauty, variety. In *Otello*, latest in a two-hundred-year parade of operas on distressed nobles, he provided the necessary solos, duets, a "handkerchief" trio and quartet, full-scale ensembles for soloists and chorus. In *Falstaff*, he referred to *buffa*'s flexibility in avoiding any extended "scene." The thing zips along, characters racing in, speaking their business, and racing out. It's one of the few Italian operas that don't excerpt well on an LP highlights disc—where to snip? There are no beginnings and ends: three acts, two scenes per act, each first scene on Falstaff's turf at the Garter Inn and each second on less defensible territory where the merry wives of Windsor and their family and friends outwit Sir John. The opera contains barely two hours of music, but Verdi darts from tune to tune, filling the ear with more than it can take at a hearing. Furthermore, Boito's text stands among the most literate, and calls for an intellectual engagement of great concentration. Most Italian operas of this century get along on a severely limited vocabulary, but Boito knows all the synonyms, and the mind reels.

What a finale! It's not unusual for a composer to improve with time and finish with a masterpiece, but there is something awesome in the close-fisted exactness with which Verdi hunted his aesthetic ideals, each opera's relevance to the next, as if they were clues in a thriller. Verdi never had to invent a nationalist style, or design an innovative theatre, or teach an old public new tricks; he and his audience knew each other virtually from the start. Except for his Paris campaigns, he never compromised *melodramma;* and even those Paris jaunts proved beneficial to his renovation of form. His themes—all variations on the urge to loving fraternity—stayed constant throughout his life, and despite his writing only two comedies (one at the start and one at the very end), it seems fitting that he draw the curtain on a huge fugue on the premise, "Tutto nel mondo è burla; l'uom è nato burlone" (All the world's a joke; man is born buffoon). *Falstaff* launches it, to the driest accompaniment, and bit by bit the other principals and the choral and orchestral divisions enter till the stage is a teeming bin of chuckles in radiant C Major.

CHAPTER TWELVE

Musical Comedy

*I said to myself that the Opéra-
Comique was no longer the
home of comic opera, and that
the idea of really gay, cheerful,
witty music . . . was gradually
being forgotten. The Composers
who wrote for the Opéra-Comique wrote little grand operas.* —JACQUES OFFENBACH

BACK IN THE EIGHTEENTH CENTURY, WHEN THEY WERE NEW, BALLAD
opera, *Singspiel*, and *opéra comique* served as popular musical theatre.
Originally as cynical and sentimental as real people are, these forms
gradually lost their naturalism and became adjuncts of the opera world:
musical and, partly, ideal. Ballad opera vanished altogether, while *opéra
comique* and *Singspiel*, typified in Auber and Lortzing, lost the satire
that made them such a menace in the good old days.

So musical comedy had to found itself all over again. In France,
the maximum leader was Jacques Offenbach, a German emigrant who
inaugurated his career as cellist in the Opéra-Comique orchestra in the
1830s. There he had a chance to assess the general run of what had
survived of Favart's irreverent and dainty form, and Offenbach was not
amused. The *genre primitif et gai* had grown smug. Determined to
strike out on his own, he ran into the brick wall of genre segregation
that assigned patients to theatres by the type of show they put on.
Naples had once had its comic theatres on one hand and serious court
theatre on the other (the San Carlo) and Venice in Rossini's youth
apportioned *seria* to the Fenice, *buffa* to the San Benedetto, and bills
of *intermezzi* to the San Moisè. Similarly, non-Italian cities had their
Italian theatres and secondary stages for local artwork. This practice

229

disintegrated during the 1800s*—*La Traviata*, for example, premiered at the Fenice and returned a year later to the San Benedetto, though it is hardly a comic piece.

But the Paris of Offenbach's youth preserved the distinctions, and the only venue open to him on a regular basis was a tiny, out-of-the-way house licensed for one-act pieces using no more than three characters. (This is history happening all over again, as the infant *opéra comique* of the fairgrounds was harassed by similar regulations.) Renaming his theatre the Bouffes-Parisiens, Offenbach opened in 1855 with a triple bill of little gems, and luck was with him: his venture coincided with the Universal Exhibition, set up nearby, and Offenbach did a brisk walk-in business. Later that year he moved his operation to a bigger theatre more centrally located, and arranged for a tacit understanding with the government that enabled him to juke the regulations. All he needed now was a smash.

Orphée aux Enfers (Orpheus in the Underworld, 1858) put him over, at the same time positing the model for reinvented musical comedy. *Orphée* was a satiric, breezy, and informal, a full-length spoof of Classical legend with full cast and chorus and constant digs at the contemporary scene, theatrical *Lebensraum* for the *gai primitif*. There is parodic allusion: a quotation of "J'ai perdu mon Euridice" from Gluck's *Orphée*. Wicked revisionism: Orpheus and Euridice are unfaithful to each other, and the musician must be pressured (by Public Opinion, a pushy soprano *en travesti*) to retrieve her from Hades. Musical burlesque: to punish his spouse, Orpheus plays her his "latest concerto" while she pleads for mercy.

A huge hit partly for its impiety and partly on the publicity generated by outraged pedants, *Orpheus in the Underworld* founded a new line in musical theatre, for Offenbach's inventive musicality was as much a factor as the comedy. This was something new. No ballad opera, no burlesque could boast such resourcefulness in its score—and no *opéra comique* or *Singspiel* was this playful. Thus in *Orphée*, Diana hectors Zeus:

> *Pour seduire Alcmène la fière,*
> *Tu pris les traits de son mari!*
> *Je sais bien des femmes sur terre*
> *Pour qui ça n'eût pas réussi!*

---

* The apotheosis of the one-theatre, one-genre rule may be seen in the erection of the Bayreuth Festspielhaus for the sole purpose of presenting Wagnerian music drama.

(To seduce the proud Alcmena,
You appeared in her husband's form!
I know plenty of mortal women
On whom that trick would not have worked!)

A like tone informed Offenbach's many succeeding works, whether classical, historical, or literary spoof, up-to-date satire or exotic romance. The material is savvy, replete with zesty anachronisms, pastiche pieces such as military or yodeling numbers, parody references to Rossini, Meyerbeer, and such, and lots of opportunities for those rare theatre talents versed in acting as well as singing. Given a performer with some crazy specialty, Offenbach would fit him in somehow, and he was especially fortunate in obtaining the assistance of leading lady Hortense Schneider, a comely mezzo-soprano comedienne, for several of his outings. Collaborating most often with the team of Henri Meilhac and Ludovic Halévy, Offenbach tackled medieval chronicle in *Geneviève de Brabant* (1859)—complete with baritone turn for Charles Martel—examined events leading up to the Trojan War in *La Belle Hélène* (1864), tamed the Bluebeard legend in *Barbe-Bleue* (1866), ridiculed militarism in *La Grande Duchesse de Gérolstein* (1867), and even spoofed Defoe in *Robinson Crusoé* (1867). So light was his touch, and so winning, that faced with a commission to write for a company stronger in acting than singing and a libretto that goes absolutely nowhere for four acts, he wrote a dream of a score devoted to the sensual mystique of the demimonde in *La Vie Parisienne* (Parisian Life, 1866), set, for once, in real-life places: a train station (where foreigners arrive, wild-eyed in "the modern Babylon"); a young dandy's lodgings (where an assortment of riffraff impersonate people of station and a pert glove seller, disguised as a colonel's widow, sums up the anarchic character of the *gai primitif* by singing, for no reason at all, an up-tempo salute to her late husband, "Es-tu content, mon colonel?" with a "Ra plan plan" refrain); a town house (where yet another party is thrown); and a restaurant salon (where the cast straggles in to assess the rhythm of Parisian life: "Et pif et pif et pif et pouf!").

Hailed as "the Mozart of the Boulevards," Offenbach began to upgrade his level of composition. He hoped to leave something of permanent artistic interest behind him, fearing that his timely comedies might not outlast their era.* He labored to make *Les Brigands* (1869)

---

* His comedies are not only alive and well today, they are still being written. To honor the American Bicentennial, Don White and Lorraine Thomas concocted a libretto on a great moment in American history, set it to excerpts from Offenbach's less well known pieces, and gave the world yet another Offenbachian

musically imposing (the satire is not stinted, balancing high financiers with a band of highwaymen), and prepared an aggrandized revision of *Orphée aux Enfers* in 1874 for a spectacular production with as much ballet as a grand opera. But beefing up his form was not the answer. He must try something completely different: *The Tales of Hoffmann* (1881).

This bizarre and brilliant work, poised halfway between opera and musical comedy, has suffered from a spurious edition concocted by the producers of its first productions, for the composer died before he could see his masterpiece to the stage. It is unlike anything he had done before, a black comedy spun out of the Romantic catalogue: the *Doppelganger*, the automaton, evil geniuses, witchcraft, Venetian poison, *Don Giovanni*, and grotesque Doctor Miracle sawing on a violin while a frail heroine sings herself to death—all earnestly displayed without a trace of lampoon. Hoffmann, of course, is E.T.A. Hoffmann, the Romantic extraordinary whose tales fed the original play, by Jules Barbier and Michel Carré, that provided Offenbach's text. One thing *Les Contes d'Hoffmann* shares with Offenbach's earlier pieces: spoken dialogue. But this was turned into recitative after Offenbach's death. Scenes were switched or rewritten, the story changed, the structure hashed, cuts imposed. Until very recently, *Hoffmann* lived a lie as an "opera" sung by vocalists who lack the fundamental theatricalism that musical comedy absolutely demands. In *Les Contes d'Hoffmann* no less than in *La Grande Duchesse de Gérolstein* or *La Vie Parisienne*, panache and illusion are everything, though certainly no quasisinger could fake his way through *Hoffmann* as he might the other two.

Hoffmann is an expansive piece. A prologue and an epilogue frame three tales, each an aborted love: for a mechanical doll, a sickly, amateur artiste, and a faithless courtesan. In the frame, set in a tavern, Hoffmann leads up to his tales and at last envisions his muse, who advises him to renounce love for his poet's art. Accordingly he rejects his fourth amour, the opera singer la Stella, who leaves the tavern on the arm of Hoffmann's enemy. All four women are one, four enemies one—and the casting for the premiere founded a tradition by which, whenever possible, the same soprano sings all four female leads and the same baritone all four "evil genius" parts. (There are also four comic roles customarily assigned, in France, to a music-hall buffoon who can't

---

satire, *Christopher Columbus* (1976). It's a bit on the frumpy side, but Offenbach would have appreciated the atmosphere: Act III discloses the hero queasily hanging over the side of the *Santa Maria*, and when Indians attack in Act IV, one girl with a gloat in her eye asks hopefully, "What do you think they'll do to us?"

sing a note.)* In fact, Offenbach wrote four very different parts for Hoffmann's loves. The robot sings high coloratura, the sickly girl a slightly fuller lyric soprano, the courtesan a darker line, and la Stella's part has been shredded into nothing for so long that most operagoers think of her as a walk-on for one of the more flavorful house ballerinas. The bass-baritone villains' roles, too, call for different sorts of voices. Still, playing one woman and one villain (plus the one comic) against Hoffmann gives the show a Romantic leverage in the visual metaphor of the poet eternally pursuing a sensual ideal, eternally defeated by his dark shadow. It also makes it easier to understand why Hoffmann finally turns away from love: la Stella is merely the latest installment in his awkward serial.†

Les Contes d'Hoffmann is a remarkably innovative work, one of the few of its day to combine the most flamboyant Romanticism with outrageous comedy—a comeback for the grotesque in opera. In its original version particularly (completely set down in piano score but not entirely orchestrated; Ernest Guiraud finished the scoring), *Hoffmann* plays romance for horror and, sometimes, horror for comedy. The Venetian episode finds Hoffmann's current flame, the courtesan Giulietta, in the thrall of the sorceror Dapertutto, who uses her to steal Hoffmann's reflection. We see Hoffmann kill his rival Schlémil (note the absurd name, rendered in English as schlemiel) to eerily lyrical music, and later, at the comic's urging, Giulietta inadvertently takes poison to the soothing strains of the Barcarolle. "Ah, Giulietta," Dapertutto comments. "How clumsy." As the curtain drops.

Even in its adulterated form, *Hoffmann* influenced much that was to follow, as did Verdi's experiment in combining romance with naturalism in *La Forza del Destino*. A real world of bad dreams, restive, lunatic voids, and mean irony was creeping into opera as the humorless

---

* These quadruple roles were cut by a third at the premiere: the inauthentic recitative so lengthened the piece that the Venetian tale was omitted. (Some of its music, including the famous Barcarolle, was transposed to other acts.)
† Despite the difficulties in vocal accommodation, numerous singers have tried to observe Hoffmann's fatalistic unity, from Adèle Issac and Emile Taskin of the premiere at the Opéra-Comique to such as Anna Moffo, Beverly Sills, and Joan Sutherland; and Lawrence Tibbett, Hermann Uhde, and Gabriel Bacquier. The results vary, however, and there is a case to be made for the all-stops-pulled, star-in-every-role treatment that this ill-used piece seldom gets. Toward the end of the seventy-eight-record era, the Opéra-Comique trotted out just about every star in the fading French firmament for a complete recording led by André Cluytens that—even in the now discredited traditional version—remains a model for style. Raoul Jobin sang Hoffman, three different sopranos and an actress played his loves, two baritones and two basses handled the villains, gifted thespians took even the smallest parts, and the wonderfully, brashly unmusical clown Bourvil did the four comic parts to a turn.

Romanticism of the early 1800s began to lose its hold. But musical comedy did not at first assume leadership, particularly in France, where Offenbach's successors aped his less satiric side, favoring sentiment, middle-class heroism, and obsequious comedy, all bound up in a little novelty. The genre was carelessly termed both *opéra bouffe* and *opéra comique* interchangeably; the *bouffe* seemed to harken to Offenbach's wit, the *comique* to Auber's marching pleasantry. But with Offenbach's pastiche and lampoon overthrown, it hardly mattered. Charles Lecocq tended to the *bouffe*, as in his immensely popular *La Fille de Madame Angot* (1872), a piece of minor charm and such little distinction that it's hard to describe from any angle. Even less special than Lecocq was Edmond Audran, whose top item was *La Mascotte* (1880). With these gentlemen an occasional oddity sufficed—a Political Duet, a Song of the Grasshopper, a Song of Pistoli Carabi (don't ask), or even, when Audran was desperate, a public presentation of a mechanical doll, in *La Poupée* (1896), that suffers by comparison with a similar scene in *Les Contes d'Hoffmann*.

Offenbach had devised his *bouffes* to counter the timid respectability of *opéra comique*, but no sooner had he departed the scene than respectability reasserted itself. Indeed, the best of Offenbach's successors, André Messager, so increased the musical valence in his work that they sometimes amounted to operatic *opéras comiques*. At his most popular, however, he waxed frothy, as in *Les P'tites Michu* (The Little Michu Girls, 1897), with its sweet sisters Anne-Marie and Marie-Anne, or in the very successful *Véronique* (1898), famed for its lovely Swing Duet, a waltz for a couple who, unbeknownst to *him*, are engaged to marry—*she* has disguised herself as a shopgirl. That sort of thing. Relatively uninterested in comedy, Messager hit his apex internationalizing Booth Tarkington in *Monsieur Beaucaire* (1919), first performed in London, in English, with Maggie Teyte as Lady Mary Carlisle. Messager, at least, had real talent, and pulled some wild stunts, such as the virtually operatic *Madame Chrysanthème* (1893), an anticipation of *Madama Butterfly* in sentimental rather than tragic mode and offering even less in the way of ethnic pastiche than Puccini's piece. Oddly, after a very lyrical evening, Messager passes the affecting final minute entirely in orchestrally accompanied speech rather than song. This emphasis on the spoken language is a French peculiarity, and Messager uses it well and sparingly.

Others were content to dwell entirely in convention. Louis Ganne's *Les Saltimbanques* (The Circus Clowns, 1899) and *Hans, le Joueur de Flûte* (Hans, the Flute Player, 1906) set down a format later identified with American "operetta," with unshakable rules on Big Tune waltz songs, Big Tune marches, and crucial reprises. Offenbach hadn't just died: he had been declared obsolete.

In England, Offenbach's influence plus the native urge to enjoy the language helped inspire the splendidly devious and often touchingly lyrical satires of Arthur Sullivan and W. S. Gilbert. The sure impudence of their fourteen collaborations (one a short piece and one lost except for its text) may owe something to the fact that Gilbert made the English translation for Offenbach's *Les Brigands,* perhaps the most aggressive of the *bouffes.* Unlike Offenbach, however, Gilbert and Sullivan preferred contemporary subjects and decor, and unlike Offenbach's collaborators, Gilbert was very, very funny on a line-by-line basis. Nothing in Offenbach compares with the Gilbertian patter song, with its references to characters and events of the time, as in this morsel of a Colonel's recipe for the character of a soldier of the Queen, from *Patience* (1881):

> The genius strategic of Caesar or Hannibal,
> Skill of Sir Garnet in thrashing a cannibal,
> Flavour of Hamlet, the Stranger, a touch of him,
> Little of Manfred (but not very much of him),
> Beadle of Burlington, Richardson's show,
> Mister Micawber and Madame Tussaud!

Nothing in all opera up to then matches Gilbert, as sharply pointed in ballads and charm songs as in outright comic numbers. Not even Felice Romani's dizzy verses for the quack's spiel in *L'Elisir d'Amore,* with a parade of ailments in iambic quadrimeter (Ei move i paralitici, Spedisce gli apopletici, Gli asmatici, gli asfitici, Gl'isterici, i diabetici), rivals Gilbert; here begins the history of the literate musical comedy libretto.

As for Sullivan, a musician trained for lofty doings, his sense of humor at times outdoes Offenbach's, though he is not so dry and commentative. He used pastiche more, festooning his scores with madrigals, choral anthems, Handelian or Bellinian reminiscences, and beautifully turned imitations of English folk song; and his scoring was subtle and tricky. He could undercut pomposity or lay a romantic spell with equal aplomb, though he never attempted to run both modes at once, as Offenbach did in *Hoffmann.* In Sullivan the two are separate, as in *Utopia Limited* (1893), wherein we move from satire to the ideal and back again at the start of Act II: first, an amusing solo from the tenor lead, Captain Fitzbattleaxe, on the problems of staying in voice while sustaining a love plot ("You can't do chromatics With proper emphatics When anguish your bosom is wringing"); next, a gently anti-Wagnerian love duet ("Sweet and low as accents holy

Are the notes of lover's lay"), where music takes the lead and the mind rests, lulled; followed by an up-to-the-minute spoof of the fashionable Christy Minstrels, seven men in a line complete with tambourines, close harmony, and "novelty encores."

But in one of his Gilbert entries, *The Yeomen of the Guard* (1888), Sullivan committed himself to a quasioperatic legitimacy of mood, constructing one of his few full-scale overtures,* resorting to a *Leitmotiv* to represent the Tower of London, and really putting his singers through their paces as singers. At one point early on, a jester and his pretty partner entertain in the street with a ditty modeled on tradition, "I have a song to sing, o!," that states the outcome of the work in miniature:

> Heighdy! Heighdy!
> Misery me, lack-a-day-die!
> He sipped no sup,
> And he craved no crumb,
> As he sighed for the love of a ladye!

Offenbach was more subversive. These Gilbert and Sullivan pieces are extraordinarily patriotic and accepting of system, whereas Offenbach was risqué, nonaligned, and rude. Not astoundingly, then, Offenbach has traveled the globe while Gilbert and Sullivan go over only among English-speaking peoples. Gilbert jibes at corruption and complacency, though: at township snobbery in *The Sorcerer* (1877), at "the peripatetics of long-haired aesthetics" in *Patience;* at British politics in *Iolanthe* (1882), at women's liberation in *Princess Ida* (1884), at Gothic horror in *Ruddigore* (1887), at egalitarianism in *The Gondoliers* (1889—"when everyone is sombod*ee*, then no one's anybody!"), at capitalism in *Utopia Limited.* But it is amusing that the most popular works, *H.M.S. Pinafore* (1878), *The Pirates of Penzance* (1879), and *The Mikado* (1885) sustain no evening-length broadside at anything.

German musical comedy, so imposing in the early 1800s when its natural sense of theatre and popular, nationalist commitment recommended it to the most gifted composers, languished in these post-Lortzing years. It, too, fell under the Offenbach influence, but produced no Gilbert, perhaps not even a Sullivan. Specialists in the march, the waltz, and the polka took it over, headquartering it in Vienna, where they featured a supple musical charm at the cost of grit. Franz von Suppé seemed to be mining the Offenbach vein in *Die Schöne*

---

* An assistant concocted last-minute potpourris in most cases; *Iolanthe,* however, like *The Yeomen of the Guard,* sports a true Sullivan overture, a wonder in the musical comedy context for its symphonic structure.

Galathea (Beautiful Galatea, 1865), a classical burlesque, but this was a rare sortie; von Suppé really found himself in the Italianate lilt of *Boccaccio* (1879). Johann Strauss the Younger, when he was still a bandmaster, received Offenbach's encouragement to turn to the stage, and his *Die Fledermaus* (The Bat, 1874) was based on a French play by Offenbach's most constant collaborators, Meilhac and Halévy. Everywhere regarded as the prototypal Viennese item, *Die Fledermaus* observes more exceptions than rules. It is a naturalistic, contemporary farce with a local setting* whereas the Viennese format seeks exotic romance set in Russia, Japan, the Hungarian outback, and even the American Wild West. The Viennese prefer nobles and peasants and love, doomed wherever possible; *Die Fledermaus* takes the middle class to a costume ball, ensnares everyone in craziness, and then begs the question with the most insouciant cop-out ending on the books: nothing is resolved. There is a prize pastiche number, for the lead soprano in disguise as a Hungarian countess, with a nostalgic slow section and a whirlwind close with manic coloratura and (all too often) a sloppy swoop up to the vicinity of a high D.

As the Austro-Hungarian capital, Vienna came to prize Hungarian pastiche as an essential of the Viennese style in musical comedy, and Strauss obliged with a more representative piece, *Der Zigeunerbaron* (The Gypsy Baron, 1885), with full rota of gypsies, buried treasure, war recruitment, stolen baby, and sole comic figure, the pig farmer Zsupan, who illustrates musical comedy's amusingly alienative temper in his overdone city accent, his more-or-less direct address of the audience, and his implausibly rustic cynicism amidst the Romantic gushing. Zsupan is Papageno revived. Strauss' most faithful successor, Emmerich Kálmán, kept the eastern flame alight in such events as *Die Czárdásfürstin* (The Czardas Princess, 1915) and *Gräfin Mariza* (Countess Maritza, 1924). Kálmán proved adaptable, slipping into the modern rhythm at the height of Germany's American cult with *Die Herzogin von Chicago* (The Duchess from Chicago, 1928), with the incredibly naïve number "Ein kleiner Slowfox mit Mary (bei Cocktail und Cherry)," and reached apotheosis in *Arizona Lady* (1954), cowboys, "Lied der Prairie," and all. Still, Kálmán's quaint grasp of hip has not endured as well as the more romantic work of Franz Lehár, whose adroitly adult handling of the love plot in *Die Lustige Witwe* (The Merry Widow, 1905) exercised a tremendous influence on this most universal element in music theatre. Obsessed with misalliances of class

---

* The exact location is ambiguous, but it is not—as many suppose—Vienna. The scene plot specifies "a watering place near a large city."

The three basic elements of musical comedy: (top left) satire (Ruth Welting as Olympia in *Les Contes d'Hoffmann*), (bottom left) exuberance (Welting as Adele in *Die Fledermaus*), and (above) true romance (Neil Rosenshein and Maria Ewing in *La Périchole*). *(David H. Fishman; San Francisco Spring Opera)*

and culture, Lehár celebrated the "alas, my darling, we must part" trope so often that it became the cliché of the era, in *Paganini* (1925), *Das Land des Lächelns* (The Land of Smiles, 1929), and *Giuditta* (1934), premiered with a flourish not at the usual musical comedy house but at the Vienna State Opera with Jarmila Novotna and Richard Tauber.

What precisely are we to call this protean genre that continually assumes properties of eloquence and penetration just when we feel we can segregate it from true opera as trivial and disreputable? It has passed under a host of rubrics—comic opera, operetta, musical, and the many foreign equivalents with their irritating nuances. And what is it, at heart, if it takes in such disparate products as *The Beggar's Opera*, *Der Freischütz*, *La Vie Parisienne*, and *Annie Get Your Gun?* For a while, we had a good answer going: it's called, in this book, musical comedy, and it has spoken dialogue, a tendency to unsophisticated music ("less" than opera), a smart resonance about its words ("more" than opera). This definition no longer holds up. No sooner do we identify such a form than it develops along operatic lines, attracting sophisticated musicians and sometimes even losing its all-important verbal emphases and naturalism, as both *Singspiel* and *opéra comique* did in the 1800s. Is *Fidelio* a musical comedy? Or *Carmen?* Obviously not. They are examples of a highly evolved form that may be traced back to musical comedy. Offenbach is musical comedy until *Les Contes d'Hoffmann*, which has spoken dialogue but a score of some operatic aspiration. Gilbert and Sullivan is musical comedy, including *The Yeomen of the Guard*, which in the end isn't all that comic. Strauss and Lehár are musical comedy, despite Americans' need to isolate their middle European format from our contemporary and urban musical by dubbing the style "operetta": there are no duchesses in Chicago. And that brings us to the country that has produced the richest and most imposing output in musical comedy, the world's capital of demotic art, the United States.

Early American musical theatre is a flotsam of English derivations like ballad opera and screwy native genres like the minstrel variety show. There was no centralization for stability (as there was in Paris and London) till New York seized power in the early-middle 1800s; by that time several types of show had established themselves: the ballet-oriented "spectacle" or "extravaganza"; the "pantomime," loosely related to *commedia dell'arte;* "burlesque," much like the Parisian fairground spoofs; and the musical farce. None of these forms had the integrity of *opéra comique* or *Singspiel*, as they depended too much on comic improvisation and the most rudimentary musical accompaniment.

Offenbach and Gilbert and Sullivan, however, made an impression and helped inspire an American *opéra bouffe,* called "comic opera." This paved the way, around the beginning of the twentieth century, for composers with more reach, mostly European immigrants such as Gustave Kerker, Gustav Luders, Ludwig Englander, and Victor Herbert, a stand-out for his bottomless well of tunes. The level of libretto writing remained low, the subjects running heavily to Ruritanian masque. Furthermore, the extinct pantomime and moribund ˇburlesque had passed on to the early American musical their particular salient, the star comedian, and his antics tended to intrude on the rest of any given work. Unlike the French musical, wherein light comedy served organically as part of the whole, or the German musical, wherein klutzy comedy was assigned to specific characters (in Strauss, *The Gypsy Baron*'s pig farmer, or a sloshed jailer who turns up in Act III of *Die Fledermaus;* in Lehár, a secondary love couple), the American musical threw its comedy into any place it could find for it.

Eventually a solution was found, by accident, when "comic opera" broke up into two distinct genres, "musical comedy," dealing in jazzy urban naturalism, and "operetta" or the "musical play," dealing in fantasy or romance. This schism is easy to spot, because the absurdly collaborative and often primitive musical comedy found room for semi-amateur or at any rate untrained composers like George M. Cohan and Irving Berlin, while the musical play began to depend on adept musical technique. This is a major point, with much bearing on twentieth-century opera—the dichotomy between the intellectual-verbal and the sensual-musical in music drama: *The Threepenny Opera* or *The Rake's Progress,* say, as opposed to *Die Frau ohne Schatten* or *Francesca da Rimini;* neo-Classicism versus post-Romanticism. One can see this on the most basic level by comparing the Ray Henderson–B. G. DeSylva–Lew Brown musical comedy *Good News* (1927), with its frivolous college setting, casual sense of self, and thin score of love ballads ("Just Imagine"), cheer-up songs ("The Best Things in Life Are Free"), comedy spots ("Baby! What?"), and dance sensation ("The Varsity Drag"), to the Jerome Kern–Oscar Hammerstein II musical play *Show Boat* (1927), with its epic tale of stasis and transformation, its ambitious score centered on the symbolic grandeur of "Ol' Man River," and its enthralling immensity.

We shall travel this two-way street of satire and romance in all sorts of vehicles from now on, and perhaps this is a good spot in which to take stock of how much the popular musical stage has given to serious opera. When new, opera was based—despite its fascination with the clarity of language—on emotional involvement. The music, in its feeling expression of the text, drew the listener into a special world. The "lesser" varieties of music drama, on the other hand, used compositional modes rooted in the everyday—folk and popular song, physical comedy, common-law sentiment and sententia. This is what Offenbach meant by the *gai primitif*. The more musical opera engages one through the senses and the unconscious, from *Orfeo* to *Parsifal*. Verbal opera, from *The Beggar's Opera* to *The Gondoliers*, never pretends that it's not an artificial event, a show. And, in a way, the fortuitous comings and goings surveyed throughout this history comprise a constant tug of war between the mythical, musical illusion of secret truths and realist, verbal satire. Genres have started at one end of the compass and edged over to the other. Or they have wavered between the two poles, favoring one or the other at different times. The Romantic 1800s officially chose musical opera: the movement began when Beethoven made *Singspiel* symphonic in *Fidelio* and climaxed in Wagner's colossal mythopoeia—the remote, the fabulous, the ideal. But now the pendulum will swing back again. Wagner's huge orchestra, superjock voices, and theatre like a great, brooding cave got as occult as opera could get, and in the early 1900s revolution will lead us back into man-scaled art. But first let's catch up on developments in the late 1800s—French exotics, German faerie, and Russian histories, folk tales, and romances.

CHAPTER THIRTEEN

Late Romantic Fantasy

> *Either murder and manslaughter*
> *or operetta nonsense or an ut-*
> *terly sugar-sweet fairy tale! It*
> *is obvious that we of the* fin-de-
> siècle *have unlearned all the*
> *laughter that Rossini, Auber,*
> *and Lortzing taught us.*
>
> —ENGELBERT HUMPERDINCK

THE LATE NINETEENTH CENTURY SAW A HEYDAY OF FAIRY TALES AND wonder stories in opera: spirits of air, fire, and water, good and evil, cunning little goblins, and magical machines proliferated. There seemed to be no interest in the spirits of earth—but realism served side by side with fantasy, if slyly.

Because *Ruslan and Lyudmila* so impressed Russian musicians with its legendary plot and folkloric musicality, it inspired a whole genera-tion of successors in similar style. Operas based on Russian history, too, proved popular. Nationalism was in the air, and one way or another a Russian opera would be created out of Russian sounds and subjects. At the vanguard of the movement strode "The Five," the *Moguchaya Kuchka* (mighty grouplet), a band of composers—Mily Balakiryef, Nicolai Rimsky-Korsakof, Modyest Musorksky, Alyeksandr Borodin, and Cesar Cui—sworn to create Russian in all things. The critic Vla-dimir Stassof advised and protected them, and Balakiryef provided the bulk of the theory, which basically rejected Western academicism in favor of Russian amateurism, the coarser the better—for the coarser, the more natural (i.e., Russian). "We are," quoth Balakiryef, "suffi-cient." They were mainly Saturday composers whose public careers led them into chemistry, the navy, and so on. Their output, then, might be small and their structures heretical, but the ethnic innovation would be authentic.

Borodin labored for some twenty years on his great opus, *Knyaz*

Igor (Prince Igor, 1890), and left it unfinished at his death in 1887. Rimsky-Korsakof and Alyeksandr Glazunof completed it, earning moues of distaste from cheap journalists, who blamed them for rewriting Borodin. In fact, they put as little of themselves as possible into the score, mainly orchestrating it (and at that in Borodin's style).* The result shows typical *Kuchka* handiwork: a genuinely Russian opera, with important bass roles for the larger-than-death villains that Slavs play so well, much chorus and ballet (the famous Polovyetzki Dances), Oriental lushness in the harmony, and an unwieldy plot dangling loose ends that any hack Western librettist would have tied up. Borodin wrote his own text (with Stassof's help), based on the war between Russians and Mongols described in the epic, *The Song of Igor's Campaign*, and, yes, it's very amateur. But the music! This is a grand piece, bluntly splendid and every bit as big as the history it covers. Unlike grand opera, which tackles history via well-made scenes and diversions in orderly crescendo to calamity, Russian opera staggers all over the place. For example, the character who at first appears to be the opera's villain, Prince Galitzky, vanishes from the piece after Act I, and we never do find out whether the Russians or the Mongols win the war.

Pyotr Chaikofsky, on the other hand, favored Western ways. The *Kuchka* shuddered at the idea of a symphony, with its Western technique of movement types and exposition-development-recapitulation (though some of them eventually wrote symphonies themselves); cosmopolitan Chaikofsky wrote six symphonies, plus a seventh (*Manfred*) with no number. Obviously his operas would show affiliation with Western usages, although he was something of an ethnicist (in melody, especially) and remained what might be called a dissenting fellow traveler of The Five. The first three of his ten operas, all cut on a national bias, offer diversity—*Voyevoda* (The Commander, 1869) a contemporary piece after Ostrofsky, the unperformed *Undina* a fairy tale, and *Oprichnik* (1874) a historical item on the *Oprochnina*, Ivan the Terrible's brutal bodyguard, the score largely taken from *Voyevoda*. Chaikofsky has the reputation, among know-nothings, as a symphonist and dance tunesmith who never got the hang of the stage; but if these first three works didn't pan out, *Vakula Kuznyets* (Vakula the Smith, 1876) shows the composer on his way to smart theatre writing, and with *Vakula's* defects cleared away in a revision, *Cheryevichki* (The Slippers, 1887), the métier takes shape. *Cheryevichki*, a "comic-fantastic" opera mined from Gogol (the same source that out-

---

* Glazunof pulled off a coup with the exciting overture, which Borodin had played for him on the piano but never secured on paper. Glazunof reconstructed it, note for note, from memory.

fitted Rimsky-Korsakof's opera *Noch Pyeryod Rozhdyestvom* Christmas Eve, 1895), accords with the Russian habit of filling out a serious work with the lowest sort of comedy without straining the heroic or romantic tone. Vakula and Oksana provide the lovers' troubles; Vakula's mother, a witch, and her suitor, a devil, add spice to the brew; and numerous village gaffers provision the buffoonery. This is a heady composite, but the music carries the action along, all the pieces in a neat jigsaw fit.

Before he repaired *Vakula Kuznyets* as *Cheryevichki*, Chaikofsky had already presented utmost proof of his musicodramatic ability in *Yevgyeni Onyegin* (1879), from Pushkin's "novel in verse." The adaptation is extreme. Pushkin's original is cynically comic, not unlike Byron's *Don Juan*, while the opera hugs romance, taking at most a cutting of Pushkin—"lyric scenes," the composer called it. He has been taken to task for changing the scope of the story, making Tatyana the leading figure when Onyegin was unquestionably the poem's protagonist. And certainly Pushkin's tale of life among Russia's upper middle class loses a great deal without the poet's playful commentary. But the opera does catch the poem's intimacy, and this, in nineteenth-century opera, is rare. There is little of the uproar we expect of Verdi or Wagner. There is a duel and some ballet, but everything is scaled down, modern, close—so much so that the work's Big Moment is no *grand duo* or massed finale but Tatyana's Letter Scene: one country girl alone in her room, writing her heart out to the imposing, worldly dandy who has turned her head with his urban panache. And if the feeling melody has conquered Pushkin's irony, his verses still furnish much of the opera's text. Act I, scene three may seem very operatic, with its sprightly girls' chorus juxtaposed with Onyegin's cool rejection of Tatyana. But virtually the entire scene is Pushkin's, word for word.

The internationalist Chaikofsky owed himself at least one full-throated Western opera; this would be the exciting *Orlyeanskaya Dyeva* (The Maid of Orleans, 1881), based on Schiller's reading of the Joan of Arc story. Accused of giving in to Meyerbeer, Chaikofsky does show an interest in ceremonial, but he mostly avoids the diversion and complexity of plot that mars grand opera. Like *Don Carlos*, *The Maid of Orleans* corrects more than imitates grand opera, heroically sized but emphasizing character rather than action. It must be one of the few Russian operas not to sound Russian in melody.* Chaikofsky quickly

---

* Cesar Cui, one of The Five, blithely produced operas on Western models, and it's a wonder Balakiryef didn't drum him out of the corps. Music historians don't like Cui much, for he ruins their chapters on "national opera" with such items as *Wilhelm Ratcliff* (1869), after Heine.

fit himself back into the native picture with the rudimentary *Mazyeppa* (1884) and *Charodyeyka* (The Enchantress, 1887), but his next opera, *Pikovaya Dama* (The Queen of Spades, 1890), found him in his element: a fantastic short story by Pushkin involving obsession, tender young love, decrepit bitterness, and magical horror.

Three, seven, ace! This is the secret of the "Queen of Spades," a Russian countess who charmed all Paris in her youth. Known as the "Moscow Venus," she spurned all suitors for her only love, gambling. At the price of a night's rendezvous, a French count gave her the secret of three cards that cannot fail to win: the three, the seven, the ace. In her turn she shared the secret twice—but a vision has warned her that a third man will wrest the secret from her at the cost of her life. *Tri karty, tri karty, tri karty!*—"the three cards"—is the idée fixe of the evening. The opera takes place many years later in Petersburg, where a prudish young man, Ghyermann, falls under the spell of the three cards and juggles a romance with the aged Countess' granddaughter Liza with a craze to learn the Countess' secret. Both the lovers die suicides. The girl throws herself into the Neva in despair, and Ghyermann, who has literally scared the old hag to death trying to worm her three cards out of her, hears them from her ghost and gambles everything on the three, the seven, and the ace. But the Countess has her revenge: the last card is not the ace, but the queen . . . of spades. Unlucky in cards and love, the gambler stabs himself.

Unlike the intimate *Onyegin*, *The Queen of Spades* is spacious and public, a modern chivalry. Chaikofsky really loved opera, and this one, with its E.T.A. Hoffmannesque avidity for hunger and fury in the midst of glittering urban society, offered him a very opera sort of evening. He added in a wholly extraneous episode, a pastoral intermezzo in a Mozartean idiom during a gala party scene, thematically relevant to the story in that it poses true love, victoriously, against materialism (i.e., the gambler's winnings). On paper, the diversion slows the action, but it has great power as musicological seduction, and lends a needed sweetness to a score that otherwise mainly broods, pines, and glowers. Chaikofsky went on to write a short work to accompany his ballet *The Nutcracker*, the medieval *Iolanta* (1892), but *The Queen of Spades* holds the summit as the work that pulls all of Chaikofsky's talent together. Like *Onyegin*, it has its special *tinta*, so much so that except in the deliberately incongruous pastorale, any note of the score immediately calls up the whole adventure, with its macabre visuals—Ghyermann's sudden appearance at Liza's balcony one night to plead his love; the exciting entrance, at the party's end, of Catherine the Great, which "occurs" just after the curtain falls (tsarist censorship forbade the depiction of imperial characters); the old Countess in négligé after the ball, throwing out her army of maids and recalling her youth in Paris, falling asleep as she sings a snatch of Grétry's *Richard Cœur-de-Lion;* Ghyermann's second eruption into the house, this time to badger the Countess for her secret; and, at last, the apparition of the Countess at the table where the hero has just gone bankrupt using her suddenly capricious three cards.

As a member of The Five, Nicolai Rimsky-Korsakof might have been expected to deal in the improvised operatic constructions of his fellow Fivers Borodin and Musorksky. But Rimsky was concerned over the group's lack of training. He put himself through a vigorous academic course to catch up, as it were, with the West, and thus was more like Chaikofsky than like his nationalist colleagues, especially in the high gloss of his orchestration. But in the end he is all Five, sworn to find a Russian opera in language, melody, form. Both history and literary adaptations attracted him, but most of all he loved the *opera-bylina,* "legend opera" on the feats of heroes, the love of heroines, and the quirks of the supernatural. Not as personally informal as Chaikofsky could be nor as latently naturalistic as Musorksky, Rimsky reflects everything through a style, an idealism.

After a look back at Russia's past in *Pskovityanka* (The Maid of Pskof, also known as Ivan the Terrible, 1873), Rimsky revivified his canvas to support the tribal anthropology of Nicolai Gogol in *Maiskaya Noch* (A May Night, 1880), which reproduces Ukrainian village life as a total entity—youngsters, old blowhards, relatives, neighbors, beliefs and gossip, flirtations and pranks, and, Gogol being livelier than life, a troupe of water nymphs. Consider it in part a revolt against all that opera has been, all that *seria* fanfare and *buffa* pertness. Here is a real-life village—again, in a style—with its grime, rashness, and superstition. Even in outright fantasy, such as *Snyegurotchka* (The Snow Maiden, 1892), after Ostrofsky, Rimsky can move easily from the enchanted revels of the green world as it reawakens under the melting snow— a wood fawn, a bird chorus, lovely Spring, bluff old Jack Frost, and their daughter the Snow Maiden—into mortal realms, bounding up in an aggressive rustic carnival. But amidst the most commonplace doings, the spirit of earth's magical otherworld hovers near, and when a comic couple offer to adopt the Snow Maiden and she bids farewell to her immortal past, a mysterious echo answers, the trees bow, and the humans scatter in terror.

Rimsky's huge legend operas (some of them as long as four hours uncut) offer an interesting contrast to *Parsifal,* first performed at about this time. Though both Rimsky and Wagner are reaching for

an incantatory folk-festival feeling, traveling religious universals deep
into some intuitive oneness of work and public, the transaction in
Wagner is misty and inert while Rimsky's is as earthy and immediate
as a "how the owl lost his tail" parable. It is not just that Rimsky uses
comedy, but that he defines the comedy in sounds that both comple-
ment and oppose the more dreamlike sequences. *Sadko* (1898) is the
best of the series, a stupendous picaresque that takes its hero from
Novgorod over a twelve-year ocean voyage (and a love affair with the
Sea King's daughter) back home to a city enriched by the Sea Princess'
transformation into a river to connect landlocked Novgorod with the
sea. A kind of Russian grand opera, *Sadko* employs Meyerbeer's
spectacle and diversions to negotiate a texture of time and place, with
merchants, laborers, clerics, sailors, buffoons, and a host of weird water
creatures backing up heroic tenor Sadko, his mezzo-soprano wife, and
the enticingly moist Sea Princess of high-floating coloratura. Daring
his melodic inspiration to the utmost, Rimsky reaches an apex of
pageant at the dead center of the opera, set in Novgorod's harbor on
the shore of Lake Ilmyen, where, at the Princess' direction, Sadko
casts his net and pulls up a treasure. Now he is ready to sail the world,
and Rimsky plays his trump with three solos, one each from a Norse-
man, a Hindu, and a Venetian, citing the marvels of their respective
lands. Obviously each solo must be a gem; each is. The bass Northerner
chills like a slow, brutal wind. The tenor Hindu preens in the silky
curlicues that used to plague piano novices as "The Song of India."
The Venetian rolls out a lusty barcarolle in a vibrant baritone.*

Rimsky also tried the small forms, and even abandoned the
conscious folklore of the Gogolian village and legend opera for a
piece somewhat like early Verdian *melodramma* in format, *Tsarskaya
Nevyesta* (The Tsar's Bride, 1899). The Tsar, Ivan the Terrible, is
only a walk-on mime here; interest focuses on a snarl of lovers and
the potions of a German chemist, purchased to help the course of false
love and hinder that of true. Yet even when not synthesizing Russianness, Rimsky remains Russian to the core, and makes full use of
two folk tunes familiar from Musorksky's use of them in *Boris
Godunof*.

Near the end of his life Rimsky produced his most immense legend
yet for his fourteenth opera, *Skazaniye o Nyevidimom Gradye Ki-
tyezhe i Dyevye Fyevronii* (The Tale of the Invisible City Kityezh
and the Maiden Fyevronia, 1907). This was to be the culmination of

---

* *Sadko* is too extravagant to travel comfortably and is seldom heard outside Russia, but a careful festival mounting might well create a sensation.

his art, so iconographic in its pagan and Christian mysticisms that commentators liken it to *Parsifal*. Yet in his last opera Rimsky turned a complete revolution, wickedly burlesquing legend opera in *Zolotoy Pyetushok* (The Golden Cock, 1909). *Kityezh* tells of invading Tartars, of the love of a princeling and a wood-wise maiden, of a cowardly traitor, of a miraculous fog that enshrouds Kityezh, fooling the Tartars and then dispersing them in panic when the bells of the city ring out in apparent void, and lastly of an occult and transfigured Kityezh like an earthly heaven, all bound up in an enthralling wash of sound colors, a chastely sensual tapestry. But *The Golden Cock* sings a vastly different tune, entirely detached from and ridiculing the action. A Magician pushed to the impossible top of the tenor range introduces the story, directly addressing the audience, and what a spoof: King Dodon is given a bird that sounds an alarm in what the Chinese call interesting times and an all-clear in peace—given it, however, by this same Magician. Answering the alarm, Dodon loses the battle, and on the bloody field meets the lovely Queen of Shemakha, whom he takes as his consort. The magician reappears, demanding the Queen as payment for his gift, Dodon kills him, the cock kills Dodon, and the Queen vanishes on a giggle. End of story. Throughout, Rimsky has given us no chance to empathize with or even believe in anyone; he had stepped into the modern mode of grotesque comedy. To complicate matters, the Magician comes before the curtain at the very end to dismiss the whole business. Only the Queen and he himself, he says—the two most grotesque characters in the lot—were "living people."

As allegory, *The Golden Cock* has been taken as a comment on the Russo-Japanese War, which ended in a Japanese victory; one might also view it as a dig at the Tsaritsa Alyeksandra and Rasputin. In any case, it is a wildly modern work for the time and place, scientifically developed out of a few basic themes in constant evolution and restatement, with the Queen and the Magician denoted in one sound style and Dodon's kingdom in another. To be just, much of the grotesque in opera, so avant-garde in the West, had been evolving in Russia since Glinka's *Ruslan and Lyudmila* and was firmly established in Musorksky's music, which Rimsky, as Musorksky's artistic executor, knew very well. It doesn't seem to have affected other Slavic repertories at this time, though. In Czechoslovakia, Antonín Dvořák found a hearty comic subplot to enhance his vision of the *Rusalka* (1901) tale, and elsewhere retrieved the sweet village pranking of Smetana's comedies. Beauty and pleasantry governed this school, not Russia's coarse realism. But one sign of changing times should be noted in Zdeněk Fibich's *Hippodameia* (1891), a trilogy composed entirely in melodrama and thus anticipatory of the neo-Classical emphasis on textual matter.

In Germany, fantasy had taken the lead from comedy, *Singspiel* now being a slighter form of *Oper* as *opéra comique* was of *opéra*. Carl Goldmark's *Die Königin von Saba* (The Queen of Sheba, 1875) was cosmopolitan Vienna's answer to Bayreuth, a tuneful Middle Eastern love tangle bespangled with processional, entrance arias and *grands duos*, Jewish prayer, and closed forms (as opposed to the ceaseless ebb and flow that defined Wagner's scores not by the number but by the act). Similarly, Hugo Wolf's *Der Corregidor* (The Mayor, 1896) borrowed Pedro Antonio de Alarcón's *The Three-Cornered Hat* for a straight-opera treatment that completely fudged its ripe comic potential. Alarcón's short novel about a pompous official's failed attempt to seduce a farmer's pretty wife calls for earthy farce, but Wolf, the composer of elite songs that only the most sophisticated ear can take in quantity, set the tale primly and at daunting length. While his lyricism impresses, the plot scenes just do not move.

As if in obeisance to Wagnerism but fearful of its size, a little era of *Märchenoper* ("fairy-tale opera") daintily erupted toward the end of the century. The kingpin here is Engelbert Humperdinck's *Hänsel und Gretel* (1893), the simple story blown up in a complex orchestral design but somehow—magically, one should say—never overstated. Indeed, the opening scene between the two leads, with the little songs that are known in America as "Susie, Little Susie" and "Brother, Come and Dance With Me," sets a tone of such correct innocence that the Wagnerian overture instantly diminishes in the memory to the scale of a merry prelude, and continued use of small solos and assorted chirpings of humans, wraiths, and animals keep the show trim. Other *Märchenopern* came and went, including several by Wagner's son Siegfried, and the quick disappearance of Humperdinck's *Königskinder* (Royal Children, 1910) closed the era. *Hansel and Gretel* is its only survivor, but *Königskinder* bears investigation. Here the scale is grander, but simplicity informs the work's moral: nobility comprises character, not costume. With a tenor prince, a soprano goose girl (with real geese), a contralto witch, a baritone fiddler, and assorted crabby townspeople, *Königskinder* observes what may be Wagner's most significant contribution to opera: the use of personality and situation as the *motion* of a work, rather than the application of personality and situation to the conventions of aria, ensemble, finale, and so on. *Königskinder*'s libretto, by Ernst Rosmer (Elsa Bernstein-Porges' pseudonym) flows, and Humperdinck flows with it, finding the special solos where they happen and otherwise letting the action find its own temporal

Hansel and Gretel at La Scala: Elena Nicolai (the Witch), Renata Scotto (Gretel), and Fiorenza Cossotto (Hansel). *(E. A. Teatro alla Scala)*

shapes. It's all so effortless that it doesn't feel novel, and by 1910 it really wasn't, except that where other early-twentieth-century Romantics often let their music billow shapelessly, *Königskinder* is cogent, firm, symmetrical. Perhaps this is because it originated not as an opera libretto but as a play; Humperdinck wrote incidental music for it, then turned it into a melodrama (1897) and finally recast it, with a curtailed text, in its present form.

France was never as interested in fairy-tale material as Germany was, but it loved the exotic. With the times hostile to Meyerbeerean extravagance, composers favored Gounod's compromise form between the grand and *comique*—"occupied" but not spectacular—with the odd reference to Gluck's purity. The unique outposts of the geopolitical sphere provided the decor, the fabled East especially. Camille Saint-Saëns cut as close to home as England, albeit in Tudor times, in *Henry VIII* (1883), but he went back to Bible days for his most popular piece, *Samson et Dalila* (1877). It was said of this gifted technician that he could compose any kind of piece in the style of any composer— except, detractors added, that of Saint-Saëns. This is a quipster's canard. Saint-Saëns stands out in a somewhat degenerate period for his vigorous Classicism. He was the most un-Wagnerian of composers, though, like them all, he was accused of succumbing. *Samson et Dalila* really shows a Gluckian influence in its emphasis on the principals and their conflict. (True, a bit of dance is useful to spread the aroma of pagan voluptuousness. Try to imagine a *Samson et Dalila* without a bacchanale.)

Eduard Lalo found the exotic virtually over his shoulder, in legendary Brittany, in *Le Roi d'Ys* (The King of Ys, 1888), Ys being a city that, in the final scene, is just saved from deluge by the suicide of the mezzo-soprano third of the love triangle. Colorful folk festivals (and a few genuine Breton folk tunes) lend the piece an ethnic swagger, and the score's most famous excerpt, the tenor's gentle aubade addressed to his bride, "Vainement, ma bien aimée," with its alternating sections of swaying flirtation and lyrical sincerity, puts a nice elegance into a heavily dramatic evening launched by a grandiose twelve-minute overture. "*Le Wagnerisme!*" they screamed—but French fantasy was seldom Wagnerian, preferring fleet pacing (*Le Roi d'Ys* contains less than two hours of music), a text easily pronounced and heard, lyric voices pleasantly raised, nonsymbolic tales of love and war, and a savor of the dervish here and there. Even that convinced Wagnerian Ernest Reyer rose above his imitative *Sigurd* to reaffirm Gallic style in *Salammbô* (1890), from Flaubert's novel about a Carthaginian princess caught between duty and desire. Gone was the epical magic, the rapturous Teutonic thrumming and pounding; French opera was now upfront about being frivolous. Another ex-Wagnerian, Emmanuel Chabrier, made the biggest about-face of all. His graduate thesis had been the Flying Dutchmanesque *Gwendoline;* now he celebrated French lightness and vivacity in a courtly historical comedy, *Le Roi Malgré Lui* (King in Spite of Himself, 1887), brimming with outrageous harmonic invention.

Perhaps the era is best viewed in the work of Léo Delibes, whose animation was sharpened in frisky ballet scores and the farcical *Le Roi l'a Dit* (The King Has Spoken, 1873), thin but gleeful. Like most of his coevals, Delibes worked in *opéra comique* without calling it that. French music theatre was all "opera" now, whether or not it used spoken dialogue and ballet and no matter which theatre it was written for. In *Jean de Nivelle* (1880) Delibes debouched in an old France of peasants and courtiers, in *Lakmé* (1883) in colonial India, in *Kassya* (1893) in a Poland filled with gypsies, Jewish merchants, and more courtiers. *Jean de Nivelle* is the best of them; at any rate, it has the Biggest Tune, the Ballad of the Mandrake, for a deep soprano voice along the late Viardot order. But all the vocal writing in this work is exemplary: a dashing tenor hero, a duke passing as a shepherd; a pliant lyric-soprano heroine; the Viardot type, who claims to be a witch; and several secondary sopranos and baritones. Delibes yields love strains, war strains, weighty ensembles, confrontations, jolly bits like Meyerbeer's *bouffe* numbers, a kind of motto theme for "Jean as eternal wanderer," and the Mandrake tune, which Delibes plugs shamelessly. The work once held the stage all over France, but today only *Lakmé* turns up, notorious for its coloratura showpiece, the Bell Song. *Lakmé* has nothing that *Jean de Nivelle* doesn't; it may even have a good deal less. But the devotion of certain sopranos (Lily Pons was the last) kept it going long after its day had faded, for the title role is simply one of the most grateful parts in opera (plus Pons got to display her delightfully impudent navel in the Hindu costumes, no small attraction to all concerned).

Are we just slogging along, or have we come to a crossroads in this history, a verge of something besides the twentieth century? In a way, we slog: Wagner and Verdi have made their separate very generative contributions, but their spaces cannot immediately (and will, it turns out, never) be filled, so late nineteenth-century opera lacks new ideas. Between Wagner's *mythos* and Verdi's reprieved *melodramma*, the art is leaning too heavily to the grandiose, emphasizing varieties of musical technique over varieties of verbal. Look at the works of the 1870s and '80s: the same love imbroglios of proud nobles that busied

Handel and Rossini, cut with fairy tale in Germany and port-of-call novelty in France—and in England, Arthur Sullivan, free of Gilbertian satire, set Scott's *Ivanhoe* (1891)! We have come to a crossroads, then, if only because we *need* one; opera has become too operatic, too complacently fantastic. And what would renovate it? Naturalism.

CHAPTER FOURTEEN

Naturalism

*All art is at once surface and
symbol. Those who go beneath
the surface do so at their peril.*
—OSCAR WILDE, *The Picture of
Dorian Gray*

*If a perfume manufacturer were
to adapt the "naturalistic" aesthetic, what kind of scent would
he bottle?*   —PAUL VALÉRY

*I don't like the type of woman
who betrays.*
—GIUSEPPE VERDI, on *Carmen*

A PREPOSTEROUS MISALLIANCE: OPERA AND REALITY. WHAT WITH CURSED
world-power rings, implausibly coincidental forces of destiny, invisible
Russian and deluged Breton cities, Huguenots, Trojans, pearl fishers,
puritans, royal children, and Italian girls in Algiers, opera does not seem
to be able to use naturalism, much less need it. Its basic condition—
that music expresses drama—is antinatural. But naturalism, like everything else in art, is a style, an approach. The opera world called for
it for the same reason that reformers in Gluck's day demanded relief
from the aria opera: the directness of communication that the Camerata
had laid down as the *dramma in musica*'s first principle had once again
been betrayed by fashion.

There were several naturalistic revolutions in opera in the late
1800s, and the most intense of all occured in Russia, where nationalist
theories posed earthiness as a component of Russian art. Russian music
theatre had easily found a place for the comic side by side with the
heroic, and one of The Five, Modyest Musorksky, pulled the two
elements into *Boris Godunof*, an epic based on history that appears to

have all Russia as its protagonist as much as its title character. But more: obsessed with the possibility of song as an extension of speech, Camerata-style, Musorksky designed a vocal mirror to reflect the tempo, inflection, and color of spoken Russian. Of his first operatic project, a setting of Gogol's comedy *The Marriage*, he wrote, "If I have managed to render the straightforward expression of thoughts and feelings, as it takes place in ordinary speech . . . then the deed is done." Musorksky dropped Gogol *in medias res* for *Boris*, based on Pushkin's play and composed in 1868–69, and offered it to the Maryinsky (today the Kirof) Theatre in Petersburg, the imperial Russian stage. This original version was lean, impulsive, almost dark: in the "time of troubles" at the end of the sixteenth century, Boris seizes the throne amidst talk that he had the rightful ruler murdered; a renegade monk impersonates the late prince and is said to have raised an army; and Boris dies insane with guilt.

One can imagine the perplexity with which the Maryinsky's acceptance committee greeted the manuscript. It had a host of uncouth minor characters, a few featured parts, and the eponymous lead role, but no love plot and no lead soprano. It had a lot of chorus work and some arias—sort-of arias; solos, anyway—but no full-scale ensemble and no ballet. And while the haunted, brooding Boris promised the stuff of great music drama, the behavior of the lesser characters shocked with rudeness, guile, brutality. In the first scene policemen force a mob to call for Boris to ascend the throne, and the crowd wails thrillingly. This is opera. But as the scene ends, Boris not having yielded, the people are told to assemble the next day in the Kremlin to await further orders. As the music peters out, the crowd disperses, saying, "If we have to scream, we might just as well scream in the Kremlin." This is opera? The committee rejected *Boris Godunof*.

Undaunted—better say possessed—Musorksky revised the work in 1871, making some cuts (including the tail end of the first scene as described above) and adding in a love plot involving the renegade monk and a Polish princess—legitimately derived from history, by the way. Now *Boris* was grander, brighter, and even more impulsive. There was some dancing—a polonaise for the new Polish act—and, to underline the epic nature of the piece, a new last scene showing the people in disorder and the passing of the former monk's army on the way to Moscow. As the mob sweeps off in its wake, a lone idiot laments the fate of the Russian people.

Even with the love plot and dancing, this posed a revolutionary prospect for any opera theatre. But under pressure from Musorksky's supporters the Maryinsky accepted *Boris* and staged it in 1874 with middling success, twenty-six performances over a period of eight years. By then Musorksky had died, a little mad himself, and his friend and fellow Fiver, Rimsky-Korsakof, undertook to ease the work of its primitive eccentricities. He was aware that those eccentricities were part of Musorksky's aesthetic, but felt that they made the music inaccessible to the average ear. Musorksky, with his irregular technique, was a genius of the *lumpen*, the hard, the grotesque; he sounds coarse because life is coarse. Rimsky smoothed out the entire score, rewriting and rescoring every single page; he neatened and razzled. Also, he emphasized the personal nature of the piece by putting the finale before Boris' death scene: personality first, epic second. He has been damned for his pains, but the operation slipped *Boris* into the world repertory, and his private hope that Musorksky's autograph sound might one day reassert itself was slowly borne out: in 1928, when the Soviet publishing agency and Oxford University Press jointly published the original version(s); on stage in Leningrad (formerly Petersburg) that same year and in London at Sadler's Wells in 1935; in London again, at Covent Garden, in 1948. In the 1960s both the Scottish and the Welsh National Operas claimed Musorksky when almost everyone else, Russians included, were sticking to Musorksky–Rimsky-Korsakof. Now the Met has joined the team, and a complete recording with Martti Talvela has affirmed interest in hearing Musorksky's less suave but infinitely more provocative original.

At least *Boris Godunof* could be rediscovered. Musorksky's other operas were left unfinished and will never be heard except in someone else's version. It was Rimsky again who completed *Khovanshchina** (The Age of the Khovanskys, 1886), begun in 1872. Vladimir Stassof helped Musorksky plan the libretto, the subject again drawn from Russia's gruesome history, and here even more than in *Boris* uncontrollable human passions, rather than traditional operatic material, guide the action. Mozart distills his characters; Verdi and Wagner express theirs. Musorksky unleashes his. These are the first operas to attempt to do what fiction, Russian fiction, especially, was doing at the time: render life, not arrange it.

Called by its author a "music drama of a people," *Khovanshchina* has no protagonist. Instead it chronicles life during the late seventeenth century, a time of oppression, religious fanaticism, and utter disorder. How can opera stretch to cover such matters, with its arias, love intrigues, ballet, and spectacle? *Khovanshchina* includes all this, yet rumbles with ambition, terror, and panic so authentically that it comes

---

* Shostakovitch also prepared a version.

off as the musical equivalent of Italian neorealist cinema of the post–
World War II years: Comrade, Obsession, The Earth Trembles,
Khovansky and His Brothers. Consider the opening scene. Musorksky
begins with an orchestral prelude, Dawn on the Moscow River, with
woodwindy bird calls and cockcrow and shimmering violins. There
is one central theme, restated slightly differently each time, like the
tune in a Russian folk song that is traditionally varied at each chorus.
The curtain rises on Red Square, closed off by huge chains; the sun
reddens the domes of the churches, and as the music fades the trumpets
of the *stryeltsi* (the army) sound offstage. A sentry yawns awake,
singing bits of a regimental song. *Stryeltsi* guards remove the chains
and talk of assassinations, their lines bumping into the sentry's song,
and all three tease a frightened scribe and wander off as a boyar comes
in to dictate a secret denunciation against Ivan Khovansky and his son.
The boyar intones in weighty baritone oration, the scribe in a giggly
tenor. Meanwhile, passing Muscovites sound a merry tune and the
stryeltsi file by. Everything happens at once, as if untimed, and when
the boyar finishes his business and the scribe scampers off, the army
roars in with a mob hailing their chief, the "white swan" Ivan Khovansky. How often opera has plumed itself on parades and cheers—
but here Musorksky overthrows the gala for a ragged, clomping march
of almost incoherent festivity. Who *is* the chief in this piece? No one.
Politicians, clerics, and lovers come and go as if ad lib, with no reference to the attitudes and set structures that opera has been dealing in
since 1700. Wagner, too, had cleaned his stage of convention, but
Wagner dealt in myth, the most extreme fantasy. Musorksky managed
to bring the epic back into worldly haunts without the heroic, magical
morale of the Bayreuth pageant.

Musorksky's naturalism, then, expands the Russian nationalist style,
building on the abstractions of ethnic folklore, character, and destiny
that Glinka and Rimsky-Korsakof used but taking in as well a quasi-
Dostoyefskyan richness of humanity. Obviously Musorksky exercised
little transitional influence at first, for Russian opera did not travel
Westward with any frequency till the twentieth century. But ultimately his work and that of some of his colleagues made a lasting
impression, not only in composition but in performing tradition as
well. Naturalistic characterization calls for naturalistic portrayals; life-
like motion needs stage directors who can move crowds the way
crowds move themselves; "real" opera demands a "real" look. All this
came slowly, for stage production in all types of theatre was defiantly
antinatural in the nineteenth century, and even in 1909 such a revolution in presentation as David Belasco's use of a "real" boarding-house

Khovanshchina as staged by the Bolshoi: the first scene, with the crowd greeting Prince Ivan. The Russians play almost everything as grand opera, emphasizing spectacle rather than naturalism. A production that showed what Musorksky describes in music, with filthy peasants, debauched boyars, and sadistic soldiers, would be considered shocking anywhere. *(E. A. Teatro alla Scala)*

room, complete to its furnishings and walls, in Eugene Walter's play *The Easiest Way*, was looked on as a stunt. Not till about 1910 in Europe and the 1920s in America—ironically, periods of revolt against theatrical realism—was staging technique able to suggest the varieties of life in acting and design. Opera always adopts such developments late, and only after World War II did directors see the possibilities in naturalizing opera. Now it is common to see Mozart, Verdi, and even Handel so treated. Well cast, it can work beautifully. *La Traviata*, with its innovative intimacy, adapts well, as does *Rigoletto*, and both were brought off in quasinaturalistic style at the New York City Opera in the 1960s by Frank Corsaro, deploying such willing naturals as Patricia Brooks, Placido Domingo, and Louis Quilico.

The most influential of the naturalist operas, Georges Bizet's *Carmen* (1875),* was a terrible failure when it first appeared. Meilhac and Halévy's libretto derived from Prosper Merimée's novel of a *fatale* and fatalistic gypsy and the high-strung Spanish officer who destroys himself and her when her heart moves on, and for this unusually sordid tale Bizet liberated himself amazingly from the exotic cuteness of his *La Jolie Fille de Perth* (1867) and *Djamileh* (1872), as well as the gossamer *Pearl Fishers*. But he chose the wrong place for his declaration, the Opéra-Comique, haven of middle-class sentimentality. *Carmen*, matter-of-factly rabid and risqué, stunned the Comique's public with its sweaty public square in Seville, its seedy café and gypsy encampment in the hills, its randy soldiers and brazen cigarette girls (smoking!), its back-alley jive. More stunning yet is Bizet's *pièce de résistance*—literally—of a heroine, who sounds a new note in opera a few moments into her entrance in the famous Habanera, teaching a theory of sensuality with a confident pragmatism not voiced since the the long-forgotten days of Busenello:

> *L'amour est un oiseau rebelle*
> *Que nul ne peut apprivoiser;*
> *Et c'est bien en vain qu'on l'appelle,*
> *S'il lui convient de refuser.*
>
> *Rien n'y fait menace ou prière.*
> *L'un parle bien, l'autre se tait;*
> *Et c'est l'autre que je préfère:*
> *Il n'as rien dit; mais il me plait.*

---

* *Carmen* lasted out forty-eight performances over the course of a year, a decent showing; critics made it a failure in their savage reviews, better remembered than the mild audience support. Because Bizet died three months after the premiere, clearly depressed, the legend grew up that *Carmen*'s failure killed him.

(Love is a wayward bird
That nothing can tame;
You call it in vain
If it doesn't want to come.

Neither threats nor pleas will help.
One man speaks well to me; another is silent;
And it's the other that I prefer:
He has said nothing, but he pleases me.)

Bizet set this to a rakish, dusky Iberian rhythm (the tune evidently springs from the folk tradition), and a proper Carmen will exploit the vocal line for its native insinuation. But she is no flirt. Total freedom is her ideology, and when, in Act II, she stresses above all *la liberté*, she means it in all its aspects. Not since Poppea had an operatic heroine been so frankly earthy. But the Comique liked its heroines fragile, their sensuality muted.

By comparison, Carmen's tenor vis-à-vis, the officer Don José, has failed to rally universal admiration. Some consider him a ninny, utterly outcolored by the gypsy's mezzo, though Caruso declared he "felt like a god" after singing the part. The librettists rather toned down Merimée's hero—but indeed the whole opera suffered vitiation by the addition of Ernest Guiraud's recitatives to replace the original spoken dialogue. José, despite a certain pallid quality in the first act, can be brought to life by a special kind of tenor with the grace for the Act II Flower Song and the strength needed thereafter (Caruso, for instance). The opera, however, needs rethinking from impresarios and singers to reinstate the more vigorous musical play that Bizet had in mind, until recently swamped in Guiraud's dull musical "continuity" everywhere but in France.

For the truth of the matter is that recitative, on which opera's inventors had based their hopes for a natural musicodramatic transmission, was getting tired. It had filled in between arias and ensembles for about two centuries, and was now a shade of what it had been in Monteverdi and Cavalli. Bizet used spoken dialogue because he designed the musical sequences to capture the sense of natural communication—the chattering of crowds, a fight in the cigarette factory, an urchins' military drill, a duel, an avowal of love, a sultry gypsy dance, a fortunetelling trio (Carmen gets the death card)—all styled from life. It is the music more than the libretto that made *Carmen* so daring in its day and so admired by the daring. Nietzsche thought it perfection, especially when compared to Wagnerian rumble. *Carmen*, he noted, "is wicked, refined . . . It is rich. It is definite. It boils, organizes, completes. Have more . . . tragic accents ever been heard on the stage before? And how are they obtained? Without grimaces! Without counterfeiting of any kind!"

Musorksky and Bizet had no immediate heirs, but at length a realist movement broke out in France and Italy, inspired by and even collaborating with such leaders of realist literature as Emile Zola and Giovanni Verga. Unlike Musorksky and Bizet, the realist composers of the 1890s and early 1900s dealt—if obliquely—with contemporary socioeconomic issues, stressing poverty, superstition and violence as inseparable components of working-class or peasant life. The French realist office never took in much business, as it allied itself suicidally with the Symbolist movement in poetry and thus found itself attempting to produce two different kinds of operas—fantasy and naturalism—in the same genre. Realist opera did establish itself briefly in Italy, with the premieres of Pietro Mascagni's *Cavalleria Rusticana* (Rustic Chivalry, 1890) and of Ruggiero Leoncavallo's *Pagliacci* (Clowns, 1892), nowadays almost invariably played together.* The two are not very similar, which is why they pair off so neatly. *Cavalleria*, based on Verga's play version of his short story of a man who abandons the woman he ruined and is then killed by another woman's husband, jumps from extremes of peace and piety on Easter Sunday to extremes of crude confrontation. The hero's murder occurs offstage, but so palpable is the sense of violence that when the curtain falls one feels released from prison. *Pagliacci*, on the other hand, is more measured, building gradually to the final horror on a thematic premise: clowns have real lives too. In a prologue one of these clowns, a baritone, comes before the curtain to warn the audience of the author's intention (unlike Mascagni, Leoncavallo wrote his own text, taken from an incident in his childhood), then steps back into his "part" as the villain of the piece, who eggs on the tenor hero, the chief of a traveling theatre troupe, to kill his unfaithful wife. *Pagliacci* shows the murder, "onstage" during a *commedia dell'arte* romp. At the very end the villain reassumes his Prologus guise, nastily informing both audiences that "the comedy is finished!"†

Italian naturalism, *verismo* ("realism"), never dealt with the Russian musical naturalism of ethnic phonography. The ingredients are

---

* Italian houses separate the two often, however. Because either *Cavalleria* or *Pagliacci* is popular enough to draw a crowd on its own, one or the other will be paired with a new or esoteric one-acter or a ballet.
† Today the tenor takes this line, reportedly because Caruso, preeminent in the role, insisted on delivering it himself. It serves the work's Pirandellian premise better if the interlocutor baritone retains it, to complete the thesis of the dualism of stage life and true life.

simple: contemporary settings, full-throated singing, and heavy emotionalism. Most of the Italian composers around the turn of the century produced such pieces, but usually only one each, and a ludicrous though common error has dubbed the entire era "the age of *verismo*" when in fact fantasy, poetic symbolism, and *melodramma* in period costume were the rule. *Verismo* was the exception. Mascagni and Leoncavallo, who founded the genre, rarely returned to it, and Giordano, Alfano, Zandonai, and Puccini, constantly labeled "*verismo* composers," wrote one or two such pieces at most.

Back in France, Gustave Charpentier put the final stamp on the movement in *Louise* (1900), the most subtle of the realist operas. Not only is there no violence, but Charpentier's own text features embarrassingly quotidian pictures of working-class life in Paris, taking in a humble family dinner, a bizarre street scene thronged with street people, a view of gossiping seamstresses, a bohemian carnival, and at last the family again in their dingy flat. Paris, as nocturnal enchantress, as beehive of workers' cubicles, and as arena of libertarian exaltation, pervades in sight and sound to the point of intruding into the plot about a dutiful girl's love for an artist despite her parents' opposition. Charpentier sides entirely with the young lovers, picturing the parents as bigoted and tyrannical—but where Italian *verismo* would have resolved the conflict with some tasty bloodletting, Charpentier's naturalism simply has Louise's outraged father throw her out of the house, then repentantly call her back. In vain. She has tasted the free life, and can no longer tolerate the family prison. In the distance the lights of Paris tactfully go out, then glimmer: youth, abandon, liberty. Carmen died for it. Louise, out of a different culture, merely loses herself in it. "Oh, Paris!" the father cries, shaking his fist at not so much a city as an idea.

There were a few more naturalistic operas after *Louise*, chiefly in Italy. Manuel de Falla contributed the Spanish classic in the form, *La Vida Breve* (Life Is Short, 1913), and one of the German variety, Eugen D'Albert's *Tiefland* (Lowlands, 1903), enjoyed wild popularity for a while. But *Louise* had the last word in terms of survival, and when Charpentier decided to write a second work to follow up on his two young lovers, he composed no sequel but a wholly different kind of work, a Symbolist dream piece, *Julien* (1913), in which Louise's beloved takes center stage. Naturalism was dead—*Julien* was no great smash, in any case—and the times now favored either the svelte, asexual, Baroque delicacy of Art Nouveau romance or neo-Classicism, in both its jazz-cum-music-hall satiric element and its back-to-Bach severity.

The realists at least left their mark in vocal writing. In Italy especially, the singers needed for the realist roles had by the very nature of the form to give their utmost in personality and drive. No one in *Cavalleria Rusticana* or *Tiefland* just wanders onstage and sings. These are dramas of guts and blood, and acting—the rawer the better— was needed as seldom before. Thus the voice types ran to weight. Sopranos commanded rich bottom and top registers, with ringing high notes to cap a scene, fierce low ones to stamp a bitter phrase in the memory. Tenors wailed and stormed as they had never done in Verdi, sometimes pounding out a series of high Gs or As; the baritones traded grace for grit. (Basses faded out of the picture almost entirely.) There was even some talking now in Italian opera. Some lines, set to notes in the score, are traditionally declaimed, such as (in *Cavalleria Rusticana*) Santuzza's "A te, la mala Pasqua!" (An evil Easter to you!) to the lover who rebuffs her. Thus *verismo* and its fellow movements ratified the trend away from *bel canto* that had begun in the mid-1800s. As in Wagner, voices of this weight simply couldn't negotiate the long-breathed lines and coloratura of old.* The tone of librettos changed, too, as the wordsmith could hardly deal in earthiness and poetry at the same time.

How much naturalism—how much honesty—was the public going to take? Musorksky's virulent primitivism startled the Russians, and if the French finally couldn't resist *Carmen*, they found themselves in over their heads when the more impetuous singers threw themselves into the two leading roles. Gluck, after all, was still in the repertory; imagine the comparison one might make between his classically composed heroines and Bizet's hot gypsy. In all Europe perhaps only the Italians accepted with equanimity the new vitality of operatic plastique —and they, after all, had had such Verdian warm-ups in that line as Lady Macbeth, Rigoletto, Hélène in *Les Vêpres Siciliennes* (more exactly for Italy, Elena in *I Vespri Siciliani*), or in Boito's *Mefistofele* and Ponchielli's Gioconda and Barnaba. Emma Calvé, the French singer of phenemonal range who cited Eleonora Duse as a formative influence, applied what she had learned singing Mascagni to her Carmen, inspiring horror in George Bernard Shaw. An overrated critic with many

---

* The confusion over *verismo*'s precise limits results partly from the use, in post-Verdian Italy, of these heroic voices in nonrealistic pieces. While Puccini wrote only an hour's worth of *verismo*, *Il Tabarro*, his other works often accord with the personality of true *verismo* acting-singing. Tosca, her artist-revolutionary tenor lover Cavaradossi, and her vile baritone suitor, the police chief Scarpia, for instance, act like paragons of *verismo*, though in a costume thriller that is anything but naturalistic.

ridiculous opinions, Shaw sounds a typical note for the late Victorian operagoing public when he called Calvé's gypsy "a superstitious, pleasure-loving good-for-nothing, caught by the outside of anything glittering, with no power but the power of seduction, which she exercises without sense or decency."

But that is precisely what Carmen should be. In this sudden leap forward into realism, opera's people, doing opera justice, pulled far ahead of what the audience thought of as operatic. Nothing outrages the inferior man so much as a candid woman who wants what she wants.

CHAPTER FIFTEEN

Turn-of-the-Century
Popular: Massenet

*His colleagues never forgave
[Massenet] for having such a
power to please.*
—CLAUDE DEBUSSY

EVER SINCE VENICE OPENED THE FIRST PUBLIC OPERA HOUSE IN 1637, opera has been a popular art, intent on appealing to theatregoers. The extent of appeal varies. At Meyerbeer's Opéra the aim was total pleasure; at Bayreuth one met Wagner on his, not one's own, terms. Still, by 1900 Wagner was as popular in his way as Meyerbeer; these two and Verdi were probably the most popular composers in the repertory.

Not long after 1900 all this begins to change. While some composers will continue to appeal to the public, others—some of the best ones—will deal in what can only be called adversary opera: contrary to what the average ear enjoys and hostile to the average spectator's worldview. Opera becomes a difficult art, increasingly so as we move further into the twentieth century. By the late 1940s, after World War II, the long-standing tradition that the repertory is continually enriched by new works which immediately win over a share of the public no longer obtains. New works are still written and performed, but most people abhor the writing and most star singers wouldn't touch those crazy vocal lines for anything.

Nothing could have looked less likely in the years just before and after the nineteenth century turned twentieth. Opera was in a golden age of vocal decor: sopranos Nellie Melba, Marcella Sembrich, Luisa Tetrazzini, Milka Ternina, Frances Alda, Lilli Lehmann, Olive Fremstad, Emma Eames, Emmy Destinn, Amelita Galli-Curci, Geraldine

Farrar, Lucrezia Bori, Selma Kurz, Johanna Gadski, Lillian Nordica; mezzos Louise Homer, Sofia Scalchi, Edyth Walker, Ernestine Schumann-Heink, Jeanne Gerville-Réache; tenors Francesco Tamagno, Jean de Reszke, Enrico Caruso, Fernando de Lucia, Giovanni Zenatello, Alessandro Bonci, Leo Slezak, Ernest Van Dyck, Léon Escalais, Edmond Clément; baritones Victor Maurel, Maurice Renaud, Mario Ancona, Antonio Scotti, Giuseppe de Luca, Mattia Battistini, Riccardo Stracciari, Titta Ruffo, Anton Van Rooy, Jean Lasalle; basses Pol Plançon, Édouard de Reszke, Fyodor Shalyapin, Marcel Journet, Vanni Marcoux. Note the international assortment: Italian training and talent, paramount in the eighteenth century, now shared the stage with Germans, Poles, Australians, Americans (often veiled in foreign names), Czechs, Britons—shared it at best and were often overshadowed by non-Italians in all but the baritone register.

The above (incomplete) list includes a number of artists as well known for their charisma as for singing velvet; not only *verismo* but an innovation in characterological presentation had recommended the "acting singer" to the public. No one could get by without a voice, but some middling voices scraped up to stardom through personal intensity or beauty. Certainly Mary Garden's reputation depended greatly on her acting and Lina Cavalieri's on her extraordinary looks, though legend has exaggerated their faults as singers. It has likewise libeled Shalyapin, one of the few Russians to travel to the West and a Boris Godunof of unparalleled dramatic and vocal splendor, as his records attest.

Increasingly the most prominent managers were seizing power, and in certain centers—in Vienna and all over Italy—the conductor had the last word on everything. But generally the stars continued to hold their carnival of egotistic leadership, though changed times presented quite an array of possibilities. In the old days, holding the crowd was a cinch: one sang (and acted, when unavoidable) in the style of the place and time. In Handel and Bononcini's London, that would be Italian *opera seria*. In Gluck and Piccinni's Paris, that would be French or Italian *tragédie*, depending on which half of the audience one wanted to address. Seldom did a singer have to consider disparate styles, genres, languages at any one time.

Until 1900. An international repertory incorporated everything from Beethoven on, a century's worth of European art replete with Big Roles from a myriad of times and places. How to proceed? Some, like Lilli Lehmann, sang everything everywhere, from Offenbach to Donizetti to Wagner, in the original languages or translations, some

170 roles from contralto to soprano.* Others, like Mary Garden, associated themselves with living composers especially. Garden sang many
roles but some of them only a few times, because some of them
weren't worth repeating. Still others, like Melba, coddled their crowd
with a few favorite parts carried on ad infinitum. Melba was known
strictly for her stupendous singing, not for personality—for that one
went to Garden or Geraldine Farrar. The latter's stock of roles
typifies the taste of the time—Louise, Thaïs, Juliette, Carmen, Marguerite, Mignon, Charlotte, Elisabeth (in *Tannhäuser*), the heroine of
Königskinder, Zerlina, Cherubino, Violetta, Nedda (in *Pagliacci*), a
healthy dose of Puccini, plus numerous oddities of Italian post-*verismo*.
If Farrar had the physical beauty, gall, flair, and pathos for anything,
her instrument had its limits—and she pushed it; she had to, to make
her passions tell. An earlier age would not have tested her voice so.
But an earlier age might not have known how to handle her vibrant
sense of involvement onstage, her realism. Farrar got so into her roles
that singing became almost secondary, and she thrilled her admirers
no less than Melba did hers on voice alone. Farrar had a shortish career
of some twenty years†—more would have exhausted an already weathered sound—and for most of it she was the most popular woman singer
alive, second only to Caruso as most popular of all. Her fame even
crossed over from opera, Callas-style, into the more universal celebrity
of all show biz.

So the singers in this golden age knew how to please, not through
the musicolinguistic clarity of early opera, nor through *bel canto*, but
through lung power, songfulness, personality, or emotional commitment. The composers did not have it so clearly laid out: sentimental
romance, fiery costume melodrama, folkish comedy, urban sophistication, fairy tale, history, naturalism, irony or pathos, smart or silly
comedy—all was more or less current, and a composer susceptible to
influences could travel an eclectic itinerary even while defining a
personal style.

Such a one was Jules Massenet, the big man of French opera in its

---

* Lehmann figures in a famous anecdote that may reassure those who wonder if
prima donnas had been getting any nicer since the era of Bordoni and Cuzzoni.
It seems that Lehmann was in Bayreuth the same summer as her American colleague Lillian Nordica, and when they crossed paths Nordica deferentially asked
Lehmann if she might pay a call on this most illustrious of Wagnerians. "I am
not taking any pupils this season," Lehmann snapped.
† Farrar made her debut not in the United States but in Berlin (in *Faust*). She
was one of the few American singers to launch a career abroad before that procedure became the norm in the 1950s.

last days as an international concern. When Massenet died, his melodic well depleted and his fame sinking, the French style was already in eclipse, leaving its creators and singers to isolate themselves at home while the Germans and Italians spread new doctrines. But while he was active, from about 1875 to 1910, Massenet set the pace for an aesthetic devoted as much to the star mystique as to the inner-directed lure of art.

Massenet really caps the late nineteenth century, for he worked most of its genres, slanting each one to give the widest possible audience the best possible time. He succeeded, though recent attempts to bring him back have not impressed today's audience. And it may be that his success owes as much to a subtle, dry precision in the setting of text as to the lushness of his musical texture. He did, of course, have a great store of melodies. But he also had rare good luck with librettos, and exploited them as much for verbal intimacy as for musicodramatic thrills.

He was diligent, composing some thirty works, including a few unperformed early tries that aren't usually counted. A romantic thriller, *Don César de Bazan* (1872), placed him publicly; a stageable oratorio, *Marie-Magdaleine* (1873), enjoyed a huge success, incidentally introducing Massenet's favorite brand of character, the sensual woman; and *Le Roi de Lahore* (1877) did even better with its obediently voguish Indian exoticism. We do not yet see much of the finished Massenet signature; he was still hunting down a mode of his own. Still, *Le Roi de Lahore* is fully developed, big, wild, and lyrical, with a lot of orchestral scene setting (a tumultuous overture), ballet, unreal story (the tenor king, murdered by a jealous baritone, is sent back to life by the god Indra to finish off the love plot), juicy lead parts for soprano, tenor, baritone, bass, and important contributions from a second bass and a mezzo (who has the opera's best tune, a limpid serenade with a Moorish tinge).

Massenet drew closer to what was to be his métier in *Hérodiade* (1881), whose exoticism compares to *Le Roi de Lahore*'s in decor but which pulled way ahead in the matter of erotic luxury. Opera's Middle Easterners are notorious for their wanton fire, but here it is only Herod and Herodias who indulge. Salome, in this retelling, loves John the Baptist chastely, and it is her mother who has him put to death. Unlike Richard Strauss, who scandalized the opera world with a more candid report on these characters, Massenet aimed to tease, not distress, his public. Many of his women are frail, some are resilient, but all are seductive—not as self-assertive as Carmen but languorous, pliant, delicately feverish.

All this found expression in the essential Massenet opus, *Manon* (1884). More faithful to Prévost's novel than Auber's earlier version and more detailed than Puccini's later one, Massenet's *Manon* offers one of opera's most foolproof roles in the heroine who rises from convent girl to toast of Paris and falls into disgrace and dies on the way to transportation to the New World. So rich is the character, so resourceful the composer in setting off her facets, so grateful the tunes, that any half-decent soprano comes off as an artist in it and every first-rate one dazzles. There have been many great Manons, Marguerite Carré, Geraldine Farrar, Mary Garden, Frances Alda, Berthe César, Emma Luart, Lucrezia Bori, Germaine Féraldy, Ninon Vallin, Fanny Heldy, Grace Moore, Victoria de Los Angeles, Bidu Sayão, Beverly Sills, and Patricia Brooks among them. Massenet emphasized the girl's vivacity when he substituted a coy, note-cluttered *fabliau* for the famous Gavotte to set off Georgette Bréjean-Silver, but in fact the role calls for several different kinds of voice in one, a lyric soprano with coloratura and *spinto* ("pushed," meaning quasidramatic) extensions. Manon is several women in one—coquette, gamine, prostitute, sister, wife—and her part reflects this from number to number. What a store of great moments: her dizzy entrance monologue ("I'm still a bit scatterbrained . . . This was my first trip"); her moving "Adieu, notre petite table" (Farewell, our little table) when she is about to trade pure love for a courtesan's career; her double aria of flowery showpiece, "Je marche sur tous les chemins," and fastidiously piquant Gavotte, delighting in the adoration of all Paris; her desperate plea to her true love to take her back, "N'est-ce plus ma main?" ("Isn't it the same hand?" she asks; "the same voice? . . . Don't these eyes glitter as they used to, even through my tears?" Who can resist?); her nervous salute to the sweet life, "A nous les amours et les roses!," sung to the thrill of the gaming tables spilling banknotes; her drooping death scene, all vivacity consumed. With so many different cards to pull out of one characterological deck, Manons naturally tend to stress particular aspects, both vocally and personally. Germaine Féraldy's light voice put forward the schoolgirl flirt. Ninon Vallin's darker sound outfitted an older, somewhat fatalistic Manon. Victoria de los Angeles found the sweet innocence. Patricia Brooks saw her as a fortune hunter obsessed with role playing, finishing off the death scene with an eerily hallucinatory reminiscence of her smashed glamor to match the composer's ironic musical reminiscence. Perhaps Emma Luart and Bidu Sayão most successfully captured all of Manon's sides, splitting the difference between Manon as victim and Manon as aggressor.

Because Massenet's operas devolve so heavily on their heroines, his music takes on a slightly feminine coloration, or so everybody said. The swooning Big Tunes that Massenet lavished on the ear became known generically as the *phrase massenétique décadente*, and he was thought to have made at least a few of his leading ladies his mistress during the period of composition. Surely he knew the value of tailoring a role to show off a prima donna's certain gifts, and anyway, it was only relatively recently that utopians such as Berlioz and Wagner had written operas with no particular cast in mind and no premiere set. A smash first night was crucial in building up the momentum to send a work on to other cities. Obviously, success-or-failure had as much to do with who sang as what was sung.

Lucky Massenet, then, to work at the height of the golden age, and to ingratiate himself with so many of the singer-personalities—Sibyl Sanderson, Emma Calvé, Lucien Fugère, Mary Garden, Lina Cavalieri, Lucienne Bréval, Lucy Arbell, Edmond Clément, Fyodor Shalyapin. The first-night cast for *Manon*'s successor, *Le Cid* (1885), boasted the two de Reszke brothers and Pol Plançon, and, as a grand opera based on Corneille's virile drama, spotlighted not vacillating women but bellicose men. A hit, it must have felt a little old-hat with its Meyerbeerean hooray—and, in a way, Corneille had already done much of Massenet's work, as the situation of two loving nobles parted because he is duty-bound to kill her father in a duel is operatically a sure thing. It directly provisions *Le Cid*'s best scene, in the heroine's bedroom, opened by a plaintive orchestral introduction with Big Tune on solo clarinet leading into the soprano's recit and Big-Tune aria, "Pleurez! pleurez mes yeux!" (Cry, my eyes), wherein she mourns both her dead father and her now inoperable engagement. As the Tune dies away, the hero bursts in, and the pair slip into a wonderfully sorrowing duet, agreeing that their relationship must now maintain itself solely on respectful hatred. But love is stronger than family honor, and, fired by her unmistakable tenderness for him, the hero dashes off at the close of the scene to battle the invading Moors with renewed spunk.

Manon and *Le Cid* together show a complete disparity of genre, the one confidential and urban-worldly, the other formal and costume-courtly. There is little doubt that Massenet felt far more at ease in the former style. Grand opera brought out the traditionalist in him, the dutiful student; *opéra comique* challenged his affinity for language, the flow of musical French. No one wrote recit better than Massenet. He abstracted the melody in speech so expressively that his *opéras comiques*, like *Manon*, use few spoken passages yet never lose that basic balance of full-out singing and dialogue. Then, too, Massenet loved to cut loose with a little pastiche every so often, and while this is endemic to *comique*, it feels irreverent in grand opera. *Le Cid*'s Spanish dances, though fine as music, cheapen that work's selfish intensity. But a tidy little minuet in *Manon* sets just the tone for time and place, and a spate of Rameau-like ballet bits in the same scene "prettifies" the piece, helps develop its fragile shimmer.

Massenet made another sortie into the grand in *Esclarmonde* (1889), but here he demonstrates yet another of the epoch's genres, *le Wagnerisme*. A medieval romance uniting a sorceress and a knight, *Esclarmonde* avoids the *Ring*- or *Parsifal*-like atmosphere of the other French Wagnerians, but in melody and scoring it bears an allegiance to the Bayreuth sound, even unto a love-music intermezzo of *Tristan*-like solipsism. Massenet cast the title role for a unique find, a young Californian of great beauty and, he later recalled, "stupendous voice . . . from low G to G in alt, three octaves both in full voice and pianissimo!" But more: "I had recognized in the future *artiste* an intelligence, a flame, a personality which were luminously reflected in her admirable features. These qualities are of the utmost importance in the theatre." This was Sibyl Sanderson, and her qualities prompted an exhausting part beyond the reach of most sopranos. Not surprisingly, *Esclarmonde* vanished quickly, living in legend till the enterprising Richard Bonynge revived it for his wife Joan Sutherland.

Thereafter Massenet favored the intimate over the public in his individual entailment on *opéra comique*. *Werther* (1892), after Goethe's famous novel of Sturm und Drang fanaticism, concentrates on its two leads in a middle-class, small-town setting; for a change of pace, Massenet had to deal with an almost ascetic woman, and, baffled, turned his attentions to the tenor, who loves mezzo Charlotte in vain. *Thaïs* (1894) also focuses on the two halves of the love plot, taken from Anatole France's tale of a monk who converts a harlot only to fall in love with her himself. (Too late: born again as a nun, she dies in his arms.) A second Sanderson vehicle, *Thaïs* gloried in showing the seamier side of old Alexandria while balancing the *phrases massenétiques* against somber tones suggestive of Christian self-denial. The piece suffered neglect for decades but never entirely faded, for if it is the most excessively *massenétique* entry, overflowing with sentimentalism and ludicrous pagan hoopla, it nevertheless proves its composer's gifts for capturing personality. Was it Sanderson or the fictional Thaïs who inspired him to create the character's imposing entrance, after a clatter of "Egyptian" pastiche has died down? Shiny, solemn chords support Thaïs as she moves forward to bid farewell to her present *protégeur;* they are a lilting reflection of the woman's confidence and beauty. Louis Gallet's text, however, betrays the secret sobriety of the guilty hedonist:

> *C'est Thaïs,*
> *L'idole fragile qui vient pour la dernière fois*
> *S'asseoir à la table fleurie.*
> *Demain, je ne serai pour toi plus rien qu'un nom.*
> (It is Thaïs,
> The fragile idol, who comes
> To sit at the flowered table for the last time.
> Tomorrow, I shall be nothing more to you than a name.)

The voice floats serenely, coolly, poised halfway between presenting and enriching the material; it burns a little as her wealthy friend responds, and at last rises ardently to a high note to drop back again and affirm her empty independence: nothing more than a name. A moment later she spots the brooding monk—and her doom is fixed.

Grand opera, *opéra comique*, Wagnerian romance, all in fancy dress—now Massenet changed over to *verismo* in *La Navarraise* (The Woman of Navarre, 1892) and *Sapho* (1897), the former in the violent mode of *Cavalleria Rusticana*, the latter a hectic but unmurderous look at contemporary bohemian Paris. The *Märchenoper* also attracted him, though his *Cendrillon* (Cinderella, 1899) was as French as can be, very Perrault in its comic household of pushy stepmother, mean stepsisters, and wimpy father, its exquisite palace, and its fairy dreamland. Still turning his kaleidoscope of Eves, Massenet requisitioned four principal women: Cinderella commands a soprano with a rich lower voice, the interloping Fairy sings high coloratura, Prince Charming is a *falcon* or *soprano de sentiment* (having, Massenet warns, the *"physique du costume"*), and the stepmother rules a hefty contralto. Yet another type, the faithful wife who passes a husband's unconscionable test, shed a glow over the medieval *Grisélidis* (1901), which, like *Cendrillon*, interlaces passionate characters with farcical ones; the Devil, a "singing" bass of *buffo* humor, has the best lines.

We have crept into the twentieth century, and considering what revolutionary items came forth in these first new years—*Pelléas et Mélisande, Jenůfa, Salome, A Village Romeo and Juliet, The Golden Cock*—Massenet begins to feel leftover. But in truth much of his aesthetic reflects the innovations of the new waves, neo-Classicism in particular. Though his characteristic form was late Romantic *opéra comique* (with a continuous musical score on which snatches of dialogue would be superimposed), Massenet's use of self-conscious pastiche intrusions, his taste for comedy, and his ability to keep textual matter in relief typify twentieth-century thinking. He also showed a marked interest in Classical subjects, another attribute of the early 1900s. Unfortunately, it was about this time that Massenet went into decline, producing more forgettable pieces than gems. A trio of exceptions cheers us: *Le Jongleur de Notre-Dame* (1902), *Chérubin* (1905), and *Thérèse* (1907): a medieval parable, a sexy farce, and a short love triangle set during the French Revolution. The pastiche is subtle but significant in *Thérèse*, a minuet introduced on the harpsichord, used for bittersweet nostalgia. But pastiche runs riot in *Le Jongleur*, filling the air with the shrill doodle-do of the pre-Renaissance soundscape, and also in *Chérubin*, the continued escapades of Beaumarchais' page Cherubino and an opportunity to "do" the dynamic, carnal Spanish idiom. Of the three, *The Juggler of Our Lady* is the only one still remembered, having enjoyed an unstoppable fashion during Mary Garden's time. Massenet composed the part—that of a humble entertainer who horrifies the inmates of a monastery by performing his act before a statue of the Virgin—for tenor, but Garden tried it in travesty and did so well by it that no one else wanted to touch it. (Lately the role has reverted to its original arrangement.) However, *Chérubin* is the prize of the trio—another Garden drag part—for its exuberant libretto and luscious *massenétique* folderol.

Perhaps Massenet's reliance on stellar talent, which made him so successful, was what eventually brought him down. Suiting his principal roles to the most gifted artists, he built in a trap of obsolescence. Who would want to compete with Sanderson's Esclarmonde, Calvé's Sapho or Anita in *La Navarraise*, Garden's juggler or Chérubin, Lucy Arbell's Thérèse? True, some did compete, and of course everyone sang Manon, Thaïs, and Werther. Still, an air of exclusivity hung over all of Massenet, and too many of his better works died of other singers' *nolo contendere*.

This was especially true of Massenet's last major try, the "heroic comedy" *Don Quichotte* (1910), for Cervantes' superb buffoon was created by Fyodor Shalyapin, a one-of-a-kind singer if there ever was one. With even more Spanish "effects" than *Chérubin*, *Don Quichotte* has atmosphere and verve (not least from the absurd Sancho Panza). But Henri Cain's episodic text lacks substance. Act I presents a festive public square and the meeting of Quixote and Dulcinea, in this version an elegant beauty; Act II the fight with the windmills; Act III a raid into bandit country to retrieve Dulcinea's purloined necklace; Act IV another festival on Dulcinea's patio, where Quixote grandly returns the bijou; and Act V Quixote's death. This may seem lengthy, but it's rather slim in performance (the whole of Act V is shorter than

Cendrillon: musical comedy mated with fairy tale. This shot of
the mean stepsisters' curtain call in Washington, D.C., 1979, ex-
hibits the *gai primitif*'s jarring juxtaposition of the lush and the
wacky. The background has the air of luxury; the foreground
finds Judith Christen and Peggy Pruett mooching for applause.
Charles Elsen, who did the makeup and wigwork, is proud of his
share in identifying the wicked spoof that hides in the wonder.
(Richard Braaten, Washington Opera Society)

some arias), though Massenet lavished one of his most beguiling scores on it. More important, *Don Quichotte* shows the composer at his most "modern," blending humor with romance in a way that anticipates his successors, even if the true grotesque of Cervantes escapes him. Massenet's Quixote is at base a Romantic hero, with a contagious nobility that transforms even his ridiculous squire, who takes greatness upon himself at the close of Act IV, defending his master from the mob's laughter "with hauteur and disgust" and a Big Tune rolling out in C Major.

Massenet marks the culmination of the nineteenth-century symbiosis of serious and comic styles in opera. Bizarre as it may sound, he is Rossini's most indebted beneficiary, and the sentinel who guards the ingress into outright Modern with both eyes cast resolutely behind him. He had contemporary *parts* but not contemporary commitment, and he practiced opera as his forebears did: as show biz. Twentieth-century composers and librettists are often going to care less about singers and audience than about pursuing their private visions, and the coming collapse of traditional rules governing melody, harmony, and rhythm will exacerbate their alienation. Massenet has warned us: parody, comedy, and a heightened response to the verbal conduits of the word-music/music-word electricity will become The Things. But Massenet's wide choice of genres is a retrospective, not a preview. New formats are to be developed for a variety of subjects and approaches that makes the next century the most remarkable in opera's history.

CHAPTER SIXTEEN

Late Romanticism Versus Neo-Classicism

Art is the result of aesthetic experience that has been powerfully felt; in contemporary creation somewhere between the impulse of the original feeling and its manifestation in art, some sort of Freudian censor has intervened. The emotion is not permitted to be communicated in modern art except in disguise —symbols, wit, and satire being the masks that are most favored by contemporary creators.

—ALFRED NORTH WHITEHEAD

I can't hear anything.

—RICHARD STRAUSS,
at a performance of
Pelléas et Mélisande

WE'VE HAD ERAS OF FLORENTINE AND VENETIAN OPERA, *tragédie* AND *opera seria*, and Romantic opera. Now comes an age of diversity. It's convenient to trace it from Debussy's *Pelléas et Mélisande* in 1902, but it's also correct. Of all works on the verge between Romantic and What Came After, *Pelléas* is the most revolutionary. Yet it, like so many others, simply intends to take opera back to its basics. *Pelléas* is Camerata-style opera at its best and, in a certain very limited way, the reply to the Wagnerian plan with its manically climactic orchestra insistently beaming emotional epiphanies at the audience. Debussy

277

learned much from Wagner, but as soon as he encountered Maurice Maeterlinck's crystalline romance in 1892, he saw how opera might escape from the corner into which Wagner had painted it. "The thing," he said, "was to find what came *after Wagner's time* but not *after Wagner's manner*."

Pelléas was the thing, a playscript set to music that understatedly hovers around the words. There is no "librettist." Rather than adapt the drama, Debussy simply cut a few lines, and that's his text. The tale takes us to a medieval Ruritania called Allemonde, where a Francesca da Rimini–like triangle unfolds in a series of short, mainly inconclusive scenes stitched together by orchestral interludes. The whole work is inconclusive, actually: though the husband, discovering his wife with his half-brother, kills the latter and wounds the former, she dies without our having learned if his suspicion had any foundation. Also, and deliberately, Debussy fails to provide the ear with a structural gloss on the action, the rise and fall of conventional operatic narrative. There's nothing like an aria, duet, or finale; there's scarcely even a high note or a Big Tune. "There's too much *singing* in opera," Debussy had observed; his aim was to express "the inexpressible," find the wonder that hides beneath the visible, the verbalized, the functional in art. Just when science had passed on to commerce the secret of the first truly realistic art—the cinema—Debussy closed ranks with Symbolist poets and Impressionist painters to find an alternate realism aimed at reproducing, not the exact appearance of things but their approximate *effect*. Like Wagner, Debussy fills his sole completed opera with natural imagery—light, shadow, water, forest. But Wagner attempts to give us musical photographs, while Debussy produces a sensograph; we *feel* his water, his light.

Debussy expanded Wagner's experiments in harmony to fashion an ambiguous sound scheme of eternally shifting tonal centers which only adds to the intangible "essence-ism" of his depictions. Water flows and recedes, shadows deepen, light flickers; Debussy's music follows these transformations. More important, he reinvented music drama as "drama in music"—as opposed to the "musical sections added up to a drama" that we have been getting since about 1690. Debussy doesn't play the story as it happens; instead, a few meaningless themes float, tremble, and interlace under a fluid recitative. It is as if the singers were presenting the material and the orchestra were dreaming about it.

It works beautifully with Maeterlinck's fey excursion, though it takes some getting used to. The only other composer who adopted Debussy's plan was Paul Dukas, and he too applied it to a play by Maeterlinck, *Ariane et Barbe-Bleue* (1907). If *Pelléas* is ambivalent,

Ariane sounds a call to action: the heroine is Bluebeard's sixth wife, locked in a castle of vast gloom with six silver keys, one gold key, and a warning to use only the silver. The seventh door is forbidden. Letting the listener "notice" the music more than Debussy does, Dukas set the opening of the doors to a theme-and-variations set, each variation designed to capture the quality of a different gem (cascades of jewels lie behind the doors). A naturally rebellious spirit—"the first thing we have to do," she explains to her nurse, "is disobey"—Ariane opens the seventh door and finds Bluebeard's other wives (Mélisande among them; Dukas shatters his own spell by quoting Debussy's). In the end she tries to take them out of the castle, but they elect to stay with Bluebeard. Maeterlinck subtitled his play "The Useless Deliverance."

Like Debussy, Dukas deals in the environmentals of impressionism, opening his score in the heavily dank air of Bluebeard's castle, lightening and quickening the "view" with the scene of the jewels, plunging back into darkness, and then pulling all the stops out for an explosion of radiance when Ariane smashes open a window in the wives' prison and the outer world of ocean, wind, pasture, and birdsong fills the ear's eye. Debussy, too, painted a wonderful representation of the return into sunlight from deep in a castle's vaults. However, the great quality of these operas is not their pictorial sensitivity but their liberation from fixed number-opera format combined with the reemphasized verbal music of the text.

These diaphanous Maeterlinck operas had an immediate effect on everybody—no one was neutral. Yet they did not kill the average taste for the fun of *comique* and the passion of full-blown opera. Such pieces as Henri Rabaud's *Mârouf, Savetier de Caire* (Marouf, Cobbler of Cairo, 1914), a thinly sumptuous Arabian night, kept the slyly exotic in gear; and Albert Roussel's more sincerely exotic *Padmâvatî* (1923) told of a Mongolian invasion of Hindustan and the virtuous princess who not only refuses to give herself to the conquerors if they spare her city but kills her husband when he suggests she comply. *Padmâvatî*, described as an "opera-ballet" but really more of a small grand opera, owes a lot to *Pelléas* in the way Roussel set off the words.

Maurice Ravel was most impressed by *Pelléas*. His two one-act operas, however, *L'Heure Espagnole* (A Spanish Hour, 1911) and *L'Enfant et les Sortilèges* (The Child and the Enchantments, 1925), are lively, urbane, and parodistic, nothing at all like Maeterlinck's somber castle in the woods. Still, a Debussyan clarity infects the conversational line. Very much the neo-Classicist, Ravel delighted in reconstructions of ancient styles (as in his piano suite *The Tomb of Couperin*), and in Spanish invocations (as in the infamous *Bolero*), for he was a technician above all, polished and exact. *L'Heure Espagnole*, which looks in on a clockmaker's wife as she juggles lovers in one lazily frantic hour, might be viewed as a study in *musical* farce: how to bend the orchestral commentary to the point, rather than the tempo, of a given scene. *L'Enfant*, too, presents a problem and a solution: how to build unity out of parodistic vaudeville. Colette's libretto gives us a naughty child who, when punished, runs wild in his room, wrecking and messing. For most of the work, his toys and furnishings come alive to berate and abandon him in self-contained musical spoofs—a fox trot for a Wedgwood teapot and a china cup (the teapot sings quaint English—"I punch, Sir, I punch your nose"—and the cup Instant Oriental—"Cas-ka-ra, harakiri, Sessue Hayakawa"), coloratura canary for the rebellious fire, a Provençal pastorale for the shepherds on the wallpaper, a beery cabaret waltz for a dragonfly. The show takes on the character of a revue. But Ravel's pastiche is so finely turned that he draws the listener through these episodes, never blocks him. Moreover, his orchestration is a marvel, setting a piquant mood in the opening for two meandering oboes—bored child—and using his huge band sparingly for variety of color rather than exhortation of the eardrums. Somewhat similar to Ravel's two short operas is Manuel de Falla's even briefer *El Retablo de Maese Pedro* (Master Peter's Puppet Show, 1923), adapted from the chapter of *Don Quixote* in which Cervantes' noble crazy gets so caught up in a chivalric thriller that he smashes Master Peter's little theatre and most of the puppet company. De Falla had come under the spell of French neo-Classicism, and like Ravel he revives old forms and keeps those forms self-enclosed. The aim of the age is to keep it small, wry, and slightly abstract in feeling. Contained.

Absolutely typical of the new wave was the group of six composers known as the Nouveaux Jeunes (New Youth), or The Six. Led by Darius Milhaud, Francis Poulenc, and Arthur Honegger, in close collaboration with Jean Cocteau and the radically droll composer Erik Satie, a specialist in the tiny piano piece, The Six conceived post-Wagnerianism as a grand opportunity to infuse established technique with popular idioms, especially American music. Like Debussy they prized verbal clarity; like Ravel they adored parody and satire. Cocteau dreamed up a scenario for a pastiche of Brazilian dances that Milhaud had composed, "achieving" either through ruthless calculation or genius instinct a major event in twentieth-century art, the ballet *Le Bœuf sur le Toit* (The Ox on the Roof, 1920), set in an American speakeasy and peopled by absurdist archetypes moving in slow motion and costumed in papier-mâché masks: a boxer smoking a huge cigar, a policeman, a bookie, a red-haired woman dressed as a man, a black dwarf, and such.

The bartender decapitates the policeman; the red-haired woman dances with his head; he revives; the bartender hands him an enormous bill. Under all this Milhaud presents a hectic rondo of Latin American dances, the rondo theme that binds them together striking off sparks of slapstick sensuality. It may not sound contained, but the theme's recurrence orders the chaos, fixes the whole so firmly that one can hear the structure as the music unfolds.

Milhaud had his serious side; they all did, with the exception of Satie. Indeed, Milhaud later regretted ever having been one of the six *enfants terribles*. His *L'Orestie*, a setting of Paul Claudel's translation of Aeschylus' trilogy, composed from 1913 to 1924, is austere and vast, and with Cocteau he overturned the lush violence of *verismo* in *Le Pauvre Matelot* (The Poor Sailor, 1927), an hour-long picture of a mariner who returns unrecognized to his faithful wife only to be murdered by her in hope of saving her husband from illness and debt. Throughout, the music assists the singers but does not force any issue; livelier than *Pelléas*, it still lets the text take the lead. Milhaud prefers irony to bombast, and draws his curtain *before* the wife discovers her mistake rather than during—as, say, Mascagni would have done.

Other Frenchmen returned to Greek material. Gabriel Fauré turned out a *Prométhée* (1900) and a *Pénélope* (1913), Saint-Saëns a *Héléne* (1904). But it felt equally Classical to reinvest the stage with the old masks of *commedia dell'arte*—Arlecchino, Colombina, Scaramuccio, Tartaglia, each with his definitive traits. Milhaud, most prolific and multileveled of composers, enters the picture again with a "sung ballet," *Salade* (1924), enacted by dancers while singers deliver the lines from the pit. His masks plotting and pranking at the gallop, Milhaud redoubles the farce with pranks of his own—lampoons, wrong or bizarrely high notes, tinny scoring, ridiculously tender moments flanked by booms and bursts, and a general air of sabotage. And of course at the end the characters address the public directly to express *Salade's* moral (love intrigues conquer all), sing tra la, take their bows, and dance away.

In other words, there was a genuine anti-Wagnerian revolution going on, not by plan so much as by art's natural urge toward transformation. Though French music had included some of Wagner's most involved supporters, the dry French style quickly recoiled from all that immensity and it was the French who contributed the most to neo-Classicism. They had learned from and in some ways would continue to admire Wagner. But they themselves moved on to smaller, sharper, more worldly concoctions. Debussy and Dukas cast wonderful spells in their operas, but spell casting was Romantic, outdated. The Six did just the opposite: they reminded you, every other note, that art was artful, an arrangement of ingredients.

In England there was no need for such a movement, for nineteenth-century English opera hadn't gone Romantic enough to exhaust itself. But here too Debussyan impressionism made its inroads in the work of Frederick Delius, a tone painter of considerable bucolic serenity. Delius could dazzle, as in his animated tone poems on Norse saga and boulevardier night life, *Eventyr* and *Paris,* but his operas ran to the sedate, failing in dramatic momentum. *Koanga* (1904), on life and love among slaves in Louisiana, has a nice bounce, owing its rhythmic vitality to Delius' stint in Florida as an orange planter. But *A Village Romeo and Juliet* (1907) and *Fennimore and Gerda* (1919), made up of scenes tied together by orchestral interludes—like *Pelléas et Mélisande*—lack *Pelléas'* internal motion, especially *Fennimore and Gerda,* whose triangle plot involving a painter, a writer, and the woman torn between them gives out two scenes before the opera ends.

But then native English opera did not enjoy a very encouraging climate in which to experiment and develop. With Gilbert and Sullivan still enormously popular but the mid-Victorian opera style moldy, the art had run down badly. The least imposing pieces found a stage if not a lasting audience, while Delius and his colleagues Gustav Holst and Ralph Vaughan Williams regularly waited years till some enthusiast got one of their compositions into a theatre. Delius finished *Koanga* in 1897 and *Fennimore and Gerda* in 1910, respectively seven and ten years before their premieres; Holst's Indian one-act *Sāvitri* (1916) had lain ready since 1908; Vaughan Williams' *Hugh the Drover,* finished by 1914, waited out ten years on the shelf, and his Falstaff piece *Sir John in Love,* ready by 1928, was performed by students a year later but not heard professionally till 1946. *Sāvitri* may move a mite slowly, but Holst's half-hour *The Wandering Scholar* (1934), Chaucerian in flavor, strikes off nimble comic sparks. Vaughan Williams was the most dynamic of the three. His opera scores sound like folk-song collections strung out for narrative, which is a strength and a weakness: they are weak in the forward push of the action, but strong in nationalist lyricism. Just when continental Europe was at its most eclectic and international, England found (rather, failed to, as Vaughan Williams' operas are only now getting their fair hearing) its great cultural archon, a king of ballads, chanteys, catches, and psalm tunes. Most of them are his own—Vaughan Williams believed in improvised as well as academic folklore—though "Greensleeves" makes a grand effect when it turns up, words and all, in Act II of *Sir John in Love. Hugh the Drover,* shortish and sweet, suffers from Harold Child's overdainty text; the music sings of bluff country humor, fairground roughhouse, and small-town bullying as much as of shy young love, but Child doesn't quite tell us what Vaughan Williams does, and performances ail. Still, the work is a delight, from its eager opening of offstage voices roaring in laughter before the curtain rises, to the thrilling full-cast cry of "God save the King!" near the end, just after Hugh and his love are united and Hugh's unpleasant rival is suddenly drafted into the army to fight Napoleon I.

While France embraced neo-Classicism and England busied itself renewing its musical forms, Italy threw itself into a fabulously Romantic superage, so rich in quality and so distinct from what the rest of Europe was up to that it takes its own chapter, immediately following. It's ironic that the *commedia dell'arte* that contributed so much to neo-Classical satire proved busier in France and Germany than on home ground; only one major Italian composer dealt with *commedia* to any extent, Gian Francesco Malipiero. But Malipiero's comedy is macabre and his ingenious scores thrill the musician more than they do the average operagoer. This is highly unconventional material, theatrically sophisticated whereas Malipiero's contemporaries of the Puccini age favored straight-on melodramas that would yield the usual mix of arias and ensembles. Malipiero's prolificacy took him into the 1970s as one of Italy's greatest composers, but he is seldom heard elsewhere.

Consider Malipiero's early masterpiece, *L'Orfeide* (Orpheus' Children, 1925), a trilogy of one-act operas composed in the years just after World War I, text by the composer and music designed—like Debussy's in *Pelléas*—to render the inexpressible that hides beneath the appearance of action. However, Malipiero's style sounds nothing like the light, almost rhythmless flow of the Frenchman. The Italian knows his *canto*, and loves to stir the orchestra up in a march or dance. Where Debussy has ambivalence, Malipiero has thrust and exuberance. What odd premises he chose for *L'Orfeide*: In Part I, *La Morte delle Maschere* (The Death of the Masks), Orpheus bows out *commedia*'s stock characters—locks them up, in fact—and brings on a new crowd of players for this new era, capable of the grotesquerie, tragicomedy, and surrealistic coincidence which twentieth-century art deals in. These new-style players then enact the centerpiece of the triptych, *Sette Canzoni* (Seven Songs), a sequence of seven sketches, each in a totally different sound style and each a bizarre happening somehow involving the singing of a song. In one scene a blind guitarist accompanies a singer to cadge alms from passersby; the song so fascinates the guitarist's companion that she runs off with the singer, leaving the blind musician to guess how well the tune has gone over. In another scene, a young

woman mourning a corpse on a bed ignores a suitor's serenade till at
last he bursts in, understands, and kneels as the woman spreads flowers
over the corpse. Seven songs, seven absurd scenes. For Part III, *Orfeo,
ovvero l'Ottava Canzone* (Orpheus; or, The Eighth Song), Malipiero
anticipates his public's bewilderment by showing a puppet show performance boring an audience to sleep.

We should discuss Malipiero here because he has more in common
with French or even German composers than with his compatriots.
Like the French neo-Classicists, Malipiero agreed that there was a
"Wagner problem"—i.e., how to get on with the next epoch—and that
the solution comprised such anti-Wagnerian activity as satire, parody,
and containment: a return to the basics of musical thinking while
pushing into the complex psychology of the age of Freud. The casual
sensuality of *L'Heure Espagnole*, the fanciful childhood trauma of
L'Enfant et les Sortilèges, the uncluttered, unsentimental morsel of Cervantes in *El Retablo de Maese Pedro*, the comic traditionalism of *Salade*
and innovation of *L'Orfeide*—all this meant that Bayreuth fever had at
last broken.

The German solutions to the post-Wagnerian challenge ranged
from continued Wagnerian imitation to de-crazed Wagnerism to outright anti-Wagnerism. It must have been a wild era to live through,
with "jazz opera" and assorted contemporary hurdy-gurdy on one side,
Märchenoper on another, "intellectual" neo-Classicism on another, and
front and center, the career of Richard Strauss, launched in *Lohengrin*-
ish idolatry—*Guntram* (1894)—carried on through stages of mega-
Romantic cacophony and quasi-Mozartean withdrawal, and finished in
the 1940s in subtle wordplay and parody.

Having already established himself as the prime mover in symphonic program music in his elaborate tone poems, Strauss was a natural for opera, and in his second work, *Feuersnot* (Lack of Fire, 1901),
had already begun to cut the Wagnerian rumpus with his own timbre.
Rumpus is the word for *Feuersnot*, a sweetly smutty folk comedy set
in old Munich and based on the ancient saw about the magician who,
humiliated by a woman, extinguishes all the local fire until she takes
him to her bed. Suddenly, in *Salome* (1905), Strauss turned wholly
Strauss, leaving Wagner behind in a blaze of paranoid impressionism
and "corrupt" harmony. In the new predilection for setting texts rather
than adapting them, Strauss used Oscar Wilde's play (in Hedwig Lach-
mann's German translation of Wilde's original French), deleting numerous lines of stichomythic repetition (First Soldier: He is looking
at something; Second Soldier: He is looking at someone). But Wilde,
telling how Salome so desires the ascetic John the Baptist that she

dances for Herod and demands the Baptist's head—to kiss—as a reward, showed only the delicate surface of debauchery. Strauss delves into its beastly core.

Salome is a horror, though it doesn't shock us as it did Strauss' contemporaries. A product of the exquisite's cult of lush carnality derived out of Poe through such as Baudelaire and Swinburne, it shows how a certifiably Romantic composer no longer connects to the ideology of the 1800s. Manfred's and Faust's quests for self-knowledge had turned rotten, seeking nihilistic self-love/hatred. Faust is dead, long live Salome, the flower of evil. Strauss places her like a jewel in a setting slimy with images of appetitive depravity. When she peeps into the Baptist's cistern prison, Strauss slips into the deepest notes of the orchestra; to balance the central symbol of the "pale moon," he unleashes sounds of skin-crawling lust; he suggests the Baptist's messianic monomania by fitting a "wrong" note into his theme; he scores the internecine yapping of religious fanatics, spilled blood sloshing underfoot, and the wind blowing across Herod's terrace, doubling this interestingly with the prophet's "madman" theme when Herod senses "the beating of vast wings."

Strauss' trajectory took a turn for the best when he began his six-opera partnership with Hugo von Hofmannsthal, a man of the finest letters who replaced *Salome*'s Wildean *Jugendstil*-Art Nouveau prurience with humanist idealism. Gradually Strauss' canvas filled with Eternal Women, heroism, genteel *commedia*, wisdom, and transcendence. Yet their first collaboration, *Elektra* (1909), from Sophocles, seemed even more shocking at first because of Strauss' orchestral vehemence. *Salome* was nasty, but *Elektra* was loud, and as they had railed at Mozart, Rossini, Bizet, and Wagner, so now did critics attack Strauss for drowning song in symphony. It became a joke—"Louder, louder the orchestra," Strauss called to the conductor during a rehearsal, "I can still hear Frau Heink!"—though Ernestine Schumann-Heink, the first Klytämnestra, vowed never to get involved in anything like it again. What had happened to opera? Where was post-Wagnerism going to take it? Despite the gravity, the Classical finesse like a steel arrow in flight, of Hofmannsthal's text, *Elektra* echoed much of *Salome*'s greedy bedlam. Elektra herself needs a voice of monstrous power, her sister Chrysothemis acts like a lyric soprano but had better sound like a banshee to cut through the din, and Klytämnestra is such a voice shredder that it has become a favorite of veteran mezzos, who figure they have nothing to lose. Even the brief role of Aegist calls for a tenor of Wagnerian capacity. Only Orest, a bass-baritone, admits the accepted operatic vocal scale—but then it is Orest who alters forever the state of things in Mycenae when he makes his fateful entrance as both deliverer and curse bringer, to avenge his father's murder and commit his mother's in the same act. So Orest must anchor the work, must reaffirm the human proportions of a story that, till he appears, has gone haywire on dark deeds, secrets, and psychosis.

As individuals Strauss and Hofmannsthal moved in different circles and were not the best match. Yet in art they blended magnificently, the nonintellectual Strauss instinctively finding the right voice for Hofmannsthal's subtle allegory, though he claimed to find it all somewhat confused and on a few occasions actually mistook stage directions for lines and plonked them right into the music. Their most popular collaboration, *Der Rosenkavalier* (The Cavalier of the Rose, 1911), however, is a radiantly nostalgic comedy set in Maria Theresa's Vienna, with little of Hofmannsthal's psychology of the unconscious. *Feuersnot*, *Salome*, and *Elektra* were longish one-acts; *Der Rosenkavalier* is talky and takes three acts to paint out its fresco of high-, middle-, and low-lives in dalliance, puppy love, social climbing, and farcical revenge. The plot revolves around an arranged marriage between the crude Baron Ochs and Sophie, a parvenu's tender daughter, and there is much, much plot—but what makes it so special is character, especially that of the Marschallin (the Field Marshal's wife) and her impetuous lover Count Octavian. It is Octavian whom Sophie eventually ends up with, as the aging Marschallin assents to the inevitable and retires with sumptuous grace. But comedy is indissolubly merged with pathos throughout the evening, a joke hidden in or near each sigh. While we empathize when the Marschallin takes her farewell of Octavian, the "reality" of the situation is stylized for us—in the eye-filling costumes, the prudent politesse of the creamy classes, and the fact that Octavian is sung by a soprano (or mezzo) in travesty. Indeed, though Octavian is the Rosenkavalier of the title, appearing in Sophie's father's mansion with full convoy of hussars and bearing a silver rose (a "customary" token of Ochs' suit, Hofmannsthal's invention) like a prince in a fairy palace, the character spends a healthy fraction of the evening disguised as the Marschallin's maid, complete with proletarian Viennese accent, travesty donned on travesty. Part of *Der Rosenkavalier*'s uniqueness is that one is never sure where the laughter ends and sentiment begins.

Having weaned Strauss away from his lurid excesses, Hofmannsthal now introduced him to the chamber scale of post-Wagnerism in an unusual project: Hofmannsthal would adapt an outdated translation of Molière's *Le Bourgeois Gentilhomme*, for which Strauss would compose the incidental score—curtain music, entrance tunes, dances, and so on. And for the entertainment that the "bourgeois gentleman" orders, the pair would create an *opera seria* on the "Ariadne on Naxos" trope, complicated by the intrusion of *commedia* clowns—the gentleman's schedule does not allow time for both opera and farce except simultaneously. Here Strauss slipped into the archeology, parody, and satire of neo-Classicism: a small orchestra,* a rehabilitation of old forms, quotations from Lully's original score for Molière, and the chance to shadow the steadfast Ariadne with her profane counterpart in the comedienne Zerbinetta. Because *Der Rosenkavalier* had made Strauss the preeminent German composer, *Der Bürger als Edelmann* containing *Ariadne auf Naxos* (1912) could take its pick of creating forces, and the authors turned to Max Reinhardt, likewise preeminent in both experimental and traditional theatre. But Reinhardt's home company in Berlin couldn't handle this combination of drama, opera, and *divertimento,* and the various talents descended—with a hand-picked coterie —on Stuttgart, elbowing the resident artists out of the way but at least assuring the work of an ideal launching pad.

It did not take off. Basically the thing is too big, too much to absorb in one sitting. Just the idea of confronting the "ideal" woman with the trollop, in all their disparate and shared facets, fills an evening, and in the end the musical components were cut out of the Molière to float on their own. The incidental score survives as a concert suite, and the opera, slightly revised (1916)† and preceded by a prologue (to explain why the *seria* and *buffa* characters share the stage), has slowly entered what might be termed the "caviar repertory," works too special to be called popular yet too frequently performed not to be.

The chance to revive the *seria* style might have prompted an all-out replica or burlesque from many a neo-Classicist of the day. But Strauss never broke entirely with Romanticism, with the feeling behind story, and he simply purified his native idiom, coming up with less an *opera seria* than a Straussian salute to the *seria* spirit. The Prologue melds song, recit, and speech—very twentieth century—as it prowls the backstage haunt to reveal musicians and farceurs in their element. The arch of the evening rises toward a comprehension of the "two" essences of woman, mythic Ariadne and earthy Zerbinetta. So Strauss

---

* Hofmannsthal had at first proposed a group of no more than twenty players, but eventually Strauss settled on somewhat less than forty.
† The most important difference, from the singer's point of view, was the easing of the last section of Zerbinetta's huge showpiece recit, aria, and rondo, which in its original form troubled even expert singers. Hedwig Francillo-Kaufman, who made one of the two records of the ur-version, comes to terrible grief in it, and though at one moment she breaks into the music to announce that she'll make it or "sing it again," she was clearly bluffing. Her off-pitch, vertiginous performance hardly constitutes making it and she gives no encore.

alternates the Romantic and the comic, bridging the two worlds in the character of the Composer, an impressionable Mozartean lad of staunch artistic extremism who somehow finds himself flirting with Zerbinetta. This bimodal outlook naturally dominates the opera proper, wherein the comedians improvise assorted flapdoodle on the desert island where Ariadne, abandoned by Theseus, waits for death. Sollipsistic Romanticism—which no one had served up better than Strauss—was sharing its space with Classicism. If the *bel canto* aria characterized opera in the eighteenth century and exotic melancholy characterized it in the nineteenth, this new blend of the heroic and the silly characterizes it in the twentieth.

Speaking of heroes, Strauss didn't at first know how to cast them, for tenors, the natural choice, gave him the horrors. *Feuersnot*'s, *Salome*'s, and *Elektra*'s lead males are baritones, while Octavian and the Composer are trouser parts. But with Bacchus, the god who brings Ariadne love in place of death, Strauss honored precedent and let the love hero sing high and, he hoped, virile. He could hardly have done otherwise: *Ariadne auf Naxos* already counts a rich Straussian soprano of considerable stamina and radiant upper register (Ariadne), a coloratura daredevil (Zerbinetta), and a darker soprano (the Composer), and the lead male comedian is a baritone. For balance, Strauss admitted the tenor into the circle, and the result, a final duet of clarion exaltation, is successful. So much so that the fourth Strauss-Hofmannsthal opera, *Die Frau Ohne Schatten* (The Woman Without a Shadow, 1919), also counts on a lead Wagnerian tenor.

Die Frau took Strauss into the deeper reaches of Hofmannsthal's symbolistic humanism; more about this astonishing piece later. As if by way of antidote, Strauss set a sturdily worldly course in his next piece —to his own text—the "bourgeois comedy with symphonic interludes," *Intermezzo* (1924). Here is opera at its most quotidian, unthinkable before *Louise:* petty spats and tender peacemaking in a household modeled on Strauss' own, even including a faithful rendering of his infamously unpleasant wife, Pauline. The musical approach would not have been possible before *Pelléas et Mélisande:* dialogues that really sound like "talking," set off by an orchestra that reserves most of its contributions for the interludes between scenes. It was as far from *Salome* as anyone could get.

Meanwhile, Strauss' fellow late Romantics were trying to pick up the pieces of their shattered style in a world growing suddenly cynical after World War I. The *Märchenoper*, the adaptations from fiction and drama, the neurotic exorcisms of troubled souls continued to fill theatres, but, except for Strauss, virtually the entire literature has disappeared. Operas by Max von Schillings, Leo Blech, Franz Schreker, Erich Wolfgang Korngold went everywhere in the century's first two decades; today a rare outing of von Schillings' *Mona Lisa* (1915), Schreker's *Die Ferne Klang* (The Distant Sound, 1912), or Korngold's *Die Tote Stadt* (The Dead City, 1920) is all that remains of a whole industry in supernatural and/or sensual tales run up in pushy vocal lines and demented orchestration.

With garish *Spätromantik* (= late Romanticism, circa 1900 on) on one hand and the various gathering forces of neo-Classicism on the other, Hans Pfitzner spoke out for reactionary renewal, most effectively in *Palestrina* (1917), his semiautobiographical picture of the sixteenth-century Italian composer who instilled the virtues of the old polyphonic style against the revolutionary simplicity of the "new music" (which, we recall, formed the basis of the first operas of the Florentine Camerata). Polyphony—the use of more than one melody at once—stands in Pfitzner's piece for Wagnerian symphony, and the threatening "new music" stands for the neo-Classicism that had found an eloquent theoretician in Ferruccio Busoni. Having no use either for the overboogie of *Spätromantik* or for Busoni's disciplined rejection of it, Pfitzner planted himself, so to speak, in the vanguard of the rear, as if hoping to lead the covered wagons westward all over again. He designed the pompous but deeply felt *Palestrina* (to his own text) to reroute the course of German opera, to purge it of decadence—in story matter and harmony both—and to save it from neo-Classical extremists. But no one followed Pfitzner.

Indeed, those who felt that Romanticism had grown turgid, morbid, and elephantine tended to abandon it entirely for the economy and clarity of neo-Classicism. Busoni, who with Paul Hindemith led the movement, retrieved the models of Renaissance *commedia* and Baroque structuring in two short works, the storybook *Turandot* and the slapstick *Arlecchino*, premiered as a double bill in 1917 in Zurich (a coincidental halfway point between the German intellectualism and Italian sensuality that comprised Busoni's warring blood stock). Whereas Puccini's version of *Turandot* (like Busoni's taken from Gozzi's play) is expensively lush, Busoni's is compressed, made of miniatures. Each little section—aria, ensemble, chorus—stands apart from the rest. *Arlecchino*, devoted to the spoofs of Harlequin, is laid out in four movements, like a symphony. It opens with a very showpiece of compression: a fanfare made of all twelve notes of the Western so-called "chromatic" scale.

Hindemith, unlike the exegetical Busoni, was something of a cutup at first, writing several avant-garde one-acts that thrilled the progres-

sive cognoscenti and scandalized everyone else. In 1921 a double bill
of one-acts at the Stuttgart court theatre disclosed *Mörder, Hoffnung
der Frauen* (Murderer, Hope of Women), whose title neatly sums up
the action of painter Oscar Kokoschka's libretto, and *Das Nusch-
Nuschi*, a whimsical Oriental marionette play about a field marshal
who must undergo castration as a punishment for having dallied with
one of the emperor's wives. (At the moment of revelation, Hindemith
lets the emperor repeat King Marke's line, "This—to me?," from
Tristan und Isolde and wryly quotes from Wagner's score.) Both
works showed the influence of Germany's radical new theatre (both
had been plays before they were librettos), and Hindemith further
distanced them from business-as-usual with his parodistic methodism,
making his scores sound as if they were as interested in their own
technical acrobatics as in narrating the action. Indeed, the intendant
at Stuttgart had chosen not to mount the third of what Hindemith
had planned as a triple bill, *Sancta Susanna* (1922), a tale of a nun's
sexual rampage, set to a theme and variations. Later, Hindemith embraced outright lampoon in two librettos by a cabaret wit, Marcellus
Schiffer, the brief *Hin und Zurück* (There and Back, 1927), an absurd
murder tale that replays its action in reverse at the halfway mark,
and the full-length *Neues vom Tage* (News of the Day, 1929), on a
divorcing couple's adventures with the commercial tie-in of show biz
and the news media.

One cannot build an operatic output on the fads of the day,
and Hindemith looked for a chance to test neo-Classicism in a more
ideal situation. This wouldn't be easy, for German and French writers
who were willing to subsume their gifts in a script for music preferred
to work in satire or horror. The most bizarre ideas were filling Hindemith's mail. "My mother sorts them out," he explained, "and my sister
reads them, and finally our dog busies himself with them in his own
way." At length, in 1925, Ferdinand Lion, who had just supplied Eugen
d'Albert with the text for *Der Golem* (1926), handed over to Hindemith a libretto he had intended for d'Albert. Hindemith had to content
himself with the bizarre after all, for Lion had based his story on
E. T. A. Hoffmann's *Das Fräulein von Scuderi*, about a Parisian gold-
smith so possessed by his own craftmanship that he kills his clients to
reappropriate his creations.

As *Cardillac* (1926) the result stands as a masterpiece of high
neo-Classicism, coming after its overcompensating introductory experiments and before it neutralized itself in stagnant fanaticism. Perhaps the 1920s interest in Handelian opera inspired Hindemith to shape
his piece in the clear-cut entities of the Baroque era, with aria, duet,

variation form, and even a *da capo* scene for Cardillac's daughter with solo lines for oboe, horn, and violin. In any case, this is no conventional thriller. Unlike the *verismo* composers, Hindemith does not always score the horror itself, but sometimes steals around it, emphasizing it by playing against our Romantic conditioning as operagoers. We expect the orchestra to scream when the action does; Hindemith's doesn't necessarily. Thus the scene in which a Knight surprises his Lady with a gift, a jeweled belt from Cardillac's workshop, proves unnervingly suspenseful in pantomime, accompanied by a steely minuet led by two flutes. We know that Cardillac will show up to reclaim his belt—and sure enough, as the Lady tries it on and the Knight begins to make love to her, a masked figure slips into the room. The orchestra continues to go its own acidly merry way, and the use of mime develops the tease: the Lady spots Cardillac but cannot get the Knight's attention in time. Cardillac stabs the Knight, grabs the belt, and flies off "like a bird of prey," and at last Hindemith allows the Lady the scene's sole employment of the human voice. She screams.

Along with parody, comedy, and structural virtuosity, neo-Classical opera loved popular music, especially American. "This was the America," Lotte Lenya recalls, "of the garish Twenties, with its Capones, Texas Guinans, Aimee Semple MacPhersons, Ponzis; the Florida boom and crash, also a disastrous Florida hurricane; a ghastly photograph, reproduced in every German newspaper, of the murderess Ruth Snyder in the electric chair; Hollywood films about the Wild West and the Yukon; Jack London's adventure novels; Tin Pan Alley songs." Lenya's husband Kurt Weill caught the reverberation of all this better than anybody, taking for his muse a jazz baby who smashed Romanticism with the shimmy, the fox trot, the saxophone riff, and the cymbal stinger. Yet Weill, who studied with Busoni, had more technique than he knew what to do with; his jazz copulated with fugue and put on variation forms like a transvestite fingering a feather boa.

If Busoni was the grandmaster of German neo-Classicism, Weill and Hindemith led the younger generation. At the German Chamber Music Festival in Baden-Baden (organized to play contemporary music) in 1927, the same bill that introduced Hindemith's *Hin und Zurück* brought forth the first collaboration of Weill and Bertolt Brecht, a short *Songspiel* entitled *Mahagonny*. There was no plot: inside a boxing ring, in front of Caspar Neher's sexily sardonic projections and occasionally spelled by orchestral interludes, the cast delivers songs of greed, sloth, fear, and despair on the subject of an imaginary place half Chicago and half Utopia. Brecht, who claimed that eventually the whole world would speak a pidgin English, wrote two of the lyrics in that tongue ("Alabama Song" begins, "Oh, show us the way to the next whiskey-bar!"), but in fact he intended to make himself understood—to the last syllable—on a number of items, and embarked on a series of full-length evenings of music theatre in his special "epic style" oathed to "the extinction of bourgeois forms of art" along with the bourgeoisie as a class in the "irreversible breakdown of the existing social order."

Weill-Brecht theatre is political theatre, though as a genre their works fall under the heading of *Zeitoper*, an untranslatable term for opera created out of the fashions of a day. *Neues vom Tage*, with its burlesque of media manipulation, was *Zeitoper*, and the *Mahagonny Songspiel*, with its crazy English, its trashing of the Bridesmaids' Chorus from *Der Freischütz* in its opening number, its boompa-boompa rhythms and Bachian surprises, was *Zeitoper* too. Perhaps the most definitive of them all was Ernst Křenek's fantastic-realistic *Jonny Spielt Auf* (Jonny Strikes Up the Band, 1927), telling of a black American jazzman trying to steal a priceless violin, and closing in a red-white-and-blue finale of jazz worshipers hailing Jonny, who plays that fiddle for the lowdown while perched on a huge revolving globe of the world.

Brecht's librettos are *Zeitoper* only by coincidence; their main intention is to expose the capitalist system as exploitation and corruption of an already base humanity. Most comfortable when setting his works in unnamed terrain stippled with the places of British imperialism—Tahiti, Benares, Tibet—Brecht moved to a very real London in his full-length collaboration with Weill, *Die Dreigroschenoper* (The Threepenny Opera, 1928), an adaptation of *The Beggar's Opera*. Technically this is a play with songs, as the score does not advance the action but actually halts it for explication. Brecht makes no attempt to fold the numbers into the libretto: he *prefers* the disjunct procedure, for that way the spectator will not take part in the performance emotionally but will retain his distance and receive the art as moral instruction. This is the famous Brechtian "alienation," the *Verfremdungseffekt*, very typical of neo-Classicism's bashing of Romanticism's magic.

The worst of Romantic theatre, Brecht thought, was the *Gesamtkunstwerk*, that "fusion of the arts" that robbed each art of its separate purpose. "The process of fusion," he wrote, "extends to the spectator, who gets thrown into the melting pot, too, and becomes a passive (suffering) part of the total work of art . . . Whatever is intended to produce hypnosis, is likely to induce sordid intoxication, or creates fog, has got to be given up. Words, music, and setting must become more independent of one another."

This independence is the alienation, and it works brilliantly. If the playwright's dissection of capitalism as a vicious conspiracy of the underworld, the business world, and the state security forces doesn't tally out, and if his hypothesis of the human condition—"The world is poor and man is bad"—is dead wrong, still his eloquence is amazing. And Weill, of course, was just the composer he needed. No wonder Hindemith's letter of query to Brecht on the possibility of a *Faust* opera led to nothing. Weill captured the pulse of pop music as Hindemith never could. Both are dry, ironic, touchy—but Weill has the oomph. Who else could have constructed an international smash hit song out of one simple tune repeated over and over with a slightly different accompaniment each time, as Weill did in *The Threepenny Opera*'s opening number, the "Moritat of Mackie Messer,"* sung by a ballad singer on a market day in Soho? (Brecht sets the scene: "The beggars are begging, the thieves thieving, the whores whoring.")

Many analysts would not rate *Die Dreigroschenoper* as an opera, and it certainly didn't act like one when it was first staged, being the product of a small nonmusical theatre company in a kitschy old house in Berlin.† This was their opening entry, and word of mouth, based on casting problems and disastrous rehearsals, boded ill. About twenty minutes into the premiere, however, as of the lively Cannon Song, *Die Dreigroschenoper* turned into a sensation, and the author quickly followed it up with a second work, staged by the same production team, *Happy End* (1929). This one takes place in Chicago and counts gangsters and a Salvation Army band as its characters. A jolly piece that doesn't face politics till its final scene, *Happy End* moves somewhat chaotically, leaving the songs—including the classic neo-Classical torch song, "Surabaya Jonny"—to strike the tone. The two men were already working on their most musical event yet (albeit retaining their roots in Berlin's cabaret theatre), an all-out expansion of *Maha-*

---

* The Moritat, or Murder-Deed Song, has no counterpart in *The Beggar's Opera*, though ballads citing the exploits of noted criminals belong to an old English tradition. Weill and Brecht's Moritat is known in America as "The Ballad of Mack the Knife."

† G. W. Pabst, filming the piece in 1931, seemed to regard it as a straight dramatic work and the score of incidental importance: he deleted most of the songs. Brecht hated the movie, even instituted proceedings against it, but Pabst does bring out the atmosphere of Brecht's setting, if not his theatre style. Best of all, Pabst preserved Lotte Lenya's really dangerous performance of "Pirate Jenny," sung perfectly motionless through all its verses till the last note, when she lifts her arm in a *louche* existentialist's shrug.

gonny, Aufstieg und Fall der Stadt Mahagonny (Rise and Fall of
Mahagonny City, 1930). Except in a few lines, music carries the entire
show, and, as in *Die Dreigroschenoper*, an unfriendly detachment
keeps one intrigued but not involved. Failing to be attracted to the
characters, one takes in Brecht's lecture as if one were left out of a
party. Brecht posits Mahagonny as a model of capitalist society—the
"city of nets"—where anything can be fixed and poverty is the only
crime. We see Mahagonny founded (on the Florida "gold coast," by
criminals on the lam), filled with good-timers and bad hats, on the
boom and in the slump. At length it collapses in a stupendous depression, but, to bring the horror home—intellectually, now—Brecht shows
us his male lead, Jimmy Mahoney, executed in the electric chair for
being unable to meet his bar bill. Even his girl, the eternal Brechtian
Jenny, won't bail him out. If *Mahagonny* is to horrify us, we have to
care about Jimmy on some level—yet how can we, when Brecht and
Weill refuse to present him as anything but a cartoon archetype like
everyone else onstage? This detachment in neo-Classical art proved
problematic for the public (as did Brecht's politics: *Mahagonny*
prompted riots). Even in a satirical (i.e., anti-Romantic) age—which we
have arguably been in ever since World War I ended—such a paradox
of procedure bewilders most people. The attempt to alienate even as
one inveigles is very, very tricky to bring off; it is what makes the
likes of T. S. Eliot and Stravinsky unique and unclassifiable.

Can neo-Classical opera work at all? Isn't opera, at heart, a
Romantic form adaptable to certain aspects of the neo-Classical men-
tality (economy, verbal clarity) but hostile to others (antiemotional
narrative)? Opera was invented Romantic and has been getting steadily
more so through the years. Could it possibly turn so completely around
in subject and approach, disconnecting its currents of psychology,
description, diversion, fantasy, and rapturous emotional involvement?
Always opera believed in people—in Arianna, Orfeo, Penelope, and
Ulisse, for starters. Is opera now to believe not in people but in ideas,
caring about the society that executes Jimmy Mahoney but not about
Jimmy himself?

As it happens, opera did not turn completely around, except in
a very few cases such as these Weill-Brecht pieces. Even Hindemith's
Cardillac, so often cited as "too" neo-Classical in its rigorous working
out of each scene on an academic plan, is fine (if different) theatre,
exciting and highly colored if seldom precisely moving. Neo-Classical
opera's achievement was to find new ways to do the same thing that
Romantic opera does. Basically, neo-Classical opera *comments* on what
happens in its libretto while Romantic opera just happens. Romantic

art in general is self-absorbed, instinctual; neo-Classical art is self-regarding, measured out logically. These are two very different ways to tell a story, and both ways work. But neo-Classicism meant more than a revolution in mode, more than a deflation of Romanic elephantiasis with an interest in the comedy and precision that Romanticism had neglected. Neo-Classicism also tied in with contemporary art in its use of political militancy and satiric naturalism. It's a complex business, and should not be thought "inexpressive" because it "lacks passion," as its detractors claim. It has different passions.

While Italy remained Romantic and France and Germany balanced Romanticism with neo-Classicism, nations less central to Western stages worked out their own varieties of Modern. In Hungary, Béla Bartók moved from Wagner to Strauss to Debussy, finding in the latter's whole-tone scale the ideal correspondence for the Hungarian folk timbre, and Bartók's sole opera, the one-act *A Kékszakállú Herceg Vára* (Duke Bluebeard's Castle, 1918), scores Wagner's ritual opera in Strauss' obsessive-compulsive orchestra, letting the vocal line unfold conversationally in the *Pelléas* manner. Bartók's compatriot Zoltán Kodály, also an enthusiast of the native sound, complements Bartók's farouche *opera seria* with basic musical comedy. His *Székelyfonó* (The Spinning Room, 1924) and *Háry János* (1926) both draw heavily from the public domain for their tunes; the later of the two stands as a preeminent folk musical, being the preposterous adventures of a veteran soldier with as much wistful epic in him as braggadoccio. Kodály troubles to assure us that every word of the tale is true. He appeals to an old Hungarian tradition: any statement greeted by a sneeze *must* be so, and *Háry János'* overture begins—with a sneeze.

At the same time the Polish Karol Szymanowski was trying to refresh Romantic opera in *Król Roger* (King Roger, 1926), about a medieval Sicilian ruler's resistance and capitulation to Dionysian cultism. Szymanowski succeeded on the grand scale, using much that is Modern in an essentially ecstatic myth-opera. Conversely, the Danish Carl Nielsen found a more severe style for his Biblical *Saul og David* (1902) and the comedy *Maskarade* (1906), two operas completely unalike in subject but sharing Nielsen's peculiar version of neo-Classicism as Romantically involved but Classically structured.

The most singular contribution to a Modern aesthetic in eastern Europe was made by a Czech (Moravian, more precisely), Leoš Janáček, more or less self-taught and like Bartók one of the great collectors and synthesizers of folk music. Janáček had matured in the nineteenth century but he shared with younger composers the twentieth century's obsession with the potential linguistic contours of composition. "The magic of the human voice!" he wrote. "The tones, the melody of human speech, of every living creature, meant for me the supreme truth." Janáček's operas "talk" even at their most musical; the orchestra whines, chuckles, shouts along with the singers, and in exactly their "words." It's a thrilling study in cultural extrapolation, all the more so because it is so bound up in a spiritual intensity. Janáček's six major operas, all produced in the last third of his life, find the humanity in troubled or disreputable human situations: in those who break community taboos (*Jenůfa*, *Káta Kabanová*), in a bourgeous philistine and coward (*The Excursions of Mister Brouček*), in the shameful carryings-on of the animal species (*The Adventures of the Vixen Sharp-Ears*), in a woman who gains eternal youth at the cost of the ability to feel (*The Makropulos Business*), and even in the brutalized prisoners of a Siberian labor camp (*From the House of the Dead*).

Starting with *Jenůfa* (1904), Janáček began to discard Western conventions, though already there is little of the aria approach that Massenet and Puccini, for example, were still using very successfully. Janáček's operas are more like Strauss': solo scenes and Big Tunes occur when they are called for, not because the audience might otherwise feel cheated. Too, *Jenůfa* (actually titled *Její Pastorkyňa*, Her Stepdaughter) is a naturalistic piece, centered on the tribulations of an unmarried mother. It seems as if every composer around the turn of the century felt obliged to try naturalism at least once—but Janáček had a vested interest, for to him only the natural in art was interesting. But fantasy often keys us into naturalism, through exaggeration and satire, and in *Výlety Páně Broučkovy* (The Excursions of Mister Brouček, 1920), he took his unadmirable hero first to the moon and then back in time to a momentous and bloody event of Czech history. Mr. Brouček fails to appreciate the high-flying lunar art and similarly fails to distinguish himself in battle, but in the end we can't dislike him, for we know him all too well from life. Janáček also energizes an animal fable with rustic, Czech-style *commedia* in *Příhody Lišky Bystroušky* (The Adventures of the Vixen Sharp-Ears, 1924), interlacing the animal and human worlds against the wondrous continuity of the natural world, and set Karel Čapek's play *Věc Makropulos* (The Makropulos Business, 1926) to detail the flinty fascination of its 342-year-old heroine as person rather than as ghoul.

From work to work, Janáček abandoned more and more those definitively musical passages that mean "opera" to most ears. He was seeking an atmosphere to carry the ear through an entire act as tunes prompt or echo the voices and reinvent themselves in endless trans-

L'Heure Espagnole in Max Bignens' bizarre designs at La Scala, 1975. *(E. A. Teatro alla Scala)*

Der Rosenkavalier, Act II; the presentation of the silver rose. Octavian (Frederica von Stade, left) meets the gaze of little Sophie (Ruth Welting), and it's love for life. Hussars and duenna look on. *(Jaap Pieper, Nederlands Opera Stichting)*

The Makropulos Business at the Welsh National Opera, 1979.
Hunting her father's elixir of eternal life, Emilia Marty (Evelyn
Lear) runs across an ancient admirer (Nigel Douglas); they last
met some fifty years ago. He's stunned—but then she's quite well
preserved for a woman who's over three centuries old. *(Julian
Sheppard, Welsh National Opera and Drama Company, Ltd.)*

formation. In *The Makropulos Business*, Janáček has already reached a point where the text feels more important than the music, though he did create one of the stand-out prima donna parts in Emilia Marty (alias Elina Makropulos, Elsa Müller, Eugenia Montez . . . every time she quaffs the youth potion she invents a new identity), done to a white-hot turn by Marie Collier in recent years. Like Debussy, Janáček saw a chance to realign opera with its origins by tossing out the arias and diversions and returning to through-composition as Wagner had reinstituted it, letting the action dictate the shape of a piece—in effect creating a new structure each time out. Thus in *Z Mrtvého Domů* (From the House of the Dead, 1930) Janáček uses his music to suggest the empty stretch of time hanging over the prisoners, filling out a lack of action with lengthy monologues (arias?) of reminiscence or fantasy plus a performance by inmates of a Slavic Don Juan comedy (diversion?). Except in the opera's opening and closing pages, there is little sense of the ongoing push of melody; everything is fragmented, distended, hollow. Yet this is no mere "theatre piece"—the music makes it go. But it is music from the period following *Pelléas et Mélisande*, not from the period before.

In Russia, a brief era of great artistic freedom followed the Revolution in 1917; everything new in the West, no matter how radical, got a hearing. But Igor Stravinsky and Syergyey Prokofyef, the most promising of the post-Rimsky composers, had left Russia, Prokofyef during the Revolution and Stravinsky some years before. In Paris, Stravinsky made history with his grotesque and primitive ballets for Dyagilyef's Ballets Russes, *The Firebird* (1910), *Petrushka* (1911), and *The Rite of Spring* (1913)—fairy tale, Pirandellian horror comedy, and tribal ritual, all scored and danced in modes that reflected the raised Western awareness of the communal id in art. This is just the sort of thing one might have expected of Russian genius after Rimsky-Korsakof had broken the ice with *The Golden Cock*—and Stravinsky's studies with Rimsky had, for a time, made a committed nationalist of him. But despite the inbred Russian sodality of Dyagilyef's company, in Paris Stravinsky became pan-Western, leaving Russian opera's destiny in the hands of Syergyey Rachmaninof, the last of the old-style charismatically egocentric virtuosos of Romanticism, a stupendous pianist whose output as a composer is often underrated. His operas, however, are a little twice-told: the naturalistic *Alyeko* (1893), the Pushkin adaptation *Skupoy Ritsar* (The Miserly Knight, 1906), and the Classical romance, *Francesca da Rimini* (1906).

Stravinsky, on the other hand, forged new paths in everything he did. His personal style underwent changes at such a rapid rate that the tiny first act of his one-hour *Solovyey* (The Nightingale, 1914),* composed in 1909, sounds rather different from the rest, composed four years later. Like almost everything Stravinsky wrote, *The Nightingale* is like nothing else by anybody. The source, Hans Christian Andersen's tale of the bird whose ineffable chant pacifies even Death, fits into the Russian tradition of the "storybook" opera—*The Golden Cock* spoofs just this genre. But no tradition prepares the ear for Stravinsky's ditsy "Chinese" suggestions, his narrator-like Fisherman who appears in each little act to outline a moral, the metal tinsel that cuts through the charm like a file gutting a pastry. Similarly, Stravinsky's one-act *Mavra* (1922), which Dyagilyef produced in Paris, borrows a farcical ploy out of Pushkin—girl brings boyfriend into household disguised as maid—and the score is dedicated "to the memory of Pushkin, Glinka, and Chaikofsky." But Stravinsky's deceptive rhythms, wryly slipping out of sync, reinvent the tone of his otherwise highly Russian-flavored melodies. And as for Greek revival, Stravinsky's "opera-oratorio" *Oedipus Rex*, another short piece, refuses to behave like the era's other classical tragedies. It doesn't "behave" at all; it just stands there and is, a Greek frieze in huge costumes and chilling masks. Only the minor characters move, and at that merely to enter and exit. Cocteau wrote the text, then had it translated into Latin as if to emphasize the international condition of the composer's disinherited ethnicity. (A narrator in evening clothes outlines the plot in the language of the audience.) Stravinsky's music has a great urgency— no one else could effect such terror so economically—but the work's premiere in 1927, in concert, had as much theatre in it as its stage debut the year after. Still, companies want to mount it, and it does thrill and move as such tales as Oedipus' must. Altogether, then, it's clear, in this protean era, that the new modes not only apply to new subjects: they may also reinvent the antique, leaving us without an essential quality of opera before 1900, authorial point of view.

Let's consider three different operas typical of this period, all fantasies: one a post-Wagnerian romance (fantasy as myth), one an example of intellectual neo-Classicism (fantasy as treatise), and one a sample of parodistic neo-Classicism (fantasy as satire). Point of view is no problem to a Romantic, and sure enough one always knows where one stands in relation to the characters in Strauss' *Die Frau Ohne*

---

* *Solovyey* is generally known as *Le Rossignol* because it was first performed in French. However, it was composed in Russian, and Stravinsky eventually recorded it in that language.

Schatten, the first of these three fantasies. *The Woman Without a Shadow* was the biggest event in the Strauss-Hofmannsthal partnership, though oddly it may represent a homage to *The Magic Flute*, as compact (if chaotic) a work as *Die Frau* is tumescent. As in Mozart's *Singspiel*, there are two couples, one noble and one earthy, a trial of sorts, even counterparts for Sarastro (in Keikobad, the ruler of the spirit world, who never appears, though in Hofmannsthal's original draft he does) and the Queen of the Night (in the Empress' vicious Nurse). But what in *Die Zauberflöte* is personal and momentous is in *Die Frau* apocalyptic; it is, in fact, a kind of rebuttal to Wagner's *Ring* in that it proposes self-reliance as the key to utopian world order, not self-denial. Strauss' Brünnhilde is the Empress, the shadowless woman—i.e., the barren—who must find a shadow in three days or her husband will turn to stone. In the end, offered a shadow, she declines it, refusing to snatch her happiness at the cost of another's. At this show of the truest wisdom, Keikobad puts all right.

A *Zauberoper*, like *Die Zauberflöte*. But that old Viennese genre, with its spoken dialogue and mean-streets comedy, is here raised up to Wagnerian proportions, with full table of *Leitmotive*, roaring orchestra (though Strauss can lure the most diaphanous effects from it when he needs to), big, brilliant voices, and a pageant of allegorical spectacle which one cannot view dispassionately. One must go with it, fall into the magic, all of it; and there is an endless supply, as a glance at the *Leitmotiv* labels reveals: themes of the Unborn Children, of Turning into Stone, of the Phantom Lover, of the Shadow, of Judgment, of Sterile Love. The action glides between the spirit and human worlds, and by the time it all ends one should feel as though Strauss had taken one through one's own dreams. That is a true magic, and it is perhaps a basic function of Romantic monster opera.

Neo-Classical opera resists involvement on the personal level. Its archetypes, unlike *Die Frau*'s spirits and mortals, are not unlike the pieces in a game of chess: one roots for a particular side but does not identify with the "players." Yet neo-Classicism has its mystical side, as in Busoni's *Doktor Faust* (1925), a searching look at the life, love, and work of the West's choice seeker. A Romantic would have (several did) set Goethe's reading of the tale; Busoni admits Goethe's mastery—in a spoken prologue he calls Goethe's *Faust* a "structure of riddles" that "shows many shapes"—but goes back in time to the medieval puppet plays on the same subject. Busoni wrote his own libretto, and his narrative involves real people—Faust, the Devil (in many guises), the Duke and Duchess of Parma, the soldier brother of a girl whom Faust ruined, opposing choruses of Catholic and Lutheran students—and yet all are, at base, pawns in the metaphysical gambits. Busoni keeps us at a remove through devices typical of the intermediary (as opposed to the strictly narrative) theatre: a prologue as well as an old-fashioned "I hope my public is satisfied" epilogue, and the musical stunts that keep one focused on the adventure as an act of art rather than an emotional experience. Busoni's magic, unlike Strauss and Hofmannsthal's, does not enchant us. It informs. In his turn as a magician at the Parmesan court, Faust conjures up images of great couples of the past (Solomon and Sheba, Samson and Delilah, Salome and John the Baptist) ostensibly to send the Duchess a flirtatious message but meanwhile keeping *our* minds alert to parallels we might use as a gloss for this classical love scene. *Doktor Faust* represented a *summum bonum* of Busoni's own somewhat Faustian journey, but, sadly, it was left unfinished. His pupil Philipp Jarnach completed the opera on Busoni's death.

The third of this trio of fantasies is the shortest, and the only comedy, Prokofyef's *Lyubof k Tryem Apyelsinam* (The Love for Three Oranges, 1921), neo-Classicism at its most antimetaphysical, a rash romp. The *commedia dell'arte* inspired it, specifically a play by Carlo Gozzi, Goldoni's old nemesis in the war between the barbaric humor of the masks and Goldoni's refined naturalism. Both Goldoni and Gozzi made their way onto the opera stage in these years, each of course demanding a different accompanimental tone. Goldoni is pliant and loving; Gozzi is crusty, savagely mocking, and Prokofyef echoes him in whip-cracking whimsy. The music wheedles when a Romantic would have been confident, saunters when it might fly. Even the love scene has bite.

Here too is magic. What else would cause the Prince of Clubs to conceive an obsession for three oranges whose whereabouts are not even known? But unlike the magic in *Die Frau Ohne Schatten* and *Doktor Faust* it is not viewed as something special, neither a means of exorcism (as in *Die Frau*) nor a symbolical communications system (as in *Doktor Faust*). Magic in *The Love for Three Oranges* is just part of the gaming, as natural to the sorceress Fata Morgana (evil) and the sorceror Tcheli (good) as pranks are to Truffaldino and love avowals are to the Prince and the third orange Princess (the first two die of thirst). Prokofyef exploits *commedia*'s precision with the slightly anarchical assistance of five groups of theatregoers: crackpots, emptyheads, and lobbyists for tragedy, comedy, and romance. All get what they want in the same evening—Gozzi brews a rich mixture—but with all the cavorting, one has even less chance to be seduced by the theatre ritual than in *Doktor Faust*. Busoni at least demands an intellectual/

emotional involvement. Prokofyef holds the emotions at bay through-out. In the love duet, one place where operagoers tend to put their hearts before their minds, Prokofyef retains the comic distance with murmured comments from the romantics and the crackpots.

It's listener's choice. Some find *Die Frau* abstruse and *The Love for Three Oranges* bracing, while others find both trivial compared to the mysterious contours of *Doktor Faust*. But it is clear that we have come, for the first time, into an era of the broadest variety. Once, composers and librettists had a choice of *seria* or *buffa*, or grand or *comique*. Now every imaginable type in size, shape, and opinion is available. And note that the old symbiosis of serious, musical opera and comic, verbal opera is still going on in the war between post-Wagnerian Romanticism with its mythic sweep and neo-Classicism with its elite jive. Comedy brings out the theatre in music.

CHAPTER SEVENTEEN

The Post-*Verismo* Era
in Italy

*In the musical world reigns the
Biblical confusion of Babel . . .
We are against this art that does
not have any human content.*

—ILDEBRANDO PIZZETTI and
OTTORINO RESPIGHI, on the
"intellectualism" of music,
circa 1930

THOUGH NATURALISM ENJOYED ONLY A BRIEF ERA AFTER *Cavalleria Rusticana* and *Pagliacci*, its influence on Italian opera in general was enormous in terms of vocal style, orchestral style, and the balance of recit and aria. The format laid down by Mascagni and Leoncavallo in the 1890s became standard for post-Verdian Italian opera, whether in costume or modern dress, whether thriller, romance, or comedy. The pushy new *verismo* vocal types competed with what survived of the old *bel canto* lyric ones, the orchestra became more and more strategic, often building up to an instrumental intermezzo (like those in *Cavalleria* and *Pagliacci*, as burnished with *canto* as an aria), and stagecraft fell in line with "realism." The centralization that had developed in the nineteenth century singled out certain houses as the major ones, and the top composers chose Rome, Venice, Naples, Turin, and Milan for their premieres, with La Scala now thought of as the top house. As *verismo*'s supercharged emotionalism radiated through the industry, singer-personalities and librettists who could supply the needed shocks won special attention. Moreover, the invention of the phonograph revolutionized the acculturation of new work, making it possible for listeners to acquire single selections and even entire operas (though in dim sound and spotty accompaniments) without having access to live performances.

All this meant that Italy had no reason to retire Romanticism, as France and Germany partly did; no reason to produce a Milhaud or a Weill. Even if it had done so, the tradition of *canto*—opera as sensual stimulation—was so ingrained that it is hard to imagine anti-*canto* making any headway. Italians wanted arias, duets and trios, finales, not experiments in verbal music like Debussy's—and when the time came, *Pelléas et Mélisande*'s Italian premiere, under Arturo Toscanini's loving supervision, was a fiasco. Even the neo-Classical Malipiero, for all his defeat of conventional subject matter and construction, never lost sight of the singing line. Italy had no Wagner to forget; it continued to honor Verdi, the composer with the most universal appeal since Beethoven, and would support not revolutions against the nineteenth century but rather new alignments with it.

Thus composers already active in the nineteenth century oversaw the transition into the twentieth. Indeed, some creators were only just now catching up to Romanticism's most passé devices. Alfredo Catalani took himself to Marschner-Weber country in *Loreley* (1890), complete with water nymph, a storm scene on the banks of the Rhine, a spirit chorus, and folkish festival. His *La Wally* (1892) ditched the supernatural but retained the rocky Germanic setting and closes in an avalanche. Catalani's contemporary Alberto Franchetti ambitiously revived the Meyerbeerean historical pageant, weeding out the diversionary niceties. His *Cristoforo Colombo* (1892), written for Genoa's celebration of the four-hundredth anniversary of Columbus' first voyage, is some big business, taking in Columbus' understanding with Queen Isabella, the sighting of new land, and two further acts (plus an epilogue) of colonization. This is tedious epic, but one moment stands out, by its very nature virtually fail-safe: the sudden cry of "Terra!" (Land ho!) that breaks up a bitter mutiny. Dividing his chorus into three groups on the *Santa Maria*, a fourth from the *Pinta*, and a lone voice from the *Niña*, Franchetti builds up a tremendous riot of *Terra! Terra! Terra!* over and over—but then dashes the whole works to bits in a turgidly innocuous Big Tune. Franchetti's *Germania* (1902), on the German unification movement, wasn't much better.

Verismo's graduates, like Bellini and Donizetti before them, turned to the French stage for inspiration, come what may. Costume melodrama came. This proved more fun than *verismo* but not that much different, as artists who excelled as *Pagliacci*'s Nedda and Canio would play exactly the same sort of people as grandees, actresses, or secret policemen. Leoncavallo fared the least well, donating a useful "theatre

piece" (meaning that the action intrigues more than the music) in
Zazà (1900), but fading away thereafter despite such idealistic entries
as the grand opera *Der Roland von Berlin* (1904)—a German commission—and *Edipo Re* (Oedipus the King, 1920).

Umberto Giordano had better luck. At the height of *verismo*, he
applied the realist technique to *Andrea Chenier* (1896), a romance set
during the French Revolution, with extravagant genre pictures—a mob
howling as it chases a filled tumbril, an old "woman of the people"
handing her adolescent grandson over to the army, a revolutionary
tribunal with a gallery's worth of Mesdames de Farge, newsboys, sans-
culottes, *carmagnoles*, snarls, screams, and death. There really was an
Andrea Chenier, a poet executed during the Reign of Terror, but
Luigi Illica's libretto veers erratically from political and artistic idealism
to blood-and-guts love triangle, coming up with a pasteboard hero.
Giordano, too, moves erratically, but his brash power pulls it off,
creating one of the great tenor roles of all time. Beniamino Gigli was
supreme in it; his 1941 recording of the opera, with Maria Caniglia and
Gino Bechi, still withstands all competition.

Giordano wrote "soprano operas," too. *Fedora* (1898), after Sardou, turns up every now and then; *Madame Sans-Gêne* (1915), also
after Sardou and a Farrar vehicle at the Met, has vanished. Giordano's
most finely realized opus, however, demands tenor and baritone leads
of a more adroit charisma than even this strikingly theatrical epoch
could supply in quantity. It is *La Cena delle Beffe* (The Dinner of
Jests, 1924), drawn from Sem Benelli's drama of bloody pranks in
Renaissance Florence. The tenor is a grotesque coward, the baritone a
feral bully, but the tenor turns the baritone's brawn against him and
changes places with him, taking his mistress to bed and driving him
insane. Giordano outdid himself in transcribing Benelli's weird blend
of comedy and horror, and if the right cast could be found, his reputation as another "one-opera composer" might be revised.

Coeval and often lumped with Leoncavallo and Giordano, but in
actuality a gifted and experimental composer, was Pietro Mascagni,
who will probably never rise above *Cavalleria Rusticana* because his
most interesting works call for a lead tenor of Wagnerian stamina, a
voice that Italy rarely produces. A year after the torrid *Cavalleria*,
Mascagni about-faced in a piece of pastoral delicacy, the tunefully
charming *L'Amico Fritz* (Friend Fritz, 1891). But Mascagni buffs
regularly cite *Guglielmo Ratcliff* (1895), produced after but written
before *Cavalleria*, as illustration of the composer's often overlooked
subtlety in word-by-word setting of the text, pulled (by Verdi's erst-
while collaborator Andrea Maffei) from Heinrich Heine. But *Gug-*

lielmo Ratcliff is if anything more preposterously antique-Romantic than *Loreley:* its scene plot takes in a Scottish castle, a thieves' tavern, and "a wild spot near the Black Rock." Mascagni's individuality is heard to better effect in *Iris* (1898), the tale of a sensitive Japanese girl who is carried off to a geisha house and destroyed by a sensualist and his pimp, then renounced by her uncomprehending father. Illica's highly symbolistic text means to examine the place of art in a crass world, and it works beautifully until the stagnant, dreamlike final act.

It soon became clear that this prolific and possessed composer was running out of melody, though his technical genius never flagged. More than anyone else in this vibrant and imaginative epoch of Italian post-*verismo*, Mascagni troubled to make the music work for, not against, the word, constantly redefining the context of recitative until —as with Ravel, Strauss, and Janáček in other lands—it became indistinguishable from the *canto* sections. However, how far could he go without Tunes? Like so many others of his day, he helped bring back the avatars of *commedia*, but despite Illica's breathlessly antic libretto, *Le Maschere* (The Masks, 1901) just doesn't happen. Sadly, Mascagni had to endure failure just when he stood at the forefront of the national scene: *Le Maschere* had the honor of receiving seven premieres scheduled for the same day, in all the major cities (Naples' first night was delayed two days) plus Genoa and Verona. The piece flopped six times; Mascagni himself conducted the Rome production, so nobody dared to boo.

From then on, Mascagni's career ran unevenly, badly so. He seemed to recover toward the end, first with the gently moving *Lodoletta* (1917), after Ouida's wildly popular and now forgotten novel, *Two Little Wooden Shoes*, and then with the French Revolutionary melodrama, *Il Piccolo Marat* (The Little Marat, 1921). For the latter, Mascagni worked with one of the great literary men of his day, Giovacchino Forzano, not only a superb theatre craftsman and vital poet but an expert on the French Revolution. Unlike Illica's carnival vignettes in *Andrea Chenier*, Forzano's really savage revolution does not embellish a tale: it is the tale. Ostensibly about an aristocrat who feigns bloodthirsty radicalism to save his imprisoned mother, *Il Piccolo Marat* presents the revolutionary condition as a confrontation of two kinds of opportunist: the hero sneakily saving lives and the villain grubbing for power. The "little Marat," one of Mascagni's most fatiguing challenges of the tenor voice, is the hero; a bass called The Ogre handles the villainy. Circling around them are a host of minor figures, including the girl who furnishes the tenor's love interest and a cowardly carpenter who suffers one of the plot's basest cruelties in having to assist in the public executions. Here is another kind of opportunist, the coward obeying irresistible orders. Confessing horror at what the revolution has reduced him to, he claims to have reached the breaking point just the day before:

> Yesterday! Yesterday!
> Little Charon, twelve years old!
> On the scaffold, the poor little boy asked the executioner,
> Are you going to hurt me?

On paper the words look a little contrived, but Mascagni forces the scene up through sorrow, nostalgia, terror, and black humor to smash outward with Forzano as if cracking the public in the face. There's nothing as keen as this in *Andrea Chenier*.

Balancing the integrity of a Mascagni were the show makers, remembered less for what they wrote than for who sang it. For years, thousands raved over Antonio Scotti's portrayal of the wicked Chim-Fen in *L'Oracolo* (The Oracle, 1905) without being able to name the composer, Franco Leoni. A *verismo* trifle placed in San Francisco's Chinatown, *L'Oracolo* retired when Scotti did, but Francesco Cilèa's *Adriana Lecouvreur* (1902), about the last two days of an actress' life, has held on through the years for the fascination of the title part. This is the soprano's evening all the way, from her dazzling entrance backstage at the Comédie-Française, intoning a bit of Racine and promptly launching a Big-Tune aria, "Io son l'umile ancella" (I am the humble handmaid of creative genius . . .), to her lush death by poisoned nosegay. Modeled on the real-life Lecouvreur, the character of Adriana holds the center of the piece as few roles do—the tenor loves her, her mezzo rival hates her, and the baritone adores her in vain. Typically, the play had recently seen service as a French straight-play vehicle, notably for Sarah Bernhardt.*

The era's most invigorating quality was its love of big, symphonic scoring, using the orchestra for an almost Wagnerian leadership in the drama. But where Wagner's orchestra comments ceaselessly, the Italians used theirs to heighten sensual texture. Few of them followed Mascagni's lead in remixing the components of recitative and song to favor both equally, to *merge* the two. Rather, some of them composed operas made up entirely of song, in no fixed aria structures. This was one

---

* The opera in turn has conveyed many a diva, most notably Magda Olivero, who made it her own over the course of a remarkable (interrupted) fifty-year career through the use of assorted vocal bizarrerie (such as the holding of the antepenultimate note in "Io son l'umile ancella" on an endless crescendo), extinct pantomime, and the *verismo* commitment that has fizzled away in jet-age hustle.

reason why the orchestra had to become more prominent: the ear needed to renew its "intelligence" from time to time with the break in the singing that recitative used to supply, and which was now supplied by intermezzos, act preludes, or even brief instrumental passages within the action.

Of these symphonists the most accomplished was Riccardo Zandonai. The subjects he chose, half favoring the medieval and half adapted from semirealistic novels, betray Italy's approach-avoidance conflict in regard to *verismo:* the public had tired of naturalism, yet needed its fire. Zandonai tried realism only once, in *Conchita* (1911), drawn from Pierre Louÿs' novel *The Woman and the Puppet* (which also turned into Buñuel's film *That Obscure Object of Desire*), about a Carmen-type and the man she uses and ridicules until he learns to win her through violence. Zandonai's true realism lay elsewhere; he knew it and moved into the quasifantastic world of doomed and strongly poeticized love. If every Italian composer wrote at least one *verismo* piece, almost every composer also set one libretto by Gabriele d'Annunzio; Zandonai's was *Francesca da Rimini* (1914).

D'Annunzio stands as central to the Italian libretto of the period as the Maeterlinck texts do to the French in the same era. The Frenchman is reticent, suggestive, fearful of contact and hypnotized by images of darkness/light, age/youth, and action/passivity; the Italian is feverishly carnal, going over and over the equal parts of conquest, despair, hunger, and worship that comprise his view of the man-woman relationship. A rousing nationalist, D'Annunzio plunged into his country's past for material, satisfying the eye with antirealist splendor while the musicians filled the ear with the big "realist" voices. *Francesca da Rimini* offers a quintessence of post-*verismo*, with its old Italy of the city states and warring families, its soprano married to the baritone but craving the tenor, its surging orchestra and Big-Tune *Leitmotive*, its ferocious language, which makes *Tristan und Isolde* look like Hansel und Gretel:

PAOLO:	*Ti trarrò, ti trarrò dov'è l'oblio.*
FRANCESCA:	*Baciami gli occhi, baciami le tempie*
	E le guance e la gola . . .
	Tieni i polsi e le dita . . .
	Così . . . così . . . così!
	Prendimi l'anima e riversala.
PAOLO:	I will take you, I will take you into oblivion.
FRANCESCA:	Kiss my eyes, kiss my head
	And my cheeks and my throat . . .

Hold my wrists and fingers . . .
So . . . so . . . so!
Take my soul and drain it.

There is even a touch of neo-Classical pastiche in the lute and fife that provide a medieval aura. But at heart this last and best of Francesca operas is Romanticism running riot. If Debussy found the inexpressible in Maeterlinck, Zandonai adheres more to the surface of D'Annunzio, following the passion expressed in the lines. He also uses far less of his source than Debussy did, for the play *Francesca* is insatiably verbose, and the heroine, "a flower in the midst of so much iron" in D'Annunzio —a pawn in the political checkmate, propelled from one fratricidal family to another—becomes more her own person in the opera, with several subsidiary characters and much of the feudal detail shorn away. Zandonai centers on the two lovers, and we sympathize with the singers attempting to bring them off, for the name part demands a soprano of Wagnerian endurance and top notes with an added dimension of doe-eyed tragedy, while her adulterous brother-in-law looks lyric on the page but must prove dramatic in the theatre. All of *Francesca* is hyper. The second act features an almost unstageable Guelph-Ghibelline battle, viewed from the top of a tower, with flaming arrows, fwhipping cross-bows, warriors berserk and expiring, brasses roaring and bells clanging, a chorus shrieking at the top of its register (the sopranos must sustain several C Sharps), and smoke rising up like a curtain over the burning city of Rimini.

This was an age of spectaculars. With the intensity of Gluck, the ambition of Berlioz, the flair of Scribe, and the utter musicality of Wagnerism, post-*verismo* opera overthrew the memory of *bel canto*, the orchestral discretion of Rossini, the aria-and-ensemble structuring of prime Verdi. Finally, just as the rest of Europe was giving it up, Italy had discovered the ceremony in opera, the mystery, pageant, myth of it. Big was not the rule, exactly. Zandonai pulled back for *Giulietta e Romeo* (1922), so concentrated that it's lighter and smaller than Bellini's version of the tale, and ooched down into the neglected *intermedio* in the very Spanish-colored *Una Partita* (A Match, 1933), an hour of contests in which Don Juan gambles with a fellow noble, wins his mistress from him, kills him, faces down the outraged mistress, and lets her inadvertently poison herself. But in general the epoch lived for the elaborately exotic. Not unlike Zandonai was Italo Montemezzi, who produced two masterpieces in the modern custom of setting rather than adapting playscripts, *L'Amore dei Tre Re* (The Love of Three Kings, 1913) and *La Nave* (The Ship, 1918). The first is Sem Benelli's

somewhat Maeterlinckian story of a beautiful, inwardly sorrowful
woman and the three men who share her—a disinherited Italian ruler,
the barbarian who invaded the land some decades earlier, and his son,
the present king. Spectacle obtains here not in decor but in passion;
this has got to be the second most intense opera of the time. Montemezzi keeps his orchestra at the boiling point, pulling it off the fire suddenly for moments of urgency so unbearable they can't be scored with
more than a few slashing chords, or turning up the heat for a love
duet of blinding eroticism. Benelli, like Maeterlinck, deals in symbols:
the heroine is Italy, susceptible to primitivism, needing to be loved,
conscious of historical booms yet resistant to the foreign authoritarian-
ism she has suffered most of her existence. The piece boasts one of
opera's most titanic curtains, that of Act II, after the king's ancient,
blind father, having caught Fiora with her lover, strangles her. He
then carries her offstage, and Montemezzi sets the picture to an ob-
stinate drumbeat over throbbing, tuneless strings that grow louder,
grander, and more aghast by the moment until at last the dismal procession of tired old man and murdered woman slips off to the loudest
pounding wail the ears can receive.

The *most* intense opera, completely out of the repertory now, is
La Nave, reduced from D'Annunzio's most radical script, about the
earliest years in the history of Venice and centered on the love/hate
relationship of two warriors, one of them a woman. The ship of the
title stands for the bellicose mercantile glory that was to be Venice,
and the action takes in blood and sex in the rawest terms, making one
wonder what the people who stormed over *Salome* were doing now
that everything was out in the open.

Zandonai and Montemezzi alone are enough to prove the new
symphonic valiance of Italian opera, but they had company in Ildebrando Pizzetti. The Wagner of his time and place, Pizzetti wrote his
own librettos and tended to the religious or mystical in his subjects;
unlike Wagner, he observed the twentieth-century absolute of the
text. Pizzetti seldom managed to write star parts, yet he outlasted
everybody. In *Débora e Jaèle* (1922) and *Fra Gherardo* (1928) he
showed his awesome stuff: huge, austere, slow-moving tapestries of
historical flux sewn into legend.

These operatic symphonists accomplished the complete reorganization of the last reactionary subgroup in European music theatre.
Now, everyone who had not turned neo-Classicist accepted late-Ro-
mantic through-composition of organic, whole-score integrity, building
a work's conceptual *tinta* out of leading themes in constant variation
or, at least, repetition. Thus Zandonai literally haunts *Francesca da*

Rimini with an all-purpose "love" or "fate" theme dominated by an off-center harmony that mirrors the out-of-sync situation of the two lovers. And Montemezzi floods *La Nave* with a "sea" motif, undulating and lowering with menace just as the Adriatic did at Venice's frontier at the *lidi* of the lagoon.

There was not much comedy in mega-Romantic Italy—most of these composers set at least one comic text, but not always competently. They apparently had *verismo* squalor or poetic nationalism down too well to adapt to fun. Giordano's *Il Re* (The King, 1929) is humdrum despite Forzano's pointed text, and Zandonai's *La Farsa Amorosa* (The Romantic Comedy, 1933) from Alarcón's *The Three-Cornered Hat*, sounds spiffy but lacks jollity. Ottorino Respighi's *Belfagor* (1923)— one of those devil-takes-mortal-wife tales ("Take mine!" cries the first stranger he meets)—though lively and suave, fails to suggest the elasticity of comedy. Respighi comes through at his best only in the super-lyrical desperation of the love plot. This surprises, for Respighi was a deft parodist (*Belfagor* includes a tiny suite of dances in the old style) and thoughtfully based the devil's music on permutations of a theme made of harmonic intervals (fourths, to be exact) that still fell oddly on the Western ear at the time. *Belfagor* has energy, sure, but few treats.

Besides Malipiero, only Ermanno Wolf-Ferrari concentrated on comedy, and he did so not in Malipiero's avant-garde grotesquerie but along lines set down by the old master of humanist comedy, Carlo Goldoni. Venetian-born, German-trained, and Italian-German by blood, Wolf-Ferrari appeased the great Romantic god *verismo* with his best-known work, *I Gioielli della Madonna* (The Jewels of the Madonna, 1911), but discovered himself in light, fond neo-Classical farce. He brought back the *intermedio* in *Il Segreto di Susanna* (Susanna's Secret, 1909), a wily little gem as old in structure as new in subject (her awful secret: she smokes), and produced a series of full-length comedies based on Goldoni's plays—much richer material, by the way, than any of Goldoni's opera librettos. *Il Campiello* (The Square, 1936) is typical, one crazy day among the inhabitants of a Venetian piazza— young lovers, old farts and flirts, and a visiting foreigner. The piece teems with life plain, from its use of the sibilant local dialect to the way Wolf-Ferrari develops the stalls, anxieties, and rushing joys that bounce the tale along. The list of principals is extensive, ten parts of about equal size (including two old women sung by tenors in a salute to the duenna figure of Cavalli's era), and calls less for vocal finish than for comic bravado, a gift for intimacy, and word-perfect diction. Diction above all: the word is coming back into style. Even as Wolf-

Ferrari laces his score with folklike ditties and dances (a wedding dinner is choreographed for ballet), he has in essence musicalized Goldoni's play.

In sum, the era let genuine *verismo* fall away into opera of fabulous poetic drive, supplemented by Wolf-Ferrari's genial and Malipiero's tense neo-Classicism. But the star composer of the day does not accord with any of these categories: Giacomo Puccini managed to touch on the vogues without ever bending his personal style out of shape. His specialty was not costume melodrama, naturalism, or fantasy, but a rarified melodrama called *morbidezza* (literally "softness"). The dynamic of this form is pathos, not gutsy action, and Puccini's most characteristic figure was the pathetic heroine—the hapless golddigger Manon Lescaut, tubercular Mimì, wan, lovesick Liù, the slave who dies for her master. Puccini could create a tougher heroine when called for —Minnie, the gunslinging, card-cheating Girl of the Golden West, or Turandot, the flinty princess who asks three riddles of her beaux, and to fail is death. But the essential Puccini heroine is the ingenue blinded by love and doomed, by rules of sentimentality, to die. Puccini is not unlike Massenet in this, though Massenet's women seem to enjoy their declines while Puccini's heroines undergo it in dazed surprise. Even Butterfly, the fifteen-year-old geisha whose prideful sense of self forces her to commit suicide when abandoned by her faithless American "husband," is really no more than a girl who should have known better than to love in vain.

Inaugurating his career in the 1880s, before Verdi had produced *Otello* and *Falstaff*, Puccini suffered two failures, *Le Villi* (The Witches, 1884) and *Edgar* (1889). He found his métier in *Manon Lescaut* (1893), daringly based on Prévost's novel when Massenet's *Manon* was only nine years old and full of fashion. *Le Villi* was a Germanic horror-pastorale with a feeling of Catalani about it, and *Edgar* was melodrama erratically mixed. But *Manon Lescaut* offers all the parts of the *dramma Pucciniana* in working order: the prototypal soprano heroine, a lyric *spinto* and her less interesting tenor lover, also lyric but with a ring (the baritone, as so often in Puccini, is a minor figure, nearly a *comprimario*); the arias placed precisely to expand the emotional line with an immediacy that sweeps the listener along; the distaste for recitative; the complementary orchestration, less voluble than that of Zandonai and Montemezzi; the swift pacing and sure touches of *frisson;* and the heroine's death, in this instance of exhaustion on the plains of Louisiana, whither her outlaw career of beauty-for-rent has taken her.

Perhaps most typical of the composer's style is the amount of labor that went into writing the *Manon Lescaut* libretto. Even Puccini's abundant musical gift would fizzle when applied to weak theatre, and the *Edgar* experience in particular taught him to do as Verdi had done, to flatter, browbeat, advise, and otherwise superintend the word men till every turn of plot, every line, every word—the *parola scenica* —felt right. As a newcomer of little reputation, Puccini was in no position to harangue Ferdinando Fontana, his collaborator on both *Le Villi* and *Edgar*, but he should have harangued, for no less than four revisions failed to bring *Edgar* to life. The music is interesting but the libretto is faulty, and at last Puccini gave up on *Edgar* permanently: "as an opera it does not exist."

His lesson learned, Puccini held out for a top-flight *Manon* text. Before he was ready to compose, at least six writers had been put through the wringer, each enduring Puccini's thorough editing and then withdrawing in despair. Rather than credit all those involved— such a string of names would have looked ludicrous—the published score credited none (not even Prévost): "*Manon Lescaut*. Lyric drama in four acts. Music by Giacomo Puccini."

For those who had doubts about *Manon Lescaut*, Puccini's next opera, *La Bohème* (The Bohemian Life, 1896), settled the question definitely. A look at the liberated world of the artist, complete with garret, starvation, temporary menial employment, free love, and pitiful death in Paris' Latin Quarter in the 1830s, *La Bohème* embraced *morbidezza* even more fulfillingly than *Manon Lescaut* had done. Again there was a literary source, Henri Murger's novel *Scènes de la Vie de Bohème*, a best-seller of the 1850s, when it was considered something of an exposé. By 1896, Murger's sometimes sordid tale came off more as a romantic comedy with a sad ending.

And there is much comedy in Giacosa and Illica's libretto, the better to set off the central love plot involving the flower maker Mimì and the poet Rodolfo. High jinks mainly occupy the other principals— Rodolfo's garret roommates and Musetta, the part-time lover of one of them—but Puccini as tunesmith works full time to incorporate farce on one hand and pliant, shimmering *amore* on the other into a "whole idea" of the bohemian experience, frolic and tenderness all one. Musetta's famous waltz, for instance, "Quando m'en vò" (When I walk alone through the streets, people stop to watch me . . .), climaxes the rambunctious second act, set outdoors on Christmas Eve, yet nothing could be more graceful, less rambunctious: in one stroke, Puccini plays both sides of the scene. Similarly, he opens the evening with two of the bohemians freezing and jesting in their loft and closes in that same loft, this time darkened by Mimì's death. "A merry life," Murger observed, "but a terrible one!"*

Doubtless it is Puccini's deft blend of the comic and the lyrical that has kept his score one of the four or five most popular operas ever. Oddly, it took some time to catch on, especially outside Italy, though Nellie Melba enjoyed singing Mimì so much that she made it, through sheer repetition, a staple of the English repertory. (Possibly Melba liked the role too much. She could never quite bring herself to give it up, and was eventually to sing it, well into her sixties, from a wheel-chair.) Even more oddly, Puccini's *La Bohème* had direct competition from Leoncavallo's adaptation of Murger's novel, also called *La Bohème* (1897). Leoncavallo had shown Puccini sketches for a *Bohème* libretto which Puccini rejected, so Leoncavallo went ahead and composed it himself; he wasn't thrilled to learn that Puccini had changed his mind after all. Leoncavallo's version was more faithful to Murger, equaled if not bettered Puccini's sense of bohemian camaraderie, really dug into the poverty and restlessness, and included a waltz for *his* Musetta. But Leoncavallo's tunes were not competitive with Puccini's. Though the French perversely favored it in the early 1900s (presumably because of its close relation to their own Murger), the work is seldom heard today. Puccini analyzed it aptly: "Too much hilarity in the first two acts and too much sadness in the last two."

If *La Bohème* is *morbidezza* at its richest, *Tosca* (1900), Puccini's next opera, marked his most telling excursion into the coarser ruts of melodrama. The source, again, was French, Sardou's *La Tosca*, a love triangle–thriller involving an opera singer, her lover—a painter with an interest in radical politics—and a vicious police chief. The change in genre is felt immediately. We move into a menacing world of royal absolutism, intrigue, and terror in the five viselike chords that shoot the curtain up on *Tosca*. An even stronger comparison: in a Big Moment in *La Bohème* the heroine overhears the tenor tell the baritone that she is dying of a lingering illness. In *Tosca* the heroine overhears the tenor being tortured by the baritone's henchmen.

Tosca has been despised as a "shabby little shocker" by a few sensitive critics, but a triangle plot concerning a raving diva, the artist who loves her but loves democracy as well, and a sadistic chief of

---

* Mimì dies but Musetta survives; she is a rarity in Puccini, a woman neither pathetic nor fierce, and she doesn't quite jibe with either *morbidezza* or *verismo-*influenced *melodramma*. Of all Puccini's operas, only the bimodal *Bohème* could contain her: it has the vivacity/tenderness that she has. The role always goes over (the waltz is the surest thing in opera), while Mimìs have to work for their applause. A really brilliant singer who knows how to feature the warmth as well as the wiles, such as Ljuba Welitsch, Elisabeth Söderström, or Renata Scotto, can walk home with the performance.

police whose job is to crush democrats and whose pleasure is to taste of raving diva is *supposed* to be a shocker. That's how Sardou wrote it, and if Puccini or his librettists, Giacosa and Illica, had diminished its shock value they would not have been doing their job. As it is, *Tosca* offers singers irresistible opportunities. Baritones feel challenged by the psychology of the sadist: shall they swagger, roar, and claw . . . or should evil wear some suave mask? Tenors are delighted with two of the most grateful arias in the repertory, "Recondita armonia" and "E lucevan le stelle." Sopranos attempt to build a reputation on their Tosca, but they face one of the most difficult, yet most taken-for-granted roles going. Anyone can cite the vocal hurdles in Norma or the test of endurance in Isolde or Elektra. But even veteran opera buffs fail to realize how complex Puccini's heroine is as a character, aside from the tricky, sometimes cruel demands on the voice alone. Of course, as an opera star Tosca has temperament, resolve, charisma. But what lies below? She has been played as tigress, madonna, vamp, coquette. Somehow, few of the uncountable divas who have played her have done her justice; one had grown so used to intriguing but incomplete Toscas that when Maria Callas got her down for good and all in the early days of long-playing records, her performance (with Giuseppe Di Stefano, Tito Gobbi, and conductor Victor de Sabata) became an instant classic and remains just about the only complete opera recording that all reasonable opinion holders concede to be one of the all-time great ones. Even forgetting thought-through characterization, the role is still hazardous in its assortment of Big Moments by which the buff tests a given singer—her laconic "Quanto?" (How much?) when she tries to buy Scarpia off, her pantomime scene with the fruit knife when she realizes that she can kill him rather than yield him her body, exploding in the knife thrust and "Questo è il bacio di Tosca!" (*This* is Tosca's kiss!) and dying down in "E avanti a lui tremava tutta Roma" (And before him, all Rome trembled) as she surveys the corpse.

If Mimì is a little darling and Tosca a spitfire, the heroine of *Madama Butterfly* (1904) is both, melting with love for her Pinkerton but ferocious with those who dare to suggest that he has left her not for a while but forever. Puccini's emphasis of the lead soprano is total; the tenor and baritone take subsidiary positions, and once she enters she is seldom off the stage. There is nothing like this marathon in Verdi or *verismo*, yet again we take it for granted because the Puccinian tune flows so sweetly. *Verismo* vocal writing really did more damage to *bel canto* than Wagner did with his bigger voices, for Wagner worked out of the German style that had cut its ties to Italian training when *opera seria* gave in to Weber and Marschner. But in Italy, Rossini, Bellini, and Donizetti maintained a *bel canto* connection. Not till *verismo* did the light voices capable of fioriture and sustained *legato* finally die out. As of Puccini's sopranos and Mascagni's tenors (perhaps Verdi's baritones as well) they are dead; it is safe to say that few Italian singers of the early and middle 1800s could have met twentieth-century Italian vocal requirements. Nowadays singers tackle Lucrezia Borgia, Amina in *La Sonnambula*, and Puccini with what they hope to be ease, but what we are hearing in Donizetti and Bellini is probably louder and rougher than what the composers had in mind. There are exceptions—Norma calls for an almost anti-*bel canto* dramatic force, and certain unusual modern voices (Callas' and Sutherland's, for example) encompass different styles in a kind of throwback progressiveness. Each sang a splendid Gilda, Amina, and Norma, among other things. But who else can?

With *La Bohème, Tosca,* and *Madama Butterfly* behind him, Puccini was king. Not all his premieres were a cinch—a hostile audience deep-sixed *Butterfly*'s La Scala production—yet the works established themselves more quickly than any do today. Puccini was to Italy what Richard Strauss was to Germany, but Strauss never held the international scene as Puccini did, being too vicious in *Salome* and *Elektra* and then too subtle in *Ariadne* and too "heavy" in *Die Frau Ohne Schatten.* Puccini never varied his style the way Strauss did, though he set *morbidezza* aside for *La Fanciulla del West* (The Girl of the West, 1910), a shoot-'em-up "meller" taken—like *Madama Butterfly*—from the work of the American revolutionary and charlatan in theatre "realism," David Belasco.

Belasco's stagy tricks impressed Puccini. But what most attracted him to *The Girl of the Golden West* (besides its *Tosca*-like imbroglio of tomboy saloonkeeper, "nice" desperado, and sneering sheriff), was the opportunity it offered for a display of ethnic coloration. Puccini loved to instill atmosphere by quoting from authentic folk themes, though he harmonized them for an Italian's ear rather than authentically. *Butterfly, Il Tabarro,* and *Turandot* try to suggest Japan, back-street Paris, and China in this way, but *La Fanciulla* is the most successful of the lot in the stalwart naïveté of its "American" themes, balanced by some beguiling experiments with the whole-tone scale associated with Debussyan impressionism. Some of *La Fanciulla*'s Americana doesn't work—having miners sing "Dooda day," for instance. Moreover, the crucial poker game in which Minnie plays the sheriff for the wounded outlaw is nothing but camp to American eyes, despite Puccini's nifty manipulation of song and speech.

By this time Italy had built up a busy but ephemeral business in musical comedy. Many of the better-known opera composers tried their hand, including Mascagni and Zandonai, and now Puccini made a deal with some Austrians to compose what Americans call "Viennese operetta," the "alas, my love, we must part" sort of thing. Complications ensued. Puccini's *morbidezza* exactly suited the bittersweet Viennese confection, but he thought its textual basis unworkably pallid; furthermore, the outbreak of World War I found him stuck with a contract with the enemy, outraging the Italians and the French. Ultimately the finished product, *La Rondine* (The Swallow, 1917), surfaced in Monte Carlo, in Italian, and it wasn't an operetta but a vaguely "popular" opera, filled with catchy tunes and shaped to include the two sets of lovers, one romantic and one comic, that have dominated musical comedy back to Viennese *Zauberoper*. The plot, an untragic *Traviata*, is forgettable and the last act horribly empty till the final "parting" duet. But the first two acts offer such melodic bounty that it is hard to reckon why *La Rondine* has never caught on. It might serve as a lesson in the twentieth century's course in hybrid synthesis, mating trained musicianship with the directness of the popular stage, except that Puccini mates the two much less vitally than such pieces as *Die Dreigroschenoper*, *L'Heure Espagnole*, or *Arlecchino* do.

Back in opera, Puccini devised an evening of one-acts as *Il Trittico* (The Triptych, 1918), premiered, like *La Fanciulla del West*, at the Met. The assortment lacks unity, being one part *verismo* in *Il Tabarro* (The Overcoat), one part *morbidezza* in *Suor Angelica*, and one part comedy in *Gianni Schicchi;* each of the trio has its partisans. But despite some eye-opening casts in its green years,* the event has not succeeded as a whole and is usually heard piecemeal. At least Puccini ditched the technicians he usually worked with in favor of Forzano; but that worthy refused to deal with *Il Tabarro*, to be drawn from a shocker of the grand guignol school. Forzano prepared *Suor Angelica*, doing the best he could for a weeper set in a convent, but he really triumphed furnishing *Gianni Schicchi* with the paraphernalia of *com-*

---

* Because each of the three operas is so different in style, ideal performances call for two or three charismatic sopranos, one dramatic and one lyric tenor, one dramatic and one comic baritone, and numerous important assistants, plus a conductor who can sculpt three mutually antagonistic atmospheres. Early mountings aimed at the ideal: the Met premiere had Claudia Muzio, Geraldine Farrar, Florence Easton, and Giuseppe de Luca; Covent Garden in 1920 had Gilda dalla Rizza, Dinh Gilly, and the superbly *buffo* Schicchi of Ernesto Badini. Still, no center held *Il Trittico* together. Beverly Sills made a gallant attempt to bind the trio by taking all three soprano leads for the New York City Opera in the 1960s, though her voice wasn't really suited to any of them.

La Bohème at La Scala: Mimì (Ileana Cotrubas) and Rodolfo (Ottavio Garaventa), perhaps opera's most essential lovers. *(Richard Braaten, Kennedy Center)*

Turandot at La Scala. Note the droll fringed headgear on the
wise men flanking the emperor near the top of the stairway.
(E. A. Teatro alla Scala)

media—the moronic doctor with the Bolognese accent, the snuffling notary, the fakes, ditsies, and young lovers, back in Florence in 1299. Schicchi's plot to slip into a warm deathbed to dictate a new will (to his own benefit) left no room for a *verismo* or *morbidezza* heroine; the soprano is present merely to indicate the love plot and sing the delectable "O mio babbino caro" (Oh, my dear daddy) when said plot hits a stalemate. But the tenor, so often subaltern in Puccini, comes into his own in an aria central to the work's premise, "Firenze è come un albero fiorito" (Florence is like a flowering tree), explaining the arch of civilization at the very moment and place when and where feudalism was just rising up into capitalism. *Gianni Schicchi* is a perfect *intermedio*, a rare foray into neo-Classical satire for Puccini, who closes the show, *mirabile dictu*, with his hero's spoken address to the audience. Dante consigned him to hell for his caper, he admits, but would the public be so kind as to grant him a theatrical vindication—applause?

Fired perhaps by this venture into comedy, Puccini finished off his canon with a flamboyant piece, half fairy tale and half grotesque farce. The combination of romance and comedy in *Turandot* (1926) stems from the source, the same Gozzi piece that Busoni used for his *Turandot*. Busoni sticks closer to Gozzi, undercutting the make-believe with the masks Truffaldino, Pantalone, and Tartaglia (dropping Gozzi's Brighella). Puccini's librettists, Giuseppe Adami and Renato Simoni, also use only three masks, and renamed Ping, Pang, and Pong they lose their traditional distinct identities, acting as a unit musically and dramatically. Moreover, Puccini draws halfheartedly on their historic role as interlopers between play and public; in *Turandot* he joined Zandonai, Montemezzi, and Pizzetti in the fabulous remote.

Vocally *Turandot* is truly daring, featuring Puccini's most heroic tenor, not only huge in sound but the catalyst of the action. It is he who demands to try Turandot's riddles, he who answers them and suggests a compromise when she refuses to honor the bargain, he who at last confronts her and turns her from haughty goddess to loving woman. In the soprano department, Puccini found room for both his tintypes, Turandot being the Tosca-Minnie tigress and Liù the Mimì-Manon *morbidezza* victim. But while Liù is a natural for Puccinian lyricism, Turandot calls for an instrument of Wagnerian breadth, bigger than anything in Puccini's colleagues' operas. The role is not long—she doesn't so much as open her mouth till the piece is half over—but it is very, very high and loud as thunder, needing steel fire to cut through the many climaxes. Great Turandots have been few—Maria Nemeth; the superb Eva Turner, who filled Covent Garden with high notes of resilient beauty; Gina Cigna, the only Italian in the list; Maria

Callas, who pointed her not-that-sizable voice to capture the evil glint in the eye of the sound; and Birgit Nilsson, Turner's only rival as all-time supreme Turandot.*

Turandot might have been Puccini's unquestioned masterpiece if he had not died before completing it, leaving the dénouement, an extended duet for Turandot and her conqueror, in sketches. Critics have uniformly damned Franco Alfano, who finished the piece, but in fact Alfano—chosen because his sound exactly aligned with the exotic *Turandot* orchestration—turned out a reasonably convincing duet and final crowd scene, working in as much of Puccini's notebook as he found room for but drawing on his own good sense as well. Apparently Toscanini, who was to conduct the premiere at La Scala, demanded that he redo the job with less Alfano and more Puccini, and the second ending, invariably used today, is tighter but less convincing. The first night (which featured Rosa Raisa, Maria Zamboni, and Miguel Fleta) faded out dejectedly at the spot where pure Puccini ends and Puccini-Alfano begins; thereafter, at La Scala and everywhere else, Alfano slips in and the story proceeds to its finish, often with stupid cuts that make Turandot's transformation incoherent.

Opera's story, too, has reached a certain incomplete cut-off point. With the twentieth century in full swing, we have seen the fixed conventions of Romantic opera—the overture, the recit and aria, the ensemble finale—blended into an organic whole, a clean sweep of through-composition that starts when an acts starts and stops only when that act ends. We have also seen neo-Classicists retrieve the conventions. But they have gone back not to the 1800s but the 1700s, marking the conventions more boldly. It is one extreme or the other: either the transparent structuring of *opera seria* and *buffa* or the apparently structureless mosaic of "conversational" opera reminiscent of the Camerata style.

Opera is digging into its past, renewing itself in the novelty of ancient custom. But now we come to a true novelty, something no one has tried before: combining the hypnotic emotionalism of Romanticism with the precise compositional discipline of Classicism. We come to Modern.

---

* Tape technology has permitted singers who shouldn't try the role in the theatre to sneak through it on microphone—Sutherland and Caballé. The stunt doesn't take; both sound as if they were fighting their way out of a huge pie.

CHAPTER EIGHTEEN

The Twelve-Tone Revolution

In Berg's music there is not the slightest trace of melody. There are only scraps and shreds, sobs and belches . . . A whole zoological garden is opened up . . . One seriously has to consider the question, whether and to what extent activity in music can be criminal.
—A newspaper critic reviewing the premiere of *Wozzeck*

Supposing times were normal— normal as they were before 1914 —then the music of our time would be in a different situation.
—ARNOLD SCHOENBERG

IT IS WORTH NOTING THAT WHILE A ROMANTIC ERA MAKES MOST ART-ists Romantic, a neo-Classical era recruits only a portion of the art community—others stick to Romanticism or try to modify it.

By the early 1900s it had nevertheless become uncomfortably clear that Romanticism had expanded itself out of workable proportion. Gustav Mahler's tremendous symphonies with their vocal parts and subtextual meanings, Skryabin's amorphous erotic tone poems, Richard Strauss' voice-drowning orchestra, and assorted neo-Wagnerian miscellany troubled theorists, especially in Germany, the spiritual and academic home of musical Romanticism. Neo-Classicism seemed only a temporary restraint on the way to further miasma.

Arnold Schoenberg found the way out. Like Beethoven, Berlioz, and Debussy one of the few influentially unique musicians, Schoenberg took his first strokes in the Wagnerian wake, composing an epic song cycle for orchestra, soloists, and chorus, *Gurre–Lieder,* in terms reminiscent of *Der Ring des Nibelungen*—doomed love, fantastic horror, and the natural world scored for a cyclic table of *Leitmotive.* But the times were moving fast, dizzy with shifting aesthetics, and while Schoenberg composed at fever pitch, he often dropped a work suddenly. When he returned to it, if he did at all, who knew what new autograph he might have acquired in the meantime? He finished *Gurre–Lieder* in 1901 but did not orchestrate it until 1911. In between he had begun to move out of late-Romanticism and into his personal Modern, so that while *Gurre–Lieder* might pleasingly fill ears bored with lean neo-Classicism, it was already outdated for Schoenberg. For his new plan involved applying principles of organization to the emotional impulsion of music.

Others had done this. But they had done it in the inherited language of Western music. Schoenberg invented a new language. He pointed out that the so-called natural laws of Western harmony are not natural at all, but an applied system. C Major, in other words, is logical only insofar as one erects a logical system upon it. Besides: if Western harmony is logical, why did it now sound so muddy, so overfull, so shapeless? Why did neo-Classicism have to step in to clean up the post-Wagnerian mess?

Schoenberg swept the mess aside and started from scratch. In conventional Western harmony, certain notes are more important than others—they imply a harmonic center, a "logic." In Schoenberg's system, called serialism, all notes are equal and harmonic logic gives way to the logic of note (more exactly, pitch) progressions. One starts not with C Major, or e minor, or whatever key, but with a set of twelve notes, the full twelve notes of the "chromatic scale" (these twelve constitute all the notes—pitches—practically available to the Western composer). As the serialist composes a given piece, however long or short, he continually restates this arbitrary set of notes and countless possible variations of them, at different pitches, in different scorings, rhythms, chord combinations, and tempos till the piece ends.

It is safe to say that nothing in the history of music sounded as difficult to the average ear as serialism did when it was new. Critics and public alike flayed Schoenberg for reckless, ugly idiosyncrasy; they called his music gibberish. But Schoenberg held that all music is, technically, gibberish: the conditioned ear "speaks"—understands—fluent gibberish of a certain kind. Western harmony, until Schoenberg, was that kind. That Schoenberg was more or less self-trained added fuel to the enemy fire, though it makes the open mind admire him all the more. His music counts among the most expressive, beautiful, and original, and his self-training reminds us that character, not education, is fate. "My music is not modern," he said. "It is only badly played."

Wrong. His music was very modern; it was the Modern that found a way out after Wagner, the ineluctable vitality that sweeps into a state of stationary befuddlement. But Schoenberg was no fanatic. "No one else wanted the job," he claimed. "So I had to take it on." His first opera, composed in 1909, was published in 1916 but not performed until 1924; apparently no one else wanted him to take it on, either. He had not yet crystallized serialism, the "twelve-tone" system (also called dodecaphonic music) and this first opera, *Erwartung* (Waiting), is a free exercise in musical expressionism, set out in what is called atonality, meaning that it has no "C Major"—no conventional harmonic center.* Much has been made of Schoenberg's debt to Debussy, and expressionism is not unlike a lurid impressionism, the latter's imagistic suggestiveness made pathological. But where *Pelléas et Mélisande* is ambiguous in its musical "narration," Schoenberg fleshes out each available moment of *Erwartung*, so that the twenty-seven-minute piece absorbs a full evening's concentration. Marie Pappenheim's carefully inconclusive libretto presents a woman wandering in a forest and stumbling upon the body of her lover; or so it seems. The scene shifts fluidly, as if projecting hallucinations, and the text takes free-associative ramble of the Freudian stage. The effect is incoherent, but the procedure, of course, is extremely controlled: the mad are precise. *Erwartung*'s one flaw lies in the excessive demands it makes on the singer, for in this experimental adoption of expressionist exaggeration in music, Schoenberg had to free the ear of its reliance on the steady rhythmic patterns and repeated tunes of tradition, had to find musical equivalents for guilt, delusion, and the like. The voice, no question, is pressed. *Erwartung* is seldom performed because few singers who can handle it are willing to. Helga Pilarczyk made herself a kind of sacrificial scapegoat in the 1950s and '60s keeping *Erwartung* in the repertory virtually single-handed. Even less frequently heard than *Erwartung* is the roomier *Die Glückliche Hand* (The Lucky Hand), composed in 1913 and first produced in 1924. Here a chorus and mimed

---

* Certain critics object to the adjective "atonal" as implying a judgmental negativism. "Tonal" sounds rigorous and efficient, "atonal" suggests infantile riot. Two legs good, four legs bad. But because tonality has already trained the Western ear, the *lack* of it is fairly described as atonalism. In the end, though, all music is equal.

parts assist the protagonist, a man who undergoes a series of ritual life experiences against an almost cinematically active lighting plot. But neither *Erwartung* nor *Die Glückliche Hand* has taken hold as has Schoenberg's song cycle of 1912 for reciter and chamber group, *Pierrot Lunaire* (Moonstruck Pierrot), the classic expressionist musical treat for its daffy, morbid, and nasty settings of French poems (translated into German) decanted, so to speak, in *Sprechgesang* ("speaking song"), a method of "talking" notes so that the voice only just touches an actual pitch, leaping off it into hollow reverberation before the next.

By 1921 Schoenberg had perfected his twelve-tone system and abandoned expressionism—so suitable for the monstrous art thrown up in the years just before and after World War I—for his impetuous science of the note series. Some people can't tell the difference between the early and later atonal styles. Schoenberg's comedy *Von Heute auf Morgen* (From Today to Tomorrow, 1930) sounds expressionistic to many, though this one-act satire on society's craze for The Latest in all things couldn't be more natural if it tried. From Freudian horror (*Erwartung*), symbolic tragedy (*Die Glückliche Hand*), and comedy (*Von Heute auf Morgen*), all in short form, Schoenberg moved into the grandiose, writing his own text for the evening-length *Moses und Aron*. This gaping, grasping, outrageously brilliant spectacle consistently outpaced the imagination and courage of managers and producers, not making it to the stage (in Zurich) till twenty-five years after Schoenberg put it down. Even so, the piece is not complete. When Schoenberg stopped work on it in 1932, the final third act consisted of a libretto but no music. And though Schoenberg lived till 1951, for some mysterious reason he couldn't bring himself to finish what is for many his magnum opus.

Spectacle in *Moses und Aron* is as much music as action, for in tracing the confrontation of austerity (in Moses' "one, eternal, omnipresent, unseeable, inconceivable God") and sensuality (in the luxurious pagan pantheon that Moses' people are reluctant to abandon), Schoenberg heightens our reception of the *tinta* in opera, the coloration in harmony and melody that dyes a work for mood and texture. Those who found *Erwartung* pointless, *Die Glückliche Hand* unfriendly, and *Von Heute auf Morgen* forced fun are surprised by *Moses und Aron*'s flamboyance as *opera*, though the work is uncompromisingly Schoenbergian. Characterizing Moses in bass *Sprechgesang* and Aron as a heroically mellifluous tenor; calling for numerous small parts, an agile chorus, full ballet corps, and sizable orchestra—Schoenberg rivets the senses as well as the mind: in the eerie opening, six solo voices quietly

Moses und Aron: the Orgy of the Golden Calf.
(Royal Opera, Covent Garden)

moaning as the curtain shoots up on Moses taking his orders from the burning bush (four-part choral *Sprechgesang*); in the sudden pause in Act II, when Moses has lingered too long on the mountain in the desert, and the orchestra cuts out in horror as a furious mob of Israelites gradually bursts onto the stage to roar for their leader; in the waltz rhythm that releases their rage a bit later as they contemplate renewing their old, creamy religion; and in the Orgy of the Golden Calf, whose detailed directions, if a producer dared to follow them to the letter, would stand unrivaled in opera for depiction of bestial debauchery.

Subtextually, *Moses and Aaron* seems clearly to tell of Schoenberg's own struggle with his inconceivable god, serialism. His music, too, seemed inconceivable when new. Charles Rosen refers to the work's irresistible sense of autobiography: "The inarticulate Moses, whose mystical vision of God cannot be translated into song, and the voluble Aron, whose view of God is entirely in terms of outward signs and miracles, are part of an allegory whose subject is the impossibility of realizing an artistic vision." Schoenberg himself refuted this line of approach: "The subject matter and its treatment are purely religious and philosophical." When he tells of God, he means, God, not art.

Still, Moses' position as involuntary and despised leader is very like Schoenberg's. The composer had many followers, some who envied the fecund psychology of beauty as terror (and vice versa) in his expressionism, some who eventually gained the upper reaches of true serialism, and some who found both styles too extreme but reveled in the libertarian freshness of antonalism. Because it does "trick" the ear, lacking the harmonic body that Westerners expect of their music, atonalism seems useful in catching the agony of the Modern, the alienation, despair, and comic horror that crop up so often in all twentieth-century art. But atonalism is not chaotic to match the chaos of the times: atonalism is not chaotic, period. Rather, one might call it "open."

After exploiting this openness, Schoenberg developed a vigorous system of composition. If he started out as a late Romantic, he achieved a qualified neo-Classicism, and a Classicist does not deal in chaos: quite the contrary. From Romanticism, Schoenberg extracted the cyclic *Leitmotiv* (which restates itself in endless variation) and reinvented it to equalize all its variations. In Wagner's *Ring*, the all-basic motive that launches the work dominates it as a concept; in serialism, the "all-basic" tone row also launches a given work—but vanishes for all practical purposes as soon as it is heard and might not be recognized again. In Wagner the *Leitmotiv* directs the art; in serialism the row merely engenders it, letting its permutations take over, one after the other as they sound.

Some of atonalism's reputation as a depiction of chaos is the result of the drastic power of the first post-Schoenbergian Modern work to enter the repertory, Alban Berg's *Wozzeck* (1925). Highly expressionistic, filled with giggly tragedy and hollow wonder, and based on Georg Büchner's *Woyzeck*, a nineteenth-century play that anticipates twentieth-century psychological and aesthetic complexity, Berg's *Wozzeck* may sound unleashed, but, as one of Schoenberg's prize pupils, Berg was hardly a primitive finger-painting in music. Büchner's intensity called for an overall discipline, a structural clarity, and Berg found it by organizing the many short scenes neo-Classically by genre. There are three acts with five scenes each; the first act is a suite, the second a symphony in five movements (including slow movement and scherzo), and the third a set of inventions (on a theme, a rhythm, a tonality). This is useful to the work's atmosphere as theatre: capricious expressionism delights in switching moods scene by scene. But unlike the neo-Classicists, Berg does not impose his self-contained forms on the ear. Even a trained musician would not discern the structures on first hearing. He would be too absorbed in the action. *Wozzeck* is Romantic opera, sharing its feelings with the audience with no contrapuntal commentary from an authorial voice. What moved Berlioz, Verdi, or Strauss moves Berg—indeed, *Salome* contributed to *Wozzeck*'s chittering violins, cavernous brasses, and bat-screaming woodwinds. (The Schoenberg circle was known to admire Strauss' opera greatly.) "Passions are no longer simulated," Berg wrote in discussing Schoenberg's expressionism, "but rather genuine emotions of the unconscious—of shock, of trauma—are registered without disguise through the medium of music."

That's why *Wozzeck* sounds so crazy: it is about craziness. The protagonist, a forgotten man, is everybody's dupe. Though he can't identify the forces that oppress him except in paranoid imagery ("Do you see that streak of light there on the grass, where the mushrooms grow? At night a head rolls around there"), the societal system closes in on him scene by scene, driving him at length to murder and his own death. Paradoxically, Berg's musical system of suite, symphony, and inventions does not in the least inhibit the action; rather, it coexists with it as a kind of "other" world of simple order to balance Büchner's real-life world of the sordid, the uncharitable, and the dispossessed.

It is proof of Berg's powers that while revivals of the play had gone over in sophisticated centers, as opera it provoked scandals of resistance wherever it went.* Was it because the play alone, undeniably radical in form and politics, could be disarmed as a "historical experiment" while Berg's intent musical realization made it bitterly realistic? Even some who tolerated *Wozzeck* because of liberal ethics didn't like it as art, seeing the modern habit of setting plays as operas without adapting them to a recognizable operatic form as an aberration. *Pelléas et Mélisande*, they felt, should have been the only, not the first. A play "set" rather than adapted has valence neither as play nor opera, they insisted: the words lose their completeness and the music is too subsidiary too often. They longed for the nineteenth-century method of adaptation, when a plot was remolded to suit aria, duet, intermezzo, finale—a *Faust*, a *Trovatore*.

How wrong could they be? This new-style opera is not failed drama or failed music. It marks a return to the *dramma in musica*, the Camerata ideal wherein a play is sung: wherein theatre is sharpened by musical penetration: wherein the listener's intellectual and emotional investment is equally keen. The Camerata never bargained for Big Tunes or *grands duos*. It argued the supremacy of text over music— the text, rather, *through* the music. And this *Wozzeck* has. The music agitates or meanders or does both at once; the vocal line has no glamor; the subject isn't pretty. But *Wozzeck*'s immersion in art, in bringing itself forward with meaning, is total. The expressionism that so horrified audiences in 1925 is useful for Berg's "shock and trauma," but his atonalism in general offers a legitimate sound style of its own, not merely a fund to be drawn on in moments of advanced despair. After all, opera can use expressionism more than "naturalism," which at best is a mannerism in opera anyway. *The Marriage of Figaro* is as reasonable and unforced as operatic naturalism can get; *verismo* was too inflexibly lurid, a fanfare of realism: unreal. Any realism, in opera, is bound to emphasize opera's natural conditions of overstatement and expansion. So which is more realistic, *Cavalleria Rusticana* or *Wozzeck?*

Wozzeck, of course. And Berg's second and only other opera—he died at fifty—is, if anything, even more exciting. In *Lulu*, Berg aban-

---

* *Wozzeck* went far afield—to Prague in 1926, where protest demonstrations led to its being banned; to Moscow in 1927; Tito Gobbi sang it all over Italy for decades; and such diverse American singers as Eileen Farrell, Marilyn Horne, Eleanor Steber, Brenda Lewis, and Evelyn Lear have sung Marie. Curiously, *Wozzeck* went even farther than Berg could send it—in a second version, premiered a year after Berg's, by Manfred Gurlitt. Gurlitt had double bad luck in choosing subjects: as Berg's *Wozzeck* erased Gurlitt's *Woyzeck*, so did Bernd Alois Zimmermann's *Die Soldaten* rub his *Die Soldaten*—from the same source— out of the lists.

doned atonal expressionism for Schoenberg's twelve-tone system, turning again for his text to theatre of an earlier epoch, Frank Wedekind's plays *Erdgeist* (Earth Spirit) and *Die Büchse der Pandora* (Pandora's Box). Wozzeck shares something important with Lulu: the two central characters do not understand the context in which they move. Wedekind's heroine is a woman of devastating charm, destructive to men and women alike. But she is innocent, in the sense of not having an opinion about herself. Lulu just is; the tragedy that stalks her associates is their own fault. In *Wozzeck*, Berg dealt with the working class. Lulu took him into society, though she herself is a person of no set milieu, and falls from the pinnacle to the depths.

It's a fascinating work, the more so because its insane lyricism—Lulu is a lyric soprano with a high-flying, decorated line—rings with vocal niceties. Too, the shrieky, grumping *Sprechgesang* reminds one that Berg is a Schoenbergian, with his roots in expressionism, as does his meticulous sense of structure. He charts Lulu's rise and fall musically, drawing "up" to a central point in Act II and then falling away in a recapitulatory culmination as Lulu's castoff victims reappear one by one to even the score. The last of them, "Jack" (we presume "the Ripper"), finishes the work of revenge by killing Lulu and her lesbian admirer Countess Geschwitz.

Until very recently Lulu's third and final act remained opera's great frustration, for though experts declared it virtually complete in short score (a shortened version of the full orchestration), Berg's widow refused to release it for performance. Berg died in 1935 and the first two acts were produced in Zurich in 1937; slowly the work gained ground as a worthy successor to *Wozzeck*. But what's an opera without its last act? Producers staged *Lulu* with a tacked-on closing scene (Berg had included this in his *Lulu Suite*); still, some fifty minutes of crucial action were lacking. Secretly, Berg's publishers commissioned Friedrich Cerha to expand the third-act manuscript, and Helene Berg's death in 1976 removed the last practical barrier to a whole *Lulu*. In early 1979 the Paris Opéra* triumphantly presented the first-ever complete *Lulu* with Teresa Stratas, Yvonne Minton, Kenneth Riegel, Franz Mazura, and Toni Blankenheim under Pierre Boulez and staged by Patrice Chéreau. The reverberations of that unveiling are still being felt: new masterpieces are in short supply nowadays.

---

* Note the reascendance of Paris in the musical community after a half-century of torpor; almost nothing of consequence happened there between Dyagilyef's Ballets Russes and the reorganization of the Paris Opéra—despite the screaming resistance of its many bureaucrats, for whom torpor is candy—by Rolf Liebermann.

CHAPTER NINETEEN

Bad Times

*National Socialism puts the per-
sonality of a creative artist before his work. The fact that before the new regime Hindemith
showed signs of an un-German
attitude disqualifies him from
taking part in the movement's
cultural reclamation work.*
—BERNHARD RUST, spokesman for
Joseph Goebbels'
Reichskulturkammer

THE 1930S AND EARLY 1940S DISHEARTEN IN OPERA AS THEY DID IN
history. Everyone, it seems, was trying to recover from or redefine
the artistic revolutions of the previous few decades. Post-Wagnerism,
whether as exhausted late Romanticism or elfin or severe neo-Classicism, still called the tune, while few really top-notch composers made
their debuts till after World War II and the one vital possiblity for a
new idiom, Schoenberg's serialism, remained forbidding to most ears.
The excitement of the early 1900s, with Debussy, Milhaud, Hindemith,
Weill, and Stravinsky all opening up different routes After Wagner,
not to mention the theatre-filling momentum built up by Puccini and
Strauss, the last of the universally popular composers, was dissipated
in a time of Depression and totalitarian menace. Some masterpieces
were produced, true, and this was the era in which American opera
rose up in *Four Saints in Three Acts* and *Porgy and Bess*. But overall,
the zesty second-rank pickings—the thick and fun of the opera output—
the *Don Quichotte*s, *Königskinder*s, and *Piccolo Marat*s—are slim.

Perhaps it is all too typical that even Richard Strauss ran downhill
in these years. Still working with Hugo von Hofmannsthal, he embarked on another mythological subject after *Die Frau Ohne Schatten*,
Greek like *Ariadne*, and—as originally planned—light and irreverent,

332

with plenty of opportunity to take up where Strauss had left off with his exercises in *parlando* recit in *Ariadne*'s Prologue and in *Intermezzo*. But somewhere along the line the project, on what happened to Helen *after* Troy fell, got deep and serious. Despite a chance to pull out his accustomed magic for Helen's soaring soprano and a willingness to see what he could do with his first really animated lead tenor (the Emperor in *Die Frau* doesn't do much more than turn to stone) in Menelaus, *Die Ägyptische Helena* (The Egyptian Helen, 1928) does not come off. The first act, mystically psychological, isn't too bad, closing with a delectable scene in which the "true" Helen is supposedly awakened from a ten-year sleep. But Act II, after Helen's opening "Zweite Brautnacht!" (Second honeymoon!), collapses in unwieldy physical action. Strauss sensed this early on; after Hofmannsthal outlined the plot of the first half, the composer remarked, "And surely that's the end of the piece. What else could happen in the second act?"

The team rallied, however, in *Arabella* (1933), a comedy not unlike *Der Rosenkavalier* but developed for darker colors. The setting, again, is Vienna, but the waltzes are less convivial and the tale of an impoverished family attempting to launch their older daughter socially —the younger is kept in boy's clothes, to cut costs—very nearly turns tragic at the end. Strauss wanted it so, but Hofmannsthal thought better. All is put to rights—both girls get their men—and if *Arabella*'s musical total tallies uneven, it has Hofmannsthal at his best . . . and last. He died just after completing the libretto.

Doubtless it's just as well; he would not have weathered the ensuing years. The upheaval of racist oppression and preparations for war made nomads of many artists discussed here, some of them creating works in exile, some composing a piece along the road from horror to haven. Strauss, as the kingpin German composer, had considerable defensive clout; but unlike some of his colleagues who resisted Nazism and some who preferred it, Strauss despised yet got along with it. Most of his later operas took on a political bias, if in behind-the-scenes ways: the comic *Die Schweigsame Frau* (The Silent Woman, 1935) offended Nazi higher-ups because Stefan Zweig, a non-Aryan, wrote the text; *Friedenstag* (Day of Peace, 1938) sings so firmly of liberty, with a look back at the catastrophic barbarism of the Thirty Years' War and a finale modeled on *Fidelio*'s, that one wonders how the Nazis ever suffered its production; and *Die Liebe der Danae* (The Love of Danae), Attic romance with satiric touches, got only as far as the last dress rehearsal at the Salzburg Festival in 1944, when Total War shut third-reich theatres, and was not again attempted till 1952.

The most audacious of the late Strauss canon is his "conversation piece," *Capriccio* (1942). Strauss and conductor Clemens Krauss wrote a libretto on opera's oldest theme—which comes first, music or words? We know the words came first originally, and nowadays singers' woolly diction renders the question academic rather than popular. But the authors set their charade in the time and place of Gluck's musical revolution, when the question really carried force. Operagoers took sides enthusiastically then—is opera a *play* in music or a *musical* play? That lays *Capriccio*'s foundation, represented in a poet and a composer, rivals for the attentions of an artistic Countess. Embellishing the foundation with in-jokes (such as quotations from operas new and old, parodistic bits, and an antiintellectual impresario who castigates Modern for its grotesquerie), Strauss and Krauss try the question from several angles—*le parole o la musica?*—and at last pretend not to answer it: torn between poet and composer, the Countess shrugs at her reflection in a mirror. There is no one answer—she needs them both. But the impresario has already answered the question for us in his big scene. Neither words nor music is supreme; good theatre, however it's managed, is what counts.

Possibly *Capriccio* is not the best theatre. It's too dry and verbose to please a multitude, though it begins promisingly with a graceful string quartet in period style and ends with the characteristic radiant Straussian soprano in the Countess' closing scene. But then this Strauss was not the one who wrote the daringly expressionistic *Salome* or the intimately Romantic *Rosenkavalier*. This was the *Ariadne* Prologue Strauss, chastely seeking self-contained structures and Mozartean tensions, a quasi-neo-Classical Strauss. He had not exactly run out of melody. Both *Die Schweigsame Frau* and *Die Liebe der Danae* offer fetchingly lyrical moments. But *Friedenstag* is a bore and *Capriccio* sounds as if Strauss had traded words for music almost all the way.

As for those former bad boys Ernst Křenek and Kurt Weill, they, at least, stuck to their guns, though both smartly realized that their *Zeitoper* days were over. Křenek attempted a retrospective of virtually every Modern style, from neo-Classical simplicity to expressionism, in his historical pageant *Karl V* (1938), while Weill, still with Brecht (in France en route to the United States), moved into opera-ballet in the one-act *Die Sieben Todsünden der Kleinbürger* (The Seven Deadly Sins of the Petit Bourgeoisie, 1933), retaining his sardonic fox trot and shimmy. Originally choreographed by George Balanchine, *The Seven Deadly Sins* takes a pair of sisters, both named Anna, on a tour of the land Brecht loved to hate, the United States, in a prologue, seven movements (one for each sin), and epilogue. As before, Brecht spits his irony in the face: practical Anna I (a singer) exhorts susceptible

Anna II (a dancer) to resist temptation—in "capitalist" terms, to think only of amassing material wealth.

Whether at home or in exile, the German composer could not sidestep politics. Paul Hindemith at length found himself so oppressed by maneuverings for and against him that he wrote an opera to explain the politics of the artist. Though willing to pull his shocking early pieces *Sancta Susanna* and *Das Nusch-Nuschi* out of circulation without Nazi prompting (no doubt feeling that they had run their timely course anyway), Hindemith tried to turn his back on *l'affaire Hinde- mith*, but eventually he was forced to flee Germany. His opera of apologia, *Mathis der Maler* (Mathis the Painter, 1938), was produced in Zurich, Amsterdam, and London. Not in Germany.

The heroes of Hindemith's three major operas are all artists, seen in proximity to or alienation from their surroundings—but none so much so as Mathis. In the composer's own libretto (based on the life of the sixteenth-century painter Mathias Grünewald), Mathis is chal- lenged to defend his vocation when his world is at war, the peasants against the establishment. "Is it possible?" asks the peasant leader. "You paint?" "Is that sinful?" Mathis replies. "Perhaps," says the peasant, "when so many hands are needed to better the world." But no war, Mathis learns, betters a world, and at length Hindemith pictures his epiphany of self-realization in a series of visions modeled on old paint- ings, including Grünewald's famous Isenheim tryptych on the life of St. Anthony. Finding the last meaning of life in the truth of art, Mathis retrieves his shattered will to create: and Hindemith defends his own way, drawn back from the world in the priority of personal out- giving that becomes, when taken, universal.

The parallel between modern and medieval Germany was hard to miss in *Mathis:* book burning, political refugees, feudal sycophants urging the arrest of dissenters, crises of faith, cowardice, heroism, and bargain striking all connected Mathis to Hindemith. "Normal" times prompted Lullian *tragédie* and *opera seria:* consensus opera. Abnormal times make for works applicable first to the creators and only then— maybe—to individuals in the audience, and many listeners who cheer for Mathis' courageous no! to history still don't find his adventure enthralling as opera. *Mathis der Maler* is a form of chronicle; it starts slowly. But the story soon absorbs one enough to care about the characters as if in the standard make of lovers' and fighters' opera (which, on a level, it is). Hindemith's third opera, *Die Harmonie der Welt* (The Harmony of the World, 1957), fails because its people don't grab us dramatically. But in the baritone Mathis, his heroic-tenor employer the Archbishop of Mainz, two high sopranos Mathis befriends, and numerous smaller parts, Hindemith assembled real lives to illustrate his philosophy. Nothing is more affecting than the opera's final moments, when Mathis, at the end of his long life, packs away his things to wait for death in peace. The greatest achievement, the smallest article, all thought, all action, pass away to dust, he says; to the punctuation of quiet chords, he displays his souvenirs of "what I aspired to" (his ruler and compass), "what I created" (paints and brushes), "what I won as honor" (a golden chain), "what distressed me" (books), and "what I loved" (a ribbon given to him by one of the two women on her deathbed). Mathis kisses the ribbon, and the curtain falls.

If Hindemith led what survived of neo-Classicism, the Swiss Othmar Schoeck has been called "the last of the Romantics"—though in actuality Schoeck played the field. He wrote operas in the comic, fairy-tale, legendary, and naturalistic modes, and changed his sound appropriately each time. The longish one-act *Penthesilea* (1927), his best-known work, accords with the new system of setting (cut down) play texts, the play being Heinrich von Kleist's version of the meeting of Achilles and the Amazon Queen. "Not a comma that's not in Kleist!" Schoeck instructed his collaborator, Léon Oswald, but more important than verbal integrity is Schoeck's flavorful scoring, lush for the central love duet, icily expressionistic during the war scenes.

Interestingly, *Märchenoper* did not die. Carl Orff breathed new life into the form with his austerely folkish Grimm pair, *Der Mond* (The Moon, 1939) and *Die Kluge* (The Wise Woman, 1943), featuring simplistic, sturdily rhythmic tunes repeated with hebetudinous insistence. Orff's *Märchenopern* (to his own texts) eschew the *faux naïf* of the Viennese genre (like *The Magic Flute*) and the rich Romantic palette of the Humperdinck school. His are shrewd, moral, quasi-Brechtian. *Der Mond* amounts to a lecture on the eternal wickedness of humankind, and *Die Kluge* shows the perils of being wise in a stupid world, though both end happily. Politics again intrudes here in one scene of ferocious anti-Nazi spoof in *Die Kluge*, slightly disguised to fool the censors.

Some composers busied themselves ratifying methods developed in preceding decades. Darius Milhaud produced another of his classical tragedies in severe style, *Médée* (1939), just before he went to the United States; Franco Alfano brought forth a *Cyrano de Bergerac* (1936), in French, reduced from Rostand's play, in the *Pelléas* mode. Peripatetically derivative was the Czech Bohuslav Martinů, whose fourteen operas include native folk pieces, *Zeitoper*, musical mystery plays, French impressionist dream opera, neo-Classical parody opera, and operas in English. His *Julietta* (1938) blended a powerful dramatic thrust with the sleepwalking ambience of *Pelléas*.

Politics caught up with Russian music (left to its own devices throughout the 1920s) in 1932, when the Central Committee of the All-Union Communist Party cited Maxim Gorky's "socialist realism" as the only acceptable approach in art. No more "formalism" or "experimentalism": from now on, Soviet art must be simple in effect and optimistic in theme, to help build the state. This oppression lay heaviest on the most gifted composers, eager to match their Western colleagues in the formal experiments of Modern—Shostakovitch, for instance. In *Nos* (The Nose, 1930), he produced one of the most gala black comedies, a satiric fantasy adapted from Gogol's tale of a nose that escapes from the face of one Major Kovalyof and runs around disguised as a civil servant. Gogol lampooned the culture—the bureaucracy especially—of Nicholas I's clumsy autocracy; Shostakovitch, who wrote *The Nose* at the time of *Wozzeck*'s Russian premiere, appears to lampoon expressionism in all its extremes—the incredibly high tenor voices, rhythmic speech, textual and musical non sequiturs, the heartfelt laments that in the context only add to the ridicule, the short scenes connected by crazy intermezzos, the gurgly woodwinds, trilling brasses, and overwrought percussion, the pointillistic scoring in which each successive note is played by a different instrument, and off pitch at that. Oddly, Shostakovitch insisted at the time that his score intended no spoof, that he sought to mirror a dead-pan narration with a straight-on approach, letting the bizarre story provide the fun. It does —but Shostakovitch's music does, too. He attacked the basic opera problem—how to set text—with such inventive élan that he couldn't resist enlivening his second opera, *Lyedy Macbyet Mtsenksowo Uyezda* (The Lady Macbeth of the Mtsensk District, 1934), a dour tragedy, with some of *The Nose*'s absurd gimmicks. But by this time the Party was prepared to put the screws on, and *Pravda* smashed *Lyedy Macbyet* for its inflammatory subject matter (adultery and murder) and musical irreverence. The composer revised the piece as *Katyerina Ismailovna* in 1963, when his political position was more secure, and it is slowly creeping into the repertory (in both versions) as his reputation expands in the West. Two other victims of Party persecution, conductor and cellist Mstislaf Rostropovitch and his wife, the soprano Galina Vishnyefskaya, made a point of performing the original *Lyedy Macbyet* when they recorded the work in London in 1978.

Syergyey Prokofyef, if anything even more formalistic and experimental than Shostakovitch, had left Russia during the Revolution, but in 1932 he returned to his homeland, unfortunately just in time for

the Stalinization of the arts. In Paris in 1927 he had completed a compelling tragedy on occult possession, *Ognyeniy Angyel* (The Flaming
Angel)—much too hot an item for the prudish Soviet sensibility. As
always, Prokofyef wrote his own text, in this case basing it on Valery
Bryusof's strange novel, and there is a weird Teutonic flavor to the
whole piece—surely Busoni or Hindemith should have handled this
subject. But Prokofyef's obvious sympathy for his disturbed heroine
carries him through, and while waiting for a premiere that never came
in his lifetime, he utilized some of the music in his Third Symphony.

Political accommodation. That is the curse of this era—Strauss
ceasing work with a gifted collaborator because the government didn't
like his genetic stock, Shostakovitch hunted from the stage for his
wicked whimsy, Prokofyef hampered then strait-jacketed, Hindemith,
Schoenberg, and Weill fleeing their native countries. The nationalist
art ethos that has guided opera through the years like a sentinel of
benignly incentive progressivism collapses in these days, cutting many
creators off from their roots and destiny as artists. Prokofyef had long
been international by choice, but it seems ineffably exotic of him to
have made an opera of Richard Brinsley Sheridan's comedy-with-songs
The Duenna, as *Obrucheniye v Monastirye* (The Bethrothal in a Monastery, 1946), completed in 1940 but not produced until after World
War II. In the end, though, he put his greatest effort into a thoroughly
Russian project, *Voina i Mir* (War and Peace), an attempt to find the
timeless epic of *patria* in Tolstoy's novel of Russia at war, which
Prokofyef composed during the great war of his generation.

War and Peace is nothing like the legendary or historical Russian
operas of the 1800s. Episodic and multistoried, without a protagonist,
it leaps back and forth from private lives to national chronicle. In
Glinka, Musorksky, and most of Rimsky-Korsakof, all action is seen
on one level as the poetry and adventure of a people. *War and Peace*
breaks up, as the title suggests, into two different kinds of opera in
one evening, certain people's love lives in peace and an entire people's
survival during war. The former scenes emphasize the lyrical, the
latter the dramatic, and since the very long work is usually performed
with substantial cuts, either the lyrical or the dramatic can overshadow
the other depending on what gets sliced off. Indeed, while the first
("peace") half reached the stage as early as 1946, in Leningrad, the
complete opera was not heard till 1959, at the Bolshoi in Moscow.

It's a thrilling piece, one of the biggest in terms of the humanist
response it engenders in the listener, for though Party stooges stood
over Prokofyef's shoulder throughout the years of composition and
revision, he somehow gave his considerable powers free rein in retriev-

ing Tolstoy's richness, eccentricity, and incisiveness. Opera does not *observe* the way a novel does; even Modern's expressionism cannot be as precise as the spoken language, and Prokofyef had retained that blend of the simple and perverse he had mixed when still an *enfant terrible*. Yet, as refracted through opera's prism, the simple can bend into the titanic. In *Les Troyens*, Berlioz portrays epic through a statuesque Classicism highlighted by personal passions; in the *Ring*, Wagner portrays epic in a series of catastrophes connected back to one essential catastrophe (the renunciation of love for power: the stealing of the gold); in *War and Peace*, Prokofyef portrays epic through the confrontation of people and history, all seen in not-quite-separate vignettes framed by a choral prelude and finale, the first defying the enemy and the second celebrating its defeat.

Though this period from 1930 to 1945 is no golden age, it does at least show that the continuous dialogue between primarily musical opera and primarily theatrical musical comedy continues to benefit both forms. We have reached a point now where many "operas" owe more to musical comedy than to opera—*Die Dreigroschenoper, Die Kluge, The Makropulos Business, The Love for Three Oranges, Gianni Schicchi*, and *L'Heure Espagnole*, for example. Twentieth-century opera, in its diversity, has reestablished the absolute importance of the text, of theatre on a line-by-line basis. And this not in place of music, but in collaboration with it. The Tunes are not as Big as they were in Meyerbeer, Wagner, or Verdi, but the experience as drama is enriched. If one views *Mathis der Maler* or *Die Ägyptische Helena* as contemporary *opera seria* and *Arabella* or *The Nose* as contemporary *opera buffa*, one must concede an immense gain in conceptual integrity. The notion that Modern opera is not good opera is not only ridiculous but false; new works often outdraw old ones everywhere except in the United States—and there the problem is a combination of timid management and bad English translations. Obviously, if an opera counts its words as heavily as its music, one must hear the words in competent renderings in one's own language. We'll take this up again in due course.

CHAPTER TWENTY

The Postwar Scene

What are the requirements for a modern opera? The answer can be given in one sentence: opera as total theatre . . . architecture, sculpture, painting, musical theatre, spoken theatre, ballet, film, microphone, television, tape and sound techniques, electronic music, musique concrète, *circus, the musical . . .*
—BERND ALOIS ZIMMERMANN

Given a good and suitable libretto, there are qualities and possibilities in nineteenth-century opera which can still stimulate the imagination.
—HANS WERNER HENZE, 1961

Opera is finished.
—HANS WERNER HENZE, 1970

AFTER THE CONFUSION OF THE 1930S AND THE DEVASTATION OF WORLD War II, the last few decades have made an amazing recovery, redefining the sectors of traditionalism and progressivism to let both breathe more freely, meanwhile building up the Western opera plant with new companies that enlarge opera's economic and cultural bases as well as give new singers the opportunity to collect experiences onstage. If tradition and progressivism don't get on well, they do check and balance, in that most of the public prefers new works that sound "attractive" while spokesmen for the musical community consider anything less than serialism trivial and corny. Yet it should be pointed out that almost everyone who works in serialism applies extensive modifications to Schoenberg's system—sometimes just enough to appease the fancy European critics.

If the postwar operagoer's hardest task is getting used to Modern, his great perquisite is the plethora of revival movements. Everything from early Baroque opera to the mistermed *verismo* has been coming back, often promoted by experts in style, so that the overlapping textures of Monteverdi, Lully, Gluck, Rossini, Meyerbeer, Verdi, and Zandonai give the ear a chance to encounter the whole historical panorama. Moreover, stage technology today—whether in "realism," traditional mannerism, or experimentalism—has the potential to bring any work home in or out of style. Truth to tell, a shortage of world-class voices has made the superdirector's ascendancy convenient, though his power over the conductor invites disaster—especially as many directors slip in crabwise from the spoken stage inadequately prepared for the musical end of things.

The opera singer has been riding out the tail end of a post–golden age, when the hegemony of vocal cords is about to be overpowered by the "all-theatre" opera that twentieth-century fascination for text, comedy, and psychological depth had brought home. Such operas as *Wozzeck, Intermezzo, Gianni Schicchi*, and *Chérubin* must be staged with the actor's, producer's, and designer's technique as much as the musician's. Thus the postwar generation has grown up in an environment somewhat inimical to the stand-there-and-sing approach. At the same time, the gradual development of television opera—broadcasting both theatre performances and stagings conceived for video—has helped acculturate opera demographically.

But whereas technology has made opera accessible on records and airwaves, it has done harm to opera's equilibrium, blowing star singers in and out of city after city on a jet schedule that forbids anyone's doing his best work and leaving the company principle, so important to the maintenance of ensemble, to the less interesting singers who stay put by default. It's notable that when *Opera News* magazine published Lanfranco Rasponi's series of interviews with Italian veterans of the post-*verismo* era, virtually all of them condemned the current opera scene as brusque and unartistic. Tancredi Pasero blasted the bureaucrat know-nothings who administer it; Gina Cigna shuddered at the speed with which young singers rush into the limelight before completing their training; Mafalda Favero deplored the bankrupt pretensions of the pushier directors. "The spontaneity is gone," she said.

Some of this is true, but it is also true that Italy, like France, has lost its international prominence for a number of reasons. This era has been colored to a great extent by the recovery of the German musical theatre (most of whose major companies were dispersed and bombed away to nothing during the war); the striking growth of interest in opera in the United Kingdom and all over the British Commonwealth, and the astonishing development of American opera from a few elite houses to a huge network of regional groups, some of which rival the Met in quality (though not quantity) of performance. Most operagoers probably noticed little of all this as it happened gradually over the course of the several postwar decades. They would have noticed the thinning out of the Italian leadership, as Renata Tebaldi, Giulietta Simionato, Mario del Monaco, Giuseppi di Stefano, Franco Corelli, Ettore Bastianini, and a few others dropped out in the 1970s with no corresponding replacements; and the paucity of new "hit" operas was hard to miss. But otherwise operagoing must have felt like a tour through a museum with the occasional "contemporary" room. Italy especially trod paths laid out long before, though the long-lived Pizzetti and Malipiero had lost none of their resonance. Pizzetti's *L'Assassinio nella Cathedrale* (1958), from T. S. Eliot's *Murder in the Cathedral*, has proved to be the composer's most popular work, and Malipiero showed top form in a pair of rather spiritual *commedie*, *Le Metamorfosi di Bonaventura* (Bonaventura's Metamorphoses, 1966) and *Gli Eroi di Bonaventura* (Bonaventura's Heroes, 1969) in which the old master put down his pen symbolically by writing himself (as Bonaventura) a death scene to finish *Gli Eroi*.

Other works were so old-fashioned they sounded obsolete even when new. Renzo Rossellini (brother of the film director) made *Uno Sguardo dal Ponte* (A View from the Bridge, 1961) from Arthur Miller's play, but despite the minor surprise of the lawyer character speaking (often over accompaniment) when he serves as narrator and singing baritone as actor in the plot, the result was tedious *verismo* cliché. Similarly old-hat is the much better known Gian Carlo Menotti (librettist and stage director as well as composer), whose good timing enabled him to supply the burgeoning American audience with the melodious thrillers *The Medium* (1946), *The Consul* (1950), and *The Saint of Bleecker Street* (1954) just when the nation was ready to tune into something new (meaning "just written") but not new (meaning post-Schoenbergian in sound). Menotti's *œuvre* consists mostly of operas written in English for American (often Broadway) audiences, so he is generally thought of as an American composer. But no one could sound less American. Having ridden shock as far as it will ride, Menotti tried satire in *The Last Savage* (1963) and *Help! Help! The Globolinks!* (1968), the former a sizable mess spoofing consumerism and the rich and the latter a "rebuttal" to electronic music, seen as ex-

traterrestrial invaders and imaginatively designed by Alwin Nicolais
to resemble accordionlike chess pieces. (The youthful Judith Blegen
charmed many with her violin playing as a heroically tonal little
heroine who neutralizes the aliens with real music.) But by this time
the composer had totally run out of the melody his rebuttal needed:
even electronic tape sounds better than late Menotti. Voguishly anti-
American entries such as *Tamu-Tamu* (1973) and *The Hero* (1976)
couldn't save his reputation, and no doubt he will dwindle into a footnote as the author of the only lead role created by Beverly Sills, that
of *Juana la Loca* (1979).*

French traditionalism at least had Francis Poulenc, who reclaimed
Dada in the short *Les Mamelles de Tirésias* (The Breasts of Tiresias,
1947), based on Guillaume Apollinaire's loony burlesque of, among
other things, women's liberation. Rich harmonies, brash instrumental
doodle-doo, cabaret whimsy, farcical death and rebirth dance around
the heroine, Thérèse, who bursts her breasts (as balloons), dons a
mustache, and abandons homemaking to her husband, who—during the
intermission—procreates 40,049 babies. Neo-Classically, the full cast
assembles at the finale to preach the moral: everybody stay home and
have babies.

Bizarre, no? But a decade later Poulenc bequeathed the world a
solemn and infinitely moving full-length masterpiece, *Dialogues des
Carmelites* (Dialogues of the Carmelites, 1957), yet another of the
countless settings of plays, in this case Georges Bernanos' look at the
martyrdom of a group of Carmelite nuns during the French Revolution. As the title suggests, this is a conversational piece, but the constant flow of sung talk yields great women's roles—the mezzo-soprano
Prioress, a natural for crashed-in voices for the raw, shouting horror
of her death scene; her austerely pious successor; the tense Mother
Marie; innocent Sister Constance; and, at the center, the quietly bewildered Blanche, who completes the final tableau of the Carmelites'
execution when she gently paces forward out of the watching mob
and joins her sisters, her prayer, like theirs, shattered in mid-phrase by
the slash of the guillotine. Another certified "French" neo-Classicist,
Manuel de Falla, rose to epic in *L'Atlántida* (1962), finished after
De Falla's death by his pupil Ernesto Halffter. This "scenic cantata"
doesn't stage well, perhaps, except with the devoted assistance of a
ballet corps. Still, La Scala mounted its premiere, letting the panoply
roll—Margherita Wallmann's direction, Nicola Benois' designs, Thomas

---

* Sills is often thought to have sung the title part in *The Ballad of Baby Doe*'s
world premiere; Dolores Wilson first sang it in Central City, Colorado, two years
before Sills took it over in New York.

Schippers conducting, Giulietta Simionato and Teresa Stratas leading the cast, and full pantomimes rousing this colossal narration (from Jacinto Verdaguer's Catalan poem) on the passing of glory from deluged Atlantis to its heir, Spain.

Some countries favored pre-Schoenbergian composition. In Russia, Soviet dictates made strict tonalism a do-or-die absolute even after de-Stalinization, while in England the momentous arrival of Benjamin Britten pushed his colleagues to find the new wave in traditional tonality, as he did. At first English opera moved sluggishly, as in William Walton's *Troilus and Cressida* (1954). A great subject, but it needed D'Annunzio's sexual compulsion, not Christopher Hassall's judicious poetry.

Each nation, it seems, has its leading Schoenbergian exponent, often expressionist and using at least some version of serialism. Argentina has—and resents—Alberto Ginastera, who with Shostakovitch and Prokofyef exemplifies the obdurate abandon of those who commit art in a totalitarian climate. He has had his greatest successes in the United States, as when a New York City Opera staging of his *Don Rodrigo* (1964) proved a vehicle for Modern's ingratiating itself with the public as well as for Placido Domingo to reach for international stardom in the title role. Ginastera's Modern compromises with tradition, particularly in *Don Rodrigo*, and his fondness for using every possible sound and combination of sounds that can be blown, plucked, or beaten out of material objects makes his operas, if nothing else, a hoot. *Bomarzo* (1967), however, shocked many with its interest in lust, sadism, homosexuality, orgiastic ecstasy, and murder. Manuel Mujica Láinez wrote the libretto (from his novel) as the flashback retrospective of a poisoned hunchback noble, and for all its episodic construction, it suits the theatre beautifully. Ginastera's Polish colleague, Krzysztof Penderecki, also exploits timbre—the "color" of sound—as an end in itself; his *Die Teufel von Loudon* (The Devils of Loudon, 1969) from John Whiting's adaptation of Aldous Huxley's novel, was if anything even harder to take than *Bomarzo*. Thirty scenes on pride, envy, alleged "possession," and monstrous ecclesiastical cruelty in seventeenth-century France do through music what Ken Russell, in his film from the same source, could not do: find some meaning in the abject bottom of human brutality. While Ginastera waxed progressively more "difficult," Penderecki got less so. On a more idealistic plane he set Christopher Fry's potted Milton in *Paradise Lost* (1978), the Chicago Lyric Opera's delayed Bicentennial offering, composed by a Pole to a Britisher's text, designed by an Italian, and staged by an Italian replaced by an Israeli. (Mediocre) Americans sang it, at least, and Nancy Thuesen and Dennis Wayne danced impressively as Eve and Adam.

In Italy, where *canto*'s maximum leadership would seem to militate against Modern, Luigi Dallapiccola wrote one of the classics of post-Schoenbergian opera, *Il Prigioniero* (The Prisoner, 1950), one hour's worth of a political prisoner's despair, wonder, hallucinated escape, and execution. Dallapiccola set it in Renaissance Spain, but the situation applies no less well to his own time; even more timely is his dilution of serialism for a thrilling commentative alchemy that reflects the interior action while heightening the effect of the lines. The construction, too, is characteristic of the generation that followed Schoenberg (though *Moses und Aron* had yet to be heard), as in a trio of *ricercari* ("investigations"—pieces expounding on a set proposition), each one built on a musical theme associated with an idea of fundamental textual significance. The first *ricercar* is on the prisoner's prayer to God for help, the second on the jailer's word of encouragement, "Brother," and the third on the name of a freedom fighter. But while *Il Prigioniero* was heard everywhere, Dallapiccola's major opera in terms of effort and length, *Ulisse* (1967), on the homeward-bound adventures of Homer's hero, has few admirers.

German lands have recycled Classical subjects far more than other nations, and the German composers share a great enthusiasm for serialism—an odd blend of the oldest and newest. If some of the better-known musicians use a free atonal style, others revel in the extreme. Gottfried von Einem leads the former group with a sharp sense of the stage and an impressionism qualified by rhythmic heft. His *Dantons Tod* (Danton's Death, 1947), from Büchner's play; *Der Prozess* (The Trial, 1953), from Kafka's novel; and *Der Besuch der Alten Dame* (The Old Lady's Visit) from Dürrenmatt's play (known in America and Britain as *The Visit*) may well stand among the postwar era's enduring entries. The last of the three is especially strong; Dürrenmatt's look at a millionairess' return to her shabby home town for revenge on the man who ruined her is one of the modern theatre's great exercises in matter-of-fact horror. Offered a fortune to kill her former lover, the villagers indignantly refuse, and Dürrenmatt supplies Von Einem with a matchless curtain line for his mezzo-soprano heroine: "Ich warte" (I can wait). But ultimately the townspeople do what is "necessary," and Von Einem thought up his own matchless final curtain, a wordless, ugly choral dance of triumph around the corpse.

Carl Orff, of the grim fairy-tale operas with repetitive folkish strains and pushy percussion, spent the postwar years divesting his sound of melody and emphasizing the repetition and percussion. He especially favors Classical subjects—but is there really a call for a *Prometheus* (1968) sung in Greek by excruciated voices? Bernd Alois Zimmermann planned to ask even more of his public. In the late 1950s, working on an opera based on Jakob Michael Reinhold Lenz' play *Die Soldaten* (The Soldiers), Zimmermann conceived of a theatre revolution to out-Wagner Bayreuth. Lenz, one of the more progressive figures of the Sturm und Drang, was something of a forerunner of Büchner; *Die Soldaten* jumps from event to event in many small scenes and opposes the establishment worldview with social critique. Zimmermann in turn was something of a successor to Berg. But rather than cut from scene to scene he proposed to draw the whole thing in on itself, so that the action might unfold on several stages and screens in a complex "happening." Chronology, he felt, was unimportant—the revelation of events was everything, the interaction that feeds inevitability. Time, for Zimmermann, was not an endless line but a "ball-shape." Could he possibly reflect this in opera?

The City Theatre of Zimmermann's native Cologne didn't think so. Cologne had officially "commissioned" the work early in its composition, but Zimmermann was asking for more than any existing theatre could supply. He laid out a simplified *Soldiers*—which remains probably the most complex opera ever—and Cologne presented it in 1965, directed by Hans Neugebauer with Edith Gabry, Liane Synek, Anton de Ridder, Claudio Nicolai, and Zoltan Kélémen under Michael Gielen. Perhaps no premiere since that of *Peter Grimes* twenty years earlier had such impact. Though only German cities attempted the work, reports filtered back of an unapproachably excellent piece, and a recording of the Cologne production plus the Deutsche Oper am Rhein's tours of their production to the Holland and Edinburgh festivals in 1971 and 1972 introduced it to an international public. Zimmermann had done what few opera authors have been able to—synthesize a new art out of old ones. From a text nearly two hundred years old, Zimmermann slammed home the very modern notion that militarism is an agency of selfish destruction; out of such ancient forms as the *ciaconne, ricercar,* and *toccata,* he constructed the motion of his music (as in *Wozzeck,* each scene takes a different musical shape); he developed a four-act plot about the symbolic degeneration of a young girl from merchant's daughter to army whore through the use of multistaged action, dance, mime, films, and projections; and he reinvented the articulate recitative of the Camerata for expressionistic serial technique. Pulling all this into his *Kugelgestalt der Zeit* ("ball-shape of time"), Zimmermann mesmerizes the spectator with the ramifications of the story line without losing hold of thesis at its center.

Musical forms actually become visual forms—counterpoint, rondo, and, in the horrifying final scene, fugue unfold to the eye as well as the ear as the heroine, a beggar whom her own father doesn't recognize, crouches motionless as the stage fills with mixed-media images of marching soldiers.

If *Die Soldaten* holds classic status as *the* new work of the 1960s and '70s, Aribert Reimann's less spectacular but no less formidable *Lear* (1978) will surely win the palm in the 1980s, for this setting of the play Verdi stalked all his life and never dared trap suits the post-Schoenbergian idiom as it did not suit *melodramma*. In this most timeless of plays, the barbarism held in check only by strong social order runs amok when a king is weak, littering the stage not with Romantic corpses but busted puppets. With the Fool's grotesque comedy and the structural symmetry of Shakespeare's pairs of characters (two bad sisters, two brothers, two fooled fathers, two betrayed husbands), *King Lear* offers the satire and neo-Classical architecture that has so enriched twentieth-century opera, and Reimann brought the whole thing home with genius. His librettist Claus H. Henneberg sharply reduced the original, shuffling scenes together and shaving away poetry to include only essentials: the curtain leaps up on Lear's abdication, and matters move with great speed till the last moment, Lear's death. For the Munich premiere, Jean-Pierre Ponnelle exposed the National Theatre's huge back wall and wing works, letting a few mounds and grass tufts on the stage floor do for "setting," as if the work were too vicious to present without keeping a visual reminder that "it's only a play."

Reimann's score is extraordinarily expressionistic. A Romantic would have harmonized the story; Modern extrapolates its horror. But Modern entails a problem: with the orchestra and voices all so ferocious, how to *build* to the calamity? Reimann does it by balancing the horror with orchestral intermezzos that still the frenzy between scenes with dazed lyricism (a lone flute crying out in the gloom; wan strings wandering homelessly), thus pulling back only to forge more deeply into tragedy as the next scene begins. He toys, too, with our knowledge of Shakespeare's plot, approaching the moment in which Gloucester's eyes are put out through a pounding drum that quickens as we shrink back in our seats. He tightens tragedy's cord by playing some of the later scenes simultaneously (a touch of *Die Soldaten* there). And at last he releases us from the power of evil beckoned loose in license in a naked, unison string theme stroking Lear's agony as he dies over Cordelia's body.

If *œuvre* is a guideline, then Hans Werner Henze must be counted as the foremost figure in postwar German opera, with seven full-length operas. This is an eye-opening count for someone who was quoted as saying that "opera is finished." Presumably he means opera as "we" know it. As Henze knows it, the opera of the future will celebrate the Marxist-Leninist revolution. It doesn't seem to trouble Henze that his highly avant-garde sound has invariably been grounds for liquidation or imprisonment in the totalitarian societies he so admires, and he disclosed his personal Modern in his first full-length work, *Boulevard Solitude* (1952), which is *Manon Lescaut* updated to the late 1940s with echoes of Stravinsky, jazz, and expressionism. This is a slim work. In *Der König Hirsch* (The King-Stag, 1956) from Gozzi's extreme *commedia* about forces of urban evil and natural-world good respectively attacking and protecting a boy king, Henze and his librettist Heinz Cramer broke the length barrier in contemporary opera. One can't blame them for wanting to retain all of Gozzi's rich interworlds of fantasy and naturalism, but critics did blame them, and Henze drastically shortened the work in an efficient but charmless revision as *Il Re Cervò* (1962). The original showed how an Italian influence can feature the *canto* in the most up-to-date idiom, and even unheard it stands as a textbook case of innovation seeking meaning in tradition.

Not yet ready to tackle Marxist opera, Henze worked with W. H. Auden and Chester Kallman on a chamber piece, *Elegy for Young Lovers* (1961), devoted to exposing the rotten heart of the creator who bleeds humankind to feed his art. The central figure is a poet on holiday in the Austrian Alps, Gregor Mittenhofer, who exploits a madwoman's ravings to get "the note that I had so vainly groped for, of magic, tenderness, and warning" (exactly the note that Henze himself hits in his score). He brings the two lovers of the title together and then arranges indirectly for their beautiful death in a snowstorm so as to inspire the elegy. At the end, as Mittenhofer begins to read his vampire's trophy before a glittering audience in Vienna, Henze blots out all verbiage and calls up the principals' voices, dead and alive, sighing in the ozone: they, not Mittenhofer's inventions, have supplied the poem. The idiom is harsh and angular, but Henze's vocal writing is supple even so, wonderfully characterful. Surely much of the work's early success depended on Dietrich Fischer-Dieskau's performance as Mittenhofer, for this baritone is the Grand Kaimakan of Lieder and this word-sharp musical play needs his pointillistic delivery. Some listeners don't like him in Italian *canto—Rigoletto*, say—where he paints words in Lieder style instead of letting each line play itself as a whole. But his ecumenical dedication to music has been crucial in a time when too many singers limit themselves to the old and tried; one wonders if Aribert Reimann would have labored on *Lear* if Fischer-Dieskau had not guaranteed to assume the lead.

Henze, meanwhile, got slyly political in *Der Junge Lord* (The Young Lord, 1965), a black comedy about how a hyped public accepts cultural leadership on the energy of vogue without examining what lies under its façade. A huge cast of supporting roles—no protagonist—helps Henze and his partner Ingeborg Bachmann delve into genre pictures of the Biedermeier township: mayor, worthies and town band greet visiting English noble; social arbiter is rebuffed in her attempts to lure Sir Edgar to her salon; an undernourished circus does a turn in the town square; Sir Edgar's young nephew is presented to the local cream, who are nonplused by, but then imitative of, his weird behavior; and at last, the black taking over the comedy, the whole town struts out in the casino ballroom, the men copying the young lord's borderline antisocial quirks and the women adoring them—until it is revealed that he is the circus ape in disguise.

A year later Henze let politics out of his closet in *The Bassarids* (1966), to Auden and Kallman's superb adaptation of Euripides' *The Bacchae*. A long one-acter, *The Bassarids* is cast as a tragedy broken up partway through by an intrusive comic intermezzo, thus recalling the old practice of brightening a *seria* evening with between-the-acts farce. Euripides pictures the dissolution of Apollonian order by Dionysiac ecstasy; Henze suggests the Revolution in a hippy Dionysus and his flower children—terrorist followers. Interestingly, the intermezzo, "The Judgement of Calliope" bears no connection to the main plot but is sung by four of its principals in rococo dress, recalling the last securely monarchical era before the revolutions began. If only Henze had waited a few years he might have set *The Bassarids* at Altamont during the infamous Rolling Stones concert and really shown his public what's in store for them; but if one can tune out the activism and concentrate on the authors' artistry, *The Bassarids* proves to be one of the era's most absorbing events. After all, *The Bacchae* is not about political overthrow, but about man's irrepressible need for the Dionysiac and the danger of imposing strict order upon the chaotic human spirit. Henze has caught this in his music, which glitters with evil beauty in Dionysius' monologue, "I found a child asleep," rages with impotent militarism in King Pentheus' music, and chuckles in the intermezzo's risqué set pieces. He shaped the work in a symphony's four movements (the intermezzo functions as a scherzo), gliding through them in Wagner's through-composition, a Romantic revision of Henze's neo-Classicism that was much commented on at the time. But no Romantic would have dislocated his lyric theatre with comedy, and Henze is not a neo-Romantic. Not that it matters. For as Peter Heyworth pointed out in *The Observer* when *The Bassarids* was premiered at the Salzburg Festival, "both [Schoenbergian twelve-tone technique and Wagnerian music drama] are rooted in the art of variation." Because Modern frequently involves use of Romantic and Classical technique—the former's musical power but the latter's disengaged commentary—these labels lose their usefulness. So do such terms as *opéra comique, Singspiel,* and grand opera: the infusion of sophisticated theatricality into musical procedures has even made the word "opera" useless. What is an opera, nowadays? Henze doesn't use the word any more. He called his latest extravaganza, *We Come to the River* (1976), an "action for music." With a libretto by Edward Bond, this was Henze's most straightforward political piece (showing lessons learned from *Die Soldaten*'s multiscene stage). Covent Garden threw its all into the premiere, staged by the composer in the disjunct intensity that informs Modern as style.

The "action for music" seems a specialty of leftist opera, and often depends more on environmental spectacle than on composition. The prim, Weill-flavored East German Paul Dessau may be the last composer who uses opera for propaganda yet calls it opera, as in *Der Verurteilung des Lukullus* (The Condemnation of Lucullus, 1951) and *Herr Puntila und Sein Knecht Matti* (Lord Puntilla and His Servant Matti, 1966), both to Brecht's texts and both respecting the value of a good "theatre" libretto and colorful musical analysis. When one has nothing to say, however, and cannot even say it to interesting music, bring on the diversions and gimmicks—as in *Houdini* (1977), a "circus opera" by the Dutch Peter Schat to Adrian Mitchell's English libretto. Schat scores for Modern, but eclectically; Mitchell, too, freewheels, calling for a big cast of dancers, clowns, acrobats, and illusionists to back up the principals and many small parts. Somehow he managed to read Houdini's biography as a great Marxist escape from "The Police Force of the World." *Houdini* is a piece of utter garbage—serial clichés, phony Brechtian *Verfremsdung,* aimlessly shrill vocalism—desperately in need of the superproduction it got from director Donya Fleur and her agile circus at its Amsterdam premiere.

In England, the controversial debut of Michael Tippett's *The Midsummer Marriage* in 1955 gave the first evidence that someone besides Britten was creating—not deriving—English opera. Always his own librettist, Tippett tackled myth and transformation in *The Midsummer Marriage,* and though his music as such is lyrical, dramatic, and distinguished by endless inventiveness, his tale really shocked the public.

Leftist opera: Dessau's *The Condemnation of Lukullus*. A matter-of-fact Brechtian central committee (on the parapet) hears the deceased Roman general tell of his deeds to decide on his after-life. In the end, they purge him, as a warmaker and exploiter, "into nothing." Note the jarring dress styles and the industrial-era backdrop. *(E. A. Teatro alla Scala)*

"Was it a vision? Was it a dream?" In a contemporary woodland setting, mixing people of our everyday with timeless mystical avatars,
Tippett proposed a nervous comedy not unlike *The Magic Flute* in
its characters and atmosphere. Through an encounter with The An-
cients, a modern couple—she cold and he carnally brazen—learn to
share their natures, meanwhile shaking off the harassment of her busi-
ness-magnate father. But all this develops through a magical union with
unseen forces that dwell in the clefts of time and space around us, and
it is precisely the casualness with which Tippett brings in his magic
that makes it so hard for some people to take. Opera too seldom mixes
the fantastical and the ordinary as radically as here. During the last of
three Ritual Dances depicting hunter and quarry, one character is so
scared by the violence that she screams, bursting the vision like a bub-
ble. And then, to regain her composure, she attends to her makeup:
"They say a woman's glory is her hair."

Those who hoped that Tippett's Straussian richness would com-
plement the sparer Britten style regretted his graduation into atonalism
in *King Priam* (1962), but as theatre this awesome tragedy is more
satisfying than anything else Tippett has done. This may be because
it is his only libretto in which he asks us to accept people as they are—
kings, heroes, and all—and to empathize with the forgivable mistakes
that destroy them, rather than to root for the voguish transfiguration
of sexual and racial identity that his other works turn on. Indeed,
King Priam stands out from all other English operas for the compelling
individuality with which it invests its familiar story: Hecuba, Hector,
Andromache, Paris, Helen, and Achilles all in place, irreversibly doing
what they did; the drums and trumpets, lamentations, and oaths of
battle (that of Achilles, erupting in fury when Patroclus is killed, comprises one of the Biggest Moments in modern opera) hemming all in
till Troy falls, a Greek runs Priam through, the destiny—a series of
mistakes—is accomplished. The action of character is Tippett's plan,
rather than either action or character, and he laid out both *The Knot
Garden* (1970) and *The Ice Break* (1977) to explore interpersonality in
turmoil and at peace. But these two lack *The Midsummer Marriage*'s
musical luxury and *King Priam*'s thrilling tragic clarity.

By the 1960s, British opera, from Vancouver east to Sydney, had
built up an empire of startling vitality, based on strong production
values, ambitious programming, and a congregation of world-class
singers unequaled for musicianship, commitment, and theatrical aplomb.
Consider the riches in sopranos and mezzos alone: Joan Sutherland,
Gwyneth Jones, Marie Collier, Amy Shuard, Heather Harper, Josephine Barstow, Joan Carlyle, Jenniffer Vyvyan, Elizabeth Harwood,

Josephine Veasey, Yvonne Minton, and Janet Baker. This is an audacious gang, prepared to tackle anything from the most voice-exposing traditional fare to the most voice-challenging contemporary sound, and English-language opera offers them the lot. Upholding tradition is, among others, Malcolm Williamson, whose *Our Man in Havana* (1963), from Graham Greene's dotty spy novel, is almost a musical comedy in its clearly outlined Big Tunes and arias as simple as songs. Williamson remixed his style for *The Violins of Saint-Jacques* (1966), from Patrick Leigh Fermor's tropical novel, its Creole sensibility chalked in with somewhat advanced harmony. Williamson is hummable. And in *this* corner, weighing in for Modern, is Humphrey Searle, whose *Hamlet* (1968), text reduced from Shakespeare in the post-*Pelléas* manner, failed to bring the material to life in a post-Schoenbergian idiom. Hamburg, a world capital of Modern opera in these years, gave the premiere, and a year later Covent Garden chimed in with a somewhat underpowered production whose excellent Hamlet, the Canadian Victor Braun, inadvertently exposed Searle's heavy-handedness with a too strong, too serious Prince: the real Hamlet is ambivalent and confused. Too, Braun exposed the perils of Modern vocal writing in his struggle to survive the workout. As Karl Heinz Wocker reported it, Braun "certainly got through the premiere, but had to cancel the next performance. A later attempt fell through after the first act. The scheduled cover was likewise ill, and the Hamlet of previous productions [Hamburg and Toronto] not available. The rest was silence."

   Hamlet is Modern in sound but not in production technique, whereas Zimmermann's multiform *Die Soldaten*, Schat's Houdini circus, and (Harold Prince's staging of) *Evita* set the style for mixed-media opera, the "action for music." John Tavener's longish one-act *Thérèse* (1979), about a saint who lived in the last years of the nineteenth century, exemplified the new music theatre as a combination dream piece, ballet, pantomime, and Christian incantation. Librettist Gerard McLarnon focuses not on Thérèse's uneventful life but on the condition of ecstasy, confronting her with Rimbaud, whom she never met but who tours her through a hell of earthly savagery, challenging her faith. A lyric-tenor Christ calls to her from the very dome of the theatre; the devil's work rumbles from its cellar; the whole auditorium becomes a cathedral. The *New Yorker* critic Andrew Porter analyzed Tavener's sweeping technical congeries: "sweet strands of mellifluous high melisma; wide-flung, complicated chords long sustained or reiterated as ostinatos; pretty children's songs decked with a tinkle of little bells; Stravinskyan, even Orffian, motifs rapped out in the violent passages; chant; rhythmic choral speech; drums crashing and trumpets pealing from the distance." The composer himself has called *Thérèse* "a tightrope opera," one that "provokes in every way." God knows, the self-enclosed mantras of His saints and demons are worthy operatic material; and Tavener and McLarnon know better than *Evita*'s Webber and Rice that the conceptual interior tells far more than the documentary exterior.

The English are rich in comedy, a handy thing to be these days. In light farce, Nicholas Maw composed *One-Man Show* (1964), to Arthur Jacobs' spoof of the art business (the man *is* the show: his back bears a surrealist tattoo), following this up with *The Rising of the Moon* (1970), atonalism feathered with loving parodies and a sometimes Mozartean nostalgia; Beverley Cross' text views late-nineteenth-century Ireland with a recondite sadness under the fun. In the crazy-vicious *commedia* genre comes Harrison Birtwhistle's *Punch and Judy* (1968), like Malipiero's puppet shows but scored for ear-blasting Modern. A more humanistic farce lights Richard Rodney Bennett's *A Penny for a Song* (1967), beautifully drawn out of John Whiting's play about assorted confusions on the British home front during the Napoleonic Wars. *Canto* is conspicuous. English comedy has always had bite, but Maw and Bennett want to extract the warmth of character from the ruckus of action.

Perhaps the most engaging of all is Gordon Crosse's *The Story of Vasco* (1974), a dark yet almost childlike comedy based on Georges Schehadé's play. Crosse had set Yeats' one-acter *Purgatory* (1966) to underline its bizarrely redemptive violence, but Schehadé's tale of an unassuming barber who accidentally becomes a hero in wartime calls for Modern's contiguous planes of fun and romance, each undercutting but finally developing the other. The cast listing of "Chorus of crows, soldiers, widows" styles *Vasco*'s brutality for us, sets it at a distance so we can follow the adventure as if it were all comedy. It certainly acts like one. On the theory that apparent heroes draw bullets while a timid barber may slip through enemy lines unnoticed, Vasco is sent on a dangerous mission. Further amusement as well as a love plot is provided by Marguerite, an imaginative girl who has fallen for Vasco without having met him. When they do cross paths, she naturally doesn't see her hero in this little barber, though Crosse urges her on with a singing theme, a "love" theme, in a more conventional work. Modern is nothing if not ironic, and not till Vasco has gone off on his mission—"So he goes on, where angels turn back," notes Major Braun, one of the opera's several nutty characters; "Is he really an idiot? Or really a hero?"—does Marguerite catch on. Vasco has dropped his scissors; picking them up, she realizes who he must be. But before she can run after him, everyone freezes and Braun comes downstage to address the public: "The position is as follows . . . BLACK!" And the lights close out the act.

This is Modern to the nth: the hero/antihero ambivalence, the sudden jolting of audience involvement by a character's abandoning his character, and the sophisticated post-Schoenbergian idiom that comprehends disparate styles from the traditional and the advanced. As Schehadé (in the poet Ted Hughes' translation) distances one with his seriocomic technique, so does Crosse carry this over into the music. He delights in making the farce hum as well as letting the sympathy sing, but like his text he takes the comedy right through the gathering horror, when Vasco is caught, threatened, achieves his mission, and is shot: he really was a hero, after all. But having to ask if he's an idiot or a hero is what makes Modern. In the Romantic 1800s, no one asked such questions in opera—everyone knew the idiot from the hero at sight and sound. Modern is not always sure.

As if all this variety were not enough, England has also led the world in the potentially vital but as yet unfulfilled (even undefined) territory of rock opera. So far, rock opera has proved a fraud, being more exactly rock song cycle, not always rock in idiom, and less a theatre form than a two-record album. (A few American rock operas conceived directly for the stage disappeared virtually on their opening nights.) Three rock operas have stood out; they are all English and they all tell of the rise and fall of messianic creatures. *Tommy* (1969), written mainly by Peter Townshend and performed by his group The Who, set the tone for the genre—mostly small numbers beefed up by instrumental improvisation and a storyline that plays as an incoherent synopsis of what would happen in a *Tommy* show: a report on theatre rather than theatre itself. That *Tommy* was staged (and filmed) is irrelevant. Anything can be staged, not necessarily well, and *Tommy*'s tale of a deaf, dumb, and blind kid who locates a communication and reception on the spiritual level as a healer does not, as written, stage well. As a Who concert, it depended more on the startling rockers' antics than on concept or plot motion. Still, it felt right, if only as a try: The Who is a fine combo (some say the best), and rock is after all a somewhat messianic form, loaded with pop mythology and raising up pop gods as surely as any cult can.

Two years later, Andrew Lloyd Webber and Tim Rice came up with *Jesus Christ Superstar*, no more a theatre piece than *Tommy* but disguised as one by Tom O'Horgan's inventive stage spectacle and a youth-oriented, now-ancient, now-modern movie filmed in the Holy Land. Webber and Rice occupied true theatre space in *Evita*, though this, too, appeared as an album (in 1976) before making it to the stage in Harold Prince's highly imaginative production. Both works debunk their messiahs through the use of cynical interlocutor figures, Judas in *Jesus Christ Superstar* and Che Guevara in *Evita;* and both works depend heavily on musical parody, reasonably enough since the Beatles had introduced parody into rock back in the 1960s. *Superstar*'s jiveass burlesque flattered fashion, but the more resourceful (and frankly nonrock) *Evita* drew critical fire for the power with which the authors endowed their repulsive heroine. She is not meant to be sympathetic, but an aria as potent as "Don't Cry for Me, Argentina" cannot help but win one's interest in the character who sings it. Librettist Rice glosses over the ugliness of the real-life Eva Perón—vanity, in his reading, is her worst crime. As far as that goes, confronting her with Guevara, who was as much of a gangster as she was, hardly puts her (or him) into historical perspective.

Rock, with its eclecticism, electronic technology, and semiimprovised performances,* takes us to the far side of format. But Igor Stravinsky takes us even further. Everything he has done in opera invents a genre—*The Nightingale* is too diaphanous to be called a *Märchenoper, Mavra* awfully Russian for an *intermedio, Oedipus Rex* so still it's barely an opera at all. His only full-length music drama, *The Rake's Progress* (1951), was another first: a tense comedy after Hogarth's famous picture series in the most schizophrenic neo-Classicism. Every scene is old syle; every note is new Stravinsky. It's a brazen, delightful, moving work, an imaginary garden with real people in it, a cartoon that breathes.

Stravinsky never quite fits in anywhere. *The Rake's Progress* might as easily have opened as closed this chapter; it might have opened or closed the whole book, or been shredded into intermezzolike bits between chapters. It is all opera, and unlike all, with its cruel naturalism and absurd whimsy, its curvy vocalism and angular, biting rhythms, its poetry and satire, its ambition and nostalgia, its everything at once,

---

* Postwar music has featured, on its outskirts, what is called aleatory music, meaning that the performer exercises certain options (such as which order to play a number of thematic fragments in). The aleatory in what is considered "legit" music is a mere stunt, a revolutionary's drivel; in rock, it is the very basis of the sound, and it is based on the old traditions of ragtime and "stride" piano, jazzman's riffs, country string band "fill," and black blues singers' imaginative coloratura, from which early rock and roll partly derived. *Tommy* retains some aleatory connections for all its polish; *Superstar* and *Evita*, however, are fully scored, their orchestration set down so that any group of musicians may play it. They are in that sense indefinitely "available" works, whereas *Tommy* is (was, after drummer Keith Moon's death) The Who, and exists only as long as their original recording does.

from prefatory fanfare to moral epilogue ("Good people, just a moment . . ."). *The Rake* is one of the few operas of recent vintage to attract voices associated with the standard repertory—Elisabeth Schwarzkopf (with Jennie Tourel, Robert Rounseville, and Otakar Kraus) sang the premiere in Venice with the composer conducting; Hilde Gueden, Erna Berger, Elsie Morison, Nan Merriman, Cloe Elmo, Rudolf Schock, and Alfred Jerger have all tried it; and for all its technique, which shivers dryly throughout the score like wire on a refinished bow, it pleases many of the more timid operagoing ears. But it also has something extramusically special, one of the best librettos ever. We have noticed that a very high percentage of the better twentieth-century operas are settings of plays—*Wozzeck*, *Lulu*, *Lear*, *Die Soldaten*, *Salome*, *Der Besuch der Alten Dame*, *Pelléas et Mélisande*, *Dialogues des Carmelites*, *Francesca da Rimini*, *L'Amore dei Tre Re*, *Il Campiello*, *The Makropulos Business*, for example. But there are many "originals" as well. W. H. Auden and Chester Kallman's black Restoration comedy for *The Rake* joins *Moses und Aron*, *Der Rosenkavalier*, *Die Frau Ohne Schatten*, *Aufstieg und Fall der Stadt Mahagonny*, *Mathis der Maler*, and *Don Rodrigo* in conception as music theatre first and only. Auden and Kallman dazzle as librettists seldom dare to. See how they scan—as when a Crowd of Respectable Citizens surveys the debris in Tom Rakewell's abandoned town house:

GROUP I: What curious phenomena are up today for sale.
GROUP II: What manner of remarkables.
GROUP III: What squalor!
GROUP I: What detail!

Rakewell's village darling appears, asking for news of him:

TUTTI: We're certain he's in debt;
         They're after him, they're after him, and they will
         catch him yet.

In the end, Anne finds Tom in Bedlam, where he thinks himself Adonis, and she, Venus, sings him a lullaby as he dies:

> Gently, little boat
> Across the ocean float,
> The crystal waves dividing:
>   The sun in the west
>   Is going to rest;
>   Glide, glide, glide
> Toward the islands of the Blest.

The Rake's Progress has found itself an edgy place in the abiding repertory, but it is one of the few new operas to find a place at all. Once the public so hungered for new work that any number of premieres could only whet, never satisfy, its appetite. Now that Modern has driven a wedge between composers' progressivism and audiences' conservatism, the public has found a new source of novelty in revivals of neglected repertory. Only one composer of the postwar era managed to enrich the stock of works with one piece after another, appeasing the suspicious ear while satisfying his personal needs in art. He too deserves his own chapter.

CHAPTER TWENTY-ONE

The Conservative
Modern: Britten

*In writing opera I have always
found it very dangerous to start
writing the music until the
words are more or less fixed.*
—BENJAMIN BRITTEN

THOUGH IT MARKED THE OFFICIAL BEGINNING OF THE STAND-OUT OPERATIC
output of the postwar years, *Peter Grimes* (1945) felt for some Britishers like a culmination. The war had just ended, the Sadler's Wells
Company had set up shop again in its out-of-the-way London house,
and here was this fusion of drama and music using vocal characterization, heavy choral involvement, orchestral interludes, rural naturalism,
and a tale of one of society's outsiders—all standard components of
opera—and sounding like nothing ever encountered before. It was a
culmination in the sense that everything that preceded it suddenly
seemed to have been preparing the British ear for the unexpected.

If Wagner is instantly recognizable for his world-shaking brasses,
Verdi for his rum-ti-tum accompanimental figures, Berlioz for his
cackling woodwinds, Mozart for his melodies floated out of basic
harmony, and Meyerbeer not instantly recognizable at all, Britten's
signature is the odd intervals in his vocal line—no one else "speaks"
quite like him. This had been a problem in twentieth-century English
opera: how to pull individuality out of characters when the national
vocal tradition leans to pious and patriotic chorale and folk song, the
most universal idioms going? Britten resolved the problem effortlessly.
His characters open their mouths and one is "placed"—at the start of
Peter Grimes, for example, at the coroner's inquest into the death of
Grimes' apprentice, when, echoing the opera's opening woodwind

359

figure, the town mayor Swallow sings, "Tell the court the story in your own words": hearty, self-satisfied, a rustic pushing for a little dignity. At that moment, one enters Britten's world whole.

It's an odd world, one that takes in Christian parable and rapt Shakespearean fantasy, ghosts, schoolteachers, sailors, lovers, tourists, rulers, the ideal and the humdrum, yet always seems rooted in the bluff terrain of East Anglia, where Britten spent the second half of his life. Certainly *Peter Grimes* belongs to such a place, with its dour fisherfolk and not so much misunderstood as altogether discounted protagonist. From George Crabbe's poem *The Borough*, Montagu Slater's text refined the original Grimes from a sadist into a proud loser who will not court the borough folk but cannot seem to make it alone. Britten saturates his score with ocean-and-shore music and folkish character, yet he qualifies this naturalism, suggests rather than photographs place, paints individuals, not classes. His chorus of townspeople is textured by featured and small roles—the tavernkeeper and her two "nieces," a religious crazy, the local quack, the rector—and though as a mass they engender much of the opera's action and provide its most stirring moment screaming "Peter Grimes!" at the close of the penultimate scene, shy, angrily despairing Grimes dominates the work without half trying, so unusual is he as a person and so unusually crafted as a character.

Britten's mastery of the art shows in every scene: the stunning impressionism of the interludes, with their bird cries and church bells mingled with tidefall and deep-six imagery, the shocking rightness of the set pieces in the overall structure, the psychological correlation of themes, singing the work's heart out in expert code. What is significant above all is the ease with which Britten builds his opera—and the fourteen to follow—out of melodic cells used as if in a theme-and-variations set. From the first moments, personal or pictorial propositions set forth in music develop and collide, defining the action psychologically. This is Wagnerian practice. But Britten spins a more congenial vocal line than Wagner did, and he never gives much to the orchestra when the characters can say more. However, he does engage in constant variation movements—a passacaglia at the very center of *Peter Grimes*, connecting the two scenes of Act II; a *Leitmotiv* so central to the plot of *Albert Herring* that it shows up at moments throughout the evening as a kind of motto theme for "Albert as May King," turning all the colors that Albert turns as he abandons milksop purity for outspoken virility; and, in *The Turn of the Screw*, a construction that lays the whole opera out as an introduction, a twelve-note theme (not unlike Schoenberg's tone row, but nonexpressionist), and fifteen variations, one for each scene.

Resisting outright Modern—or, rather, deriving his own version of it—Britten retreated from *Grimes'* grand scale for chamber opera in *The Rape of Lucretia* (1946), suitably unveiled at what may be Europe's most pleasurable summer festival, Glyndebourne. Other festival jaunts are run on the order of Studio 54: for the rich and fancy. Bayreuth, Munich, Aix-en Provence, and the like are big, expensive, celebrity-crazed, and prohibitively hot-ticket; Verona, Rome's Caracalla, and other open-air theatres are more accessible but artistically not worth the trip. Glyndebourne is the caviar company, small, careful, and audacious: just the place to launch the "other" Britten of the small orchestra (*Lucretia* calls for five strings, five winds, harp, and percussion), small cast (no chorus), and word-clear presentation. One could see the gentlemen of the Camerata enjoying this robust reading of a morbid subject—Classical, going back to Ovid and Livy—on the violation of a woman so proud of her chastity that she kills herself rather than recover. They would have relished Britten's prologue, rather like their own, sung by a Male and Female Chorus duo, and if Britten's little instrumental combo comments more effusively than a Florentine band ever did and his vocal ensemble was just the sort of thing the Camerata wanted to overcome, the communication still rests on the singers' ability to deliver the poetry.

Albert Herring (1947), another chamber-sized event, counters Modern's grotesque comedy with an elatedly confidential burlesque of insular village ways. It makes a pair with *Lucretia* as its comic counterpart: both tell of chastity debauched. Eric Crozier's upbeat adaptation of a bitter De Maupassant tale culls the types of the English county. There are the rich autocrat Lady Billows, the fluttering schoolteacher Miss Wordsworth, the vicar, the mayor, two slightly **worldy cutups** named Sid and Nancy, three blatant children, and a spate of patois. At the center of it stands bewildered Albert, the May King (Lady Billows finds the village girls too immoral to crown) who gets drunk on spiked lemonade (a deft *Tristan* quotation as he drinks: the "potion" theme) and goes off on a binge. Everyone assumes that he has come by some ghastly accident, and when his smashed May wreath is brought in on a tray—"found on the road to Campsey Ash . . . crushed by a cart!"—all nine principals on stage burst into the famous Threnody, "In the midst of life is death," one of Britten's most brilliant structural studies and a potentially most moving piece save that the spoof has been so carefree that we *know* that Albert is going to wander in (hungover, no doubt) as it ends. Some listeners have balked at this manipulation of emotion, but such congruence of horror and fun enlivens Modern art. For those who can take the joke, it stands as one of the Big Moments in contemporary *buffa*.

Another significant item in the Modern catalogue is the parody or revival of old forms or works; Britten tried his hand in a new edition of *The Beggar's Opera* (1948), quite faithful to Pepusch's original plan in melody (a few numbers omitted, a few others combined) and nimble Britten in a new orchestration. This work still awaits acclamation (it is one of Britten's few stage works not to be recorded), but at least *Billy Budd* (1951) has come into its own of late, partly because of a 1960 revision that smoothed out its contours, centering it in two instead of four acts. This is Britten's most symphonic opera, yet the vocal line still retains dramatic leadership while the instruments pose and answer subtextual questions. Taking Crozier and E. M. Forster's adaptation of Herman Melville's sea parable as a metaphysical battle of good and evil, Britten symbolizes the duel in two conflicting chords, a high G Major against a low G Minor. Billy is the good, a sailor of artless, easy nature; Claggart, the Master-at-Arms, is the evil. But one might also see Billy as an innocent pawn trapped between evil Claggart and "good" Captain Vere, the man who ultimately, with guilty rationality, condemns Billy to death. With the entire action set on board H.M.S. *Indomitable* Britten had to distinguish his all-male cast to relieve a possible sameness of vocal texture, and achieved a host of small plums backing three leads of absorbing power. Vere is a "Pears role," long associated with the quintessential Britten stylist, tenor Peter Pears; Claggart, a bass, is a resourcefully abstracted villain with enough depth to raise twenty *verismo* marplots; and Billy, a lyric baritone, calls for a rare charm of athletic, ingenuous youth. The trickiest of the three to cast well, Billy came to life memorably in the work of two Americans, Theodor Uppman, who sang the Covent Garden premiere and an early broadcast on American television, and, more recently, Richard Stilwell.

By this time, Britten's lightning-quick interaction of vocal and instrumental information so pointed his operas that one hearing might not be enough to grasp the whole. The first time, one would be entertained and engaged; only a second or third time might one comprehend. This is sadly contrary to many operagoers' taste: they want their art served neat and facile. Even Wagner, the most complex of creators, held that everything must be clear the first time, instinctually (through music's evocations) if not intellectually. But who "gets" the *Ring* or *Tristan*, on any level, the first time?

Nonetheless, audiences seemed to demand an easier Britten than they got in *Gloriana* (1953), a "coronation" commission to celebrate the ascendancy of Elizabeth II by reviewing the reign of Elizabeth I. William Plomer's libretto portrayed both the woman and the monarch, interweaving her quasiromance with Essex with historical events; Britten filled out the pageant with a pastiche of lute songs spry and passionate, fanfares, dances, choruses and such, and the two authors pooled their specialties in a controversial epic finale designed to epitomize the Queen's last years in tiny scenes of mingled song and speech closing in a last reprise of the opera's choral motto, "Green leaves are we, Red rose our golden queen." Undeservedly neglected for its subtle character stitching on a broad tapestry-like background, *Gloriana* may one day take its place among Britten's acknowledged masterpieces. It is not so dramatically charged as *Peter Grimes*, nor so portable as *The Turn of the Screw* (1954), another chamber opera and, in Myfanwy Piper's adaptation of Henry James, a clear-cut ghost tale rather than James' ambiguous ghost-or-paranoia? proposition. *Grimes* is a classic and *The Turn of the Screw* the least ethnically xenophobic of all Britten's operas. Both travel while *Gloriana* is little celebrated even at home. Perhaps the piece has never recovered from the *querelle* it inspired on its coronation premiere, when progressives hailed Covent Garden's mounting a new work, on a suitable Festival subject, by one of England's greatest—and *living*—composers, and when reactionaries maintained that a repertory potboiler with a fancy cast would have filled the occasion better. But a superb revival at Sadler's Wells in 1966, with the great Sylvia Fisher, past her prime but in her element as Elizabeth, put the work over for all those with open minds and ears.

After *Gloriana* came a new little era in Britten's career, that of one-act "church operas." The first of them, *Noye's Fludde* (1958), taken from the Chester Miracle Play in sixteenth-century English, was intended for performance in church mainly by children (except for the lead parts and a few key instrumentalists). A less deft hand might have made too adorable a setting; Britten's is perky, not cutesy. The parade of animals solemnly intoning "Kyrie, Kyrie, Kyrie eleison" to a bumpy percussion figure as they pass up the aisle to the ark ranks as one of the most piquant Little Moments in opera. Despite its huge cast, *Noye's Fludde* is a compact piece, and seems to have dared the composer to exploit the resources of chamber organization. At the same time, music and theatre experiences in the East enriched his aesthetics, and the combined result was the Three Parables for Church Performance, *Curlew River* (1964), *The Burning, Fiery Furnace* (1967), and *The Prodigal Son* (1968). Deceptively simple in appearance on stage, this trio furthers Britten's urge to economy, tightness, and exemplifies postwar opera's experimentally derivative threatricalism. But in the interim Britten had produced his first full-length opera since *The Turn of the Screw*, *A Midsummer Night's Dream* (1960).

This work is anything but experimental; perhaps its conservatism is what brought it home as one of the few superb Shakespearean operas. Chamber-scaled in feeling, it projects its compressed text cleanly, yet makes the most of Shakespeare's implicit music. There is no bottom to the passion, the magic, the comedy; what play offers more opportunity to the tone painter? Britten exploits it, and his vocal casting is an opera in itself. Tytania and Oberon sing high Baroque lines, the latter designed for a countertenor,* whose references to the arcane herb that smooths or roughens the course of true love are scored for a sumptuous quivering unlike anything else in music, a rotten beauty that even Strauss' *Salome* neglected to disclose. Puck, planned for an acrobat, speaks his lines to drum and trumpet. The solo fairies call for boy sopranos. The four Athenian lovers—mezzo and tenor, soprano and baritone—deal in angular but lyrical lines as interwoven as the four themselves. The crude craftsmen who perform Pyramus and Thisbe are clumsies, Bottom winningly pushy, with a real heehaw for his famous "translation" into an ass. For an opera within an opera, Britten turns their play into a sendup of operatic convention, from the mad-scene flute cadenza to *Sprechgesang*. Even the forest sings, in a string scoring that heaves and pulses with living sorcery.

A Midsummer Night's Dream may be Britten's best opera—it is certainly his most imaginative. It might have been his most popular, for he has found the music for the queer antique of Shakespeare's beauty, humor, and grotesquerie right to the note. But how are non-English speakers to appreciate the English? German performances utilize Schlegel's classic Shakespeare translation; still, can Schlegel catch "The honeybags steal from the humblebees, And for night tapers crop their waxen thighs, And light them at the fiery glow worm's eyes" just so? In Italian at La Scala in 1961, a devoted staging with an earnest Elizabethan look under conductor Nino Sanzogno labored to achieve both Britten and Shakespeare, but Margherita Roberti's Tytania, Irene Companeez' Oberon, Gabriella Tucci, Biancamaria Casoni, Alvino Misciano, and Antonio Boyer's lover quartet, and Vladimiro Ganzarolli's Bottom sounded just right for something else entirely. Here is where the domesticated technology of the postwar age comes in handy, for the long-playing record has preserved Britten's own performance with singers of the Britten idiom. This is a major docu-

---

* Britten wrote the part for Alfred Deller, who created and recorded it; elsewhere and since, mezzos and tenors have filled in.

ment, a manual of style for future generations.

Modern is, like Baroque, Romantic, and neo-Classic before it, in evolution. By this point in Britten's career, fifteen years after *Peter Grimes'* premiere, the opera scene had shifted remarkably in terms of repertory, vocal customs, production styles, and the popular response to new work. Was Britten Modern? He was no throwback, certainly. His overall rhythmic-harmonic approach was relatively conservative, flirting with atonalism but stopping way short of expressionism. In format, he never got into Modern's "action for music," though the Three Church Parables offer an unusual experience and *Owen Wingrave* was conceived for television. Nor did Britten accede to the fashionable in subject matter; indeed, all his adaptational sources are either ancient or several generations old. One quality does mark him as a Modern: his word-oriented musicality, his insistence on making opera a theatre experience at the cost of the Big Tune. The Tunes slip in all the same, for Britten was the supreme melodist of his day. But they slip in through the *theatre* of it, inextricably dependent upon the text, the dramatic motion, the effect in performance. In his work, the symbiotic tango of the musical (in opera) and the theatrical (in musical comedy) has at last made it to the clinch.

A television opera was inevitable. As the last opera composer to hold a broad audience, Britten took an earned advantage of the home screen in launching *Owen Wingrave* (1971) before a first-night public numbering in the millions. Since then the piece has been staged in theatres, but that first taping really did use video's capacities for close-ups, split-screen shots, and montage. Britten and his librettist Myfanwy Piper turned for a second time to Henry James, drawing on a tale of the scion of a military family who denounces war as a profession, and to prove his courage faces down the family ghosts—and dies. Almost all the action takes place in the Wingrave seat, Paramore, and because the house and its brutal past provide the story's atmosphere, it filled the screen, outside and in. The splendid opening sequence could hardly be duplicated onstage: the camera prowled through Paramore's portrait gallery to pick out glorious Wingrave warriors dead and gone; at each one Britten sounded a variation on a theme not yet heard, each variation scored for a different instrument. We seemed to be moving forward in time from picture to picture; the tenth showed Owen's father, and the eleventh, suddenly, was no portrait at all but Owen himself. *Now* we heard the theme, quietly valiant on solo horn. And the action proper had begun.

Death in Venice (1973) closed the Britten account with another large opera whose orchestra does not envelop the senses so much as prompt them. Working with Piper again, and carefully avoiding the improvident homosexualizing of the beautiful but faithless Visconti film, Britten steered close to Thomas Mann's novella, effectively re-creating its battle of Apollonian and Dionysian forces for the soul of novelist Gustav Aschenbach. A large cast of singers and dancers fills an almost cinematically fluid action, two acts splitting seventeen short scenes. The Modern style uses the stage not as a fixed arena but as a "space" to be remodeled each time out, and the company that scores with *Peter Grimes* or *Albert Herring* must rethink its technique to bring off *Death in Venice*. (This amorphously liquid piece does not adapt well to a large theatre, as its Covent Garden and Met perform-ances proved. But better to see it outsize than not at all.) Musically, too, *Death in Venice* is advanced Britten, defter than ever in his use of theme cells in variation, in the voices bearing the dramatic freight, in atmospheric naturalizing. Aschenbach is bashful, a "Pears tenor" given to piano-accompanied monologues on notes pitched but not metered; his seven nemeses, sung by one baritone, run a gamut of personae, as lugubrious gondolier, oily barber, flaming pop-tune fop; a vibraphone shimmers for Aschenbach's Ganymede (a dancer); and Venice itself billows with rankness, disguised at first in a lapping barcarolle but later heard as if decomposing in musty stillness. Visconti used the slow movement of Mahler's Fifth Symphony to embellish Aschenbach's decline; Britten is austere, more a reporter than a beautician, and much that he must deal with here falls into Modern's choice land of the absurd. Visconti outdid Britten in the strolling players' performance (Britten's scene ten), one of the most intriguingly repellent moments in Italian cinema. But then Britten's absurd was never Modern's: he sees the misshapen as human, not humanoid, and his many eccentrics charm or at least enlighten rather than disgust. Remember the opening theme in *Peter Grimes* or Bottom in his ass' head—that is the utmost of Brit-ten's satire, nowhere nearly like the true Modern bizarre.

Then was Britten Modern? In some ways he was—so are we all in some ways Modern. Unlike the reactionaries and confirmed serialists of the time, he didn't classify. Neither did Mozart, Gluck, Berlioz, or Schoenberg suit the terms of their eras. They set unique terms. Britten set his as a rigorously eliciting dramatist who subordinated symphony to language. If Modern is seriocomedy in the post-Schoenbergian twelve-tone idiom of Romantic emotionalism and neo-Classical struc-turing, Britten was not Modern. But Modern's great facet, from De-bussy on, is its cultivation of text, and in the end Britten did lead a subgroup of Modern: his own.

CHAPTER TWENTY-TWO

Opera in America

My hope in putting Gertrude Stein to music had been to break, crack open, and solve for all time anything still waiting to be solved, which was almost everything, about English musical declamation.

—VIRGIL THOMSON

I made up my mind that [the development of an American opera] could only take place on Broadway, because Broadway represents the living theatre in this country, and an American opera, as I imagined it, should be a part of the living theatre.

—KURT WEILL

ECLECTICALLY DERIVATIVE, EARLY AMERICAN OPERA GOT NOWHERE FAST. In the eighteenth century English ballad opera held sway, in the nineteenth century foreign and native companies dispensed the established European masters, and the early twentieth century saw a whole generation of Wagnerian, Straussian, and other imitators. But never did any American come up with a native classic to compare with *The Beggar's Opera* or *The Bartered Bride:* all the operagoing energy was invested in European style.

Yet there are textbook references aplenty for those who wish to trace the history of American music theatre. Old American ballad opera certainly existed, though it lacked the rash gusto of the British model even when dealing with Indian life, as many did—John Bray's *The Indian Princess; or, La Belle Sauvage* (1808) is best thought of as James Nelson Barker's play (on the Pocahontas-Captain John Smith story) with Bray's music added. There are solos and ensembles as well as an overture and incidental underscoring, but the vocal numbers tend to go to subsidiary characters, as if the score didn't have much to do with the play. As for full-out opera, citation for first American piece performed in public usually goes to William Henry Fry's *Leonora* (1845), drawn from Bulwer-Lytton; a concert of excerpts in 1929 revealed little to admire. Nor is George Frederick Bristow's Marschner-flavored *Rip Van Winkle* (1855) worth hearing except as a curio, though at least somebody had tackled an American subject.

The fact is, there was little call for American operas. For one thing, by the middle of the nineteenth century every major eastern city had opera in quantity, in European languages (not always the appropriate ones) as well as in English. With current Bellini, Verdi, and Meyerbeer fresh off the boat—*L'Africaine* got to New York seven months after its Paris premiere—who needed a *Rip Van Winkle?* For another thing, the democratic American style emphasized popular art in a way no European nation did, and the host of musical theatre forms (from minstrel and music-hall variety shows to burlesque, farce, so-called pantomime, and the ballet-rich extravaganza) kept American theatregoers busy on the first principle of "good theatre." Opera, whose first principle in those last days of Romanticism was "good music," occupied a subordinate position in the culture.

This is what stunted the growth of American opera: the theatre composers were weak in composition, but the music (i.e., trained) composers had no stage tradition to draw on. So their work continued drably eclectic. Wagner sat heavy upon Frederick Sheperd Converse's one-act woodland fantasy *The Pipe of Desire* (1906), Horatio Parker's anti-feminist *Mona* (1912), and Deems Taylor's *The King's Henchman* (1927), to Edna St. Vincent Millay's libretto. Other works, such as Walter Damrosch's huge *Cyrano de Bergerac* (1913), were merely heavy. Said one critic of the latter, "It offers nothing which points even remotely to a solution of the problem of English or American opera." The problem was seen variously as: what subject is American, what source (if any), what shape, what ethnic *tinta*, what class of characters? One possibility was Indian opera, but Victor Herbert's *Natoma* (1911), despite Mary Garden's desperate efforts as the heroine, and several entries by the Indian folklorist Charles Wakefield Cadman suggested more problem than solution, not least in their obsession with tragic white-red miscegenation.

The odd thing is that management intransigence was *not* a problem. Most of the important managers were hungry for native opera. But in years punctuated by the most exciting avant-garde develop-

ments abroad, American composers turned out such antiquated make-
weights as Henry Hadley's *Cleopatra's Night* (1920) or jumped the
gun on contemporary and gave the most conservative audience in the
Western opera world Hamilton Forrest's *Camille* (1930). It's sad that as
late as the first years of the twentieth century, an American composer
who hit on a plausible solution to The Problem was denied a hearing and
his opera not performed till many years after his death. But his was a
special case: he was known only for short piano dance pieces, and he
was black. As the "king of ragtime," Scott Joplin had identified himself with what the status quo viewed as a countercultural proletarian
incitement, and the idea of a "ragtime opera" made some guffaw and
others fume. The ragtime craze was in full swing, so Joplin cannot be
thought *musically* ahead of his time: his time lagged behind him. After
enduring countless rejections—he had to publish the score himself—
Joplin finally held a piano-accompanied concert runthrough of his
opera, *Treemonisha*, in 1915, hoping to interest backers. Nothing doing.
Joplin died unredeemed.

In recent years the tenacity of the musicologist Vera Brodsky
Lawrence brought Joplin back into the active music scene, and the
momentum of the ragtime revolution plus the changed racial climate
at last made the production of *Treemonisha* possible, even essential.
Morehouse College in Atlanta staged it in 1972, and three years later
came the Houston Grand Opera's pace-setting production in Gunther
Schuller's orchestration of elated cheek, Franco Colavecchia's look of
story-book primitivism, Louis Johnson's choreography, and Frank
Corsaro's direction. Houston toured *Treemonisha*, making it something
of a national experience, and while it is no masterpiece, its confident
sense of self still placed it ahead of the general run of American opera
some sixty years after its composition. An indictment of superstition
closing with the advice that people improve their morality through
education, *Treemonisha* is no "ragtime opera" after all. It uses recit,
solos, ensembles, choruses, dances, and instrumental passages in styles
ranging from story ballad to more expansive forms.

In short, though no one knew it at the time, Joplin had come up
with the first workable aesthetic for American opera: draw folk-
lorically on the Afro-American subculture. George Gershwin attempted such a piece in his Frankie-and-Johnny-like one-actor, *Blue
Monday* (later called *135th Street*), composed to B. G. deSylva's libretto for George White's *Scandals of 1922*. *Blue Monday* predates
Gershwin's large-scale formulations applying legit technique to "jazz"
and it unfolds clumsily as a kind of blues medley with trivial recit;
moreover, it had no place in a legs-and-yoks revue, as White belatedly

realized. He cut *Blue Monday* after opening night. Still, there were possibilities to be explored here. Louis Gruenberg took up the challenge in *The Emperor Jones* (1933), from Eugene O'Neill's play that pictures the degeneration of a badass black dictator in a West Indian forest as his former subjects hunt him down. O'Neill had already used Gruenberg's most striking effect in the hypnotic terrorism of offstage drums, but at least this work stood out from the other two American operas the Met presented in its 1933–34 season, Howard Hanson's *Merry Mount* (1933), after Hawthorne, and Deems Taylor's asinine *Peter Ibbetson* (1931), after George du Maurier. (Lawrence Tibbett lent a touch of unity to the trio by singing leads in all of them.)

The black, with his keen musicality and tragic role in the American destiny, replaced the Indian as the fittest subject for art's exotic alchemy; to balance Gershwin's aborted and Gruenberg's halfway naturalism (not to mention Joplin's folk stylization), Virgil Thomson and Gertrude Stein provided fantasy-dada in *Four Saints in Three Acts* (1934). The authors are scamps; they term *Four Saints* "an opera to be sung" and fill the scene with incoherent rituals and reenactments of a high-chic tommyrot and endless charm. More important, Thomson took this as the main chance to establish a procedure for the setting of English words. In Stein's libretto, Thomson wrote, "with meanings already abstracted, or absent, or so multiplied that choice among them was impossible, there was no temptation toward tonal illustration, say, of birdie babbling by the brook or heavy heavy hangs my heart." Again, again, and again nowadays: the words matter. Even Stein's words, which obey their own logic as sure as—to quote *Four Saints*— "moon follows June and June follows moon and moon follows soon and it is very nearly ended with bread." The Friends and Enemies of Modern Music mounted the premiere in Hartford, Connecticut, in a now-legendary production staged by John Houseman and Frederick Ashton, designed for dotty cellophane origami by Florine Stettheimer, and sung (for no reason except that Thomson wanted it so) by an all-black cast. *Four Saints in Three Acts* is not a black opera by any ruling, yet no one wants to hear it done any other way; the dignity of the original singers, many of whom had been recruited from Harlem church choirs, perfectly matched Stein's declarative insistence ("Pigeons on the grass alas" and "It was a magpie in the sky") and Thomson's hymns and ballads. For the composer, an American opera called for middle-American tunes.

Four Saints went on to a sensational New York run of six weeks in a Broadway house—how many operas ancient or modern could last out forty-eight consecutive performances in a full-sized auditorium?—

American prime: *Four Saints in Three Acts* as first seen in 1934.
(RCA Victor Records)

and one year later Gershwin came back with *Porgy and Bess* (1935), likewise produced in commercial precincts rather than in an opera place. A story has it that the Met had wanted to stage Gershwin's only evening-long opera, based on DuBose Heyward's novel *Porgy*, but we have only Gershwin's word for it—though he *had* signed a contract with that company in 1929 for an opera on Sholem Ansky's play *The Dybbuk*. (The pact was dissolved when the rights to *The Dybbuk* went to Ludovico Rocca.) It is hard to see how the Met could have even rehearsed a piece calling for a large black cast deeply versed in their racial vernacular, let alone mount it. The Theatre Guild, which had staged Heyward and his wife Dorothy's adaptation of his book, produced the opera, carrying over the very gifted Rouben Mamoulian, who had directed the play *Porgy* in 1927. As with *Four Saints*, casting turned up people who had little or no stage experience, but the original production, for an enlightened few, cast a spell of wonder as much for its historical achievement in the synthesis of a native style out of the work of underclass artists (black subject matter, black singers, Jewish composer) as for its experience as entertainment.

The achievement was obscured for years, partly by sleazy critics' putdowns—for as so often with something truly out of the way and not yet in mode, reviewers felt safer if they disdained it. It takes talent and guts to consider the revolutionary in art, and people who answer that description are usually too busy creating it to write about it. Newspapers sent both music and drama stringers to *Porgy and Bess;* the music men said, "My, my, my" and the drama critics said, "What's an opera?" Moreover, *Porgy*'s heavy running costs—a given in privately- or state-sponsored opera but a cause for putting up closing notices in the commercial theatre—kept it from being profitable. It lasted about four months in New York, and for some time after it closed it lingered in the ear mainly through spot performances of its many popular solos and duets. The turning point came in the early 1950s, when an international tour featuring Leontyne Price, William Warfield, and Cab Calloway kept the work in the news. A Hollywood film and scattered revivals contributed to a *Porgy* cult, and at length a major American revival toured from Houston to New York in 1976. This time vogue ran with the show, and the suggestion that *Porgy* was not an opera was hooted down as a racist slur. Two complete recordings (one of the Houston staging and another conducted by Lorin Maazel in an underpowered "conservatory" approach) helped solemnize the event, and *Porgy and Bess* was at last conceded to be a masterpiece.

We'll get to this ridiculously trivial question of whether certain instances of music theatre are opera or Something Else at the end of the book. Right now we should consider for a moment why a work so characterfully dramatic and musical as *Porgy and Bess* took so long to fit in. There is a technical reason: the trouble and expense of mounting the show. There is a cultural reason: Gershwin captured the black idiom so well (the barbaric drums that open the picnic scene startle even today) that many people who had not yet acquired the taste for the true black idiom were bewildered by it. There is a tragic reason: Gershwin died two years after the premiere, and so was not around to urge the work on his colleagues in the arts. In music, very often, being recently dead is to invite neglect. And there is another reason: *Porgy* is unique, and opinion makers hadn't yet figured out that American opera would be either derivatively mediocre or imposingly different from anything in other cultures. Thomson and Stein's entry could be excused as a cubist irrelevance, something to be patted on the head and forgotten. But *Porgy* was bold and knew it—Gershwin was arrogant, the Theatre Guild proud, the cast imposingly gifted. *Four Saints in Three Acts*, like it or not, was elite stuff. But *Porgy* was the solution to The Problem, and the solution's name was Proletarian Art. Take it in the context of 1935: the composer is a graduate of Tin Pan Alley and rag-into-"jazz," the librettists are his lyricist brother Ira and the Charleston aristocrat Heyward. The cast, except for a few very small nonsinging white men's parts, is black. And these are not the juking-comic or naïve-and-sentimental black that whites had condescended to in Harlem shows, but subcultural, in-depth blacks living in their own world on their terms. Except for Heyward, the whole project had subversive written all over it, and it was as much WASP supremacist reaction that rejected *Porgy*'s first night as it was the honest panic of the hack journalist faced with something new. Such people don't even know how *La Traviata* works; how can they possibly analyze *Porgy?*

Porgy inspired the art community, however, pointing the way to an American opera, American in look, plastique, and musical and verbal idioms. The next few decades saw an industry opened up in opera Americana, a complete overthrow of the *Cyrano de Bergerac* and *King's Henchman* school. Aaron Copland plied his melting-pot ethnicity—he manages to sound the urban hustle and rural panorama almost in the same breath—in *The Second Hurricane* (1937), a work for high-schoolers to perform about high-schoolers engaged in a rescue mission who learn a sense of community by suppressing their individualities. Edwin Denby's libretto, replete with the sneaky Popular-Front communism of the 1930s, has kept this brief piece from earning much of a following. The more energetic historical Americana proved more worthy, in such short works as Douglas Moore's *The Devil and Daniel Webster* (1939), libretto by Stephen Vincent Benét, and Lukas Foss' *The Jumping Frog of Calaveras County* (1950), from Mark Twain. Thomson and Stein turned out another landmark work in *The Mother Of Us All* (1947), a crazy-quilt pageant on the feminist leader Susan B. Anthony. This time Stein worked out a more discernibly narrative format and a less abstruse poesy, though she amusingly gathers together an assortment of figures from different epochs—such as Daniel Webster, Lillian Russell, Anthony Comstock, and Ulysses S. Grant, who at one point lets fly an observation about Dwight D. Eisenhower. Thomson's nostalgic parody ranges more widely here than in *Four Saints*, opening, in his own words, "a memory-book of Victorian play-games and passions . . . with its gospel hymns and cocky marches, its sentimental ballads, waltzes, darned-fool ditties, and intoned sermons." Moreover, Thomson had so sharpened his already acute gift for Camerata-like revelation of language that Stein's tricky lines come through to the syllable. *The Mother of Us All* provided one of the American Bicentennial's few thought-through operatic endeavors in Santa Fe, New Mexico, where a stylishly inventive production directed by Peter Wood, designed by Robert Indiana, conducted by Raymond Leppard, and sung by natives (Mignon Dunn as Susan) made authentic contact with the audience (Indiana's parade floats matched Thomson's musical pastiche with the *look* of the past) while certain other companies busied themselves with commissions from foreigners.

This all-American period reached its culmination in Douglas Moore's *The Ballad of Baby Doe* (1956), to John Latouche's account, taken from chronicle, of the rise and fall of a silver miner and the young adventuress for whom he casts off his prim New England wife in the wide-open days of the pioneer west. Moore was not a great composer of opera, yet he and Latouche created something ingenuously paradigmatic in *Baby Doe*, something whose overall reach far exceeds the end-to-end expanse of their eleven episodic scenes of personal and political upheaval in a "memory-book" of sounds comparable to Thomson's. Thomson set English more naturally, and Gershwin sang Bigger Tunes; but *Baby Doe*, more than *Four Saints*, *The Mother of Us All*, and *Porgy and Bess* (all of which are vastly superior to it) is the ecumenical American opera, embedded in the all-cultural highway. From dance-hall girls to stuffy arriviste wives, from miner camaraderie to smoke-filled-room cronyism, from the main drag of Leadville, Colorado (where Baby Doe first meets Horace Tabor), to the Willard Hotel in Washington, D.C. (where President Arthur salutes their scandalous marriage) to the Matchless Mine (where Baby, who promised Tabor she would never part with it, freezes to death), this opera sweeps the land for material, images, abstractions. Like Thomson's and Gershwin's operas, it does not reduce to a formula—as so much opera does—because its detailed trappings, its Americana, comprise its action more than the central triangle love plot. *Baby Doe* isn't the tale of a rich man, a fortune hunter, and his discarded spouse, but a saga of changing times seen against two unshakable obsessions: Tabor's for silver, and Baby's for Tabor.

Formula had kept American opera down; now, rejection of formula brought it up. And most of this rejection came out of a raised theatre consciousness, one that exploited native emotional dynamics in musical idioms and representational technique. But where was the newly fledged opera to find its librettists? This is a historical opera quandary. Obviously composers write the music; but who exactly is a librettist? Poets, journalists, unmusical playwrights, all-around theatre people, and composers themselves have all supplied the texts at various times; consider the very different backgrounds of Da Ponte, Scribe, von Hofmannsthal, Stein. A paucity of librettists combined with the newly developed theatre flair sent American composers to the play catalogues for their librettos, and the 1950s saw a raft of scripts set to music, most of them quickly forgotten. More operas were being produced, mainly by the New York City Opera in its old home at the City Center (which still bears its old name, Mecca Temple, as a testament to its original use as caravansary for an occult order). But the practice was rooted in duty, not pleasure, the kind of thing foundations do. The American public's opera attitude was unenterprising, and much of this was the fault of the nation's first opera institution, the Met. No longer the committed emporium of new work it had been under Giulio Gatti-Casazza, Rudolf Bing's Met in the 1950s and '60s was a house of fat, thickheaded and potbellied in its extremely unthe-atre-minded singers, heavy-handed in its self-righteous management.* Its look was moldy or garish and its ideals consisted of Zinka Milanov's floated pianissimos. Attacked for its heavy-cream diet of *Lohengrin*s and *La Bohème*s, Bing would, once in a blue moon, sullenly unveil

---

* Early in his tenure, Bing proposed to refresh house style by bringing in thespian directors—Margaret Webster, Alfred Lunt, Cyril Ritchard—and commissioning English translations of *Die Fledermaus* and *La Bohème* from Howard Dietz. Except for Dietz' forced but funny Strauss, none of this worked well. The worst of it was an alleged *Così Fan Tutte*, translated into High Cockamamie by Ruth and Thomas Martin, staged by Lunt, and sung by Eleanor Steber, Blanche Thebom, Patrice Munsel, Richard Tucker, Frank Guarrera, and John Brownlee. Despite the efforts of Mozart stylists Steber and Brownlee, it played like an evening in monkey city.

The Rake's Progress or *Wozzeck* for four or five performances and
say, "So?"

The Met's idea of contemporary American opera was Samuel
Barber. In one of his very few world premieres, Bing presented Barber's *Vanessa* (1958), to Gian Carlo Menotti's libretto about smolder-
ing women wearing purple gauze veils in a frigid country mansion
with all the mirrors covered, waiting for lovers who won't return.
It might work better if the setting were changed to a gay bar, but in
any case Barber's music, passionately neo-Romantic, believes in itself—
more than one can say for many a coeval score. Barber's one other
opera, *Antony and Cleopatra* (1966), inaugurated the Met's Lincoln
Center quarters in Franco Zeffirelli's insistently sumptuous production
and with all-American cast (Leontyne Price, Jess Thomas, Justino
Diaz). Ambitiously Shakespearean in its diverse features, it seemed to
lack a center; a revision pruned it of impedimenta but failed to center
it, and, on second thought, the impedimenta of 1966 at least made for
ear- and eye-filling fun.

By the 1960s, the upsurge in national opera activity announced a
second epoch, one that tested the Met's supremacy not just in long-
established or revived institutions in San Francisco or Chicago but by
some dozen other companies from Boston to San Diego, with much
supplementary action in smaller cities. With strong local boosterism to
draw on, impresarios increasingly mounted new work, though the general style hugged the neo-Romantic idiom and realistic linear narratives. This was dangerously timid after Gershwin's blackness and
Stein's helter-skelter. Typical of post–World War II American opera
is Jack Beeson (who by coincidence was born in "Middletown," the
prototypal American city, later revealed to be Muncie, Indiana, in
Robert and Helen Lynd's famous sociological study). Beeson's career
takes in a setting of William Saroyan's one-act *Hello, Out There*
(1953), a domestic tragedy based on American legend in *Lizzie Borden*
(1965), and an adaptation from turn-of-the-century pop theatre in
Captain Jinks of the Horse Marines (1975). Any of these might have
made interesting operas; they didn't, because Beeson's often carefully
worked out musicodramatics simply don't engage the ear. He knows
how to vary his flow, knows where the grand scene is needed, as in
Lizzie Borden's great confrontation between the heroine and her tyrannical father, "What am I forbidden now?," a gruesome neurotic ritual
in which she cowers on the floor and he lists her demerits in what
appears to be a secret litany the two have shared in love and hatred
while, upstairs, Lizzie's nasty stepmother is heard practicing her singing. Great stuff: concise, fleet, distinctive. But then, alone, Lizzie closes

Act II with a lengthy monologue, bouncing off the "What am I forbidden?" rite into a complex of bitterness and fantasy. Dull stuff: dramatically right but musically empty. *Captain Jinks*, from Clyde Fitch's comedy about an opera star* taming a rakehell fireman in little old New York, held more promise, for here Beeson worked with Sheldon Harnick, a gifted Broadway lyricist and one to whom that special *parola scenica* of Broadway is an absolute. Strangely, the piece quacks and gobbles; even more strangely, considering Harnick's experience in Broadway polish, the authors tolerated an abysmally amateur production for *Captain Jinks'* Kansas City premiere.

If European opera production suffers from mindless innovation—resettings in modern dress or weird climes, relentless leftist politicizing of innocent texts, "actions for music" imposed on old works whose aim was music first and action second—American opera production is still in the throwback stage. This has in turn influenced composition. If production is so unoriginal, how can the material itself be anything else to start with? If Kansas City couldn't launch an old-fashioned well-made, proscenium-bound-with-transparent-fourth-wall *Captain Jinks* decently, what would it have done to a *Death in Venice*, a *Bomarzo?* One composer who has divined the crucial theatreness of opera, Carlisle Floyd, still holds his work to a pre-Schoenbergian idiom, no doubt aware that anything more advanced would be cultural suicide. His own librettist, Floyd turned out one of the major folk operas in *Susannah* (1955), whose simple but highly characterful scoring reflects the rural southern setting. But he held to the same idiom in *Wuthering Heights* (1958) and *Of Mice and Men* (1965), respectively not at all and only incidentally folkish in sound. Floyd's idée fixe is the outcast, a basic American trope, and this has led him to both standard and bizarre situations. The heroine of *Bilby's Doll* (1976) believes herself to have entered into carnal union with a demon—*opera natura*, one might say. But *Of Mice and Men's* love plot, faithful to the John Steinbeck novel, brings two men together, drifters who dream of a small farm to settle down on, and Floyd's current project in the early 1980s is an adaptation of Robert Penn Warren's novel *All The King's Men*, roughly modeled on the career of the Louisiana demagogue Huey Long.

Outcasts are the meat of American opera—Gershwin's Charleston ghetto, Thomson's feminists, Moore's couple going down with silver. An outlaw format, too, has done well—Gershwin's "taint" of blues,

---

* The role is a Big one: Ethel Barrymore became a star playing Madame Trentoni (a continental pseudonym—she's from Trenton) in the original 1901 production.

Stein's dingbat wordorama, *Baby Doe*'s unexpected final scene, a potpourri flashback dream sequence on Tabor's life. We have even had
an outcast institution, the Minnesota Opera Company, whose experimental outlook would have made it famous if it were resident in a
media-approved cultural capital instead of in the Twin Cities. Minnesota's *Gulliver* (1975) is typical of its work: small cast, chamber orchestra, a free (even unhinged) structure based on Swift but admitting
contemporary correspondences, tape, film, spoken dialogue, and no
less than five authors. The company has enjoyed an enduring relationship with the composer Dominick Argento, which presumably accounts for the strong theatre imagination in his work: he demands the
most from *acting* singers. His *The Shoemaker's Holiday* (1967), a ballad opera after Thomas Dekker's play, is actually intended for actors
rather than singers (Minnesota's first-night cast included Douglas
Campbell, Michael Moriarty, Len Cariou, and Patricia Elliott), and
Postcard from Morocco (1971), with its phantasmagoria of travelers
and their suitcases of secrets, its Algerian palm-court orchestra in
fezzes, its parody and nostalgia, seems more creditable as a "theatre
piece" than a musical experience. Surely it was theatre that led Argento
to the unusual proposition of *The Voyage of Edgar Allan Poe* (1976),
a ghostly trip over water into the poet's mind and work, deliberately
unclear about whether a character is a legitimate being or a Poe fiction.
Or, it *is* clear: all are both. To Charles Nolte's* libretto Argento applied a misty brush, observing the waking dream while not losing sight
of the intensity of Poe's art, which led directly to the Symbolist-and-
degradation school of French poetry.

Listeners regularly comment on Argento's similarity to Britten in
sound, in technique, and in the refreshing "unsuitability" of their source
material. With his long-time collaborator John Olon-Scrymgeour,
Argento hit upon an enticing prospect for *Miss Havisham's Fire*
(1979): an inquest into the death of Dickens' celebrated old spinster in
Great Expectations who, abandoned on her wedding day, shut herself
in to decay amid the unused wedding appurtenances. Rather than adapt
the novel, the librettist plucks some action and character from it to go
his own way with them in ternary structure: prologue (the fire), inquest, and epilogue (an unconventional "mad scene"). By the time

---

* Nolte, as a youth, played Billy Budd in a stage adaptation on Broadway in 1951,
an odd credit for an opera librettist. Even odder is the backstory—as they put it in
Hollywood—on Jack Larson, librettist of Virgil Thomson's *Lord Byron* (1972):
Larson played the overeager rookie reporter Jimmy Olson on the Superman
television series in the 1950s. Still, the record for all-time unique librettist is held
by Lorenzo da Ponte, as his rather wild memoirs attest.

the work was unveiled at the New York City Opera,* Argento had become the great hope of American music. The highly portable *Postcard from Morocco* was doing nicely on the chamber-opera circuit, his song cycle *From the Diary of Virginia Woolf*, as premiered by Janet Baker, impressed many as a surething for the standard repertory, and the "songs for orchestra" *In Praise of Music* was making successful rounds. Much lay on *Miss Havisham*'s first night—too much. Everyone expected the piece to invent, enthrall, and elucidate like a classic on one hearing. It isn't that kind of work—it has niches, moods, circles— and the generally disappointed reports most likely would have been more favorable if the reporters had remembered that art is not necessarily efficient product for consumers. *Parsifal* doesn't impress the uninitiated on one hearing, either.

Floyd, too, will have to wow 'em pronto with his *All the King's Men* piece; but at least he and Argento have the public's willing ear. Those who work in more advanced harmonic idioms do not. Roger Sessions, for instance, is counted among the few major American composers today, but it was Berlin's Deutsche Oper that premiered his *Montezuma* (1964), to G. Antonio Borgese's sometimes insufferably poetic libretto. Even then the work was not heard in Sessions' homeland till the conductor Sarah Caldwell staged it in Boston in 1976. Heard and not liked. Sessions is Modern, no question, yet even conservatives should concede Modern's theatrical savvy. *Montezuma*'s Act II ends with the Aztec king in shackles and Cortez shouting, "Caps down, caballeros! Caps down! The king passes!"—and Act III begins with a narrator taking up that theme to the same music to retrieve the irony across an intermission. "Kings pass," he admits. "But better dead than humbled majesty." Similarly, Harold Farberman's *The Losers* (1971), to Barbara Fried's hip libretto on the California bike subculture, had nowhere to go after its premiere at New York's Juilliard School, for Farberman's uncompromisingly Modern score simply cannot please an American crowd. Worse yet, two interesting events like *Montezuma* and *The Losers* are lumped together, in audiences' mind, with such inept Modern as Leon Kirchner's *Lily* (1977), based on Saul Bellow's *Henderson the Rain King*. Attempting to recall its historic role as America's "contemporary" house, the New York City Opera mounted *Lily*, prudently scheduling only three performances and even more prudently calling in director Tom O'Horgan for some expert

---

* Originally Beverly Sills was to have sung Miss Havisham, but in the end the role was divided into a younger and older self, taken respectively by Gianna Rolandi and Rita Shane. The latter scored a great success for her authority in coloratura, portrayal, and diction.

theatre wow. *Lily* stumped even O'Horgan.

Because opera cannot be decorated with theatre, not successfully. Opera must have theatre built into it: theatre is what opera is, music theatre. Conrad Susa's *Transformations* (1972) seems to know this. A setting of Anne Sexton's grisly Mother Goose poems, *Transformations*, like Gulliver, was a Minnesota project, and sharp acting-singers can bring it off, though Susa's score doesn't add as much as it might to Sexton (sometimes it even obscures her). Theatre without music is not good opera either. And what are we to make of *Einstein on the Beach* (1975), a blend of not-exactly theatre and not-exactly music—or, let us say, a blend of theatre that moves too slowly and too mysteriously to matter and music so well coordinated with it that it, too, fails to matter?

Einstein is the work of Robert Wilson, who treats the stage as a place for arcane surrealist collage and whose lengthy works call for such dedication and Wilsonian training that only his own troupe can present them. (The troupe is protean; a Wilson piece often swells as it tours.) Shown at various festivals, the five-hour *Einstein* arrived at the Met for two performances in late 1976 at the height of the Wilson vogue, and *le tout New York* turned out cooing to see. But is it music theatre? Wilson will almost certainly influence others, and his collaborator, Philip Glass (who wrote *Einstein*'s lyrics and music), is ingenious; their mutual experiments in the rhythm of theatre, the calibration of its motion, will take a proud place in the indexes of theatre history. But all of *Einstein*'s spectacle amounts to very little in the way of sheer material. It was fun in spots, but most of it simply wasn't there. Few critics were willing to risk their rep at the time and question the emperor's clothes, but in *Harper*'s magazine F. Joseph Spieler wrote: "To see *Einstein* is to be invited for dinner. You arrive. The china, the silverware, the flowers are beautiful. You sit down. It is only after some time has passed that the intentions of the host become clear: you were to have brought your own food."

Another team that deals like Wilson and Glass in what might be called the neo-Classical surreal—dreamily free form at first glance but precisely constructed—is Stanley Silverman and Richard Foreman. Foreman has his troupe, the Ontological-Hysteric Theatre, but when he works with Silverman the results are not so recondite as Wilson and may be staged by any company. The billing on the front cover of the recording of *Elephant Steps* (1968) gives some idea of the style: "A fearful radio show with pop singers, opera singers, orchestra, rock band, electronic tape, raga group, tape recorder, gypsy ensemble, and elephants." This is not hype—*Elephant Steps* has everything. If Silverman's enthusiasm for parody and Foreman's mysterious text put some people off, the collaborators do give full measure in entertainment. Their material is dense and eclectic, but it's *there;* you don't have to bring your own food to the feast.

For the most part, American opera is not as inner-directed as *Montezuma* or *Elephant Steps;* it fears Modern. How much richer contemporary European opera is—Henze's clowns in *Der König Hirsch,* to be played by real clowns in real clown improvisation; the cinematically shifting decor in *Erwartung* and *Die Glückliche Hand;* the kaleidoscopic soundscape of Ginastera and Penderecki; the imagistic timelessness of *Il Prigioniero* and *Moses und Aron;* the ineffable archeology of *The Rake's Progress.* By comparison, *Baby Doe, Vanessa,* and *Susannah* are so *naïve.* Yet America had sophisticated an extraordinary technology for emphasizing the theatre in music theatre, even at the expense of the music. American opera should be the most, not the least, inventive.

But American music theatre made its heaviest investment in musical comedy, and that's where the main action is to this day. The term "musical," as ambiguous as *opéra comique,* invokes the collaborative with the auteurist, distinguished musicians with nine-day wonders, and the finest calculations with flukes. Yet out of the Broadway womb of backer's auditions, tryout tours, and weekly running costs sprang more than a few out-and-out operas: works in which the bulk of the dramatic motion is carried through song. In the decade that saw both *Four Saints in Three Acts* and *Porgy and Bess* to Broadway, Marc Blitzstein attempted a piece of agitprop in the Weill-Brecht style, *The Cradle Will Rock* (1937), long a legend for its disheveled opening night. Blitzstein, as librettist as well as composer, laid out a scenario for revolution, revealing capitalism in cross-section through cartoons rather than characters—villains Mister Mister and family, stooges Editor Daily, Reverend Salvation, and Doctor Specialist, victims Moll and Gent, hero Larry Foreman. As staged by Orson Welles, *The Cradle Will Rock* was a project of the Federal Theatre, one of President Franklin D. Roosevelt's New Deal employment programs, and with the times riven by real-life strikes, Blitzstein's intended incitement was declared counterproductive and its theatre padlocked at the last minute. But cast, staff, and audience filed up Broadway to an abandoned house on the northern fringe of the theatre district (at the owner's invitation). To add to legend, unions sided with the government in forbidding their members to enter the pit, work the wings, or mount the stage.

Blitzstein accompanied the piece himself on a battered piano, lighting designer Abe Feder manned a bitter spotlight, and the actors delivered their parts from seats in the auditorium. In such an electric atmosphere, the work was bound to go over, but in truth Blitzstein's savage, black-and-white conception is too unfriendly to enjoy. *The Threepenny Opera*, too, had failed earlier in the decade in its American premiere, and here was an American version of the same format and content. *The Cradle Will Rock* passed into legend and stayed there; every revival has collapsed in its own hostility.

Blitzstein tried again, more musically, in a completely different sort of thing, *Regina* (1949), after Lillian Hellman's play *The Little Foxes*. Here, for once, was an adaptation rather than a setting of the original. Blitzstein expanded Hellman's revelation of entreprenurial southern greed with scenes and bits of his own devising, including ragtime, blues, and spirituals for the blacks. Blitzstein was no melodist. *The Cradle Will Rock* is notable, as music, only for the way the score matches the words in bite, and *Regina* has more places for Big Tunes than the Tunes themselves—as in the title part, which lacks an attractive line but nonetheless captures the energy of selfishness so well that a singer has to be pretty dull to flop in it. (The *Little Foxes'* Regina, too, is strongly written; it pulled from Tallulah Bankhead one of her few really brilliant performances.)

Melodist or not, Blitzstein found the music in Hellman's melodrama. The bads (Regina, her two scalawag brothers, and her giddy nephew) roll and hop with tough tunes; the goods (Regina's dying husband, their daughter, the alcoholic Birdie, and the black servants) comfort each other with hopeful lyricism. A real inspiration is the Rain Quartet, only latent in Hellman, in which the goods exult in their fellowship and, for a refrain, imitate the pitter-patter of raindrops in wordless vocalizing. First produced on Broadway, *Regina* eventually entered the City Opera repertory; in each case the casting took in both legit and Broadway voices, reflecting America's lack of separation between opera and musical comedy. European musical comedy (except British) calls for trained voices; as Offenbach noted years ago, it's too often just a lighter form of opera. But America's theatre-oriented musical comedy only *draws from* opera, when necessary: when the emotional thrust of the theatre needs musical penetration. It is both separate from yet highly dependent on opera. On occasion it *is* opera—just as twentieth-century opera has on occasion been musical comedy.

Broadway is presumably an odd place in which to get an opera on —who can guarantee that musical values will get a fair shake? Does

Broadway have the musicians, the voices? In fact, it does,* and it is noteworthy that between *The Cradle Will Rock*, an opera for actors, and *Regina*, theatre for singers, Broadway's most typical show-shop hustler, Billy Rose, produced one of the few authentic productions of *Carmen* to be heard before the revival of Bizet's original *opéra comique*. Oscar Hammerstein II translated the libretto, Robert Russell Bennett scaled Bizet's orchestration down to pit size, and the whole thing was done with a black cast in a southern setting as *Carmen Jones* (1943). Still, it was *Carmen* as few (if any) opera houses could stage it, *Carmen* alive. Don't ask if theatre has the voice; ask if opera has the theatre. Because *Carmen* in someone else's language, with clumsy recit that the composer never wanted, and with singers who can't get inside their parts as people is half an art.

Kurt Weill had no qualms about trading the trained voices for which he sometimes wrote in Germany for the singing actors of Broadway. On Broadway he slipped out of his dry Brechtian idiom and went sentimental without losing his power. He dispatched what was left of the German acid in Paul Green's play with songs, *Johnny Johnson* (1936), an antiwar fantasy with Brecht's irony ("Captain Valentine's Tango") but American naïveté ("The Rio Grande," sung by a Texan in the trenches). Thereafter Weill continued to write for "popular" singers—Gertrude Lawrence in *Lady in the Dark* (1941), Mary Martin, Kenny Baker, and John Boles in *One Touch of Venus* (1943), Nanette Fabray and Ray Middleton in *Love Life* (1948). Yet Weill remained Weill. *Lady in the Dark*'s score comprises—except for one song, "My Ship," whose theme provides the heroine's *Leitmotiv* —three one-act operas, each a dream that turns into a nightmare: the heroine as New York's most glamorous woman; as bride; as star attraction/defendant in a circus/trial. *One Touch of Venus* featured some compelling ballet music. *Love Life* trotted out a whole evening of American parody—barbershop quartet, torch song, folk chorale, radio scat trio. Weill always did his own orchestrations, too, a practice lapsed since the days of Victor Herbert. Furthermore, he saw no im-

---

* The musical has drafted an array of trained voices, not even counting "operetta," which naturally demands sopranos, tenors, and a full-throated chorus. No doubt the appearance of such as Cesare Siepi in *Bravo, Giovanni!* and Patricia Neway in *The Sound of Music* proves nothing artistic about the scores they sang; certainly Helen Traubel's stint as a bordello madam in Rodgers and Hammerstein's would-be Steinbeckian *Pipe Dream* only proved the incompatibility of art and pop. But the voice-rich sound of the original version of Leonard Bernstein's *Candide* confirms that work's musical depth, and the participation of Ezio Pinza in Harold Rome's *Fanny* and of Robert Weede (Giorgio Tozzi in the recent revival) in Frank Loesser's *The Most Happy Fella* point to that unclassifiable territory between the theatre musical and musical theatre.

portant distinction between opera and musical comedy. He was for music theatre, period, and he put his oar in on the question of "Broadway opera" in two major entries, *Street Scene* (1947) and *Lost in the Stars* (1949).

Street Scene doesn't quite work, though its documentary value as historical experiment is immense. The trouble lies in its source, Elmer Rice's play of the same name, an exercise in microcosmic urban naturalism that was already on the verge of obsolescence when it first appeared in 1929. The scene is a dull street peopled by tenement inhabitants, passers-by, and visitors; the atmosphere is claustrophobic; the outcome is violent; but the life goes on. Weill stretched too far to include a huge cast in recit, aria, parody specialties, and ensemble: these people aren't that interesting. But he made his point—there is opera even in this disjunct, humdrum piece. Weill's music and Langston Hughes' lyrics poeticize the realism, crooning a violin lullaby over a "blues piano" bass to hymn crowded loneliness and soaring in birdlike woodwinds in dreams of escape. More adaptable to the fantasy of modern opera staging was Alan Paton's novel *Cry, The Beloved Country*, which in Maxwell Anderson's libretto and Rouben Mamoulian's eloquent direction made *Lost in the Stars*' original New York run an experience of inextricably blended parts of "opera" and "Broadway." No revival has been able to repeat the trick, though Paton's subject, the oppression of blacks in South Africa, later gained in topical resonance and thus thrust the work into vogue. But by now the idea of opera working out a destiny on the popular stage feels less pioneer than in 1949, less like "operetta" with a sensory overload. So producers don't work as hard at it; also, frankly, the Mamoulians are gone.

Popular opera isn't in the least pioneer in any case. It's as old as Grétry and Mozart. But unlike Grétry's *opéra comique* and Mozart's *Singspiel*, the Broadway musical has not yet shown much sign of losing its popular connection. Even when sung throughout, like Jerome Moross' *The Golden Apple* (1954), the ambitious musical retains its roots in the vernacular sound style. Maybe it feels it has to, to keep the words clear. And what words! *The Golden Apple* retells the Iliad and Odyssey in an America just on the cusp of global industrial mastery. In John Latouche's astonishingly witty libretto, the apple symbolizes power; ultimately his modern Ulysses rejects it, retaining his innocence in a world going vicious on hunger, greed, envy, and hatred.

This is the Romanticism of Broadway opera, neo-Classically dependent on self-conscious spoof and pastiche but in its sweet little heart as potently idealistic as any Wagnerian worldquake. Broadway is popular, and people want to believe, to envision, to be intoxicated. This is why audiences the world over prefer *La Bohème* to *The Threepenny Opera*. Even an angrily Marxist reading of the building of the first New York City river tunnel, Earl Robinson and Waldo Salt's *Sandhog* (1954), avoids Brechtian alienation for a Romantic *verismo*, and in so doing shares its polemic with us all the more effectively. *Sandhog* has been an in-crowd Broadway joke for years because of its unfortunate title, but the work itself is a lost classic, with titanic choral writing (the sopranos' top line is a voice killer, but thrilling to hear) and an incisive Irish ethnicity to capture the idiom of the people in it. *Sandhog* is simple, dangerous, and profound, one of the few American operas that is *not* naïve. Perhaps that's why no American company wants to mount a revival.*

Ever since *Porgy and Bess*, analysts have worried over what terminology to apply to the varieties of Broadway opera; such concern shows an amazing ignorance of opera's history. The "popular" in such opera bothers them. It didn't bother Haydn, Mozart, Rossini, Weber, Auber, Smetana, Ravel, Orff, and many others. Yet no one attacks their pieces for not being operas. This snit over genre exists entirely because critics have nothing to say about the substance of art—all they can do is call it names. The questions are: does a piece of music theatre work or doesn't it?; and what makes it go? If *Lost in the Stars* isn't opera because it has spoken dialogue, then neither is *The Magic Flute*. If *Sandhog* isn't an opera because Hershey Kay did Robinson's orchestrations, then neither is *The Tales of Hoffman*. If no work staged on Broadway is opera because it must accord with commercial show-shop techniques, then all of Bellini, Donizetti, and Meyerbeer is not opera.

In fact, show-shop techniques have consistently liberated opera from an overmuch of stagnant concert. At their worst, in the age of Scribe, they were hackwork device, perhaps. But good theatre practice revitalized Florentine theorizing, dismantled the aria opera for Gluck's sweep, helped Rossini create *melodramma*, ushered *opéra comique* into its golden age, inspired artists like Viardot and Pasta, stoked the fires of Russian, French, and Italian naturalism, reemphasized the text, revived comedy, and provided the wonderful diversity of subject matter that Modern chooses from. Without show-shop techniques, how could any creators in any era devise such a remarkable piece as *Pacific Overtures* (1976), the sole masterpiece to fall out of the Bicentennial. Here you have a work of music theatre that exploits

---

* Like *The Golden Apple*, *Sandhog* was staged by the Phoenix Theatre in its old home on lower Second Avenue—technically off-Broadway, but full-scale in size, decor, and professional acumen.

music and text to the fullest within an innovative presentational concept, the whole detailing a theme of epic action: you cannot make
history, nor prevent its being made. History happens.

How did composer and lyricist Stephen Sondheim, librettist John
Weidman, director Harold Prince, choreographer Patricia Birch, and
designers Boris Aronson and Florence Klotz make this statement? Using an Oriental cast, they invented a hybrid genre: Kabuki musical
comedy. This was not an American musical staged Kabuki-style, nor
Kabuki theatre with a musical comedy overlay: they actually blended
the two styles into one so that only a very few moments—such as a
geisha madam's patter song and the fluid dance of her cohort, "Welcome to Kanagawa"; or the all-Western pit orchestra opposed to the
onstage Japanese band—showed the styles nestled but identifiably diverse. Their subject was the nineteenth-century reopening and subsequent Westernization of Japan, and their characters for the most part
oppose or lead this development—both to no effect: history is force of
time, place, and culture, not a human force. At the evening's center
point, a quartet called "Someone in a Tree" brings this out in a discussion about the signing of a treaty between the Japanese and the Americans under Admiral Perry. This is the climactic event in the history,
for while the Japanese believe it is the end of the Westerners, it in
fact marks the beginning of a mercantilist invasion. The temporary
treaty house was closed to outsiders. Who knows what occurred in it?
An old man who peeked in from a tree (but heard nothing) and his
younger self, a hidden samurai who heard scraps (but saw nothing),
and an "epic theatre"-style narrator review the event, each from his
fragmentary vantage. To the audience, seeing in under three hours the
turning of the geopolitical gyres, history is an inexorably shifting
panorama. To these characters, history is existential: "the pebble, not
the stream." Their ludicrous solipsism thus dramatized for us, we rise
above the human mistake and now take the narrator's point of view:
history is the stream, not the pebble, no matter how big or how many.
As the rest of *Pacific Overtures* unfolds, we follow the panorama
as well as the personal, and when the finale, "Next," cites the twentieth-century denationalization of Japan in lyrics, sound, motion, and
look, the ear cuts back to the show's opening, "The Advantages of
Floating in the Middle of the Sea," and notes that its obsessive but
restrained three-note bass theme is now driving the turmoil of "Next."
History happens.

Pacific Overtures might be thought of as a modern American
equivalent of the *opéra comique* of Auber and Scribe, though Sond-

heim is a vastly superior musician and Scribe the very pattern of art-fearing bourgeois consumerism. What *Pacific Overtures* has in common with *Le Philtre*, *Marco Spada*, and *Fra Diavolo* is an urge to good theatre that sweeps all elements along with it. Show-shop technique is far advanced from what it was in Scribe's day, but the aesthetic is the same, and it has to a great degree directed the course of opera for the past seventy-five years or so. Once one went to certain theatres for musical comedy, certain others for opera; but Walter Felsenstein's Komische Oper in East Berlin did everything, putting the same amount of effort into *Fiddler on the Roof* and *Barbe-Bleue* and *La Traviata*. Felsenstein had no star-class voices to work with; his was a theatre opera, and it is typical of the state of the art that his operation was universally praised yet merrily regarded as a fluke, an exception. Opera is many things today—conductor's sensation, director's spectacle, stars' vehicle, propaganda, artifact, funeral. It is seldom a coherent and penetrating event of theatre in music.

This is what *Treemonisha*, *The Emperor Jones*, *Porgy and Bess*, *The Mother of Us All*, *Regina*, *The Golden Apple*, and other such have that most operas don't: a theatre atmosphere so patent that opera companies that are weak in theatre (which is most of them) generally avoid them. True, fools will rush in. To pick only one example, the Met could not rise above that American naïveté in its *Aufstieg und Fall der Stadt Mahagonny* in 1979, could not quite shuck the sentimentality that Brecht's epic theatre abhors. The cast was capable and willing and James Levine's baton in style to the last dinky note. But director John Dexter kept trying to show the secret tenderness in the "love plot"—as if Jenny and Jim were just grouchy versions of opera's age-old Boy Meets Girl. There is no tenderness in *Mahagonny*, no "love," not even on the sly. Astrid Varnay, a veteran of more confident German *Mahagonny* revivals, kept her head as Leocadia Begbick; Teresa Stratas (Jenny) and Richard Cassily (Jim) should have sued Dexter for degradation of talent.

Still, the presence of such committed artists as Varnay and Stratas on the opera scene does at least keep opera's theatre connection alive, though great acting-singers are always fewer than the singing-actors that Broadway used to produce in such quantity. Who, for instance, will play the two leads in Sondheim's *Sweeney Todd* (1979) when it enters the opera repertory, whither its lush-sarcastic, Romanticized-satiric score is bound to take it? With this work Sondheim abandoned his vernacular roots for more fully developed constructions, and it is no longer clear where the theatre quality yields to the music quality: in other words, opera. But does the opera world have the thespian power to cast the protagonist (a baritone with a high lyric extension), who must project first a bottomless weary bitterness, next an ecstatic blood-thirst, and at last, as tragedy overtakes him, a transcendent humanity? Could it cast his accomplice Mrs. Lovett (a Broadway husk), the blowsy baker who complements Sweeney's self-belief with inadvertent self-satire? Sweeney is Romantic, Mrs. Lovett straight out of Gozzi-esque vaudeville, their surrounding apparatus Victorian *grand guignol* within a commentative Brechtian frame. What opera house could bring it off?

Sweeney *Todd* is theatre opera at the apex. Its source, a play by Christopher Bond, leads back to Victorian melodrama and the popular imagination. There may have been a real Sweeney Todd, of sorts, and it is Sondheim's contention that we are all failed Sweeney Todds—"everyone does it and seldom as well." (Leftist opera's most consistent and irritating convention holds that the audience is no better than the worst creeps on stage; *Evita* and much of Brecht also accord with this rule.) Sweeney is a barber so radicalized by the corruption of indus-trial-age world order that he sets up shop in London as the absolute moralist of the times, slitting his customers' throats so Mrs. Lovett can cook the corpses into pies, dog eat dog. However, what starts as a per-sonal revenge plot and turns into an indiscriminate bloodbath ends back on the personal level; in *Sweeney Todd*, as not in Brecht, character matters. We know opera singers can create character. But could they balance *Sweeney Todd*'s several dovetailed styles, stalking Sweeney's emotional route while grasping Mrs. Lovett's music-hall *buffa*? Angela Lansbury, who first played the latter role, is unique and unreplaceable even in the Broadway milieu; what opera singer could take over for her? Even the two stand-out acting singers of the postwar era, Maria Callas and Janet Baker, belong to the Classical line in acting, one car-ried more through vocal accent and gesture than through stylistic sleight-of-texture. Callas was Norma, Violetta, Lucia; Baker is Dido, Dorabella, Walton's Cressida, Britten's Lucretia. How often does this style apply to contemporary opera?

Sweeney *Todd* is a fit piece to close with, as it points up the end-less symbiosis of opera's two formal energies, the vernacular-theatrical and the elite-musical. It also reminds us that this back-and-forth con-stantly fragments into forms emphasizing one or the other, so much so that the result creates something that no longer relates to its antecedent, cannot be performed by the same file of artists, does not appeal to the same public. Yet Offenbach, Gluck, Janáček, Wagner, Stravinsky, Brit-ten, Spontini, Zimmermann, Lully, and all the rest, from their very separate branches, swing off the same trunk. The form is music theatre —call it opera—and it is simply drama of a musical procedure. *Le parole o la musica?* Remember *Capriccio*'s advice: neither the words nor the music should dominate. Good opera is good theatre.

A Very Selective
Bibliography

F̲O̲R̲ GENERAL REFERENCE, TWO WORKS STAND OUT: "KOBBÉ" FOR SYNOPSES and "Oxford" for data. The former is officially known as *The New Kobbé's Complete Opera Book* (New York: Putnam, 1976), Gustav Kobbé's 1919 classic revised and updated by the Earl of Harewood and a rich mine of potboilers and specials (*Giulio Cesare, La Donna del Lago, Mireille*) set down in almost moment-by-moment detail. *The Concise Oxford Encyclopedia of Opera* (second ed., New York: Oxford, 1979), by Harold Rosenthal and John Warrack, is the *vade mecum* for quick reference (listings include composers, librettists, singers, and significant others; works, literary sources, terms, and places). The article on Shakespeare alone, with its play-by-play citation of countless Shakespearean operas, is worth the ticket.

To bone up on specific periods, try starting with Michael F. Robinson's *Opera Before Mozart* (New York: Morrow, 1967) and Simon Townely Worsthorne's *Venetian Opera in the Seventeenth Century* (London: Oxford, 1954), the latter quite elaborately produced. Unfortunately, the Classical terrain (roughly the last half of the eighteenth century and the first few years of the nineteenth) remains largely untapped by opera historians as well as impresarios. Haydn's many operas, for example, are only just coming into limited currency on Philips' superb series of complete recordings. Then, in the Romantic 1800s, the territory is too vast and various to leave to a single volume; this is better handled by genre, as in Martin Cooper's excellent, brief, and sumptuously illustrated *Opéra Comique* (London: Parrish, 1949) or by composer (see below). Winton Dean has edited Edward J. Dent's Cornell University lectures on the period's formative years as *The Rise of Romantic Opera* (London: Cambridge, 1976); this is a little doughy but worth investigating. In the twentieth century, George Martin's oddly titled *The Opera Companion to Twentieth-Century*

Opera (New York: Dodd, Mead, 1979) offers essays on provocative subjects followed by plot synopses-cum-musical analysis, which seems to me to give short weight on two completely different books: the essays don't delve much, and those who want synopses are going to want more than these. I recommend my own *Opera in the Twentieth Century* (New York: Oxford, 1978).

Perhaps the best way to achieve expertise is to immerse oneself in the stylistic idiosyncrasy and development of one composer, work by work. You may find that reading an authoritative biography and then gliding through the music via recordings and a keenly interpretive, book-length analysis will bring you closer to an understanding of how opera functions than a decade of aimless operagoing. Sadly, because the market for such work is limited, many foreign-language biographies (of, say, Mascagni or Meyerbeer) have not been translated into English, and the field is spotty. Try Paul Henry Lang on Handel (New York: Norton, 1966); Herbert Weinstock on Rossini (New York: Knopf, 1968), Bellini (New York: Knopf, 1971) and Donizetti (New York: Pantheon, 1963). Weinstock is dryly competent, Lang brilliant but stuck with a subject whose life is much less interesting than his music. A more ideal entry—ingenious biographer and intriguing subject—is Frank Walker's *The Man Verdi* (New York: Knopf, 1962), still the standard work in its line for its layered research (including much quotation of letters to and from Verdi). For a sampling of the famous letters by themselves—Verdi was a forthright and highly personal correspondent—try Charles Osbourne's collection (New York: Holt, Rinehart, and Winston, 1971). Those who like to know everything should make the acquaintance of Ernest Newman's four volumes on Wagner, recently reissued in paperback by Cambridge University Press. But for a real treat in biographical art, for a comprehension of period, a meeting with the nabobs of the day, and a pen that soars above everything else of its kind, seek out Eleanor Perényi's *Liszt: The Artist as Romantic Hero* (Boston: Atlantic, 1974). Liszt is not known for opera,* but his influence on dramatic music was acute; anyway, Perényi doesn't go into the music. Just read; you'll never forget it.

There are fancier pickings in the line of musical analysis. As most authors go through an *œuvre* piece by piece, with full introduction (sometimes a biography in little), one can charge a composer's canon in chronological order or slip in and out for favorite works. Winton Dean tackles *Handel and the Opera Seria* (Berkeley: University of

---

* He did write one: *Dan Sanche, ou Le Château d'Amour* (1825), produced in Paris with Adolphe Nourrit.

California Press, 1969), Cuthbert Girdlestone offers *Jean-Philipe Rameau, His Life and Work* (London: Cassell, 1957), and Patricia Howard explains *Gluck and The Rise of Modern Opera* (London: Barrie and Rockcliff, 1963); Howard's book is too thin. Dent's absorbing *Mozart's Operas* (London: Oxford, revised ed., 1947), still around in paperback, deals almost entirely with the "big seven," but two complete Mozart volumes present a choice of texture. Charles Osbourne's (New York: Atheneum, 1978) is concise; William Mann's (New York: Oxford, 1977) takes its time. I recommend Mann for his breadth, detail, and considerable charm. William Ashbrook supplies both a life and a discussion of the work in his *Donizetti* (London: Cassell, 1965). Rossini and Bellini, as far as I know, still await such treatment.

Comes Wagner. Here the material is so rich that no one book can cover it all; perhaps Ernest Newman's venerable *Wagner as Man and Artist* (New York: Vintage, 1952) serves as a good introduction for its enticing (if sometimes benighted) psychobiography. It would appear that Newman didn't appreciate how original an artist Wagner really was, yet Newman's *The Wagner Operas* (New York: Knopf, 1949) is still the best all-around one-volume guide on the musical side. Verdi can have no complaints. He has been royally feted in Julian Budden's three-volume series, stupendously informative as analysis and a smashing good read. Only two volumes have appeared so far; the first moves through *Rigoletto*, the second through *La Forza del Destino*, and Oxford is the publisher. As he did to Mann's Mozart, Charles Osbourne offers a slimmer alternative to Budden in a one-volume *Verdi* (New York: Knopf, 1970).

On Richard Strauss, however, even Mann's grand entry (London: Cassell, 1964) plays second fiddle to another excellent three-volume set, Norman Del Mar's "critical commentary on his life and works" (Vol. I, New York: The Free Press, 1962; Vol. II, Philadelphia: Chilton, 1969; Vol. III, Chilton, 1973). Mosco Carner gives us Puccini (second ed., London: Duckworth, 1974), Michael Evans hones in on *Janáček's Tragic Operas* (London: Faber and Faber, 1977), and Eric Walter White assesses Britten (Berkeley: California, 1970), though *Owen Wingrave* and *Death in Venice* had not yet been written at the time.

Many buffs hold to the one-opera, one-book persuasion in the name of intoxicative saturation. E. M. Batley's *A Preface to The Magic Flute* (London: Dennis Dobson, 1969) is rather an introduction to early *Singspiel*, and while Batley has little to say about *The Magic Flute*, his excursion into the form that produced the work gives one a rich perspective on Mozart and Schikaneder. Generally these books tend to musical analysis, though there is the odd item. *The Rape of*

Lucretia, "a symposium," (London: The Bodley Head, 1948) offers
Ronald Duncan's libretto, Eric Crozier's report on the opera's first
impact, articles on text and music, John Piper's Sunday quarterbacking
of his own designs, and luxurious color illustrations. Karl H. Wörner's
dig into *Moses und Aron* (New York: St. Martin's, 1964) yields a
discussion of Schoenberg's philosophy along with musical guidance and
the libretto. Perhaps the most stimulating of such volumes is Donald C.
Daviau and George J. Buelow's look at *Ariadne auf Naxos* (Chapel
Hill: University of North Carolina Press, 1975), heartily recommended.

Wagner has inspired the biggest body of work, *The Ring* in particular. George Bernard Shaw's classic and thoroughly debunked socialist interpretation, *The Perfect Wagnerite* (fourth ed., London:
Constable, 1923) is available in a Dover reprint; this is amusing and
inciteful for all its wrongheadedness. Robert Donington's detailed
Jungian writ, *Wagner's Ring and its Symbols* (New York: St. Martin's,
1969) is extreme. Donington's typology of the unconscious shocks
some; other find him highly relevant. My money is on Deryck Cooke's
I Saw the World End (London: Oxford, 1979), the first half of a projected study interrupted by Cooke's death. Even as it is, Cooke is stupendous, refreshingly revisionist (his rediscovery of the all-important
"love" theme that develops Wagner's central thesis of "power conquered by love"), exacting (a handsome dig into Wagner's mythic
sources), fascinating (he seems to know the work better even than
Wagner in some respects). Cooke's wonderful title, incidentally, is
drawn from lines omitted from Brünnhilde's Immolation Scene:

> The blessed end
> of all things eternal,
> do you know how I reached it?
> Deepest suffering
> of grieving love
> opened my eyes:
> I saw the world end.

Cooke's own translation. Others have published English-language
*Ring*s: Stewart Robb's (New York: Dutton, 1960) is for reading, in
modern English, retaining Wagner's scan but little of the Germanic
alliteration. Andrew Porter's (New York: Norton, 1979), for the theatre, is superb; those who enjoy it should consider investing in the
complete *Ring* recorded live by the English National Opera in Porter's
edition with Rita Hunter, Alberto Remedios, and Norman Bailey under the shatteringly immense Reginald Goodall. You'll hear the world

end. (If you want a sample before plunging in, the *Siegfried* is the best.)

Now to the miscellany. Alfred Lowenberg's *Annals of Opera* (second ed., Geneva: Societas Bibliographica, 1955) makes a distinctive supplementary reference work (in two volumes, the second an index), listing opera premieres year by year from 1597 on, with annotations of all kinds. Henry Pleasants' *The Great Singers* (New York: Simon and Schuster, 1966) traces their contributions "from the dawn of opera to our own time," and aficionados find endless entertainment in George Steane's huge, astute, and loving review of vocal recording, *The Grand Tradition* (New York: Scribners, 1974). Those into the words-versus-music question might make a double-header of Joseph Kerman's composer-oriented *Opera as Drama* (New York: Vintage, 1956) and Patrick J. Smith's *The Tenth Muse* (New York: Knopf, 1970), "a historical study of the opera libretto." Gary Schmidgall delves into the art of adaptation in *Literature as Opera* (New York: Oxford, 1977), including in his purview not only such obvious choices as *Le Nozze di Figaro, Macbeth*, and *Wozzeck* but *Maria Stuarda, Benvenuto Cellini*, and *Death in Venice*. Schmidgall's polymath exuberance shows in a sampling of his chapter titles: "Handel's Wig and the Furioso Operas," "Bel Canto and the Sir Walter Disease," and "The Sources of Decadence: A Genealogy" (for *Salome*). As for living opera in the flesh on stage, try *The Making of an Opera* (New York: Atheneum, 1978), John Higgins' look at Peter Hall's staging of *Don Giovanni* at Glyndebourne in 1977, from casting to critics' reviews. Profusely illustrated, the book closes with Da Ponte's libretto in Italian and English. And for an *envoi*, let me offer Marcia Davenport's novel, *Of Lena Geyer* (New York: Popular Library, 1978), the best of several novels on the "backstage" of the opera world.

Glossary

aria: "air," a solo song, usually of some length and development.

arioso: "arialike," meaning halfway between declamation (recitative) and real song (aria).

atonal: having no fixed harmonic center.

ballad opera: an eighteenth-century musical comedy form, usually satiric in subject and having a score comprised of original lyrics and traditional or popular tunes.

bel canto: "beautiful song" or "singing," referring to the technically accomplished and extremely heartfelt singing style of *opera seria* in the eighteenth and, to an extent, early nineteenth century. *Bel canto*'s pedagogy, repertory, and traditions had totally died out by about 1870. (See also *canto*.)

bouffe: see *opéra bouffe.*

buffa, buffo: "comic," the feminine form *buffa* referring to *opera buffa* and the masculine *buffo* referring to the male character (usually a fat and ridiculous bass) associated with *opera buffa*, or to typical *buffa* business.

cabaletta: the second, livelier section of a full aria scene, following the *cavatina*, often after an interval of recitative.

canto: "song," meaning the vocal line that emphasizes expressive and attractive melody.

cavatina: (1) a short solo song, not sufficiently developed to be called an aria; (2) the first, slower section of a full aria scene. (See also *cabaletta*.)

coloratura: the repertory of vocal embellishments. Also called *fioratura* ("floweration").

commedia dell'arte: an ancient Italian form using archetypal characters such as Arlecchino (Harlequin), Colombina, and Capitano Spavento (Captain Horrible) for burlesques of the human condition. The characters are sometimes called "the masks."

comprimario: originally the second singer in a particular vocal category, now used to denote any small part in an opera.

dodecaphonic music: see serialism.

Fach (plural *Fächer*): "department," in-group opera argot for voice type; e.g., the baritone *Fach.*

falcon: a sturdy female voice with a soprano's bright top range but a mezzo's rich lower range. Named for Marie-Cornélie Falcon.

Gesamtkunstwerk: "work of all the arts," Wagner's term for a theatre piece that would fuse all artistic elements into an organic whole.

grand opera: a form mainly of the early and middle nineteenth century especially associated with the Paris Opéra, featuring a historical setting, a full cast of principals, dancers, and chorus, a certain amount of entertaining diversions, theatrical effects, and spectacle.

intermedio (plural *intermedi*): a one-act comic intermezzo.

lazzo (plural, *lazzi*): "jest," a piece of comic business habitual in *commedia dell'arte.*

legato: "connected," a smooth, even way of singing.

Leitmotiv (plural *Leitmotive*): "leading theme," a musical germ of vocal or instrumental melody, rhythmic figure, or harmonic pattern, associated with a character, place, act, or idea.

lieto fine: "happy end," the Baroque convention of the happy plot resolution, usually through the *deus ex machina*—the intervention of a friendly deity.

Märchenoper: "fairy-tale opera."

melodrama: (1) spoken dialogue accompanied by music; (2) a theatre form which is characterized by emotional extremism and which emphasizes action over character.

melodramma: the nineteenth-century modernization of *opera seria,* retaining its noble characters but in a Romantic conception and in a more fluid, less aria-dominated format.

monody: music composed of one basic melody, as opposed to polyphony, music composed of simultaneously conflicting melodies.

morbidezza: "pathos," contemporary with and much like *verismo* opera, but emphasizing sentimentality over violence.

opéra-ballet: a late seventeenth- and early eighteenth-century form of opera with a pronounced dance component.

opéra bouffe: a form of musical comedy of satiric subject and thin musical composition. Especially associated with Jacques Offenbach.

opera buffa: "comic opera," a form using recitative instead of dialogue and drawing its characters and situations from the *commedia* tradition.

opéra comique: (1) originally a form of musical comedy like ballad opera; (2) later, a form having less satiric subjects and more accomplished musicality; (3) still later, an opera form leaning to sentimentally romantic subjects. The one constant is the use of spoken dialogue between numbers.

opera seria: "serious opera," the major operatic form in the eighteenth century, dealing with noble characters in a historical setting, favoring happy resolutions (usually through the clemency of a monarch in place of the older *deus ex machina*), and composed almost exclusively of arias separated by recitative.

parlando: "speaking style."

passacaglia: a complex variation form in which the variations are sounded over a set and repeated thematic pattern.

pastiche: (1) an opera derived from miscellaneous sources or from several works of one composer; (2) the recreation of outdated or alien musical styles, as for example the imitation of Baroque ballet music in Act III of Massenet's *Manon*.

recitative: a declamatory singing style designed to stimulate speech, the most basic element in early opera; later, different types of recitative were developed, spanning a wide range between quasi-speaking and quasisinging. There were also *recitativo secco* ("dry"), with the barest accompaniment, and *recitativo accompagnato* or *stromentato*, more fully scored.

rondo: "round," a form built around a recurring main theme.

semi–opera: a late-eighteenth-century English form denoting a play that has been decorated, so to speak, with operatic scenes but not wholly adapted to opera.

serialism: Arnold Schoenberg's system of atonal composition in which a given piece is based on ceaseless variations on a "row" of twelve pitches arranged in fixed order.

Singspiel: a form of musical comedy emphasizing (in the late eighteenth century) fantasy and comedy, (in the early nineteenth century) Romantic adventure, and (thereafter) usually folkish subjects.

spinto: "pushed," a lyric voice, usually soprano, capable of heroic statements.

Sprechgesang: "speech song," a method in which a singer "talks" rather than sings his notes; used interchangeably with *Sprechstimme* (speaking voice), though *Sprechgesang* really denotes the method of composition and *Sprechstimme* the singer's use of the voice.

stretta: "tightening," the final, intensified section of a finale.

through-composition: a method of composing the acts of an opera not in numbers, each with a clear beginning and end, but in a ceaseless musical flow.

tinta: "hue," usually denoting a given work's particular sound colorings.

twelve-tone composition: see serialism.

verismo: "realism," the naturalistic school of Italian opera, popular from about 1890 to 1905.

Zauberoper: "magic opera," a type of *Singspiel* emphasizing magical effects in plot and decor, popular in Vienna at the end of the eighteenth century.

Zeitoper: "opera of the day," a hip, cynical form of opera, dating from the 1920s, exploiting fads of the time.

Index